MICROLEVEL SCHOOL FINANCE

MICROLEVEL SCHOOL FINANCE
Issues and Implications for Policy

Edited by
DAVID H. MONK
Cornell University

and

JULIE UNDERWOOD
University of Wisconsin-Madison

**Ninth Annual Yearbook of the
American Education Finance Association
1988**

BALLINGER PUBLISHING COMPANY
Cambridge, Massachusetts
A Subsidiary of Harper & Row, Publishers, Inc.

International Standard Book Number: 0-88730-291-2

Library of Congress Catalog Card Number: 88-29202

Printed in the United States of America

Library of Congress Cataloging-in-Publication Data

Micro-level school finance : issues and implications for policy / edited
  by David H. Monk and Julie Underwood.
     p.   cm. — (Ninth annual yearbook of the American Education
  Finance Association)
     Includes indexes.
     ISBN 0-88730-291-2
     1. Education—United States—Finance. 2. Education and
  state—United States. I. Monk, David H. II. Underwood, Julie.
  III. American Education Finance Association. IV. Series: Annual
  yearbook of the American Education Finance Association : 9th.
  LB2825.M434 1988
  379.1'21'0973—dc19   88-29202
                                                              CIP

CONTENTS

v

LIST OF FIGURES

LIST OF TABLES

PREFACE

The phrase "microlevel school finance" has several interrelated meanings, and it is sensible to begin with their discussion. First, the phrase makes implicit reference to the self-evident facts that resources are allocated for educational purposes at a variety of organizational levels, that resource allocation decisions made at one level have bearing on decisions made at other levels, and that these decisions can have a reciprocal influence on one another.

Second, those interested in microlevel school finance place a special emphasis on what transpires at decentralized levels of decision-making. An important question is what happens at local levels when resource allocation decisions are made at state and/or federal levels. The local level itself can be and is broken into a variety of levels including schools, departments or teams within schools, classrooms, and groups within classrooms.

Third, microlevel school finance research tends to focus on behavioral interactions among different actors involved in schooling, including government officials (governors, legislators, state education department officials), businesspeople, professional educators (administrators, teachers), parents, and taxpayers.

Fourth, the term "finance" is construed broadly to include the allocation of fiscal as well as other kinds of valued resources, including the time of students and teachers. Microlevel school finance research recognizes that more is involved in financing schools than the formulaic distribution of fiscal resources from one level of government to another, although such traditional school financing phenomena can certainly be examined from a micro perspective.

Finally, the study of microlevel school finance involves a wide variety of disciplinary perspectives. In large part this is because of the emphasis on decentralized levels of decisionmaking and the interest in interactions between people in various decisionmaking positions. It is difficult to think of a social or behavioral science that cannot be brought fruitfully to bear on resource allocation behavior within educational systems.

The present volume is one of the first to address explicitly microlevel school finance phenomena.[1] The elements described above can be found in the chapters collected herein. The chapters are drawn from a wide variety of disciplinary perspectives (economics, philosophy, political science, psychology, and sociology) and address a wide variety of resource allocation issues at one or another level of the educational system. These chapters provide a state of the art tour of where we are in this important and rapidly developing branch of educational finance.

LINKAGES AMONG DECISIONMAKING LEVELS

Part I of this book deals with broad issues that arise out of the realization that resources are allocated at a variety of levels for education and that important interactions occur across levels of decisionmaking. The recent reform movement provides an excellent source of data about these interactions, and the first two chapters deal with the reform movement.

In Chapter 1, Susan Furhman, William Clune, and Richard Elmore, examine the reform movement in six states and look explicitly at how changes in state policies have been reacted to within local education associations (LEAs). They argue for new interpretations of how innovation occurs and how increased state funding interacts with local autonomy. They found that many districts do not merely adapt

---

1. For an important earlier collection, see the 1983 American Education Finance Association yearbook: Allan Odden and L. Dean Webb, eds. 1983. *School Finance and School Improvement: Linkages for the 1980s*. Cambridge, Mass.: Ballinger.

to changes in state policy but instead orchestrate and amplify policies around local priorities. Furhman and her colleagues use the
phrase "strategic interaction" to describe this phenomenon. That the
impacts of reforms and decisions at local levels are highly context-
bound is a recurring theme throughout this volume.

In Chapter 2, Susan Rosenholtz continues to look at multilevel
aspects of the reform movement and focuses on reforms designed to
establish minimum competency standards for students and career
ladder programs for teachers. Rosenholtz stresses the importance of
the linkage between state and local levels and draws attention to the
importance of the local context, including the magnitude of the
resource base. One of her major theses is that many of the reforms
currently being put in place are inimical to what has been learned
from research on school improvement and the professionalization of
teaching. She goes on to argue that the effects of the reforms vary
widely depending on the internal characteristics of the schools involved. She draws a distinction between successful and unsuccessful
schools and reports on her study of how these different kinds of
schools have responded to state initiatives. She pays explicit attention to the role financing plays in the success of the reforms and
finds that the resource base is an important ingredient for successful
implementation.

Milbrey McLaughlin picks up on the theme that at the local level
there are new sources of resources, particularly those arising out of
the private business sector. She considers the implications of this
growing involvement of business for the governance of schools. She
provides an overview of trends in business involvement in the schools
and draws attention to the role being played by Local Education
Funds (LEFs). According to her analysis, the key difference between
traditional business involvement and the new LEF form of involvement is that LEFs see dollars and activities in instrumental terms, as
part of a political strategy of coalition building, and not as an end
in themselves. She considers implications of this type of business
involvement for equity and governance based on her study of LEFs
from around the country and concludes that business support represents a potentially powerful substitute for a traditional political base
of public schools, namely parents. She largely dismisses fears that
businesses are pursuing their own narrow agendas regarding schools
and sees their current involvement as a healthy and promising development for most public schools.

Claude Tibi's chapter addresses the multilevel theme from an international perspective. He calls into question the common view that outside the United States and Canada education is highly centralized and tightly governed with little local autonomy in the allocation of resources. He shows that substantial variation exists among nations in how centralized their systems are and that even in highly centralized countries there is considerable internal variation in the distribution of resources. He pays particular attention to interactions between the concerns of teachers, local officials, and central authorities in the distribution of fiscal resources. As evidence, he points to variation across nations in the degree to which variables such as the size of a school are capable of explaining per pupil funding levels. He interprets weak links between size and per pupil expenditure levels as evidence of the external factors that can intervene and reduce the ability of central governments to dictate practice at local levels. His chapter makes the important point that even in highly centralized systems, resources are allocated at different levels and that complex interactions exist across levels, which have implications for efficiency and equity.

Stephen Hoenack's provocative chapter looks not so much at how resources are currently being allocated across levels, but at how performance incentives could be used to change resource allocation behavior. He brings an economic perspective to bear on the problem and distinguishes sharply between a good incentive system and incentives that can produce unfortunate results. He is particularly mindful of the costs that can arise from the serious pursuit of an incentive system, but justifies them in terms of the superior outcomes that could be obtained. He proposes an experimental incentive system that moves the locus of decisionmaking to the school and even the subschool level.

Hoenack's analysis makes it clear that an incentive system requires explicit valuations of different kinds and distributions of learning outcomes. These value judgments are embodied in the reward structure creating the incentives that he stresses have so much to do with how teachers and students behave. But he understandably has little to say about how these value judgments are to be made. Such questions raise philosophical issues, and we have the benefit of Kenneth Strike's insights into the ethics of resource allocation as our guide here.

Strike's ambitious analysis distinguishes between competing interests in justice, legitimacy of process, and goodness of result in his study of ethical issues in resource allocation for education. One of his major concerns is with limits on what can be determined legitimately, using democratic decisionmaking processes. Returning to Hoenack's emphasis on the importance of reaching agreement over the kinds and distribution of learning outcomes encouraged through the structuring of incentives, Strike's analysis reveals the role and limits of making such decisions democratically, using voting mechanisms of various kinds. Strike's chapter addresses the question of who should decide what and how in the allocation of resources. He also provides a critique of the utilitarian conception of justice he sees inherent in much of the modern reform movement in education.

MICROLEVEL EDUCATIONAL PRODUCTIVITY

Parts II and III of this book focus on specific although interrelated topics that are important within microlevel school finance. From a variety of disciplinary perspectives, Part II deals with the transformation of schooling resources into distributions of outcomes, with emphasis on the point at which the transformation actually occurs—namely, the classroom and the interaction between students and teachers.

Byron Brown examines the microeconomics of classrooms and simultaneously provides an introduction to how economists think about classroom production as well as the results of applying an economic perspective to important and timely policy matters. Again there is an emphasis on the importance of context that is reminiscent of both the Fuhrman, Clune, and Elmore and the Rosenholtz chapters. He also points out the importance of value judgments teachers must make in their resource allocation behaviors; recall that these are issues Strike deals with in Chapter 6.

Adam Gamoran provides the sociological perspective. His chapter includes an overview of past efforts and notes that sociologists have moved away from trying to look at what resources are easiest to manipulate toward looking first at what resources are most likely to matter. Gamoran reports promising results. He describes the strong ties being found between resource allocation and resource use as well as between resource use and student achievement. Gamoran's message is positive and encouraging. Sociologists are discovering systematic differences among classrooms in characteristics that make differences for learning. As this research goes forward and more is learned about what does and does not matter, the issues dealt with by Strike, and the multilevel resource allocation phenomena explored in Part I of the yearbook will become increasingly important.

Bettye MacPhail-Wilcox examines the psychological perspective and explores compatibilities between economics and psychology. It is one thing for the various disciplines to be applied to a common problem; it is quite another for collaborations to occur across the disciplines. In this light, MacPhail-Wilcox's thesis that there is a compatibility and almost an affinity between economics and psychology is heartening. She examines psychological theories of motivation in considerable detail and finds numerous instances of ideas that are compatible with economic principles. Given what appears to be a revival or at least a growing interest in the role performance incentives play (see the chapters by Hoenack; Kirst; Hentschke; Boyd and Hartman; and Ehrenberg, Chaykowsky, and Enrenberg), and the contributions psychology can make to the understanding of how reward systems operate, the finding of these compatibilities has important implications for future research.

William Boyd and William Hartman adopt a different tack and structure their chapter around a presumption that while we may not know all there is to know about how to produce learning outcomes, we do know enough already to make it impossible to avoid responsibility for our educational policies. They then ask why it is that the performance of schooling systems is not better, and seek an answer by examining the politics of education as it is practiced deep within school systems. They are sensitive to the importance of incentives, and their chapter is thus linked to the other authors with a similar view (such as Kirst; Hentschke; Hoenack; and Ehrenberg, Chaykowski, and Ehrenberg). They end by noting the promise offered by the new applications of economics to the study of nonprofit-making organizations. Thus, their political analysis takes on a political-economic character, and the blending of the two perspectives is a further indication of the importance of collaboration.

RESOURCE ALLOCATION AT MICROLEVELS

The final three chapters deal with specific instances of resource allocation at decentralized levels of educational systems. Guilbert Hentschke deals with budget preparation and stresses the importance of understanding the underlying distribution of authority in the preparation and implementation of budgets. According to Hentschke's thesis, changes in budgeting occur because of changes in the overarching authority structure, not the other way around.

He goes on to describe five possible reforms in the authority structure that have important budgeting implications. Some of these are in place in school systems around the country, and he provides insights into how they are being implemented. These are experiments, and it is too early to assess the long-term consequences, but the early findings are encouraging and fit nicely with the incentive arguments made by Hoenack.

Ronald Ehrenberg, Richard Chaykowski, and Randy Ehrenberg describe their empirical study of merit pay for school superintendents. They were puzzled by the large amount of attention given to merit pay for teachers and the lack of a corresponding interest in assessing the degree to which chief administrative officers are in fact rewarded for superior school district performance. They developed two indicators for assessing school district performance: a test score indicator and a tax rate indicator. The district's performance was assessed in terms of the degree to which its test scores were higher and tax rates were lower than would otherwise be expected given the district's characteristics.

Their results, based on New York data, show that superintendents are rewarded for performance but that the magnitude is small. They also found little evidence suggesting that superintendents made a significant difference in terms of the performance indicators they used to assess districts.

Michael Kirst's chapter provides an overview of trends in school finance with particular emphasis on the study of microissues. He is dismayed with how little attention has been devoted to the subject and concludes that the issues will become more important as budget pressures and pressures from the private sector for accountability increase. He points to the significant increases in funding that accompanied the reform movement (and that were largely unexpected by those within the school finance research community) as setting the stage for future concerns over what was actually done with the resources. He reports on the California State Department of Education study of what a California district spends as an example of the kind of tracking of resources that can and needs to be done in response to the accountability questions he expects to be raised increasingly in the future.

Ithaca, New York   David H. Monk
June 1988   Julie Underwood

ACKNOWLEDGMENTS

As is always the case, an edited volume reflects the labors of many people. Patrick Galvin, an advanced graduate student in educational administration at Cornell, provided invaluable assistance while the senior editor was out of the United States on sabbatical leave. Galvin provided all of the early follow-up work with authors and helped achieve coherence across the chapters. Sidney Doan, as is her custom, provided cheerful highly competent secretarial support and kept the numerous drafts of chapters flowing between authors, editors, and the publisher.

We are also indebted to the Department of Education at Cornell and the two chairmen, Professors Joe P. Bail and Richard E. Ripple, who provided support for the project. A book such as this requires a substantial amount of institutional support and could not have been produced without the cooperation and encouragement of these fine colleagues. The Institut de Recherche sur l'Economie de l'Education (IREDU) at the University of Burgundy in Dijon, France, and its director, François Orivel, also provided institutional support during the early development of the book. Both Orivel and Professor Jean-Claude Eicher reacted to ideas for the volume and provided much-needed and welcomed encouragement.

The earliest ideas for the micro theme grew out of discussions with Allan Odden, James G. Ward, and William E. Sparkman, all past presidents of the American Education Finance Association. Their counsel was instrumental in choosing topics and structuring the volume, and we are indebted to them.

Finally, the editorial support at Ballinger was timely, high quality, and forgiving. We are all grateful for this often hidden but enormously important contribution.

We hope this yearbook will stimulate further efforts to explore micro aspects of educational finance. Much remains to be done, and if this book serves its purpose, it will help chart directions for future research and policy development.

CONCEPTUAL AND EMPIRICAL LINKAGES AMONG DECISIONMAKING LEVELS

1 RESEARCH ON EDUCATION REFORM
Lessons on the Implementation of Policy

Susan Fuhrman, William Clune,
and Richard Elmore

Education reform was the major state policy activity of the 1980s. Beginning in the early years of the decade and continuing with new momentum following the publication of *A Nation at Risk* and other reform reports, states increased their standards for student performance, revised their systems of teacher certification, improved teacher compensation, and enhanced accountability mechanisms. Virtually every state made new policy in these areas; some, such as Indiana, embarked on comprehensive reform as recently as 1987. The reforms were accompanied by substantial increases in state aid, on the average about 21 percent in real terms between 1983 and 1987 (Odden 1987).

The reforms pose numerous distributional and allocational issues. For the most part, state dollars that accompanied reform packages were funneled through equalized school aid formulas but special incentive programs, pilot efforts, and categoricals raise questions about the distributional equity of state aid, as discussed in other

The Center for Policy Research in Education (CPRE), a consortium of Rutgers University, Michigan State University, Stanford University, and the University of Wisconsin, is funded by the Office of Educational Research and Improvement (OERI–G008690011–88) to study state and local policies to improve schooling. An important part of its mission is research on the implementation and effects of state reform. This chapter draws on that multiyear study conducted by the authors and colleagues at Rutgers University, the RAND Corporation, and the University of Wisconsin. The opinions expressed are those of the authors and are not necessarily shared by CPRE or the U.S. Department of Education.

chapters in this book. Early evidence indicates that the new policies are contributing to a reallocation of resources at the school level to support more course taking in academic subjects by all students. We explore these tentative findings below in the section concerning reforms of student standards.

However, the main focus of this chapter is on a reallocation of a different sort—namely, new definitions of roles and relationships by state and local policymakers. The reforms are not just about academic excellence and teacher quality, they are also about the distribution of political authority among units of government. At stake in the reform movement, along with school curriculum and the nature of the teacher workforce, are issues about leadership and initiative in education policymaking (Clune 1987).

As we examine changing patterns of state and local relationships evident in the shaping and implementing of the reforms, we are acquiring a new understanding of the policy process. The paths taken by these reforms are not entirely consistent with histories of other educational changes. They differ from what we would expect from past research on policy enactment and implementation.

In this chapter, we report findings about the reform process and initial effects in Arizona, California, Florida, Georgia, Minnesota, and Pennsylvania where we interviewed state and local policymakers and educators in twenty-four districts and fifty-nine schools. These interviews, which took place between April 1986 and June 1987, constitute the first phase of a five-year study of the reforms. We compare our findings about the reform process and local implementation to what we expected from past research in policy implementation and suggest a new model for the implementation of state reform that accounts for the trends in this current reform movement.

A few cautionary words are necessary as a preface to the discussion. We do not suggest that these six states are representative of the entire nation. Rather, they represent a range on particular characteristics we expected to affect the translation of policy into practice: the scope and volume of reform and the instruments used to address policy problems. California and Florida were among the first states to enact comprehensive reform packages; Georgia followed two years later. These states addressed dozens of reform issues in one massive piece of legislation. Pennsylvania and Arizona took more incremental approaches, considering one or two reform issues at a time. Minnesota undertook few state-level policy innovations; one policy it did adopt was a unique choice plan, quite unlike other current state reforms.

The states also vary in the policy instruments or strategies used to deal with reform issues. For example, Georgia and Pennsylvania rely heavily on mandates to local districts. California's program was marked by the use of incentives or financial inducements to districts to participate in programs; over time Florida shifted from mandates to an approach more dependent on incentives.

Our study is also limited because we visited only four districts in each of the states, on the average. Finally, what we report is based entirely on perceptions of policymakers and practitioners. Much of the objective evidence of reform impact, such as course enrollment statistics and dropout rates over time, were either not gathered systematically by states and districts in the study or would not yet reflect the effects of reforms that are just being phased in.

LESSONS FROM PAST RESEARCH

When we began our research, we realized that the state reforms of the 1980s might take different paths from the education policies that had received the attention of policy researchers in the past. We knew that past research would provide only partial guidance for understanding this new set of policies. Most research on education policy formation and implementation had concerned federal policy. Although states had long been active in several policy areas, such as finance and school district consolidation, the federal government provided much of the programmatic leadership in education prior to the current wave of state reform. Also, previous research centered on individual programs, many of which were for special need students and were more peripheral than central to core elements of schooling. They were discrete and amenable to study. By contrast, the current reforms deal with central issues of who shall teach, what shall be taught, and in what manner. Furthermore, the state reforms of the 1980s typically came bundled together; they were packages that delivered tens of new policy initiatives at once in the most comprehensive states and several in the states that acted more incrementally. However, we expected that lessons from past research would provide a solid foundation for understanding the nature and course of the state reform movement.

Drawing on earlier studies,[1] we made the following predictions about the new state reforms:

1. State political culture and context would lead to wide variation in the choice of policy instruments and implementation strategies; states would take pieces of the national reform agenda that best fit their own goals and capacity.

2. Participants in the policymaking process would be those with the most stake in the outcome—that is, interests would participate in proportion to their stake in the policies being shaped.

3. There would be wide variation in local response; some local districts would resist reforms or refuse to comply; some would comply literally to the reforms; and most would adapt, taking from reforms the elements that best suited local goals and shaping them to local context.

4. Implementation success would be enhanced to the extent that reforms delivered clear, coherent signals to local districts.

5. Local actors would more readily adopt policies that match their technical expertise.

6. The effects of reform would be lagged; there would be little impact in the short term as people adjusted and began to translate policy into practice and much more actual change in the long term over years of phase-in and application.

7. The reforms would be mixtures of the symbolic and the actual; some reforms would result in real changes in school practice, others might give the appearance of change but would mean little in the course of a student's school career.

8. The implementation process at the local level would be smoother to the extent that local actors were involved in shaping the state-level reforms; ownership would be important.

9. The amount of state policy activity and the increase in state aid would translate roughly into an enhanced education policy-making role for the state. Increased state regulation in areas such as curriculum would mean diminished local control.

The model suggested by these lessons depicts a reform process that is heavily dependent on context at both state and local levels, that relies for success on the active engagement of those most interested in reform outcome, and that predicts little in the way of real change without such participation. We expected few significant impacts within the first few years; rather, we expected to see some evidence of resistance, and many changes that were more important on paper than in reality. We anticipated that even though some districts would resist, the modal response would be mutual adaptation (McLaughlin 1976), whereby the district and the state each adjusted its goals to find an accommodation satisfactory to both. Even if part of the reforms were without real bite or substance, we thought they embodied enough new state regulation to translate into a widespread perception that the state role was increasing to the detriment of local autonomy.

Our actual findings suggest a much more complex picture. In the following sections, we detail these findings in four areas: the politics of reform, the state role, student standards, and policies related to teaching. We then return to the original model and draw new lessons that provide a richer understanding of the reform process.

THE POLITICS OF REFORM

As indicated, the reforms enacted by the six study states vary in their scope, in the policy instruments used, and in their comprehensiveness. Arizona enacted two major education reforms: a pilot career ladder and new graduation requirements. The career ladder was passed in 1985. Its proponents wanted a statewide plan but resorted to a pilot to save money and avoid facing the state's constitutional spending limit. Initially five, and later fifteen, districts received competitive grants to implement a plan that, by state law, must include student achievement and classroom performance as promotion criteria. In 1983, the state board increased graduation requirements from sixteen to twenty credits. The changes included a rather large (2.5 units) and specific social studies requirement. Other recent reforms, enacted in serial fashion—one or two a year—include the imposition of teacher testing, changes in the criteria for approval of teacher education programs, yearly student assessment, and the establishment of competencies for grade to grade promotion.

California's 1983 SB813 was an $800 million dollar reform package that was extraordinarily complex. It included the imposition of statewide graduation requirements; provision for state board definition of competency standards; incentives for a longer school day; continuing education requirements for teacher certification; a mentor teacher program of annual stipends for teachers who help new teachers or develop curriculum; increased beginning salaries; an alternative certification route for high school teachers; reforms in personnel management that made it easier to dismiss and transfer teachers; expanded authority for expulsion and suspension of problem students amid dozens of other provisions. The comprehensive legislative education reform had become a familiar feature in the California education policy landscape; other notable "big fixes" were the introduction of compensatory education in 1964, early childhood education in the late 1960s, school finance reform and school improvement in the 1970s.

The Florida legislature passed comprehensive education legislation in 1983 after at least a decade of fashioning and enacting a new, major piece of education legislation each session. The reforms included mandated statewide standards for high school graduation and a mandated seventh period of instruction; a minimum gradepoint average; the Florida Quality Instruction Incentive Program (merit schools); the Meritorious Instructional Personnel Program (the master teacher plan); and improvements in math, science, and computer education. Funding, derived primarily through a unitary corporate tax, amounted to $73.8 million in 1983-84 and $130.5 million in 1984-85. In the last several years, the legislature tinkered with or fine-tuned a number of the original provisions: The mandated extended day became an incentive, the minimum gradepoint requirement was delayed, and a career ladder program was enacted in place of the master teacher program. The career ladder, which called for locally designed systems expired as funding was not provided during the 1988 session.

In 1985, the Georgia legislature enacted the Quality Basic Education Act (QBE). The legislation gave statutory confirmation to a variety of previously adopted regulations, including graduation requirements, student testing, teacher testing, and beginning teacher evaluation. It extended testing to veteran teachers, provided for a statewide basic curriculum, instituted a school readiness test, required statewide norm-referenced testing, established incentives for structural changes such as the creation of middle schools and the consolidation of school districts, and completely overhauled the school financing system. QBE was the third attempt at major education reform undertaken by Georgia governors and legislatures since the 1970s but the first to be funded. Georgia's astonishing economic growth provided the $2 billion necessary to fund QBE without a tax increase.

Minnesota's reform program is quite unlike those in the other study states. Pride in the high achievement of its students and schools and widespread trust in school personnel combined to restrict the inclination of state policymakers to regulate schooling. Consequently, Minnesota did not institute major statewide increases in student standards. It embarked on several other reform initiatives including a $3.2 million a year incentive and training program in technology, yearly local student assessment, and district-run programs of competency testing and remediation. The reform that has attracted the most attention is the Postsecondary Enrollment Options Act, which permits any eleventh or twelfth grade student to attend a postsecondary school free of tuition. The state education aid allotment follows the student and goes to the postsecondary school in an amount proportionate to the student's percentage of full-time status. The program's proponents saw it not only as a way to increase student opportunities but also as a means to shake up the educational bureaucracy by introducing competition. Other choice programs including statewide open enrollment were enacted in the 1988 session.

In Pennsylvania, the major reforms were embedded in the 1984 revisions of two chapters of state code. Chapter 5 was changed so as to increase high school graduation requirements from thirteen credits in grades ten to twelve to twenty-one in grades nine to twelve. Additional years of math and science were required. Chapter 49 requires tests for new teachers in four areas; district-conducted induction programs; and continuing professional development credits (CPD) for certification renewal. Subsequent legislation exempted teachers with a master's degree from the CPD requirements and permitted districts to design programs to meet those requirements in lieu of university courses. Another important reform was the establishment of TELLS, a program to test and remediate students in math and reading in grades three, five, and eight. With the exception of TELLS, unique in its categorical nature, the reforms were funded by yearly increases of 8 percent and then 6 percent in the basic state aid formula.

Despite the important differences between the states, some key aspects of the reform process were similar across the states. First, legislators and governors played critical roles in reform in each of the states (McDonnell and Fuhrman 1986). The academic excellence reforms, like the school finance reforms of the 1970s, did not initiate in the education community; in fact educators and representatives of state-level education associations in many of our states complained that the reforms were "done to" them and defined them as part of the problem rather than the solution. Although some chief state school officers were important reform proponents, the impetus came from outside state departments and state boards of education.

In five of the states, legislative chairmen and leaders shaped and shepherded packages, some of which were designed by gubernatorial task forces. Where governors were not actively involved in designing reforms, their support was important in securing funding. In California, SB813 was legislative reform although it swept along with it a number of the student standards and curricular policies of Superintendent of Public Instruction Honig. The package was constructed by the Senate education chair, who cosponsored it along with the House education chair. The governor's assistance was important in securing the support of Republican legislators, although the price for his activity was less funding than Democratic sponsors wanted. Florida's 1983 reform united three themes, each initiated by one of the major reform actors: the master teacher and merit pay ideas of the governor; the Senate-initiated increased high school graduation requirements and longer school day mandate; and improvements in math, science, and computer education that stemmed from the House Speaker's task force. Georgia's reform resulted from a gubernatorial task force, the Education Review Commission, whose recommendations were translated into legislation that was unanimously endorsed by the legislature, under the guidance of its leaders. In Arizona, the major reform component, the teacher career ladder, was entirely a product of the legislature; interestingly, it was implemented by the staff of the Senate Education Committee rather than the State Department of Education. The governor in Arizona was not an initiator, but his support for increased teacher salaries and increased spending provided important pressure. Finally, Minnesota's Post-Secondary Options Program is seen as a joint product of the governor and legislature.

Pennsylvania is the only study state in which the reforms came primarily through state board regulation. However, Governor Thornburgh's agenda, as carried by his Secretary of Education Wilburn, determined the substance of the reforms. The board had been considering expressing high school graduation requirements as competencies instead of courses; with Wilburn's movement from the Department of Administration to Education specific course requirements were adopted. The legislature traditionally defers to the State Board of Education in making substantive education policy, preferring the flexibility afforded when policy is embedded in regulation rather than statute. Legislative comfort with state board control was considerably enhanced by the addition of the legislative education chairs to state board membership in the early 1980s. However, the legislature can be a court of appeals for interests dissatisfied by board action and pending legislation can exert strong leverage on the board. In the case of the current reforms, legislation embodying the revised graduation requirements was dropped only when the board adopted a virtually identical package. The legislature's influence on the reforms in the area of teaching policy was even stronger. After the board revised the portion of code dealing with certification, Chapter 49, unhappy teacher associations successfully petitioned the legislature to exempt teachers with master's degrees from the requirement for continuing professional development credits as a condition of maintaining certification and to permit local districts discretion in designing continuing education programs. State board regulations were then made to conform to legislative directive.

Educational associations joined state departments and boards of education in playing a secondary rather than a leading role in the reforms. Business interests predominated in most of the states, in comparison to past years when businesspeople showed little interest in education policy except to stop tax increases. Business groups were prominent in Minnesota's PSOE reform, Florida's Master Teacher and Merit Schools Programs and in the process leading up to Georgia's QBE. Even where they continued to oppose increased spending, as in Arizona, business leaders were key in certain aspects of reform. Business leaders serving on the state board led the effort to increase graduation requirements.

In contrast, education interests were not active players in the reform process, despite the centrality of reforms dealing with curriculum and teacher certification to their professional interests. Teacher associations accommodated to reform rather than shaping it. Their influence prior to reform passage was limited, in part because of the ascent of other groups, especially business. Although not strong supporters of reform, they also did not wage all-out opposition for the most part. They were able to veto or block parts of reforms they particularly disliked, but they determined that the probability of pay off from virulent resistance was low. In addition, the reforms did carry increased education funding, often for the first time after several years of recession. This factor and the strong backing for the reforms from policymaker and business elites led the associations to suppress their antagonism. In some states their strategy was to voice opposition privately to policymakers but to take no position or a mildly supportive stance in public (McDonnell and Pascal 1988).

Finally, even though there were important differences from state to state, the reforms everywhere were the products of coalition politics. They were born of many motives and were amalgams of many ideas. Most had components that appealed to fairly diverse interests so that enough support for passage could be aggregated. In spite of public enthusiasm for education reform and the national fever of reform activity, designing winning coalitions was a challenging task. The reforms had to pass without the active support of education interests, over their opposition in some cases, and they often involved substantial new sums of money.

Although most reform rhetoric referred to improving the United States' competitive position and striving for academic excellence, some reform leaders had more particularistic motives. For example, California Senate Republicans were primarily interested in curbing the power of organized teachers. A number of Pennsylvania legislative leaders were concerned with increasing state aid to local school districts; the reforms offered a political opportunity to do something they might have pursued in any case.

Similarly, the same reforms were supported for varied reasons. For example, while some state policymakers in Pennsylvania imbued new student standards with significant promise of enhancing student performance throughout the state, others saw the same standards as explicit statements to "laggard districts," to the 20 percent of districts who did not already meet the new minimum requirements; still others expected their impact to be primarily symbolic, sending a signal to students and districts that academics was important. In like manner, Arizona's career ladder garnered the support of the governor because it meant higher teacher salaries; eventually the teacher's association came to support it for the same reason. Legislative sponsors had a variety of other goals: to improve the quality of teaching and teacher morale, to provide a more collegial atmosphere in schools, to improve the quality of teacher evaluations, and to strengthen public support for schools.

Much like their counterparts in Arizona, Georgia policymakers came at the Quality Basic Education Act from different perspectives. Most were primarily concerned with improving Georgia's economic competitiveness and ability to attract industry. However, some also saw reform as a not so subtle pressure for school district consolidation, on the theory that school districts unable to meet new standards would seek merger and seize upon the component of the legislation that provided incentives for consolidation. Others intended the reform as a strong signal to elected local school superintendents who were not trusted to seek quality education. Still others saw QBE as an opportunity for reform of school finance and the introduction of a more equalized funding system.

Not only did the reforms satisfy a variety of different goals, the reform packages also combined several different, and sometimes disparate, approaches to improving schools. In addition to new standards, they carried significantly increased funding, which for some of the sponsors was the key to fixing the system. To these actors, the standards were either exchanges for the money, part of a "big bargain"; ways to pacify other interests, such as the business supporters who agreed to increased spending and taxation only because of accountability guarantees; or window dressing. For example, key legislative actors in California saw SB813 as a way to increase funding for schools in return for some relatively innocuous reforms. They grafted together Honig's student standards provisions, the Senate education chair's teacher development proposals that he had been generating over several years, and the relatively punitive teacher evaluation and credentialing requirements supported by opponents of the major teacher association. Mentor teachers were seen as a reasonable alternative to merit pay, since teachers were being paid more for additional work, rather than judgment about their quality. Student standards were seen as affecting few districts, but as giving a clear signal about the importance of student performance. So-called personnel management provisions were seen as having relatively little effect, but as delivering a clear signal to teachers' organizations that they were not as powerful as they thought.

To summarize, the education reforms of the early 1980s were strongly reflective of state political context. Nonetheless, in each state studied, legislators and governors, with the powerful support of business groups, played leading roles. Education interests were at most supporting players, accommodating to rather than shaping reform. The reforms are often discussed as if they are seamless, speaking with one voice about improved schooling through higher standards. However, the reform packages were complex bundles of many approaches and were supported by policymakers with diverse motives.

THE STATE ROLE

Common wisdom about the reform movement characterizes it as a landmark in state control of education. Several factors lend support to this theory. First is a tendency to equate the amount of state policymaking activity with influence over local district behavior. It is certainly true that the reforms represented a significant increase in state activity by sheer volume alone. For example, legislatures considered over 1,000 pieces of legislation dealing with teacher certification and compensation during the 1980s, an unprecedented amount. Virtually every state enacted policies to reform teacher education, licensing, and compensation in this period (Darling-Hammond and Berry 1988).

The reforms signaled a surge in state activity at a time that the federal government was retiring from policy initiation and reducing education spending (Kirst 1987). Many observers link increased state leadership directly to federal retreat, arguing that the states were filling a vacuum (Clark and Astuto 1986). Similarly, some commentators interpret state ascendance as a reaction to an abdication of local responsibility. They cite visible failures of large, urban school districts, high dropout rates, and disappointing test scores as evidence of the need for state action.

As the reforms build on two decades of significant increases in state education spending, they can be interpreted as natural impulses to ensure accountability for the ever larger state aid dollar. The state share of spending on elementary and secondary education went from almost 40 percent in 1970 to 48 percent in 1983. The 1985–86 state share is estimated at over 50 percent (Center for Education Statistics 1987).

Another factor cited by those who believe that the reforms signal the end of local control concerns the nature of the reform policies. Several specific reforms appear to be very directive of local behavior. For example, many states that had left compensation issues entirely to local discretion and negotiation entered into the field of setting teacher salaries for the first time (Darling-Hammond and Berry 1988). The student standards policies incorporated a number of elements that could be expected to drive school curricula: increased and more specific course requirements, new exit exams and other statewide assessments, state-developed competencies for each subject, new curriculum guides. In some states, new sophisticated monitoring techniques could permit state policymakers to track the progress of individual students, as well as schools and districts.

Finally, what most appears to alarm spokespersons for local interests is that they were left out of the reform policymaking process. Leaders of state-level local associations in the study states say they were represented on task forces and commissions, but that they do not feel they were able to have any real input or role in shaping the result. They claim reactive victories, successes in blunting what they saw as some of the more onerous aspects of reform. For example, the Pennsylvania School Boards Association pressed to have new funding distributed through the Equalized Subsidy for Basic Education (ESBE) formula, rather than in categorical programs. ESBE represented a well-compromised and politically supported distributional scheme; it also delivered general aid, without restrictions on use by local districts.

Local concern about exclusion from the reform process and the top-down nature of the new policies suggested a rocky road for the reforms as they reached the schools. Some analysts of reform legislation predicted widespread resistance; on the other hand, some predicted total loss of local independence (Doyle and Finn 1984; IEL 1986). The choice posed for local districts was sometimes depicted in tones almost as solemn as those used when Americans first faced the same dilemma: disobedience or loss of self-governance.

However, our research has revealed a much more complex picture about state-local relations than is portrayed by forecasts of the death of local control or assumptions about massive local resistance. There was, in fact, not much resistance to many of the reforms in most places.[2] The ease of compliance has a number of roots. First, examination reveals that many of the new standards were already met by local districts prior to state legislation. In fact, new state high school graduation requirements were met or surpassed by most districts in most states (CPRE 1988); the reforms simply legitimated local practice. For example, in Pennsylvania, a state department study revealed that 75 percent of districts already exceeded new state requirements; in Georgia the new requirements were already in force for all students in the state who pursued an academic diploma prior to the Quality Basic Education Act.

Compliance was also made easier by the widespread public support for the intention of the reforms and the fact that most of the new policies called for changes that school personnel were comfortable with and knew how to achieve. They knew how to add courses in math and science and how to incorporate new testing into their programs. Many, if not most, of the reforms were well within the technical expertise of school personnel, and in fact, required them merely to do more of what they were inclined and educated to do.[3]

One of our most interesting and important discoveries is that many local districts are going far beyond compliance; they are responding very actively to state reforms. In over half of our local districts, administrators saw opportunities in the state reforms to accomplish their own objectives, particularly as the state reforms provided significant funding increases. Local districts are actively orchestrating various state policies around local priorities, strategically interacting with the state to achieve local goals. For example, one major urban district coordinates almost all state teacher policies, including its mentor teacher program and alternate route, to meet the prime objective of hiring a large number of new teachers. Another district in the same state uses the mentor teacher program for curricular and staff development activities that are current district priorities. Mentor positions are advertised to attract applicants interested in working in these specific areas. In like manner, a Florida district has expanded the state merit schools program, adding criteria for success and supplementing state funding with local dollars in order to reward all schools reaching their own goals.

In the states we studied, state student standards policies have provided opportunity for and lent momentum to a significant movement already evident in many local school districts of varying size: centralized curriculum regulation and alignment of curriculum, tests, texts, teacher evaluation, and other mechanisms. Districts throughout the nation are standardizing their curricula for a variety of reasons. Pressure from minority parents can lead to a desire to make curriculum more uniform across a district; so can concerns about high mobility from school to school. Technological advances, such as computer programs that map standardized tests against major texts in key subject areas, support the movement. However, it is clear that the state reforms furnished an influential lever. For example, administrators in one Pennsylvania district stated that the new definition of a planned course located in the Chapter 5 revision was "a good excuse" to address curriculum revision. New state testing affected the curriculum to some extent in every district we visited. In approximately half of them, state testing was cited as an important impetus for district-level curriculum standardization. Student standards have also been used as levers for more resources, such as adding more central district personnel in curriculum and assessment and more teachers where the standards meant that a longer school day was needed.

Another phenomenon we observed was the tendency of some local districts to get out ahead of the new state reforms in a way that distinguishes them from their peers. For example, several districts in our study raised high school graduation requirements beyond new state increases in deliberate attempts to stay ahead of other districts. This includes districts that did not already exceed the new state criteria and those that did. One California district that had a requirement of 120 units raised its requirements to 160 units when SB813 was passed. This placed it thirty units ahead of SB813's 130-unit requirement and five units ahead of the state board's model requirements. A Pennsylvania district that had nineteen credits to the state's thirteen raised to twenty-two when the state went to twenty-one. Two districts we visited, one in Georgia and one in Florida, are developing career ladder plans in anticipation of state programs. The Georgia district is designing a student-achievement-based teacher evaluation scheme, expecting that the state would use such criteria and preferring to fashion its own system than to respond to a mandate. The Florida system included career ladder development in a landmark professionalization effort jointly undertaken with the teachers' union.

Many local district personnel are actively engaged in networks that influence state policy before it is formalized. Several of the new state programs were modeled after practices already underway in local districts. Florida's Meritorious Schools Policy is very similar in spirit and requirements to policy previously enacted by a county well-known for its school improvement program. Florida's effort to develop subject-area tests draws on the experience of a major district that is now under contract to the state to develop subject matter standardized tests for statewide use. Sometimes, state policymakers learned about local initiatives through customary information networks; for examples, legislators frequently turn to the superintendents in their legislative districts for information about practice and potential policy impact. In addition, reform commissions often included leading local actors. The superintendents of two Georgia districts we visited were members of the Education Review Commission and, as much as possible, shaped QBE to the needs and capacities of their districts.

Increasing sophistication among local actors means that they increasingly engage in strategic interaction with state actors both in responding to and affecting the content of state policy. Although it is too soon to draw a balance sheet on state-local roles in the wake of reform, it is clear that it would be a vast oversimplification to chalk up the movement as a massive increase in state power.

STUDENT STANDARDS

Student standards were the most popular type of policy intervention in the recent waves of state reform. State graduation requirements were increased in forty-three states; other types of student standards, such as longer school days, minimum gradepoint averages and new exit tests, were also popular. The increases in standards were well supported by theory. High standards represent high expectations, and high expectations are an important component of effective schools (Purkey and Smith 1983; Cohen 1983). Standards are also supported by the concept of "opportunity to learn"—that is, students learn more if they are exposed to more content (Wolf 1977; Good, Grouws, and Beckerman 1978; Brophy and Good 1986; Raizen and Jones 1985). However, from the start vigorous questions were raised about the potentially negative effects of increased standards on dropping out and student success (Cusick 1984; McDill, Natriello, and Pallas 1985).

Early in our research we learned that the graduation requirement reforms were not as large as they looked on paper. As pointed out above, most local districts already met the new state requirements. They were more sensitive to increased university and college admission requirements. Even when local requirements fell below the new level, college bound students were already taking at least, if not more, than the new requirements. However, even those districts that exceeded state requirements generally had to add courses to meet the specific subjects highlighted in the new reforms. Most districts in our study had to add an extra course in math and science, and sometimes in social studies, language, and fine arts. The remainder of districts added additional sections of existing courses (Clune 1988). For example, a major urban district had to split a generalized "science" offering into separate classes for physical and biological science. Another urban district across the country added an environmental science course as a new third-year science course that was not chemistry or physics.

School-level respondents told us that the state reforms were leading to more students taking courses in academic subject areas. In fact, because more students, including the noncollege bound, are taking more math, science, and social studies, enrollments have declined in vocational education, business education, and, in some cases, art and music. The high school curriculum has become more concentrated around core subjects, with students taking fewer electives and having less time for career preparation, particularly where the day is short. However, even though the new courses added are in major academic areas, most have not been academic. They have generally been basic or remedial, with titles like "Math Applications," and intended for the noncollege bound. The college-bound third- or fourth-year courses in these subjects were already in place prior to the reforms.

Increases in student standards present both benefits and hazards for at risk students. Higher standards represent higher expectations, expose marginal students to more academic content, and marshal resources for previously underserved students. However, increases in standards may also be related to increased pressure on many students and a reduction of choice for students with special needs and goals, such as those who need remediation or who want vocational education in high school. Practitioners report that higher course requirements, and related reforms like minimum grade point averages, make graduation a more difficult goal for at-risk students while limiting the time available for remediation and retaking failed courses. Such effects depend strongly on the responses of individual schools, on whether schools have a five-period or a seven-period day, for example, and on how students are counseled. School responses and the course-taking patterns of different types of students will be important to document over 1987–88 and 1988–89 as juniors and seniors in many states first become subject to new requirements.

The addition of new courses did impose some expenses on districts, but none reported major costs. Some districts had trouble finding teachers, particularly in math and science, and initiated programs to recertify teachers, such as business education teachers. Others had facilities problems, including insufficient laboratory space. However, the implementation problems were minor. The real questions about student standards policies concern the nature of courses students are taking, whether in fact they provide a more academic curriculum as reformers hoped, and how different students are affected.

In summary, the new student standards posed few problems for school districts. Course requirements led to modest adjustments without much dislocation. Important questions about how individual schools are responding to the needs of individual students remain unanswered, but school personnel believe that the reforms accomplished a major purpose: creating a more academic secondary school experience for all students.

TEACHER POLICIES

State efforts in the area of teacher policy were much less coherent than the student standards reforms. States seem to be going in several different directions at once. The six states we studied stiffened requirements for entry into the profession with tests, course, and grade average requirements. At the same time, they provided for alternative routes that required no specific course preparations. Some tried career ladders intended to make teaching more of a profession by differentiating responsibilities and creating a career structure. However, many teachers found the evaluation instruments and criteria demeaning and unprofessional. There is still little agreement on what a teacher ought to be able to do, the nature of teaching and the roles of teachers. Some policies view teachers as professionals relying on an abundant knowledge base, while others view teachers as workers needing extensive direction (Darling-Hammond and Berry 1988).

Initial analysis of the implementation of state teacher policies indicates that the conflicting assumptions embodied in different approaches are reflected in implementation problems in the field. Particular difficulties are associated with career ladder plans. Such plans are very sensitive to the validity of evaluation. Teachers in Florida complained bitterly about the master teacher program, a 1983 reform that has been scrapped in the wake of severe first-year substantive and administrative difficulties. A number of the issues contributing to the program's demise concerned the evaluation procedures: Tests were available in some subject matter areas and not others, so that some teachers could advance without testing; the observation instrument was designed for beginning, not experienced teachers; nonclassroom personnel were subject to evaluation as classroom teachers; trained teacher evaluators became very savvy about doing well on their own evaluations, causing others to resent them; some principal-evaluators were suspected of stealing good teachers they evaluated in other schools; and part of the process called for teachers to be evaluated by their own supervisors, leading to dissension.

The Arizona career ladder suffered from fewer administrative problems and aroused less concern about evaluation procedures than Florida's plan. However, Arizona teachers and evaluators complained about enormous paperwork demands and the vast amounts of time required to prepare and evaluate portfolios.

The difficulties in Florida led to a decision in 1986 to create a career ladder program that would permit local districts to design their own approaches. Although state funding for the new career ladder was not provided, the concept of local design seems important for differentiated staffing and reward plans. The issues of eligibility, criteria for promotion, and how and by whom teachers should be evaluated are immensely difficult. Some of the problems are related to a weak knowledge base; for example, educators are just beginning to develop assessment instruments that appraise important aspects of teaching, such as teachers' ability to reflect on practice (Peterson and Comeaux 1988). Many problems are political. Differential reward schemes involve constructing consensus on key values, like what constitutes "good" teaching, and matching desires to recognize success to available resources. Such issues have proven at least somewhat troublesome in every district we visited where a state career ladder exists. It may be the case that these questions need to be resolved locally, with each district creating solutions to suit its needs. Al-

though we have no experience in our study states with locally designed career ladders, the mentor teacher program in California,
where districts set their own definitions of exemplary teaching,
appears to have better support than schemes in which states determine advancement criteria. The mentor program is not free of implementation troubles and perceptions of its success and utility vary,
with many respondents seeing it as an insignificant and peripheral
program. However, the widespread dissension surrounding state
career ladder plans is absent.

District response to state teacher initiatives is heavily dependent
on local needs, even more so than in the case of the student standards policies. In particular, those districts that were hiring new
teachers in significant numbers or had concerns about retaining
teachers were most enthusiastic about policies they could use for
recruitment and training of novices. Diverse policies were put to such
use by districts in several states. For example, the induction program
in Pennsylvania was relevant only in the one district that needed to
hire several hundred teachers a year and was experiencing shortages;
that district volunteered to pilot the induction program in 1986–87
and was eager to expand it to a full program in 1987–88. The district
also used the state's alternative route, an old program that has been
recently revived and expanded, to fill shortages. The Arizona district
that found the state career ladder most appealing made new teachers
as well as more experienced teachers eligible in order to increase
retention in the beginning years. Similarly, respondents in the California district with the great need for and problem finding new
teachers were the most positive about the state's various teacher
programs including the mentor teacher, teacher trainee, and minimum salary provisions.

In the districts we visited, teacher associations and unions participated in the implementation of teacher policies. For example, they
were active members of committees designing induction programs in
Pennsylvania, developing career ladder pilots in Arizona, and selecting mentor teachers in California. However, with a few exceptions,
they saw these policies as fairly insignificant compared to their key
concerns about salary and working conditions. They accommodated
to them rather than seizing leadership. Although the reasons for the
stance of unions varied considerably, ranging from their limited influence in some states to the rather narrow scope of the reform policies
in others, it seems clear that union accommodation and acceptance

was vital to the local implementation process. Local unions could easily have blocked reforms had they decided to; they did not (McDonnell and Pascal 1988).

In summary, teacher policies in the six states were encountering significantly more difficulties in implementation than other types of reforms. Some, like the Florida Master Teacher Program, were poorly designed and administered. The issues posed by differential reward schemes are so difficult that they may require negotiation and resolution at each site, suggesting the need for local discretion. However, our findings indicate that state teacher policies were put to enthusiastic use by districts that had a critical need for new teachers and that local teacher associations participated in implementation, even in the cases of policies they opposed at the state level.

A NEW IMPLEMENTATION MODEL

Our findings about reforms in these six states suggest several new ways of thinking about policy implementation. We found that certain factors were less important to implementation success than we predicted based on past research; other elements were more important than we predicted. Finally, some developments were simply different than we expected.

Among the factors less critical than our original model posited is ownership stemming from participation in the reform process. Our findings suggest strongly that policymaker and educator support for reform, which is key to successful implementation, does not depend on participation in reform initiation and design. State departments and boards were generally not reform leaders, yet they have actively engaged in reform activities such as designing tests, establishing course competencies, and assisting and monitoring districts. In fact, although they may have felt their role usurped by legislators and governors, they were by no means left without portfolio. In many cases reform legislation gave them more to do by mandating that they respond to broad legislative directives.

In none of the six states did associations representing local actors inaugurate or mold the substance of the reforms to any significant extent, yet in every state there was substantial compliance and frequent examples of districts that seized the reforms and embellished upon them. Similarly, teachers unions barely controlled their opposition to reforms at the state level but participated in their local implementation. Even though the unions were not enthused about the potential of the reforms to affect teachers' lives or district ability to recruit and retain good teachers, they ultimately helped make the reforms happen.

A second factor that was less critical than expected in the implementation process is the clarity of the policy. Student standards mandates were notably more straightforward and understood and more easily implemented than teacher policies that predictably ran into trouble, but they were not entirely unambiguous or without multiple meanings. We found widespread compliance with reforms of student standards and testing policies, even though those reforms did not give unclouded, unadulterated signals. School personnel easily absorbed the new standards, and even sought to exceed them, knowing that the standards were often carrying messages other than or in addition to academic rigor and knowing that they were sometimes proxies for distrust of local districts, concealed goads toward consolidation, or sops to business supporters. The fact that reform packages combined several different programs, some leading in different directions, also did not appear to cause local districts problems.

Two factors turned out to be more important to successful implementation than we predicted and account in large measure for the extensive compliance and lack of resistance encountered. First, compliance depends heavily on the extent to which relevant technical knowledge exists and school personnel feel competent to make the change. Although the student standard reforms often caused disruptions—more sections, more teachers in shortage areas such as math and science, more facilities—and were not "easy" in that sense, they were policies with which educators felt comfortable. Creating more academically oriented high schools was a task for which their training and school experience had prepared them and toward which they were favorably disposed. In contrast, the weaker knowledge base supporting career ladder and teacher evaluation policies contributed to implementation problems.

District context was also more influential than we predicted. The importance of local context, the extent to which policies coincide with local goals and capacity, has long been appreciated by researchers. However, our findings suggest a much less passive role for districts than past implementation research posits. We have tended in the past to view districts as reactive—first to federal and then to state policy—determining which pieces of policies from other governmental levels districts to accept and modifying such policies to suit their needs. But many of the districts we have observed are busily making their own policies, engaging in networks with and borrowing from other local districts. Such districts do not merely adapt to state policy, they orchestrate and amplify policies around local priorities, whether or not any of the other conditions that would make those policies easy to implement exist. Active districts do not wait for state policies to happen, they make them happen. To the extent that district activity is related to the political, social, and economic milieu, district context appears not only important but paramount.

Finally, we discovered that certain of our predictions about the effects of reform and governance in the wake of reform simply did not come true. For example, we did not find long delays in translating reform policies into practice or widespread resistance. Past research led us to expect long lags in implementation and little short-term impact. However, the student standards reforms, for example, were swiftly translated into new courses and sections and new state-tested competencies were incorporated into curriculum. What remains a question is whether this immediate response is the precursor to further change, or whether it represents the extent of reaction in itself. If modifications in the high school curriculum amount to the addition of basic or general courses in academic subjects rather than a more fundamental overhaul of content or course sequence, then reform in this area will have had an immediate but fairly modest impact.[4]

Of particular interest is our finding that the reforms do not signal the end of local control. States are certainly making more policy in more areas of education than ever before, but so are local districts. States are increasing standards and testing; so are local districts. Locals are ahead of states in standardizing curriculum; both states and locals are actively experimenting with teacher evaluation and reward systems. What we have found is not a zero-sum game but a net increase in governance. Every policymaker is making more policy. A key question for the future, and one we have posed for ourselves in our continuing study in the six states, is the extent to which all this policymaking impinges on teacher or student discretion or autonomy. What does the surge in policymaking mean for classroom practice?

Our findings about local response to reform significantly extend our understanding of the implementation process. We anticipated that the range of local behavior would be captured by three concepts: resistance to policy change, formal compliance, and adaptation. Instead we have observed performance that may constitute a new point on the continuum of response by implementing agencies, behavior that we have begun to call "strategic interaction." Strategic interactors seize policy opportunity, coordinate and expand state policies to meet their needs, and anticipate and actively shape state policy. Because we deliberately visited a number of districts that were judged to have a high capacity to respond to reforms, our sample may overrepresent strategic interaction behavior. However, conversations with policymakers throughout the nation and accounts by journalists and researchers of innovations in districts like Rochester, New York; Dade County, Florida; and Hammond, Indiana, lead us to believe that such local activity is increasingly apparent.

When we contrast what we are finding in our study of state reform with what implementation research predicted, we find a more complex model of the process. Although policy formulation and implementation are strongly shaped by context and are therefore extremely variable, other maxims now seem to hold less force. Ownership is possible without participation in the shaping of policy; and short-term reactions can be expected, especially where technical capacity exists. Traditional modes of describing local response to policy interventions—resistance, compliance, adaptation—fail to account for the active appropriation of policy we are witnessing. The nature, extent, and reasons for the strategic interaction behavior we have described are among the issues we intend to explore in our continuing research.

NOTES

1. For a very recent summary of research on policy implementation, see McLaughlin (1987). Earlier research and reviews include Bardach (1977), Berman and McLaughlin (1978), Elmore (1978), Sabatier and Mazmanian (1980), and Van Meter and Van Horn (1975).
2. See Odden and Marsh (1987) for a study of California reform that reaches the same conclusion based on a larger local sample than CPRE's in that state.
3. To a number of reform critics the student standards reforms are merely marginal adjustments that do not penetrate the core of the teacher-centered classroom (see, for example, Cohen 1987; Cuban 1984, 1988). These analysts would probably relate ease of compliance to the conformance of the reforms to existing structures—that is, the reforms were quickly implement-

ed as much because they were peripheral as because they were easy to understand.
4. We are indebted to our colleague Marshall Smith of Stanford University for making this point.

REFERENCES

Bardach, Eugene. 1977. *The Implementation Game.* Cambridge, Mass.: MIT Press.

Berman, Paul, and Milbrey McLaughlin. 1978. *Federal Programs Supporting Educational Change.* Santa Monica, Calif.: RAND Corporation.

Brophy, Jere, and Thomas Good. 1986. "Teacher Behavior and Student Achievements." In *Third Handbook for Research on Teaching,* edited by M.C. Wittrock, pp. 328-75. New York: MacMillan.

Center for Education Statistics. 1987. *The Condition of Education: A Statistical Report.* Washington, D.C.: Office of Educational Research and Improvement, U.S. Department of Education.

Center for Policy Research in Education. 1988. "Graduating From High School: New Standards in the States." *CPRE Policy Briefs.* New Brunswick, N.J.: Rutgers University.

Clark, David L., and Terry A. Astuto. 1986. *The Significance and Permanence of Changes in Federal Educational Policy 1980-88.* Bloomington, Ind.: Policy Studies Center of the University Council for Educational Administration.

Clune, William H. 1987, "Institutional Choice as a Theoretical Framework for Research on Educational Policy." *Educational Evaluation and Policy Analysis* 9: 117-32.

_____. 1988. "Educational Reform: The Effects of Graduation Requirements and Other Student Standards." New Brunswick, N.J.: Center for Policy Research in Education. Rutgers University.

Cohen, David. 1987. "Educational Technology, Policy and Practice." *Educational Evaluation and Policy Analysis* 9: 153-70.

Cohen, Michael. 1983. "Instructional, Management and Social Conditions in Effective Schools." In *School Finance and School Improvement: Linkages for 1980s,* edited by A. Odden and L.D. Webb, pp. 17-50. Cambridge, Mass.: Ballinger.

Cuban, Larry. 1984. *How Teachers Taught.* New York: Longman.

_____. 1988 (January). "A Fundamental Puzzle of School Reform, *Phi Delta Kappan* 69: 340-44.

Cusick, P.A. 1984. *The School Reform Movement's Impact on School Dropout and Retention Efforts.* East Lansing, Mich.: Michigan State University.

Darling-Hammond, Linda, and Barnett Berry. 1988. *The Evolution of Teacher Policy.* Prepared for the Center for Policy Research in Education. Santa Monica, Calif.: RAND Corporation.

Doyle, Denis P., and Chester E. Finn, Jr. 1984. "American Schools and the Future of Local Control." *The Public Interest* 77 (Fall): 77–95.

Elmore, Richard F. 1978. "Organizational Models of Social Program Implementation." *Public Policy* 26: 209–17.

Good, T., D. Grouws, and T. Beckerman. 1978. "Curriculum Pacing: Some Empirical Data in Mathematics." *Journal of Curriculum Studies* 10: 75–81.

The Institute for Educational Leadership, Inc. 1986. *School Boards: Strengthening Grass Roots Leadership.* Washington, D.C.: Institute for Educational Leadership.

Kirst, Michael W. 1987. "The Federal Role and Chapter I: Rethinking Some Basic Assumptions." In *Policy Options for the Future of Compensatory Education: Conference Papers*, edited by D. Doyle, J. Michie and B. Williams, pp. 89–105. Washington, D.C.: Research and Evaluation Associates.

McDonnell, Lorraine, and Susan Fuhrman. 1986. "The Political Context of Reform." In *The Fiscal, Legal, and Political Aspects of State Reform of Elementary and Secondary Education*, edited by V. Mueller and M. McKeown, pp. 43–64. Cambridge, Mass.: Ballinger.

McDonnell, Lorraine M., and Anthony Pascal. 1988. *Teacher Unions and Educational Reform.* Prepared for Center for Policy Research in Education. Santa Monica, Calif.: RAND Corporation.

McDill, Edward L., Gary Natriello, and Aaron M. Pallas. 1985. "Raising Standards and Retaining Students: The Impact of the Reform Recommendation on Potential Dropouts," Report 358. Center for Social Organization of Schools. Baltimore, Md.: Johns Hopkins University Press.

McLaughlin, Milbrey W. 1976. "Implementation as Mutual Adaptation: Change in Classroom Organization." In *Social Program Implementation*, edited by W. Williams and R. Elmore, pp. 167–80. New York: Academic Press.

––––––. 1987. "Lessons from Past Implementation Research." *Educational Evaluation and Policy Analysis* 9: 171–78.

Odden, Allan. 1987. "The Economics of Financing Education Excellence." Paper presented at the American Educational Research Association, Washington, D.C., April 20, 1987.

Odden, Allan R., and David D. Marsh. December 1987. "How State Education Reform Can Improve Secondary Schools." Policy Analysis for California Education, Policy Paper no. PC87-12-145DE. Berkeley, Calif.:

Peterson, Penelope, and Michelle Comeaux. 1988. "Assessing the Teacher as a Reflective Professional: New Perspectives on Teacher Evaluation." In *The Graduate Preparation of Teachers*, edited by A. Woolfolk. Englewood Cliffs, N.J.: Prentice-Hall.

Purkey, S. C., and M. S. Smith. 1983. "Effective Schools: A Review." *Elementary School Journal* 83: 427–52.

Raizen, Senta A., and Lyle V. Jones, eds. 1985. *Indicators of Precollege Education in Science and Mathematics: A Preliminary Review.* Washington, D.C.: National Academy Press.

Sabatier, Paul, and Daniel Mazmanian. 1980. "The Implementation of Public Policy: A Framework of Analysis." *Policy Studies Journal* 8: 538–60.

Van Meter, Donald, and Carl Van Horn. 1975. "The Policy Implementation Process: A Conceptual Framework." *Administration and Society* 6: 445–88.

Wolf, Richard M. 1977. *Achievement in America*. New York: Teachers College Press.

2 THE EFFECTS OF EDUCATION REFORM ON THE PROFESSIONALIZATION OF TEACHERS

Susan J. Rosenholtz

Since the report of the National Commission on Excellence in Education prophesized an omen of doom for public education some five years ago, educational policymakers in nearly every state have scrambled to predict and conquer educational events and practices that appear most out of control. Underlying much of the present flurry of reform activity is the assumption that teachers' lackluster performance in no small way accounts for the inadequacy of student learning.

Teachers have become the focus of every imaginable contemporary debate on education, particularly as a target for political assault. Policymakers think that they have too much freedom: all engine, no brakes, the great vehicle careening all over the road, the lowest common denominator at the wheel. With the current onslaught of commission reports, a number of prominent Americans at the moment believe that public education is not merely doomed but undeserving of survival. A great many Americans have come to sympathize with the problem, anxious about the loss of fixed points, wishing for simpler, more orderly times. Much negative publicity has resulted, and the public climate of opinion has become increasingly hostile: an abrupt and utter evaporation of confidence has occurred in the nation's teachers, and they in themselves.

This harsh and subversive judgment of teachers has resulted in greater demands for accountability. Also driving some of the current education reform movement, at least from professional educators, is the call for the enhancement of teaching as a profession including serious reflection and critical analysis by teachers about the meaning and scope of their work. This possibility is being entertained, albeit grudgingly in many quarters, by policymakers, too. However, most state reform efforts have been subjected to little critical analysis and even less evaluation. In addition, the plethora of interventions appear to rest on no solid base of valid and reliable knowledge about the teaching occupation—knowledge revealing that several approaches to school reform currently underway are blatantly inimical to school improvement and the professionalization of teachers. The unchecked pursuit of change tends to generate harmful policies, policies that injure both teachers and students.

In this chapter I argue for the necessity of research and analysis for present education policymakers so as to encourage good ideas, discourage bad ones, and permit wise midcourse corrections. To illustrate how cumulative research and analysis can provide sound information to foster and support further school improvement, I examine in some detail two education reforms that have gained considerable currency among policymakers nationwide. My purpose here is twofold: (1) to elucidate ways in which policy intervention may affect teachers' academic success with students, their sense of teaching efficacy, their commitment to the reform, and their professionalization, and (2) to examine the interaction of reform efforts with varying school contexts. The analysis concludes with specific policy recommendations.

EDUCATION REFORM

Max Weber once posed a critical dilemma when he asked how you control organizational participants to maximize effectiveness and efficiency and minimize the unhappiness this very need to control produces. This same dilemma exists today, not only in large-scale organizations but in schools as well, lending new urgency to age-old conflicts: those of standardization versus autonomy, management by hierarchical control versus facilitation of professionalism, mandatory versus voluntary change, and so forth.

The view of school improvement advanced here attempts to deal with these conflicts by applying a broad base of knowledge about the social organizational conditions necessary to improve teacher quality and professionalize teachers to a detailed analysis of how these conflicts are played out in two current reform efforts—minimum competency testing for students and career ladders for teachers.

It makes sense to filter the effects of current reforms through the lenses of teachers involved because teachers are the ultimate arbitrators of education policy. That is, how teachers experience policy changes will affect their commitment to them and the extent to which these interventions will have salutary effects on their professionalization. To explore teachers' perceptions, I turn to qualitative data from my study of the organizational context of teaching (Rosenholtz in press) conducted in Tennessee where a career ladder plan and minimum competency testing were concurrently under implementation. Data collected from extensive interviews with a random sample of seventy-four elementary teachers stratified by school quality will illuminate many of the conflicts embedded in these reform efforts. Our measures of school success parallel classical definitions of professionalism. Successful schools in the sample are those (1) where teachers seek control of their work in light of their own shared standards and common identity, (2) where colleagues mutually render technical advice and assistance, (3) where both teachers and students learn and grow, and (4) where teachers owe allegiance to their peers and profession.

MINIMUM COMPETENCY TESTING

Of fundamental importance to any policy study of education reform is the definition of student learning itself, and a pivotal part of the current reform movement, at least in the elementary school grades, is the understandable focus on students' basic skill mastery and the means to assure content coverage. Policymakers herald minimum competency testing (MCI) as a viable means to exercise hierarchical control over teachers' curricular choices by establishing clear instructional objectives and systematically detailing their attainment through standardized testing. Indeed, Dornbusch and Scott (1975), in their oft-cited study of organizational authority, found that evaluation of work was the pivotal mechanism through which control was exercised. Control through evaluation was found most effective when those being evaluated believed the evaluations were important, central to their work, and capable of being influenced by their own efforts. Herein lies a fundamental challenge confronting MCT: Where teachers perceive it as both soundly based and negotiable—that is, where policymakers strive to procure consensus with teachers—their commitment to the reform and their classroom curriculum should be aligned closely.

Task Conceptions as a Potential Source of Conflict

This challenge, however, looms large indeed when we examine teachers' task conceptions—the goals of their work and the technology available to attain them. Quite apart from children's mastery of basic skills, teachers may define student learning as developing students' problemsolving skills; raising youngsters' self-concept; encouraging friendly interpersonal behavior; instituting peace and quiet in the classroom and corridors; and so on. Except in the most successful schools, teachers seldom use objective test results to gauge their teaching effectiveness (Ashton and Webb 1986; Rosenholtz in press). With MCT, then, teachers and policymakers may hold highly divergent task conceptions about the nature of their work.

Moreover, confronted by the same task demands, constituents may hold entirely different conceptions about the way work should be carried out. Policy makers tend to emphasize task uniformity, whereas some teachers stress the need for task diversity; policymakers tend to emphasize task simplicity and routinization, whereas teachers stress complexity and uncertainty (Scott 1981).

To complicate the issue further, task conceptions held by different constituencies are associated with preferred work structures (Scott 1981). Teachers who view their work as uncertain and complex will naturally desire more autonomy and discretion to carry it out; policymakers who view teachers' work as more routine will prefer hierarchical work arrangements that both centralize decision-making and promulgate directives for teachers to follow. All of this means that given disparate task conceptions held by teachers and policymakers, there is a fundamental and profound basis for conflict over MCT. In the section that follows, I explore these conflicts as manifested in Tennessee's MCT program, but first a caveat is in order to explain the circumstances under which Tennessee implemented MCT.

MCT in Tennessee

Two Tennessee task forces, each consisting of approximately five state Department of Education personnel, five education professors, and five elementary school teachers (hand-picked by the state) initially developed a MCT program for elementary grade students. Although four of the five teachers came from suburban or urban districts ranked statewide in the top 14 percent by per-pupil expenditure, over two-thirds of the districts in the state are rural and poor, many, in fact, ranking among the poorest in the nation (Fowler 1985).

Using assorted grade-level curriculum guides and basal texts, the task forces identified 708 skills in reading and 661 skills in math and, to measure pupils' mastery of these, constructed 241 reading and 435 math tests. Tests were to be administered individually and orally to kindergarten and first-grade students to avoid reading difficulties.

During the first year of mandatory implementation, districts chose to institute either the reading or the math Basic Skills Program. The state assigned districts the task of monitoring teachers' compliance with the program; district reports, in turn, were scrutinized by the state. Compliance was assured, as open systems theorists would quickly point out (Scott 1981), because the state ultimately commanded, and could thus just as easily withdraw, the fiscal resources vital to the survival of districts and schools within them. Accordingly, interviews we conducted with teachers at the end of this initial year revealed uniformly high conformity to the standards statewide, as well as some accompanying realignments in their instructional emphases.

Unintended Consequences of MCI

But because of conflicting task conceptions and preferred work structures, MCT was not welcomed by the majority of Tennessee teachers, resulting in varied negative and unintended consequences. Teachers voiced concern that their loss of task autonomy constrained their ability to deliver appropriately paced instruction. Standardized curriculum, they explained, impaired their discretion to match appropriate learning objectives to particular student needs (see also Darling-Hammond and Wise 1985). Over three-fourths of the teachers from successful schools expressed this objection, compared to slightly less than a fourth from unsuccessful schools:

> "You can't possibly teach every child all the skills required. For some they are too easy. For others they are too difficult. Teaching has to be done so that students are given work they are capable of doing. If I were to use it the way the state wanted, it would ruin children's motivation altogether."

> "It used to be that we would take up where the kids were [at the beginning of the year] and you would go as far as you could with them. Now they say we are not to do that anymore."

With the implementation of MCT, then, these teachers confronted a dilemma between the *coverage* of basic skills on the one hand, and *mastery* of them, on the other. As it turns out, the problem of inappropriate instructional pacing is the villain of the piece in many teaching and learning problems (Barr 1975). Proper pacing means striking the critical balance between students' achievement levels and their successful task experiences, an undertaking that takes on exponential complexity as the heterogeneity of students' achievement levels within a classroom increases (Beckerman and Good 1981). This latter point is particularly meaningful for the present analysis. More than 80 percent of our sample taught academically heterogeneous classes, and almost all worked with low-SES students in varying proportions (ranging from 20 to 80 percent). Not unexpectedly, inappropriately paced instruction—directly associated with emphasis on coverage of material—has been found to account for poor reading performance on the part of low-SES students (Dreeben and Gamoran 1985). That teachers from the most successful schools would worry more about student mastery than coverage is reasonable and intuitively sound.

In addition to problems of mastery versus coverage, the most intriguing contrasts between successful and unsuccessful schools came in teachers' response to questions about their morale. Even among those from successful schools who voiced high morale (65 percent), responses were often tempered by negative sentiments about the state's educational tinkering with MCT:

> "It's high because of the other teachers in the school. And the parents who work for the school to fund raise and help do the paperwork. You know this Basic Skills Program sounds great on paper but trying to do it means so much paperwork! So the principal gets parents to come in and do the paperwork for each teacher so we can concentrate on teaching. I don't know what I'd do without the help."

"I'm proud to be in this school system. It's the things imposed by the state that are creating problems for us. Our system expects teachers to be at the top. I don't know this for sure, but that seems to create different attitudes among us toward our work. We take things very seriously, and the school system helps in the extra paperwork. I think this attitude must be very different in systems that do not support their teachers that way."

Underlying these teachers comments are their collective, shared values within the school, and the conditions shared orientations permit that save them from despair about new state mandates. That principals, teachers, and parents mobilize against a common enemy—interference with instruction—is illustrative of successful schools.

Another fundamental difference between teachers in successful and unsuccessful schools was revealed in their concerns about the teaching profession resulting from MCT. Lowered morale from concerns for the profession was identified by 60 percent of those from successful schools but by less than 20 percent of their counterparts in less successful schools. The following comments are illustrative:

"Lower. I think the system is becoming all too dictatorial. I mean I ask myself all the time, 'I wonder where all the creative teachers will be in ten years?'"

"With everything prescribed now, sometimes I ask myself, 'Will we have only desk-sitters in the future?' I'm really afraid all the good teachers are going out of teaching."

"Our assessment of what students need doesn't seem to matter any more. That hurts students and teachers. I'm really afraid all the good teachers are going out of teaching."

"His [the governor's] programs have destroyed the morale of teachers. I often think of new generations of teachers and what they'll be like. With all the rules and regulations, I think they'll be robotic, less creative, and less personal in dealing with children."

Each of these teachers' concerns involved threats to their efficacy posed by the state—a sense of loss in their governance and control of work. State mandates, they argue, now bureaucratize the workplace with fixed jurisdictions, expropriating teachers' vastly more skillful and accurate judgments. These changes are interpreted as a loss of professional trust and an erosion of their profession with its distinct stock of technical knowledge teachers once proudly enjoyed.

The delicate and situational nature of teacher commitment is another salient inference to be drawn from these comments. These same teachers, who only a year before in our questionnaire data reported high job involvement and satisfaction with their work, who exercised judgment and discretion on a daily basis, now perceive teaching as a bureaucratic obstacle course, a treacherous interval between classroom success and failure.

That successful teachers worry aloud about a concomitant loss of commitment by the teaching profession itself follows logically. As the gap widens between what they think appropriate and what the state demands, they envision that their future colleagues will also become dissatisfied and alienated and that the profession will be less able to attract or retain good teachers. Significantly, this latter fear is buttressed by evidence from Chapman (1983), who found that the most highly qualified teachers were those most dissatisfied with a lack of autonomy and discretion and thus more likely to defect from the profession.

A critical question in the study of state-mandated MCT, then, is the extent to which it allows for local variation in students' skill levels, local deviations from statewide standards, and the importance of curricular discretion to teachers. State-mandated curriculum predicated on assumptions about students performing at grade level will almost certainly fail in academically diversified classrooms, unwittingly programming students for less rather than greater basic skill mastery. The extent to which teachers suffer professionally from this policy, however, depends at heart on the school context in which they perform.

For some, the consequences of this problem may be far more extensive than one might imagine. To understand the deleterious affects of MCT on teacher attitudes and behaviors, we turn to the social psychological literature on workplace commitment. The contributions of Hackman and Oldham (1980) and Gecas and Schwalbe (1983) inform our discussion of the way people's commitment is shaped by varying organizational conditions.

Conditions of Workplace Commitment

Performance efficacy is one of the primary feelings that account for work commitment (Gecas and Schwalbe 1983). With performance efficacy, prople's feelings are closely tied to how well they perform on the job; good performance is self-rewarding and provides the incentive for continuing to perform well. Alternatively, poor performance is an occasion for distress that causes high-efficacy people to search for a way to avoid such feelings in the future and to regain those pleasurable feelings that accompany good performance (Hackman and Oldham 1980).

As shall become clear throughout this chapter, several organizational conditions enhance performance efficacy. The first is task discretion and autonomy (Hackman and Oldham 1980). Jobs that give people autonomy and discretion require that they exercise judgment and choice; in doing so, they become aware of themselves as causal agents in their own performance. Losing the capacity to control the terms of work or to determine what work is to be done, how the work is to be done, or what its aim is to be widens the gap between the knowledge of one's unique contributions to work and any performance efficacy that can be derived from it.

Accordingly, with the advent of MCT, respondents in our sample, particularly those from successful schools, took considerable umbrage at the state's confiscation of their professional autonomy: "For someone else to tell me what they think is needed when I can see some other things that are needed myself is infuriating." And this:

> What really bothers me is that the teacher's judgment is not considered important any longer. We used to be able to decide things. . . . Now we teachers are frustrated.

This dysfunctional conflict was no better illustrated than in the classroom curriculum resulting from MCT. The need to ensure that their students passed competency tests forced teachers, especially those from unsuccessful schools, to reluctantly deemphasize other content areas deemed important to them (see also Darling-Hammond and Wise 1985). Over one-third of the teachers in this group voiced this complaint:

> "I am not able to do things that are good for kindergarteners. I feel like I have to hide in my room to let children have show-and-tell."

> "The Basic Skills Program has destroyed all the important things in my teaching. I can't help children learn to get along, or raise their self-esteem, when all the state wants is memorization of facts."

Recall from earlier discussion that task conceptions shape the structural arrangements within which work is performed. Whoever controls that structure, as Scott (1981) points out, can fundamentally alter the task conceptions of people who work within it. The specific point here is that with MCT, teachers may deflect attention and effort from earlier task conceptions to a narrower or altogether different set of goals embodied in the evaluation system (see Shannon 1986; Resnick and Resnick 1985).

Lest readers question the value of alternative learning opportunities, they need only consider the effects of MCT on the language arts curriculum alone. Writing instruction and practice in some classrooms have been replaced by rote exercises in sentence diagramming (Suhor 1985). Although such exercises are arguably ineffective in helping students better their writing skills (Sherwin 1969), they are nonetheless most likely to appear on minimum competency tests (Suhor 1985).

Where students' opportunities to master a broader base of knowledge are undermined because teachers must divert their instructional emphases to material that is tested, to material that many consider inappropriate, and to material that they have had no hand in shaping, their performance efficacy and professional commitment inevitably suffer (see Shannon 1986).

The Absence of Buffering. Performance efficacy also depends on organizational conditions that facilitate the attainment of work goals; for teachers, these are conditions that optimize student growth. In the most successful schools, principals or districts buffered teachers by averting intrusive managerial tasks that pull them away from instruction. Because of greater fiscal resources, districts and schools within them acquired additional and vital teaching materials, paid aides or parent volunteers to handle new paperwork and testing demands, and used district office personnel to calibrate state and district requirements to avoid duplicative testing.

In poorer districts and unsuccessful schools, however, not only was Tennessee's MCT program at odds with those in basal texts, but because of fiscal constraints, outside resource materials had to be located and purchased by teachers themselves. Moreover, in most districts, teachers tested for mastery both in their own basal series to meet district requirements and again tested for mastery to meet state requirements.

Given all this, it is not surprising that the most onerous aspect of MCT to almost all teachers in unsuccessful schools was the time needed to acquire materials to teach state-mandated skills, the overwhelming burden of additional paperwork, and the time required to test, all of which they perceived as needless encroachments on their teaching. Over each of these points there was nearly unanimous accord: "It seems to be that Basic Skills is more testing than teaching. That is all I do." "I am actually teaching less." "I'm just not sure with all this testing that the kids are learning more." Teachers chronicled precisely how they accommodated these new extraneous demands by reducing their instructional time with students:

> "With the amount of paperwork, I can't take all that home with me. We have to have personal lives, too, you know. So I take the time for testing out of my teaching time."

> "It's pretty common around here to let kids have extra time at P.E. so that teachers can catch up with their paperwork. The testing does take a lot of time, so kids get shortchanged in the end."

Rather than providing students greater opportunity to master basic skills and testing them to ensure mastery, MCT instead robbed them of access to their most critical learning resource—teachers' instructional time. Overburdening paperwork reduced both student-teacher interaction and student learning, and in this way the tyranny of testing stunted the professional lives of teachers. Furthermore, to the extent that schools have become more concerned with bureaucratic responsibilities at the expense of their educational obligations, they will have an increasing difficult time attracting and retaining good teachers (Chapman 1983). Thus the imbalance in resources between teachers from successful and unsuccessful schools, given these new state directives looms impressively large.

The Negative Consequences of Low Commitment

Covert actions recommend themselves to people feeling the loss of their professional strength. The absence of conditions that allow people to feel efficacious in their work, therefore, has profound and negative consequences for their professional commitment (Gecas and Schwalbe 1983). People recognize the real constraints and deprivations on their performance and have a clear sense of their low efficacy. Because they usually have the need to make self-enhancing judgments about themselves, however, the definition of success in these settings is often recast among people in terms of behaviors and values that still allow them opportunity to derive a sense of self-esteem, status, and control. Instead of fulfillment through work, people redefine their goals as simply to "make out." "Making out" behaviors—providing temporary relief from boredom, finding ways to leave the job, focusing more on social than on work relationships with co-workers, and so forth—are, of course, antithetical to organizational efficiency. Stated differently, work becomes devalued and at the same time oriented toward satisfactions other than those that come from successful job performance (Gecas and Schwalbe 1983).

In a like manner, teachers who lack opportunities to attain work-related goals, who feel professionally disempowered and unefficacious, become disaffected, absent themselves from work, or defect from the profession (Rosenholtz in press). As a mediating step along the way, low-efficacy teachers converse more with their colleagues about poor working conditions than about teaching problems and their solutions (Ashton and Webb 1986; Rosenholtz in press). This pernicious type of talk presents a paradox for teachers. Where they regularly complain about difficult working conditions—such as insufficient resources with which to teach and a lack of understanding by the state of the teaching realities that they confront—they buttress their beliefs that any lack of teaching success is attributable primarily to external causes over which they have little control. Indeed, when we asked teachers what they generally talked about with their colleagues, many of those from unsuccessful schools replied unhesitantly:

> "The Basic Skills Program and all the testing it requires. None of us feel that it will help students learn more because it takes so much more of our teaching time away."

> "We talk about the governor's new Basic Skills Program. Everyone here just hates it. All it is is testing and more testing. Children won't learn more by being tested more. The state has put so many requirements on us that it's not worth being a teacher."

Because colleagues convince each other that confronted by such overwhelming odds, no one can reasonably expect to succeed, teachers more readily give up (Ashton and Webb 1986; Rosenholtz in press). It is not unexpected then that 30 percent of our respondents from unsuccessful schools either openly contemplated leaving the profession, or reported others doing so, directly because of MCT:

"Actually, I want to leave teaching. It's not because of the kids, but because of all the outsiders who are making teaching impossible. With the Basic Skills Program, I'm doing so much testing that I'm not enjoying teaching at all anymore."

"Some teachers I know are so frustrated with all the extra things we have to do now that they are going to quit teaching and get into something else. I know one who already left to become a construction worker."

Further, over 60 percent of the total sample complained of lower faculty morale brought about by MCT. The next two teachers capture the essential difference between successful and unsuccessful schools:

"[From an unsuccessful school:] Teachers' morale couldn't be lower than now. We are burdened by so much to do other than teaching. All we seem to do is complain. There doesn't seem to be anyway out of it, either. We have one instructional aide but she is spread so thin she can't really help any one teacher with the extra work."

"[From a successful school:] Teaching used to be different. You could decide what you needed to do and handle the work. Now everything is decided for us. We have no say in what it is we are supposed to teach. Everybody's morale has dropped because of that."

In the absence of a self-regulated professional culture, teachers have had to accept policymakers' formulations and forge policies and programs within their boundaries.

According to these results, reduced teacher commitment is a potential byproduct of education reform, one that is poorly understood and worthy of additional study. If policy changes pose too great a burden, teachers may further disassociate themselves from their work and receive social support from colleagues for the divestiture. The possibility that increased demands that serve as barriers to classroom effectiveness may cause some teachers to defect must also be entertained and examined. In sum, researchers who chart policy changes need be mindful of a fundamental paradox revealed by this study of MCT: The administration of a reform may create new demands that generate additional problems—such as lowered teacher commitment—that worsen the very professional services reformers intended to improve. Problems that arise from the implementation of new policy are, of course, not intractable, but without research to assess the effects of policy changes on the teacher workforce, and without proper procedures that feedback essential information and recommendations to policymakers, it is not likely that corrective action will be undertaken.

Benefits of MCT

Slightly more than a fifth of our respondents—those from highly successful schools—embraced and derived benefit from MCT, whereas less than a handful of teachers from unsuccessful schools did so (see also Darling-Hammond and Wise 1985). Most who found benefits came from settings closely resembling those of the original developers of the Basic Skills Program—suburban districts with comparatively greater fiscal resources, far less heterogeneity in students' social class and academic backgrounds, and decidedly most relevant, greater emphasis on and consensus about the importance of basic skill mastery. Three points arise from this. First and foremost, teachers' task conceptions in these districts were more closely aligned with the goals of MCT, reducing the potential for conflict. Second, the large majority of these teachers enjoyed relatively less academic diversity in their classrooms with more students performing at grade level guaranteeing a better fit between MCT and youngsters' learning needs. Third, almost all teachers reported sufficient buffering with which to implement MCT. Because of these factors, MCT posed fewer threats to teachers' task autonomy and discretion. As teachers succeeded in meeting minimum competency standards, they accrued greater performance efficacy from their work. Under precisely these conditions, as Dornbusch and Scott would readily agree, evaluation of work served as a successful device for organizational control. In fact, teachers in these schools judged their own district's basic skills curriculum as even more comprehensive than the state's. For example, consider the following representative comments:

> "Our district was doing basic skills mastery long before the state got into it. Our program is better than the state's. It's more thorough and flexible."

> "The state's plan covers only the minimum. Our curriculum goes way beyond the minimum. It's more comprehensive and allows for individual differences."

Among this group, 35 percent found the standards and tests necessary for teachers to detect students' learning difficulties and, of far greater significance, to modify the way learning was perceived by both students and teachers. As they explained,

> "Most teachers today have strayed too far away from the basics. So this program should shake them up into realizing that they have a responsibility to teach their students this material."

> "The [MCT] program will, I think, change the way students see their work. I think they will take it more seriously and maybe work harder at learning."

Others stressed the meliorative effects of MCT on poorer teachers: "I think the standards are more effective for teachers who need guidelines." "Teachers who used to ignore the basics will have to take this program seriously. It'll change what they teach for sure." In fact, some teachers hailed the program as a way to orient their *own* classroom instruction, thereby ensuring that the most important skills received adequate time and attention:

> "The Basic Skills Program helps me judge how well I am teaching each skill. Some of the district skills are not as fully covered as I'd like. That goes for some of the state skills too. So when I compare the two, I can see things I ought to stress more in my teaching."

Some additional factors in the study of MCT, then, at least at the elementary school level, include the extent to which standards gradually alter teachers' task conceptions, what they come to emphasize in their classroom curricula, and how they subsequently gauge their effectiveness. That is, where standards for student mastery are clearly specified and shared, and where teachers are evaluated by their students' success in reaching these standards, instructional content becomes driven by newly implemented standards and their measurement.

But any such investigation depends at heart on the contextual conditions in which teachers are embedded. A goodly portion of the differences between those who applauded the Basic Skills Program and those who disdained it may be explained by the fit between teachers' task conceptions and MCT, and the resources at their disposal to execute the reform, including the distribution of raw materials—the students themselves. In other words, both the nature of the problems that teachers confront, and the nature of the strategies that are conceived to remedy those problems, are shaped by the circumstances under which they occur.

To review, MCT embittered teachers from successful schools because of hierarchical decisionmaking about teaching problems and solutions over which they exercised no control. Teachers in unsuccessful schools, contrariwise, bemoaned their schools' insufficient resources to implement the reform; rather than collaborate to solve the problems created by MCT, these teachers filled the void caused by these conditions with counterproductive communications.

In the next example of education reform—career ladders—we will confront some of these same issues. Specifically stressed are the consequences of decentralized decisionmaking versus the state's hierarchical control for teachers' professional commitment.

CAREER LADDERS

Interpreted most generously, career ladder plans (CLPs) intend to bring about a salutary effect on schools through functional assignments in which talented teachers take on additional school-system responsibilities—in return for increased pay and status—to help their colleagues improve. To examine the potential of these assignments, and to illustrate how research knowledge can be usefully brought to bear on policy decisions, I contrast two examples of CLPs currently under implementation. The cases illustrate rather dramatically that the success of reforms in helping teachers become more efficacious and contribute more productively to schools depends in large measure on how carefully they are designed and implemented.

In the first example, Hart (1985) instructively details one Utah district's attempt to institute a CLP from twenty-seven interviews she conducted with principals, teachers, and the superintendent. Here the CLP was developed by a task force of administrators and teachers from each of the district's schools. Explicit in the plan was a commitment to the *individual school* as the most promising organizational level for improvement and change, and the desire to marshal the resources of experienced and talented teachers within it to bring about such improvement. Ideas were negotiated with faculties through task force representatives; at the time of its implementation, 80 percent of the district's teachers voted in its favor.

The career ladder consisted of four steps. The two highest levels— teacher specialist and teacher leader—carried with them salary increments of $900 plus pay for additional contract days to work on instructional improvement projects, clinical supervision, mentoring, and assisting probationary teachers with professional development. Individual faculties selected teacher leaders and specialists on the basis of instructional collegial leadership. Each school defined teacher specialist roles, their number allocated by school size with an eye toward serving specific faculty needs (such as the number of probationary teachers needing assistance and supervision, specific program needs, and faculty expertise). Empowered by their expertise, teacher leaders shared (albeit in sometimes intimidating ways) decisionmaking responsibilities with building principals.

Several benefits reportedly accrued to schools during the CLP's first year:

1. During the extended contract days, planned opportunities for teacher collaboration were organized that resulted in increased faculty interaction and group cohesiveness.
2. Teacher leaders provided inservice programs based on topics identified by individual school faculties.
3. Probationary and experienced teachers began to request technical assistance *on their own initiative* from teacher leaders, who also reported benefitting a great deal from these interactions.
4. Teachers at *all* levels received reinforcement for the quality of their work. Teachers gained more knowledge of their colleagues' skills and talents.
5. Principals and faculties confronted and communicated with each other on professional issues; faculty meetings evolved into substantive decisionmaking arenas.

Several structural features implicit in the plan accounted at least in part for its initial success. First, teachers were given considerable task autonomy and discretion to both formulate and implement the CLP, and this better ensured their commitment to it. As a result, teachers' task conceptions were closely aligned with program goals. That is, because teachers collectively constructed the plan, it came to have shared meaning and value.

Second—and this requires a brief caveat—inservice needs were defined by teachers themselves. The agenda evolved from problems to be solved or goals to be accomplished at specific schools. To understand why this particular feature may have engendered greater commitment to the CLP, we again consult the literature on the organizational conditions under which people experience high performance efficacy.

Teachers' Learning Opportunities

If job commitment is to be enhanced, work must provide challenges and opportunities to deal successfully with them. Opportunities that allow people to grow and develop, to perfect current skills, and to learn new ones develop a sense of challenge, progress, and personal accomplishment that increases the meaningfulness of and commitment to work (Hackman and Oldham 1980).

For their part, teachers often complain of monotony, professional stagnation, and a lack of direction. Where they have continued to use the same instructional techniques and practices year after year, they quite often become bored, unenthusiastic, and unable to motivate students (Blase 1986; Kasten 1984). We can then understand more fully why the absence of opportunities for professional growth is a common explanation teachers offer for their absenteeism and defection from work (Kasten 1984; Rosenholtz in press).

Most schools provide only limited opportunities for teacher learning. The average inservice teacher receives fewer than three days of "staff development" each year, and little of that training deals with instructional problemsolving (Joyce, Bush, and McKibbin 1984). Moreover, the most common types of inservice training are one-time "pullout" programs designed by district office administrators that have little, if any, immediate or sustained effect on teachers' instructional improvement (Little 1984; Walberg and Genova 1982).

In the CLP studied by Hart, learning opportunities were intentionally decentralized: Teachers not only specified goals according to their own learning needs, they also designed school inservice programs to help meet these needs. This means that personalized rather than standardized help was available. Assistance was therefore useful enough for teachers to avail themselves of opportunities for professional growth and challenge. And because the district granted individual faculties the autonomy and discretion to shape their own learning opportunities, teachers were more likely to implement new techniques, strategies, and ideas, thereby enlarging their instructional repertoires.

A third possible explanation for the CLP's success—one that requires more substantial exposition on the latter theme—is that criteria for advancement on the district's career ladder included instructionally related collegial leadership. That this element was viewed as central to the plan's success represents a marked departure from the experience teachers typically confront in schools. Working in professional isolation, where they seldom see or hear each other teach, teachers rarely communicate about task-related matters—especially by requesting or offering professional advice and assistance in efforts to improve instructionally (Rosenholtz in press).

Professional isolation occurs, at least in part, because, as teachers act to protect their self-esteem, they shy away from situations where any conclusions about professional inadequacy may either be publicly or privately drawn. If the call for aid raises some question about how capably teachers can render such assistance, if they might be found wanting or deficient, they will frequently and unconsciously forgo helpful efforts on behalf of a colleague rather than sustain possibly negative evaluations. Likewise, teachers avoid requests for assistance where they are viewed as potentially embarrassing or stigmatizing and where they threaten disclosure of any professional inadequacy.

However, to the extent that teachers believe that anyone, even the most capable colleague, might need help in a similar situation, it becomes unnecessary for them to draw causal inferences about their own teaching adequacy. That is, if teaching is collectively viewed as an inherently difficult undertaking, it is both necessary and legitimate to both seek and offer professional assistance. And this is exactly what happens in the most instructionally successful schools. Here, because of strong administrative or faculty leadership, teaching is normatively defined as a collective rather than an individual enterprise, and requests for and offers of assistance among colleagues set the conditions under which teachers improve instructionally (Rosenholtz in press).

We see, then, that the criterion of instructional leadership in the CLP studied by Hart explicitly underscored the importance of teachers' collaborative exchange. Mindful of the importance of teachers' learning opportunities for their commitment, we can understand why the CLP produced greater exchange of advice and assistance among colleagues.

There is a fourth possible reason for the success of this Utah plan. Integrating leaders' interactions with colleagues into regular workday activities heightens teachers' consciousness of learning as a continuous process. Nowhere in Hart's data is this more poignantly illustrated than in experienced teachers' requests for advice and assistance from teacher specialists and leaders. For these teachers particularly, a repository of new ideas, techniques, and models, like a centripetal force, pulled them toward a mission of professional improvement essential to their commitment to the CLP.

That teacher learning is experienced as a collective, recurrent aspect of school life seems equally important for new entrants to the school; beginners offered help, beginners who see requests and offers of assistance continuously exchanged among colleagues become socialized to the ways in which one learns to teach. That is, norms of collaboration establish themselves in situations where newcomers observe colleagues engaged in some mutually accepted definition of the way teaching is done. Hence Hart found that in implementing the CLP, novices more readily solicited and accepted advice and assistance. But where beginners observe few instances of teacher collaboration, they learn that teaching is more an individual than a collective endeavor. Because requests for advice and assistance in isolated settings are interpreted more as signs of teaching inadequacy than as eagerness to learn, in times of trouble novices seldom ask.

Finally, the initial success of this Utah district's CLP may also result from the benefits teacher leaders accrued as they supported the work of others. In helping their colleagues improve, teacher leaders were apt to confront new work challenges and feelings of greater efficacy. Indeed, there is ample evidence that providing teachers with the opportunity to assume responsibilities, initiative, and authority commensurate with their talents and abilities, and acknowledging a job well done, increases their professional commitment (see Rosenholtz in press).

Unintended Consequences of CLPs

We also find unintended and pernicious consequences in the forging of CLPs that provide grist for the policy researcher. When combined with the proper feedback mechanism, these consequences can result in guidance for the reform itself. Next I identify some of the problems that states and localities confront in their efforts to implement CLPs.

Evaluation Standards. States and districts can and are identifying evaluation criteria that, because they are based on the teaching effectiveness literature, may differentiate effective from ineffective teachers, at least in basic skill instruction for low SES youngsters. The challenge to devise means that distinguish competent from exceptional teachers, however, has yet to be met successfully. And if exceptional teaching remains more a reputational than an observable phenomenon, the implications for changing good teachers into great teachers are few. Of equal importance, if teachers do not accept evaluation procedures as a legitimate gauge of their classroom effectiveness, there is little basis for organizational control without alienating its members (Dornbusch and Scott 1975).

The Tennessee teachers we interviewed were confronting the state-developed evaluation and selection procedures for career ladder advancement for the first time. Prior to implementation of the CLP, the NEA affiliate, representing some 80 percent of the state's teachers, had exercised sufficient political leverage to have the CLP delayed one year for legislative study. The confrontation between teachers and state policymakers was made all the more painful when the governor retaliated by denying teachers any salary raises for two consecutive years.

The CLP that eventually came to be implemented contained four steps with supplemental salaries of $2,000 to $3,000 for advancement to the two highest career levels, plus additional pay for extended contract duties. Developed over an eight-month period, the CLP, like its MCT counterpart, permitted teachers no meaningful involvement. And any policy that is concealed from teachers always runs the risk of conferring enormous power on individuals who may abuse it or confuse it with their own overly zealous imperatives. It was primarily for this reason that the NEA affiliate again actively but this time unsuccessfully campaigned against passage of career ladder legislation the second time (Handler and Carlson 1985).

A newly created state Board of Education was appointed by the governor to oversee and monitor CLP implementation. A specific criterion for appointment to the board was that members hold no prior association with the education profession. After five months of study, the board's chairperson testified in legislative session that policymaking for the CLP was "not based on proper information, not based on knowledge, not based on experience, but *absolutely* based on recommendations by the State Department of Education." He further testified that he and other board members understood neither what they were doing nor the ramifications of their decisions. "One of the things we have not done enough is listen to teachers," he confessed (Morgan 1985).

Teacher Evaluation

Classroom Observations. Because decisionmaking in the Tennessee CLP was so deliberately centralized, explicitly excluding teachers from either formulating or overseeing its implementation, nearly two-thirds of the sample we interviewed—from both successful and unsuccessful schools alike—challenged the fairness and legitimacy of the evaluation system. Over half of our respondents, for example, charged that the classroom observation procedures better measured teachers' cunning and endurance than their effectiveness: "The evaluators only make three observations, two of which are prearranged with the teachers. You can fool anybody for a couple of days." "The observations are a farce. Any teacher can put on a good show for a few days." (For identical quantitative findings, see Morgan 1985.) Three-quarters of the teachers from successful schools—among them those who had already been promoted to one of the two highest career levels—felt that a significant number of mediocre teachers could reach these levels by deceiving evaluators. In interpreting these findings, it is well worth noting that these same teachers felt that their own school or district evaluation process gauged their effectiveness with high accuracy and helpfulness, regardless of its outcome (Rosenholtz in press). Teachers' complaints instead focused on the inadequacy of the specific state evaluation system used (see also Morgan 1985). In truth, the evaluation practices, like the Education Department's entire CLP was no model of pedagogical clarity.

Of equal relevance, 60 percent of our respondents from successful schools voiced the complaint that the observation system was *not* designed to help them improve instructionally. By contrast, only 22 percent of teachers from unsuccessful schools voiced this specific concern. These findings again evidence strong contextual effects. Where evaluative feedback is used to help them improve, teachers in such schools accept this "fact" as taken-for-granted reality. But in schools where evaluation is performed perfunctorily, with little usefulness, and at the discretionary pleasure of the principal, teachers come to anticipate no useful assistance or guidance as their given workplace reality (Rosenholtz in press).

If evaluation practices offer few learning opportunities—that is, means by which teachers can either identify improvement needs or redirect their energies toward betterment—we can clearly anticipate a decline in teacher commitment to the CLP. Two teachers from successful schools, for instance, underscored this point rather poignantly:

> "The [CLP] evaluation is totally useless. We get no information about how well we performed. Our district evaluations are much better in that way—you know exactly where you need to work a little harder, and you're given the help that's needed."

> "Compared to the evaluations done by my principal, the state's system is ridiculous. With my principal, I know I will get the kind of feedback I need. With the state's, I don't think the kind of nit-picking they are doing will help at all to make me a better teacher."

The Portfolio. The applicant for the two highest career levels—Level II and Level III—was required to submit a "portfolio," an astonishing array of materials from five previous teaching years including sample lesson plans, behavioral objectives, test items, disciplinary standards, and teacher-made materials, which the state weighted more heavily than actual classroom observations (Morgan 1985). According to almost all teachers in our sample, these could be fabricated without the dimmest glimmer of relevance to one's actual classroom performance. We again hear from teachers in successful schools:

> "The things you have to put in your portfolio—lesson plans, sample tests, teaching materials, and documenting of everything—doesn't show whether or not you're a good teacher. People who can put materials together well may really be lousy classroom teachers."

> "The portfolio is really a dumb idea. Who can tell how well someone teaches by looking at sample lesson plans? Teachers can make all these materials up if they really wanted to, and no one would ever know."

Worse still from the perspective of teachers, and parallel to Tennessee's Basic Skills Program, was their pervasive complaint that the construction of the portfolio robbed students of applicants' time and attention (see also Handler and Carlson 1985; Morgan 1985). What is contextually remarkable about this complaint, however, is that despite the burden of additional work, teachers in successful schools appeared nonetheless to carry on with the business of classroom teaching; in unsuccessful schools, teachers merely resented the diversions from work. We hear first from two teachers in successful schools, followed by two from unsuccessful ones:

> "I spent hours and hours and hours putting together my portfolio. It took a lot of time away from my family. Fortunately, my children are older. I don't know how someone with very young children at home could get all this work done."

> "My husband really complained about all the time I was putting in to develop this stupid portfolio. My time with him was really cut short for weeks and weeks. Even my weekend time, where we always do things together."

> "The hours necessary to develop a great portfolio take a lot of classroom time. It's time away from students in order to get promoted. Isn't that kind of ironic?"

> "The portfolio requires too much time and paperwork to be worthwhile. It took me hours and hours to get all that stuff together and I felt guilty sometimes that it took so much time away from my students."

Teachers—proportionately more from successful than unsuccessful schools (43 percent versus 19 percent)—further reported that the time-consuming nature of the evaluation procedure was one reason that many had chosen not to apply. They cited either themselves or their best-performing colleagues as choosing to devote their year to students rather than to developing a portfolio (see also Handler and Carlson 1985; Morgan 1985).

> "[From a teacher in a successful school:] I know that I am a master teacher and I don't need any ridiculous document to prove it. With all the time it takes to even apply, I think that time is better spent preparing to work with my students."

> "[From a teacher in an unsuccessful school:] I didn't apply for the career ladder because of the time it took away from my students. My principal really thought I could get to Level IV and so he encouraged me to apply, and I started to, but it's such a waste of time I decided to quit."

Distributive Justice. Quite apart from the organization's inability to exercise control, additional deleterious consequences result from centralized decisionmaking about evaluation standards and teachers' subsequent unwillingness to accept their legitimacy. Simply put, if career promotions are based on faulty evaluation practices—and if the best teachers are not selected for promotion—teachers experience a sense of injustice. That is, if the procedures by which the distribution of rewards are perceived as unjust or unfair—that is, if the contributions of rewarded teachers are perceived as no greater than those of the unrewarded—problems of distributive justice arise. Unrewarded individuals react to injustice by attempting to restore equity in the setting. Typically, they may alter the level of their own contributions downward in the direction of lower commitment, or they may leave the situation altogether.

In our study, teachers' persistent challenge to the soundness of evaluation practices caused many in both contextual settings to forebode trouble when rewarded teachers begin to make substantially higher salary than others: "The best teachers have not applied in this school. If the other ones make it, there's going to be real trouble among the faculty." "If some of the best teachers here are not applying, and the mediocre ones are, what's going to happen if *they* are promoted? I'll tell you one thing for sure—the better teachers will resent it."

Teachers' apprehensions were confirmed through interviews conducted just after career ladder selections had been officially published in newspapers throughout the state. Most respondents expressed grave reservation, surprise, and dismay about those chosen to advance and provided evidence of distributive justice, regardless of school context (also see Handler and Carlson 1985; Morgan 1985).

"[From a teacher in a successful school:] The teachers who have been selected for Level III or IV are not the best teachers in the school. The rest of the faculty resents it—she has had to put a lot of distance between herself and other teachers. It makes the rest of us feel like maybe we shouldn't work as hard. Let *her* do all those extra things for the school we used to do."

"[From an unsuccessful school:] We really feel that there has been a lot of politics involved in the selection. The best ones in our school who applied didn't make it—even to Career Level III. Another teacher who does a mean job controlling her students advanced to Level IV. We resent her, even though she tries not to act superior. Everyone knows she's had past problems with parents. I wonder how she feels about it all [the promotion and hostility]. It's definitely affected the morale of teachers in this school; they seem less motivated to work as hard."

Problems of distributive justice are significant not only because they reduce the professional commitment of the unrewarded; they also inhibit school improvement if colleagues consider master teachers' advice, assistance, or suggestions illegitimate. That is, if teachers come to resent those who are promoted, school improvement becomes an activity restricted solely to the chosen few. How teacher selection for career ladders alters faculty interaction, then, carries profound consequences for the ethos of the school and for the subsequent commitment of teachers who work within it.

Evaluation and Collaboration. Another serious and consistent forewarning by the majority of teachers in successful schools, unlike those from unsuccessful schools, was the threat to positive collaborative relations they presently enjoyed. Here teachers predicted or reported an end to offers of and requests for assistance and exchange of ideas and materials among colleagues because all portfolio material submitted by applicants had to be accompanied by documentation of its originality:

> "Before the career ladder, teachers were more open and willing to share their ideas and their plans and work together. Now it's kind of like 'Let me do my thing and make it as good as I can so I can make a good mark for me.' I really think it's detrimental for the children."

> "Because of the [CLP], teachers have become unwilling to share their ideas and to help each other. It used to be a very professional staff—we exchanged ideas and problem-solved together. Now that individuals are being singled out, all that has changed."

Thus the competitive principle does have its downside for teachers' professional development, one to which policymakers must immediately attend. That is, if the means to select teachers for career ladder advancement are poorly designed, if they are not thoroughly informed by an understanding of the nature of organizational behavior, then they are not apt to succeed. Should the costs of career ladders turn out to be the collegial relations needed to enhance teachers' learning, their performance efficacy, their commitment, and ultimately their professionalism, in them we have the makings of a national educational failure at the very point in our history when we need a major success. Indeed, Tennessee's CLP and MCT have come apart recently with a crash so resounding it threatens to discredit the previous governor's entire school reform package.

The evolution of changes among teaching colleagues, especially under different contextual circumstance therefore becomes critical to document. Under what conditions will collaborative exchange among teachers be affected by CLPs? What additional training will be needed to help master teachers succeed in their varied functional assignments? What are the best mechanisms for providing such training? What are the characteristics of functional assignments that appear most promising in bringing about school improvement, given different school contexts? How can competent teachers who are not selected for advancement still be made to feel appreciated? What will ultimately happen to their school commitment? In raising these and other issues throughout this analysis, I have made implicit assumptions about the nature of policy research: that it is primarily designed to assess tractable variables. Accordingly, the section that follows makes specific policy recommendations.

POLICY RECOMMENDATIONS

MCT

Given that public schooling by its very nature serves the interests of society, when policymakers perceive that fundamental reading and computational skills have not been taught—the skills on which the society depends most earnestly for its survival—it is reasonable that they take measures to ensure that basic skill mastery receive appropriate curricular emphasis. It could hardly be otherwise. But where education policy hierarchically prescribes a standardized curriculum, and where it tightens surveillance to assure compliance, it unwittingly secures the academic progress of but a few and almost certainly condemns the rest. In other words, compliance with MCT does not ensure that teachers will respond rationally or willingly to the program. To the contrary, an ironic legacy of this strategy, ostensibly designed to restore educative order, has actually accelerated its demise. What teacher, after all, is (1) prepared to accept the charge that denigrates their adequacy or (2) willing to accept a political polemic that excoriates their intelligence?

There is a viable alternative to hierarchical decisionmaking and its pernicious and unintended consequences, as by now the reader has surely surmised. If the goal of MCT is to improve, support, and ensure the capacity of schools to deliver appropriately paced instruction, states should rely on *delegated* authority, precisely because schools confront such complex and uncertain work. Galbraith (1973) describes this arrangement as "targeting" or "goal setting," meaning that control, rather than being secured by minute descriptions of tasks and their procedures, is specified by desired outcomes appropriate for the organization. That is, the work of teachers takes place within a structure of guidelines that they help shape, and they are granted considerable discretion over pedagogical decisions concerning means and techniques. Considerable research suggests that teacher involvement in decisionmaking of precisely this sort is essential to successful educational change (for a review, see Purkey and Smith 1985).

But for delegated authority to lead to task-related progress instead of organizational chaos, Glabraith argues, two structural mechanisms must be set in place. The first he calls *augmented hierarchies*, where teaching efforts are coordinated by adding specialized administrative and clerical personnel charged with enabling instructional endeavors and gathering and summarizing information needed for future decisionmaking about students' learning needs and how best to fulfill them. The second Galbraith labels *lateral connections*, where colleagues work in groups to coordinate and share technical information, to save them from floundering, and to assist in error-correction.

To restore a sense of engaged citizenship between teachers, administrators, and policymakers, and to reestablish the proper relationship between rights and duties are one and the same project: the project of creating stronger and more participatory policymaking. Strategies to implement MCT must maximize teachers' control of the instructional process while administrators find participatory ways to mobilize teachers' efforts in addressing basic skills problems, and then provide appropriate resources that respond directly to those problems.

CLPS

The reader will immediately see that the same problems and solutions inhere in career ladder implementation. States and localities may in earnest seek to reward outstanding teachers and through their selection augment school resources to help other teachers improve. Centralized decisionmaking about how this should be accomplished, however, leads to outcomes that both jeopardize the success of the reform and dampen the spirits of even the most enthusiastic teachers. Delegated authority, by contrast, where district administrators galvanize local staff participation in the design and implementation of CLPs to meet specific teacher learning needs within their respective schools, yields a higher probability that CLPs will result in instructional improvement.

The Role of the State. In three ways, state education agencies (SEAs) assume a critical role in delegating authority for the implementation of reform efforts. First, they must specify broad parameters for the development of programmatic goals and permissible variations for local adaptation. Second, they must monitor local implementation efforts and provide helpful feedback directed at improvement. Third, SEAs must set up "augmented hierarchies" by allocating sufficient resources—both fiscal support and appropriate technical assistance—organized around programmatic goals. Resources include not only teaching materials, but also information on model programs for dissemination, replication, or adaptation; release time for local staff to observe exemplary practices; personnel who steer local staff toward useful resources; and specialists who furnish information and training (Turnbull 1985). On this latter point, Turnbull (1985), in reviewing research on SEAs' efforts to improve school quality, notes that most contain some sort of intermediate unit between themselves and districts for resource allocation, a structure particularly well suited for states such as Tennessee with many small and isolated rural districts. Successful intermediate units deliver direct technical assistance to schools and establish networks for information sharing and coordination between districts.

The Role of the District. Successful implementation of new programs, Turnbull also points out, requires that districts clarify at the onset the locus for school change—that is, what they want to accomplish in specific schools, convey this sense of direction, help schools set programmatic goals, and monitor goal attainment. More, in utilizing the resources states offer, the most successful implementation efforts provide someone designated as the "local facilitator"—a member of the district staff who both organizes and advocates the improvement effort in much the same way that intermediate units deliver assistance. That is, local facilitators mobilize the commitment of teachers and administrators, arrange learning opportunities for school personnel, acquire materials, handle schedules and procedural details for implementation, evaluate changes in schools, and plan for ongoing change. In fact, local facilitators, working closely with inter-mediate units, usually produce more positive and enduring change than either working alone (Turnbull 1985). These are but a few rec-ommendations to reverse the deleterious effects already surfacing. Whatever scenario is followed, however, one can be sure that an end to bureaucratic control will only be an opportunity to establish pro-fessionalism, not a guarantee that it will flourish.

CONCLUSION

The next decade will be a time of enormous turmoil in the teaching occupation. A majority of our teaching workforce in 1992 will be people who are not presently employed (NCES 1984). This means that well over a million new teachers will be entering the classroom during the next six years. Who they are, how they will be trained and selected, what kinds of experiences and abilities they will bring with them, and what kinds of conditions they will encounter in schools are questions of more than academic interest. This huge turnover is beginning just as the issue of the unsatisfactory quality of American schooling has seized the interest of policymakers at all levels—policy-makers who intend to make changes to improve that quality. And the major object of these changes is the teaching workforce itself.

The combination of demographic forces and conscious policy de-cisions makes for a period of extraordinary volatility within and around the teaching force. There is also the eager anticipation—and hope—that through the many permutations of policy interventions, we will ultimately improve the current performance of schools. In reality, however, not enough information about teachers and the contextual setting of their work is utilized to provide a steadfast base on which to implement policy changes. Where purposive efforts to improve quality are mounted, they have hit with highly uneven impact because their effects have not been properly anticipated. At present it appears that educational policymakers, having misdiag-nosed school problems, prescribed the wrong educative medicine.

Further, without a satisfactory feedback mechanism, there is no avenue to supply continuing insight, constructive criticism, and dis-passionate scrutiny to assist policymakers in knowing whether their efforts are well designed interventions that solve actual problems or merely cosmetic changes that never penetrate beneath the surface.

The task of buttressing policy changes with real information, accurate analysis, and sound recommendations falls on the research community. Such an ambitious enterprise has many dimensions: Tracing and monitoring reform decisions in varied school contexts; providing thoughtful and informed comment about them; offering technical advice to those who will be designing, implementing, and evaluating them; and keeping in the public eye the conditions in education generally, and the teaching occupation particularly, that create a compelling rationale for well-conceived changes. Only then can the promise of current policy intervention become more than just another episodic chapter in the history of American education.

REFERENCES

Ashton, Patricia T., and Rodney B. Webb. 1986. *Making a Difference: Teachers' Sense of Efficacy and Student Achievement*. New York: Longman.

Barr, Rebecca C. 1975. "The Effect of Instruction on Pupil Reading Strategies." *Reading Research Quarterly* 10: 317–27.

Beckerman, Terrill M., and Thomas L. Good. 1981. "The Classroom Ratio of High- and Low-Aptitude Students and Its Effects on Achievement." *American Educational Research Journal* 18: 317–27.

Blase, Joseph L. 1986. "A Qualitative Analysis of Teacher Stress: Consequences for Performance." *American Educational Research Journal* 23: 13–40.

Chapman, D. W. 1983. "A Model of the Influences on Teacher Retention." *Journal of Teacher Education* 34: 43–49.

Darling-Hammond, Linda, and Arthur Wise. 1985. "Beyond Standardization: State Standards and School Improvment." *Elementary School Journal* 85: 315–35.

Dornbusch, Sanford M., and W. Richard Scott. 1975. *Evaluation and the Exercise of Authority*. San Francisco: Jossey-Bass.

Dreeben, Robert and A. Gamoran. 1985. *Race, Instruction and Learning*. Paper presented at the annual meeting of the American Educational Research Association, Chicago.

Fowler, Francis C. 1985. "Why Reforms Go Awry." *Education Week* (November 6): 24.

Galbraith, Jay. 1973. *Designing Complex Organizations*. Reading, Mass.: Addison-Wesley.

Gecas, Viktor, and Michael L. Schwalbe. 1983. "Beyond the Looking-Glass Self: Social Structure and Efficacy-Based Self-Esteem." *Social Psychology Quarterly* 46: 77–88.

Hackman, J. Richard, and Gregory R. Oldham. 1980. *Work Redesign*. Reading, Mass.: Addison-Wesley.

Handler, Janet R. 1987. *Teacher Questionnaire Data: Career Ladder Evaluation System*. Paper presented at the annual meeting of the American Educational Research Association, Washington, D.C.: April 20–24.

Handler, Janet R., and Deborah L. Carlson. 1985. *Shaping Tennessee's Career Ladder Program—1985*. Report to the Secretary of Education, U.S. Department of Education, Knoxville, Tennessee: University of Tennessee.

Hart, Ann. 1985. *Case Study Prepared for the Utah State Office of Education*. Salt Lake City: University of Utah.

Joyce, Bruce, Robert Bush, and Michael McKibbin. 1984. *Information and Opinion from the California Staff Development Study: The Compact Report*. Sacramento: California State Department of Education.

Kasten, Katherine L. 1984. "The Efficacy of Institutionally Dispensed Rewards in Elementary School Teaching." *Journal of Research and Development in Education* 17: 1–13.

Little, Judith Warren. 1984. "Seductive Images and Organizational Realities in Professional Development." *Teachers College Record* 86: 84–102.

Morgan, Barney. 1985. "Career Ladder Plan Not Working, Survey of Teachers Indicates." *Chattanooga Times*, August 15, p. 35.

National Center for Education Statistics. 1984. *The Condition of Education*. Washington, D.C.: U.S. Department of Education.

Purkey, Stewart C., and Marshall S. Smith. 1985. "School Reform: The District Policy Implications of the Effective Schools Literature." *Elementary School Journal* 85: 353–90.

Resnick, Daniel P., and Lauren B. Resnick. 1985. "Standards, Curriculum and Performance: A Historical and Comparative Perspective." *Educational Researcher* 14: 5–20.

Rosenholtz, Susan J. In press. *Teachers' Workplace: The Social Organization of Schools*. New York: Longman.

Scott, W. Richard. 1981. *Organizations: Rational, Natural, and Open Systems*. Englewood Cliffs, N.J.: Prentice-Hall.

Shannon, Patrick. 1986. "Merit Pay and Minimum Competency Testing." *Reading Research Quarterly* 21: 20–35.

Sherwin, John. 1969. *Four Problems in Teaching English: A Critique of Research*. Scranton, Penn.: International Textbooks.

Suhor, C. 1985. "Objective Tests and Writing Samples: How Do They Affect Instruction in Composition?" *Phi Delta Kappan* 66: 635–39.

Turnbull, Brenda J. 1985. "Using Governance and Support Systems to Advance School Improvement." *Elementary School Journal* 85: 337–52.

Walberg, Herbert J., and William J. Genova. 1982. "Staff, School, and Workshop Influences on Knowledge Use in Educational Improvement Efforts." *Journal of Educational Research* 76: 69–80.

3 BUSINESS AND THE PUBLIC SCHOOLS
New Patterns of Support

Milbrey Wallin McLaughlin

Business has been involved in the U.S. public schools at least since the turn of the century, through such activities as support for vocational education, charitable donations, and contribution of equipment or facilities. However, since the early 1980s both the nature and the level of private-sector involvement with the schools has changed as a consequence of trends in the political economy and stark assessments of the adequacy of U.S. education. The "rising tide of mediocrity" detailed by the 1983 National Commission on Excellence and companion reports on the condition of schools in the United States highlighted the relationship between education and economic growth and focused business's attention on public education.[1]

Concerns that the United States was losing its global competitive advantage and a belief that the public schools were both part of the

Much credit and appreciation goes to Nina Bascia and Kim Ford, graduate students in administration and policy analysis at Stanford's School of Education. They were extraordinarily helpful in tracking down the diverse sources used in this essay and never failed to provide insightful comment on the problems taken up here.

This chapter draws on data collected since 1983 in the more than forty districts receiving support from the Public Education Fund for Local Education Funds (LEFs). The PEF evaluation team, comprised of Paul Nachtigal (team leader), Toni Haas, Kent McGuire, and myself, has monitored LEF activities through annual reports and site visits. An overview of this activity is available in Nachtigal et al. (1988); a volume of in-depth case studies describing LEFs in six districts is forthcoming.

problem and essential to the solution motivated these reports. For example, the Research and Policy Committee of the Committee for Economic Development framed the rationale for its research project in these terms:

> Three years ago, a study of our nation's flagging competitiveness motivated CED to undertake this study. We became convinced that one important reason for our growing inability to compete in world markets was the inadequacy of our education.

One critical consequence of such assessments by corporate leadership was the creation of a national, regional, and local business culture that made support for public education a top priority for private-sector philanthropy. Response to this new business culture was swift by any standard of social change. In 1987, scarcely four years after the Commission report, of 130 major corporation surveyed, nearly two-thirds—64 percent—listed primary and secondary education as their number one community affairs concern.[2] Small business mirrored this focus. In 1986, at the second White House Conference on Small Business, education was rated as the sixth top priority, "at the top of the list with the liability insurance crisis and capital formation. Clearly, the small business community believes that the education of our youth is of critical importance" (Hoffman 1987).

Government acted quickly to reinforce private-sector interest. At the national level, conclusions about the need for a more active business role in public education were bolstered by President Reagan's admonition for private enterprise to step in and "fill the gap" left by shifts in his administration's education policy. For example, the president launched the National Partnership in Education program in October 1983 with a strong appeal to business:

> I'm issuing a challenge to America to insure our children get the best education they deserve. Let us resolve that every one of our country's public, private and parochial schools and community colleges—all 110,000 of them— will have formed a partnership in education (O'Connell 1985: 7).

State government followed suit and moved energetically to encourage school/business alliances. Only one year after the National Commission report was released, forty-two states had appointed task forces to build bridges between education and industry (Inman 1984).

A BROADENED RATIONALE FOR BUSINESS
INVOLVEMENT IN EDUCATION

In response to these urgings and activities, the business sector increased its financial support for elementary and secondary schools by shifting funds from other charitable purposes or by adding new dollars. This new level of support for precollegiate public education builds from a changed perspective on the rationale for business involvement.

Prior to the National Commission report and related accounts, private-sector giving to the schools was viewed sometimes as "philanthropic paternalism"[3] but more often in terms of relatively narrow "enlightened self-interest." Corporate gifts to precollegiate education traditionally were justified as an enhancement of the corporate image in the community or as an investment in the education of local young people needed to fill entry-level positions (Payton 1985; Inman 1984).

Although this form of enlightened self-interest continues to stimulate corporate giving to the schools, the conclusions of reports prepared by the National Commission on Excellence, the Committee on Economic Development, and others cast private-sector support for public education in broader terms. They framed education as a *collective good*, of direct import to the self-interest of *all* Americans—whether parents or direct consumers of the products of the schools. The language chosen for corporate position papers reflects a view of youth as society's responsibility, not just the responsibility of parents or educators, and of the schools as essential partners in the nation's future. For example, the CED report *Investing in our Children* (1985: xiii) insists on this perspective:

> all of us have an obligation to provide our children and our children's children with the best possible public education. We have a responsibility to see that our schools develop the intellectual skills and reinforce the positive attitudes and behavior that will serve our children well.

The private-sector involvement that emerged during the 1980s, in sum, takes a broader perspective on the focus and rationale for business support of public education and moves from narrow notions of self-interest to adopt conceptions of education as human resource development and an essential collective good (see also Council on Foundations 1987).

Furthermore, this collective good, many corporate leaders add, is rooted in values as well as economic competitiveness. As Stephen Chaudet, member of the California Business Roundtable and founding board member of the Los Angeles Educational Partnership, put it: "no institution is more fundamental to democracy than education."[4]

NEW FORMS OF BUSINESS INVOLVEMENT

The broadened motivation underlying corporate giving to the schools triggered change in the *form* of corporate giving and involvement. Philanthropic relations between business and education have evolved in ways that recast old relationships and define new ones. These business-school alliances operate in diverse organizational forms that embrace different strategies and purposes and define different relations between business and the schools. This essay distinguishes among three general forms: a partnership model, a banking model, and a political model.

The *partnership model* or the interinstitutional collaborations represented by the "join-a-school" or "adopt-a-school" programs go back many years. This form of school/business collaboration typically sends executives, technical assistance, and equipment to the schools. Earlier efforts provided support for career awareness in a specific industrial area (the local industry or corporate interest, most typically) or endeavored to "raise the parent, teacher and student understanding of the free enterprise system" (Nordgren and Gabriel 1981).

The school/business collaborations underway today have expanded the range of specific programs being sponsored, involve teachers from every discipline, span grade levels, and take more general aim at improving the overall quality of education (Freedman and Ascheim 1986–87; Roberts 1985; McCormick 1984). For example, whereas former alliances focused in large measure on enhancing the education available to the noncollege bound, business is now supplying equipment and expertise not only to machine shops but to AP science laboratories and mathematics classes as well.

ARCO in Los Angeles pioneered this mode of support for the schools by donating science instructors and tutors to the public schools. In Cincinnati, AT&T programmers taught COBOL to high school students. The Indianapolis Water Company collaborated with science teachers and students to develop a pond and stream on the school grounds for an environmental education course. Boeing and Honeywell engineers worked with Seattle high school teachers to develop a specialized mathematics curriculum (Shelton 1987). Texas Instruments trained "TI Champions" who serve as the contact person for the school district and broker for personnel to teach science, mathematics, and computer education in schools with a shortage of qualified teachers. Tenneco in Houston also supported a citywide program, Volunteers in the Public Schools (Inman 1984).

This partnership form dominates school/business collaboration. A 1986 mail survey of *Forbes* 500 corporations found that over 73 percent participate in partnerships and 45 percent describe those activities as adopt-a-school programs. A third of these partnerships were initiated by the corporations (in most cases by a vice president for community affairs or a public relations officer). Adopt-a-school programs sponsored by these large corporations were spread across grade levels: 62 percent worked with comprehensive high schools, 25 percent with specialized or vocational high schools, 40 percent with junior highs, and 28 percent with elementary schools. These activities generally were not expensive. Over half the respondents report that their involvement costs less than $10,000 a year, excluding the value of donated time and materials (Shakeshaft and Trachtman 1986–87). Interinstitutional collaborations or partnerships, in short, are a popular mode of private-sector support for the schools because they are inexpensive and because they are comprehensible and have clear boundaries. That is, whereas wholesale reform of public education is not a reasonable or appropriate goal for business involvement, support for a high school computer laboratory might be.

The *banking model* of the past, where corporations wrote checks to their local school system, also has been recast. Some of these shifts are purely locational. Corporate precollegiate philanthropy previously tended to favor the cities and communities where a corporation was located, but today's corporate giving has been amplified in these settings and has extended to the educational foundations springing up primarily in the middle-class communities where corporate executives live.

These "banking" organizations channel corporate and individual contributions to school systems for activities of the district's choice—

such as teacher workshops, specific curriculum projects, or general support for educational materials. In the larger urban areas, "Percent Clubs," which originated with the Minneapolis Five Percent Club, create an expected level of involvement for all member companies and rely on peer pressure to stimulate corporate giving. In the suburbs, educational foundations rely on individual gifts to the school, often supplemented by corporate matching grants. For the most part, these activities entail the "checkbook" mode of philanthropy and do not represent a significant level of direct involvement between the schools and the business community. Instead, educational foundations of this stripe comprise a modest new bank account for the schools.

However, some education foundations have programmatic interests and move beyond checkwriting to provide a vehicle for more direct involvement of corporate personnel or businesspeople in the schools through sponsorship of specific activities. The program committee work associated with these activities can play a consequential education function. For example, businesspeople learn much about their community's schools when teachers' applications for small grants are reviewed, as awards ceremonies are planned, or as school district needs are assessed for purposes of allocating foundation dollars. The Boston COMPACT is a well-known and successful model of this fiscal collaboration between the schools and the private sector and features the active and direct involvement of business sponsors. The Boston COMPACT also illustrates the positive consequences of this engagement. For example, a significant factor in the John Hancock Insurance Company's gift of approximately $1 million to the Boston public schools was the participation of Hancock executives on a committee reviewing small grant applications from teachers, which documented the extraordinarily difficult conditions of teaching in the public schools.

In addition to these programmatic and fiscal alliances, which recast earlier forms, a third form of school/business relations has emerged. It represents fundamentally a *political model* of building support for the schools, one that goes beyond dollars and specific programs to foster a broadened base of political support for public education in the private sector and in the community. These third-party intermediaries, best represented by the Local Education Funds (LEFs) sponsored by the Ford-supported Public Education Fund, provide both dollars and in-kind or direct support to the schools, and so fuse the activities of the partnership and banking models.[5] But unlike most partnership or banking forms of support, LEFs see dollars and activities in largely instrumental terms, as part of a political strategy of coalition building, and not as an end in themselves.

Like the banking model, they rely on a third-party intermediary agency as "boundary spanner" to move between the different cultures of the private sector and the public schools to establish a mutuality of interests. LEFs adopt a highly leveraged view of cash and noncash resources. The LEF convenes representatives from business, the community, and the schools, brokers private-sector resources (both cash and noncash), and takes responsibility for overseeing the use of these resources. The LEF thus reduces the transaction costs for both contributors and beneficiaries by assuming the information-search costs as well as the administrative overhead associated with private sector philanthropy. The LEF accordingly helps establish a set of preconditions necessary for any significant degree of direct corporate involvement—a vehicle for communication, standards of practice, and a neutral forum for accommodation and reciprocity between the culture of the school and the culture of the private sector.[6]

The mode of organization represented by both education foundations and by LEFs—an intermediate agent or coordinating structure—is familiar in the grantsmaking world, the United Way being a well-known example. An unwelcome cost sometimes associated with this approach has been the alienation or distancing between donor and recipient because nonprofit service providers often insulate the donor from the problems of the beneficiaries (Galaskiewicz 1985: 46). LEFs and many education foundations have managed to retain the benefits of an intermediary agent and to reduce if not eliminate these costs. They have done so by involving private-sector representatives directly in the affairs of the schools through board memberships and through activities such as program review committees. These intermediary organizations thus foster knowledge, understanding, and identification, rather than alienation or distancing from the public schools. Indeed, the educational function they perform, in the long term, may be their most important contribution.

IMPLICATIONS FOR SCHOOL FINANCE

These diverse forms of business involvement in the schools have implications for the financing, administration, and instructional practices of the public education and so frame questions for school finance, broadly conceived.

Equity was the issue most frequently raised about new levels and forms of business involvement, especially as these new ventures were taking shape in the early 1980s. Equity concerns associated with business/school alliances take two forms—interdistrict and intradistrict. Interdistrict questions center on the consequences for equalization-based measures such as California's *Serrano*-motived school finance strategy. Are they being undermined by the enhanced support available to some, but not all, communities? Available evidence suggests that to some extent, the rich do get richer. Communities such as Palo Alto have a wealthier base from which to solicit support for their community education foundation than do less advantaged neighborhoods down the road. However, these dollars are relatively small compared to total district budgets and do not underwrite inequities of the scale that sent John Serrano to court.

Figures for urban areas suggest that, while somewhat unevenly distributed, the majority of the nation's large cities receive support from the business sector. For example, 80 percent of the largest districts (over 25,000) had partnerships or school/business collaboratives in 1985; that number has certainly grown since then (Roberts 1985). LEFs sponsored by the Public Education Fund are located by design in more than forty of the nation's large urban school districts.

Rural areas or small communities generally do not benefit from business contributions to the schools and are the losers in this new form of private-sector support for the schools. There are a number of reasons why this is so. Communication between business and the schools is not the problem it is in urban areas, so new structures to facilitate business/school exchange are unnecessary. The general store or local coffee shop provides for easy interaction between businesspeople and educators. Little has changed where "resources" are framed in terms of community or local business goodwill in rural communities.

More critically, the commercial base of rural areas is slim—the base of economic support for the schools generally is not available in these locales. Because companies prefer to give near their operating locations, rural areas and small communities do not get an equal share of business support for the schools (Inman 1984). Even though the expanded view of enlightened self-interest that stimulates business support for the schools in the 1980s *ipso facto* embraces all of the nation's schoolchildren, businesses still tend to support the schools in their own backyards both for reasons of public relations and for some measure of oversight.

Intradistrict equity questions generally turn on the organizational form of school/business involvement. Third-party intermediaries—educational foundations and LEFs—frame their mission in terms of support for the *district* and strive to ensure that all schools benefit from the resources available. Some have even taken steps to channel resources to the less-advantaged schools. The Los Angeles Educational Partnership, for example, gives "bonus points" to applications for small grants from teachers in inner-city schools. Business resources also are used to support programs that benefit the district as a whole—workshops, incentive programs for students, and math/science collaboratives, for instance.

The arrangements seen in the partnership or adopt-a-school models spread the benefits less evenly within a district. "Adoption" is a discrete resource from which nonparticipating schools derive no benefit. Teachers and others associated with the "unadopted" schools sometimes complain about unfairness or special treatment: "In some cases the good have gotten better, while the sources of everyone's discontent remain untouched and unchanged" (Mann 1984: 21). However, expressions of concern about intradistrict inequities appear to be the exception. In most districts, partnerships are forged between corporate and district leaders in a manner that embodies both corporate and district interests.

Governance is a second concern raised about increased private-sector involvement in the public schools. Would contributions by the private sector buy influence in decisions about what goes on in the schools? What some observers termed the "camel's nose" problem apparently has not come to pass.[7] Representatives from business and the corporate world have, in most cases, elected to leave the business of education to educators (Mann 1987: 127):

> Businesspeople know as little about schools as schoolpeople know about investment banking, and they will not embarrass themselves by presuming to tell a superintendent how to accomplish the main work of the school: teaching and learning.

In their association with the public schools, businesspeople generally behave in a way that is consistent with the norms of the business community—respect for expertise and specialized functions. More pragmatic reasons preclude heavy-handed business control as the price of involvement—time and resources. Most private-sector contributors to public education are not corporate giants. They are small businesses with insufficient personnel to run the schools in addition to their commercial interests.

In particular, business generally has not exchanged their collaboration with the public schools for programs and activities that served their narrow self-interest. For example, a recent examination of school/business collaborations (*Public/Private Ventures News* 1988: 3) concluded:

> We saw no attempts to focus education on serving employers job-specific needs. Businesses' anticipated emphasis on vocational education has not materialized, no attempt has been made to override the schools' emphasis on well-educated students.

Further, the tension inherent between business sponsorship of particular programs (such as those discussed earlier as examples of school/business collaboration) and the autonomy of school administrators has been reduced or eliminated in most cases by collaborative planning and conferral about the ways in which business support could be most useful to the schools. In fact, most partnerships are initiated by school leaders, not by the private sector, and proceed from the "mutual commitment [of] . . . all active participants" (Walkenshaw and Crain 1984: 29).

In short, by all reports, the new relationships between business and the schools have *not* upset the balance of private-sector interests and public-sector responsibilities. Nor have they resulted in "philanthropic particularism" to any significant extent.[8]

A third issue raised about the new level and forms of business support for public education concerns the *stability* of these relationships. In the fashion show of public policy, is business interest in the public schools simply a passing fancy? Can the schools count on the support of business in the years to come? Evidence on this point is mixed. Only a quarter of the superintendents surveyed in one study thought that business involvement represented a long-term commitment to support public education (Mann 1987). In many districts, teachers, too, expressed cynicism about the enduring interest of their new corporate partners.

Yet these assessments are uneven and appear related to the organizational form of involvement. The one-shot or episodic involvement seen in many education foundations and some school/business part-nerships is unlikely to grow or to be sustained. There is little about the strategies employed in these approaches to build the commit-ment of business partners or to educate them about the importance of sustained involvement. Many of the temporary business partners seem to feel that "once is enough" or that the concern that moti-vated their initial support can be discharged by a single contribution: "I gave at the office."

In contrast, the involvement nurtured through the alliances that build on the direct, ongoing involvement of business with the schools, or that frame their objectives in terms of coalition building, receive somewhat different forecasts. These relationships appear to be mov-ing toward a degree of institutionalization. For example, Boston COMPACT evaluators comment that relations between Boston's pri-vate sector and the public schools are "becoming accepted as a way of life." Federal Reserve Bank officials take it for granted that high school youth will occupy part-time jobs; schoolpeople take it for granted that everyday in every school a nonunion person will be teaching a class—a remarkable thing in a time of teacher layoffs. COMPACT participants say that there are so many people and insti-tutions linked to the COMPACT, through a deliberate media and public relations campaign, that it would be hard for them to renege on their agreements—"too many people have their feet in" (Farrar and Cipollone 1988).

The continuing strong support of corporate leadership for an active private-sector role in support for public education also sug-gests that the 1980s shift in level and form of business involvement will be more than passing fancy. For example, Reginald Jones, re-tired General Electric CEO (Committee for Economic Development 1982: 81), felt deeply that

> public policy and social issues are no longer adjuncts to business planning and management. They are in the mainstream of it. The concern must be perva-sive in companies today, from the boardroom to the factory floor. Manage-ment must be measured for performance in economic and noneconomic areas alike. And top management must lead.

The 1985 CED report (Committee for Economic Development 1985: 81) asserted that

> There is a legitimate role for the business community in the public schools. Business has much to gain from improvements in the quality of the schools,

and it has a responsibility for helping to support and maintain that quality. Business also has a role to play in supporting adequate public funding for the schools.

The business culture that emerged in the early 1980s to make education a priority, then, appears to have the continuing, strong support from private-sector leadership. Where decline in established corporate interest is evident, it generally represents economic slowdown, not shifts in priorities (see, for example, Calhoun 1988), nor, as *Public/Private Ventures* (1988: 3) reports, has business support "appeared to wane in the absence of concrete results."

Yet these optimistic predictions may be premature. It remains to be seen whether or not the concerns of private-sector leadership will be translated into sustained support. In particular, it is not clear whether or not the continued support of leadership coupled with local strategies will be capable of fashioning stable, confident, long-term business support for the public schools. It is too soon to assess the future of business interest and support as expressed in the new organizational forms of the 1980s.[9]

CONSEQUENCES OF BUSINESS SUPPORT

It may be too early to tell whether business support for public education will or can be sustained. But it is possible to say something about the actual and potential consequences the 1980s new patterns of business support for the schools.

The private-sector support stimulated by the National Commission Report and the subsequently strengthened private-sector priorities for precollegiate education has brought multiple new resources to public education. The new dollars apparently are among the *least* important of these resources.

The 1980s form of business support for the school has less to do with relaxing tight budgets than with building broad-based support for the public schools, expanding school district boundaries into the community, and eroding the isolation of classroom teachers. Business involvement in the schools brings not just additional revenue, but a different kind of revenue. Practitioners argue that the "resource" most important to them and to the vitality of the public education system is not the financial support but the political support and recognition business involvement conveys (Cuban 1985; Leiter 1985).

In some areas, business involvement in public education has created an important new *political voice* for the schools. In California, for example, key figures in shaping the state's Business Roundtable focus on education and subsequently the state's massive new education reform measure (SB 813) were veteran board members of Oakland's LEF, the Marcus A. Foster Educational Institute. (Oakland also contributed two MAFEI members to the National Commission on Excellence.)

LEFs and those educational foundations that have provided for the direct involvement of the business community in the schools have educated their corporate members about the needs, constraints, and problems of the public schools. Some LEFs, in fact, take this function as a central mission. A founding member of Oakland's fifteen-year-old Marcus Foster Institute says, for example,

> We all know about the deep-seated problems of the schools, but that is not what I want that young Touche Ross executive to experience [while attending the Institute's awards dinner on behalf of the company]. I want him to catch a vision of what could be. And, then, maybe ask him to sit on this committee or that. And, years later, when he is in a position of power, he'll be much better informed about the schools and willing to put in a word with the governor or his legislator.[10]

Business involvement in all forms has been a powerful factor in *mediating the isolation* of the classroom teacher. Dr. Harry Handler, the former superintendent of the Los Angeles Unified School District, believes that the "windows into the community" provided by collaboration between business and the schools not only connects educators with the community but also brings critical sources of energy and support for new ideas and practices. Teachers in Los Angeles concur. They detail the stimulation and reinforcement they find in working with the private sector on activities such as the urban math collaborative, professional development for science teachers, and technology development efforts.

But beyond benefits based in professional exchange between teachers and the private sector, in community after community, teachers underscore the value of the *recognition and approval* implicit in active business support. This significance of private-sector involvement extends far beyond enhanced "happiness quotients" for teachers. Almost every study of teachers' satisfaction and commitment highlights the alienation that U.S. teachers express because they feel undervalued, unappreciated, and beleaguered. This sense of alienation, as much if not more than any other factor, drives teachers from the classroom into other occupations (McLaughlin et al. 1986). Perhaps it is a sad commentary on the state of U.S. education that so little could mean so much, but in district after district, the import of business interest in the schools for teachers' self-esteem and enthusiasm is undeniable (Nachtigal et al. 1988). From an Oakland administrator, for example:

> I don't see how we could function without the Marcus Foster Institute. It is not just the money, it is the boost to the morale. It is easy to feel you are alone, especially in a district like Oakland. No one knows the good things teachers do, no one comes to see them, no one cares. There is a tremendous sense of isolation. . . . The Institute is important to the schools because it is something from outside the school system—recognition and a chance to celebrate the schools.[11]

Minigrant or small grant programs have been an especially effective vehicle for conveying business's support for teachers' efforts. These modest awards (usually of no more than a few hundred dollars) yield disproportionate benefits in terms of teachers' renewal, development of new ideas for the classroom, and sense of recognition. The *source* of support—the private sector—makes an essential difference. To be sure, few districts have the slack to provide such funds for teacher-initiated projects. But even if district resources were available, it seems unlikely that the effect would be the same. Teachers and administrators agree that the impact of these small grants lies as much if not more in the cachet of private-sector sponsorship as in the dollars they contribute. One important implication of these experiences is that business can make a particular and central contribution to retaining talented teachers in U.S. classrooms.

But the continued involvement of business in the public schools has even more fundamental significance for the *fiscal future* of precollegiate education. The country's changing demographics mean that fewer and fewer Americans have any direct interest in the schools: Fewer than 15 percent of today's citizens have children in the schools. In some areas, those whose children attend the public schools often are among the least influential in lobbying for support for education, as many parents able to do so fled the troubled public schools for private education. The weight of individual self-interest does not favor schools in the face of competing demands on public dollars. Without strong private-sector advocacy for public education, it is difficult to imagine how the schools can compete effectively in local, state, or national legislative marketplaces.

A lesson of the new patterns of business/school relations is that the organizational form this support takes at the local level matters. The weak links typical of the traditional checkbook mode of support for education are insufficient to sustain or stabilize private-sector involvement. The hallmark of the new form of business involvement is a direct link between business and the schools that operates through an intermediary structure. This third-party institution, established expressly to support public education, engages multiple actors in multiple activities, provides highly leveraged resources, and takes building support for the schools as an objective. In this organizational context, the significance of dollars moves to the background as important resources take the form of political support, brokered access, and a broadened community for the schools.

In sum, business support is essential not only because it can provide additional, marginal resources to the schools. It is essential because it can *leverage* political support and so the base funding necessary for a healthy, productive public education system. Without the currency of influence and effective political voice, tomorrow's school finance picture likely will be bleak.

NOTES

1. Among the most widely reviewed reports were those of the National Commission on Excellence in Education, the Carnegie Commission report on the High School, the Education Commission of the States Task Force on Education and Economic Growth, the report of the Twentieth Century Fund, and the several reports of the Committee for Economic Development.

2. The timing for strengthening school/business alliances was right in terms of trends in corporate giving, which has been the fastest-growing sector of philanthropy for some time. During the past decade, the growth of corporate contributions has been remarkable, nearly tripling from $1.5 billion in 1976 to approximately $4.4 billion in 1986 (Platzer 1987: 1). Educa-

tion traditionally has been the primary benefactor of corporate philanthropy, collecting more than two-fifths (or 40.7 percent) of corporate dollars (Useem 1987: 342). This corporate support, however, focused primarily on higher education, with 97 percent of corporate educational philanthropy going to colleges and universities (Justiz and Kameen 1987).

3. See Salamon (1987) for a general discussion of this concept.

4. Personal interview.

5. The Public Education Fund was created in 1983 as an independent national organization. PEF was initiated to foster private-sector and broader community involvement in the schools by facilitating the creation of and support for third-party intermediaries at the local level called local education funds (LEFs). Both PEF and LEFs followed a strategy of using limited resources to leverage business and community resources for the schools. A $6 million grant from the Ford Foundation provided primary support for PEF and initial funding for the LEFs selected for participation. Consistent with its design as a temporary organization, it closed its doors in December 1987, after five years of operation. For a detailed report of the PEF's activities and the more than forty LEFs eventually supported by this strategy, see Nachtigal et al. (1988).

6. In many districts, LEFs facilitate communication *within* the district as well. In Los Angeles, for example, where relations between teachers and administrators have been strained for more than a decade, the Los Angeles Educational Partnership plays a valuable intradistrict communication function. A district administrator commented: "LAEP programs are beginning to address the problems of lack of trust between teachers and administrators. Teachers are beginning to see that the principals want what they want. LAEP [can help this happen because it] serves as an organization both can trust. In this sense, the neutrality—not being seen as having a vested interest—is critical. LAEP is not perceived as part of the political power structure so they can serve as an occasion for teachers and principals to really listen to one another" (personal interview).

7. Let the camel's nose into the tent, the aphorism goes, and the whole camel is sure to follow.

8. Lester Salamon (1987) discusses philanthropic particularism as both a strength and a drawback. It is a strength because it focuses philanthropic efforts and so increases the possibility of discernible impact. It potentially is a problem because of the issues raised here—uneven or inequitable distribution of philanthropic resources, change in the service mix offered by the schools, or diffusion of responsibility for the system as a whole.

9. The absence of experience with these organizational forms is matched by lack of a firm theoretical base. See Salamon (1987).

10. Personal interview.

11. Personal interview.

REFERENCES

Calhoun, S. 1988. "The Two Percent Solution." *Foundation News*. (January/February): 48–49.

Committee for Economic Development. 1982. *Public-Private Partnership*. New York: Committee for Economic Development.

_____. 1985. *Investing in Our Children*. New York: Committee for Economic Development.

Council on Foundations. 1987. *Corporate Issues* (September): 1–11.

Cuban, L. 1985. "Corporate Involvement in Public Schools: A Practitioner-Academic's Point of View." In *The Private Sector in the Public School: Can It Improve Education?*, edited by M. Levine, pp. 22–23. Washington, D.C.: American Enterprise Institute.

Farrar, E., and A. Cipollone. 1988. "After the Signing: The Boston Compact 1982–1985." In *American Business and the Public Schools*, edited by Marsha Levine and Robert Tractman, pp. 89–120. New York: Teachers College Press.

Freedman, S., and B. Ascheim. 1986–87. "Industry-Education Partnerships." *Metropolitan Education* (Winter): 33–43.

Galaskiewicz, J. 1985. *Social Organization of an Urban Grants Economy*. New York: Academic Press.

Hoffman, E. 1987. "Education of Youth Is Critical to the Small Business Community." *Directions Newsletter* 5, (3) (Spring): 6.

Inman, D. 1984. "Bridging Education to Industry: Implications for Financing Education." *Journal of Education Finance* 10 (Fall): 271–77.

Justiz, M.J., and Kameen, M.C. 1987. "Business Offers a Hand to Education." *Phi Delta Kappan* (January): 379–83.

Leiter, M. 1985. "Going Public: A Labor-Education Perspective." In *The Private Sector in the Public School: Can It Improve Education?*, edited by M. Levine, pp. 18–19. Washington, D.C.: American Enterprise Institute.

Mann, D. 1984. "It's Up to You to Steer Those School/Business Partnerships." *American School Board Journal* (October): 20–24.

Mann, D. 1987a. "Business Involvement and Public School Improvement, part I." *Phi Delta Kappan* (October): 123–28.

_____. 1987b. "Business Involvement and Public School Improvement, part 2." *Phi Delta Kappan* (November): 228–32.

McCormick, K. 1984. "These Tried-and-True Alliances Have Paid Off for the Public Schools." *American School Board Journal* (October): 24–26.

McLaughlin, M.W., R.S. Pfeifer, D. Swanson-Owens, and S. Yee. 1986. "Why Teachers Won't Teach." *Phi Delta Kappan* 67 (February): 420–26.

Nachitgal, P., T. Haas, K. McGuire, and M.W. McLaughlin. 1988. *Public Education Fund: Five Year Report*. Pittsburgh: Public Education Fund Network.

Nordgren, S., and A. Gabriel. 1981. "School Days for Big Business." *The Nation* (September 19): 235–38.

O'Connell, C. 1985. *How to Start a School/Business Partnership.* Bloomington, Ind.: Phi Delta Kappa Educational Foundation.

Payton, R. 1985. "The Taming of the Corporation." *Change* (January/February): 27–30.

Platzer, L. C. 1987. *Annual Survey of Corporate Contributions, 1987 Edition.* New York: The Conference Board.

Public/Private Ventures News. 1988. (Winter).

Roberts, A. W. 1985. "Partnerships in Education: An Executive Summary." *School Business Affairs* (January): 20–21.

Salamon, L. M. 1987. "Partners in Public Service: The Scope and Theory of Government–Nonprofit Relations." In *The Nonprofit Sector: A Research Handbook*, edited by W. W. Powell, pp. 99–117. New Haven: Yale University Press.

Shakeshaft, C., and R. Trachtman. 1986-87. "Business as Usual: Exploring Private Sector Participation in American Public Schools." *Metropolitan Education.* (Winter): 25–31.

Shelton, C. W. 1987. *The Doable Dozen.* Alexandria, Va.: National Community Education Association.

Useem, M. 1987. "Corporate Philanthropy." In *The Nonprofit Sector: A Research Handbook*, edited by W. W. Powell, pp. 340–59. New Haven: Yale University Press.

Walkenshaw, S., and J. Crain. 1984. "Procedures for Creating Partnerships in Career Education." *Journal of Career Development* (September): 27–32.

4 THE INTERNAL ALLOCATION OF RESOURCES FOR EDUCATION
An International Perspective

Claude Tibi

There have been few international comparisons of how resources are distributed for education at either regional or institutional levels of the educational system. For this reason, from 1981 to 1984, the International Institute for Educational Planning undertook a micro-analysis of educational expenditures in countries[1] where expenditures were linked to general characteristics of the learning process, the set of norms and regulations in force, and the organization of teaching at the institutional level. A primary goal was to understand the process leading to the ultimate distribution of resources to teachers and students.

In more precise terms, the studies aimed at three complementary objectives:

1. To record all current resources received during one complete school year by a sample of institutions drawn from several countries. All current resources were of interest, whether they were public or private in origin and whether they were allocated to or collected by the institutions being studied.

2. To understand how total and unit expenditures were determined, by studying relationships between

    a. Expenditures and activities carried out within the institution, the organization of teaching, and the set of relevant norms and regulations; and

    b. Resources allocated to the institution and collected directly by it on the one hand and its enrollment, expected and actual, on the other.

3. To analyze from an economic and pedagogic viewpoint how resources were used at both the institutional and national levels and to show the nature and extent of disparities of resources among institutions.

The institution was chosen as the unit of analysis because it is the basic unit of organization of educational services and distribution and mobilization of resources, and because only at this level is it possible to measure precisely and exhaustively receipts and expenditures and to analyze how resources are used. The studies were limited to primary and secondary education. They were also limited to current expenditures because of the difficulty and cost of collecting information on capital expenditures. Collecting comprehensive data only on current resources, both physical and financial, posed numerous problems because it was the first time, in most of the countries concerned, that such a study has been undertaken. Finally, it must be added that no effort was made to link available resources at institutional levels with indicators of the outcomes of the teaching process. The studies were all based on random samples of representative primary and secondary institutions and may be classified as either one-year cross-sectional studies or longitudinal studies, based on two school years, successive or not.

The first part of this chapter presents an analysis of unit expenditures with an emphasis on (1) financing mechanisms and internal processes of resource allocation and (2) the norms and regulations pertaining to the organization of education in each country.

Attention turns next to a discussion of the principal results of in-depth case studies. These country-by-country studies explore the consequences of financing and resource allocation mechanisms on disparities in resources among institutions. This exploration includes discussion about the efficacy with which resources are utilized. Particular attention is paid to variation in unit expenditures according to institutional size.

DETERMINANTS OF UNIT EXPENDITURES

Regardless of the level of analysis (national, regional, or institutional), the average unit expenditure of a group of institutions at a certain level of education is determined by the relationship between available resources and actual enrollment. This is the result of an interaction between two decisionmaking processes: (1) one that determines the physical and financial resources of institutions and (2) another that determines enrollments.

At the national level, for example, available resources stem from both the political-administrative allocation of public resources and decisions that bring about a financial or physical contribution from families or other agents to the institutions concerned. Enrollments are determined by individual and institutional decisions governing the registration of students in schools and their subsequent movement from one level to the next, including graduation and dropping-out. The same approach may be taken at regional, district, or institutional levels. The processes that occur at these different levels mutually complete and influence each other.

The analysis should be envisaged from the point of view of financial and physical resources because in countries with centralized financing, for example, resources allocated by the ministry of education to geographical areas and then to institutions are nearly all physical resources (such as teaching and nonteaching staff, equipment, furniture, and textbooks). Moreover, staff deployment in many countries is affected by preferences of teachers for cities and is sometimes limited by regulations preventing redeployment when civil servants object. These factors may have a significant impact on the distribution of staff between institutions.

If the study is carried out on an annual basis, emphasis must be given to the budgetary process and to its interactions with student registrations and preparations for the coming school year. From a longer-term perspective, the determinants of demand for education and the allocation of resources to education over a long period need to be analyzed.

The interaction between the outcome of these two decisionmaking processes may be analyzed from a technical and political-administrative viewpoint. The organization of education in each country is governed by a set of norms and regulations that foresee, for example, average number of pupils per class, the programs and teaching hours, conditions of recruitment and remuneration of staff, teaching load per teacher, and so forth. These parameters, which result from choices aimed at best resolving pedagogic imperatives and economic constraints, are the basis of budgetary demands, once enrollments expected for the next school year have been estimated. This demand for resources is considered in conjunction with often inflexible levels of resource supply, emanating from financial organisms (ministries of finance and planning or their equivalent according to the country and the administration levels concerned).

After negotiations, cuts often must be made in proposed budgets. In developing countries in particular, these cuts are often made first in capital expenditures, then in nonsalary current expenditures, and lastly in salary expenditures, of which the major part is already committed. In different countries, total salaries are sometimes reduced in real terms by the effects of inflation. Adjustments in salaries are made late and do not compensate for rises in prices. This situation, which concerns the entire public sector and not only the staff of the educational system, has prevailed in most developing countries, to varying degrees, during the last twenty years. The practice has become even more prevalent recently in all countries where debt servicing and its consequences on public-sector deficits have necessitated adoption of structural adjustment plans. In any case, the budget is approved in general before enrollments are known, and their control is not entirely in the hands of the government.

One conclusion then is that the availability of resources at microlevels is much more determined by supply than by demand. There is also at the same time a time lag between the two processes and a difference in the capacity to control resources on the one hand and enrollments on the other, even if additional budgets could be subsequently approved.

In countries where institutions can directly mobilize resources (school fees or other contributions), the situation depends on the results of the public resource allocation process, the mobilization of private resources, as well as on the subsequent interactions between the two. In the period preceding the start of the school year, adjustments between demand and supply of places take place in order to accept new pupils in the schools where they have applied or to assign them to a neighbouring school. Parallel with this are adjustments between demand and supply of resources on the basis of actual enrollments, whenever possible. These adjustments have consequences for parameters such as the number of pupils per class or the teaching load per teacher. These parameters, which were used in the first stage to prepare budgetary demands, are thus affected by the subsequent supply of resources. The values they assume at national, regional, and institutional levels indicate the outcome of the interaction between the processes of determination of resources and enrollments. The diversity of local constraints and decisionmaking criteria, both technical and political, explain to a large extent the diversity of situations that prevail in different institutions and hence the variability of their unit expenditures.

The above analysis shows that, in the study of determinants of unit expenditures, emphasis should be placed on decisionmaking processes, most especially on those with implications for the allocation of resources at the local or institutional level. For example, decisions pertaining to the acceptance and teaching of pupils are very important in this context. The organization of the teaching process within schools and unit expenditures is a result of the confrontation between those responsible for finance and those responsible for providing education at the local level.

Before analyzing expenditures, it is therefore important to examine closely mechanisms of financing and resource allocation to institutions, in all their diversity. It is equally important to consider the principal indicators reflecting the consequences of norms and regulations that have bearing on pedagogical practices locally.

MECHANISMS OF FINANCING AND RESOURCE ALLOCATION

These vary a great deal by country and, within each country, according to the level of education and the network involved.[2] Because it is not possible here to provide an in-depth comparative analysis, the following discussion presents a typology for the countries studied,[3] accompanied in each case by a summary of significant complementary information from the point of view of consequences for resource allocation.

Typology of Financing[4]

The categories chosen (see Table 4-1) are based on four characteristics:

1. The number of separate public networks, for the same level of education as well as the origin of resources allocated to education in each network;

Table 4–1. A Typology of Financing of Primary and Secondary Education.

	One Public Network			Several Public Networks		
	No private network	*One or more private networks without public funding*	*One or more private networks with partial public funding*	*No private network*	*One or more private networks without public funding*	*One or more private networks with partial public funding*
Public financing by one level of government only	Algeria Congo	Morocco Sudan Tunisia Thailand	Indonesia Kenya	—	—	—
Public financing by several levels of government	—	Colombia (primary) Nepal	—	—	Brazil Colombia (secondary) Mexico Philippines Venezuela	—

2. The number of separate private networks and the contribution of the public sector to their financing;
3. The mechanisms for the distribution of public resources between geographical areas and educational institutions, in the public network;
4. The presence or absence of a regular contribution from parents (in the guise of school fees or other forms) in public networks.

Analysis by Country

Morocco. In this country, where the public network is financed totally by the central government, the distribution of resources between regions and provinces within regions for primary and secondary education is the result of a budget preparation process that is itself the outcome of an assessment of school needs for the coming school year by the Planning Office of the Ministry of Education and its regional and provincial offices. Each year in February, educational institutions send to the central level, via the provincial and regional delegations, information concerning their enrollments and resources. Later, they send results of end of the school year examinations (in June) and the new registrations. On this basis, the opening or closing of classes and schools is decided by the central office of planning and the necessary means are included in the budget under preparation. A margin of growth for the following school year (the financial year goes from January 1 to December 31, while the school year goes from September 1 to June 30) is typically included. The process ensures a quite equal distribution of resources on a per pupil basis among institutions and a good utilization of resources.

Other countries in French-speaking Africa have a similar financing mechanism except that parents make a limited contribution to schools in the Congo. In Algeria and Tunisia, the geographical distribution of resources is also made by aggregating school needs at regional and national levels.

Colombia. Since 1973, the financing of primary education and health services in the public sector is mainly assured by the *situado fiscal*, which stipulates that a determined percentage of national ordinary revenue (current receipts minus receipts earmarked for other uses) is devoted to it. This percentage equaled 13 percent in 1973.

It rose to 14 percent in 1974 and 15 percent in 1975 and the law stipulated that it could increase from that time by 2 percent each year up to 25 percent, if ordinary revenue increased by more than 15 percent compared to the average of the three preceding years. These resources are distributed between departments and national territories such that 30 percent of the total is distributed equally between territorial units while 70 percent is distributed proportionally to the population of each unit according to the 1964 census. Seventy-four percent of the sums received are earmarked for primary education and 26 percent to health services.

Secondary public institutions in Colombia depend for funding on the national, departmental, or municipal level. Up to 1975, each administrative level looked after the financing of the network it controlled. The law to nationalize the financing of secondary education, approved in 1975, changed this so that the financing of the three networks is ensured by the central government by retaining, at the national level, a part of sales tax revenues that were previously ceded to departments and municipalities. After numerous modifications, the present situation takes the following form:

1. Thirty percent of the global product of taxes on sales (value added tax) is given back to departments by the central government. The distribution between departments is done according to the same regulation as for the *situado fiscal* (30 percent equally, 70 percent in proportion to population). These sums are allocated between the municipalities forming the department in proportion to their population.

2. Of these sums, 3 percent are intended to pay for social benefits for civil servants working in the departments, while the remaining 27 percent is allocated to the municipalities for their current expenditure. However, as a consequence of the law on the nationalization of financing of secondary education approved in 1975, the central government retains the following proportion of this 27 percent to cover educational expenditures: 50 percent of the total amount (27 percent) for municipalities with more than 500,000 inhabitants, 30 percent of the total amount (27 percent) for municipalities with 100,000 to 500,000 inhabitants, and nothing for other municipalities.

There are no school fees in public primary schools, but parents have to pay a high percentage (around 90 percent on average) of nonsalary expenditure in public secondary schools, through the so-called *Fondo de Servicios Docentes.* Departments and municipalities may also contribute to the financing of primary and secondary education, but this support has diminished substantially over the last few years, especially for primary education.

Evaluations of the *situado fiscal* have revealed two results. First, distribution criteria have tended to favor the least populated territorial units and those where private primary education is the most developed. The 1964 census results for distribution of the 70 percent do not take account of important internal migrations that took place during the period. The *initial* distribution, calculated on the basis of foreseen receipts at the time of approval of the budget, is done on the basis of regulations set by the law, but *subsequent* distributions linked to new resources obtained from additional budgets are made on different bases. Given all these factors, the amount received under the *situado fiscal* per primary school pupil in the public network varies considerably according to the territorial unit (from 1 to 30, approximately).

Second, regulations of the *situado fiscal* have contributed to inefficiency in the utilization of resources. For example, one regulation makes it impossible to modify the allocation of resources between territorial units and to utilize the corresponding resources to assist private education and to reallocate a part of the resources in the favor of other levels of education.

Nepal. Public primary and secondary schools receive resources from several sources. The central government pays 100 percent, 75 percent, and 50 percent respectively of teachers' salaries according to the level of education (primary, first, and second cycle of secondary). In addition, the central government covers the totality of primary expenditures, and all the salaries of secondary teachers in zones with difficult access. The central government also allocates a specific sum to primary schools for the purchase of supplies and distributes textbooks to pupils free of charge.

Districts and villages provide resources in the form of gifts. These gifts are used for the construction of classrooms, repairs, and purchase of furniture. In addition, there are "revolving funds" established at the district level from a grant coming initially from the central government. Each institution may receive a loan, reimbursable in five years without interest, from this fund for improving facilities.

To this support may be added school fees paid by parents at the secondary level (primary education is free) and possibly revenue from land owned by the school and the surplus (or deficit) from the preceding year. In secondary schools, resources from the local level and from parents represent 30 to 50 percent of the total and this structure of financing leads to marked disparities of resources among individual institutions.

Indonesia. Four networks of primary and secondary schools coexist in this country: public, subsidized, assisted, and private schools. School fees were abolished in public primary education but continue in public secondary as well as in all other categories of institutions. Their amount (in the public network) varies from one to fifteen times according to the level of development of the province; 85 percent of fees collected by the school are returned to it and may be assigned to specific expenditures. Because the amount of fees received by the school varies considerably according to its size, location, and percentage actually returned, very marked disparities result among institutions. Utilization of these funds is not so strictly controlled as those from budgetary credits, so that the difference between resources and declared expenditures is sometimes very significant.

Public secondary schools have their staff paid for by the Ministry of Education and receive budgetary credits for their current nonsalary expenditures. Resources from school fees complement teaching staff salaries for overtime. They may also help recruit administrative and service staff and complement the government credits for nonsalary current expenditures.

Subsidized schools receive a regular government contribution, which may cover the salaries of part of the staff. For *assisted* schools, the public contribution is less important and more irregular, while *private* schools receive nothing from the public sector. The criteria establishing eligibility for a subsidy and its subsequent magnitude are not very clear. Each year, many privately established schools try to enter the category of assisted or even subsidized schools by showing that they fulfill the conditions set by the Ministry of Education. However, only some of these schools succeed in making the change.

Kenya. Strong demand for education, associated with a long tradition of self-help, has brought about the creation of Harambee and assisted schools. These relatively new forms of schools parallel the network of maintained schools whose current expenditures are taken care of to a large extent by the central government. In many villages where there is no maintained school or whose capacity is insufficient, parents conduct fund-raising to build, equip, and run an entirely privately financed Harambee school. It may subsequently happen that the government will provide some assistance. If this support becomes regular and takes the form of posting teachers paid by the Ministry of Education, the school can evolve into an assisted school. One may also find maintained schools with Harambee streams, when the government has not financed expansion of the school. In each case, parents contribute to school expenditures by paying admission and school fees as well as boarding fees where applicable.

Brazil. At the first and second levels of Brazilian education, there are federal, state, municipal, and private schools. The financing of public schools varies according to the levels of government and education. The budget of the Federal Ministry of Education is financed by general revenues and the part assigned to the federal level from taxes on salaries assigned to education.[5] Expenditures of the Federal Ministry for primary education (covering federal primary schools and certain federal programs in states and municipalities) are financed by federal revenues from the salary tax and general revenues. The budget of the Education Secretariat in each state is fed by the fiscal revenues of the state, its share of the salary tax, participation of the state in federal revenues, and different federal transfers to education.

Primary state schools are financed by each of these sources but salaries may be financed only from fiscal state revenues. Local governments receive primary education revenues from local taxes, block grants, and direct and indirect competitive project grants from the federal government. Municipalities are required to spend 25 percent of federal block grants on education; spending less than 25 percent disqualifies them for some additional support. In addition, the law requires municipalities like states, to spend 25 percent of tax revenues and transfers on education. Most federal project grants are given indirectly to the municipalities via the state secretariats of education. In addition, collectively, municipalities directly receive 25 percent of the federal share of education salary tax revenue; these funds are not passed through the state secretariats. In addition to cash transfers, both state and municipal governments receive in-kind transfers of textbooks and school lunches from the federal government for primary level students.

Mexico. In each state a federal and state primary and secondary network coexist in addition to private institutions. Each level of government finances its own network. Transfers from the federation to the states allow them to balance their budgets; transfers may also be used to finance state education expenditures. The rapid increase in federal revenues and the priority that the federation gives to education has resulted in the federal network developing much more quickly than the others. It receives, at present, approximately 80 percent of enrollments.

CONDITIONS OF ADMISSION AND EDUCATION OF PUPILS

Different norms and regulations governing internal and often pedagogical matters have important consequence for education resource allocation. Among the most important (or significant) factors are:

1. The minimum number of pupils that an institution may have;
2. The pedagogic grouping of primary school pupils in schools located in areas of low density of population, including decisions regarding multigrade classes, one-teacher schools, and so forth;
3. The organization of teachers' work in primary education including single or multiple shifts, departmentalized grouping, and the salary scales of teachers responsible for two shifts as compared to those who only take care of one shift;
4. The number of teaching hours per week to be carried out by secondary teachers and any regulations concerning overtime; and
5. Decisions regarding class size (average, minimum, and maximum number of pupils per class), curriculum, teaching methods (distribution of pupils in a class in groups for practical work in laboratory or workshop), conditions of recruitment and remuneration of faculty and staff (full-time, part-time, per hour salary scales and differentials of salaries linked to qualifications and seniority, modality of remuneration of overtime, and so forth), and regulations governing the use of monetary resources held by

the directors of institutions (such as budgetary credits, resources from school fees, and revenue from boarding).

The relationship between current unit expenditures in an institution and some of the parameters mentioned above may be easily shown by simple equations:

If *TUE*   = total current unit expenditures
    UETS   = total current unit expenditures for teaching staff
    UENTS = total current unit expenditures for nonteaching staff
    UENS   = total current unit expenditures on nonsalary inputs

$$TUE = UETS + UENTS + UNENS$$

$$UETS = \frac{\text{Teachers salaries}}{\text{Enrollments}} \text{ may be changed to obtain}$$

the following formula:

$$UETS = ATS \times \frac{PCL}{ATL} \times \frac{1}{PUCL}$$

where

    ATS   = average teachers' salary
    PCL   = weekly average number of periods per class
    ATL   = weekly average teaching load (per teacher)
    PUCL = average number of pupils per class

This formula holds for each institution as well as for any group of institutions (at district, regional, state, or countrywide level). The parameters included in it may be determined by regulations or may result from practice. Their values within a particular institution depend on decisions made by the level of control and the head of the institution. They may vary according to institution as a function of the results of the process of allocation of resources and the level of discretion enjoyed by the head of the institution regarding the organization of teaching in the school.

For example, if the director of an institution does not have the number of teachers considered necessary for enrollment, adjustments may be made in the average teaching load and number of pupils per class. Fewer periods per week for some subjects may be offered, a response that directly affects the average number of periods per class.

Moreover, the average values of each parameter—at the institutional level—may hide internal variations due to diversity of cycles, as well as other factors. For example, individual class sizes may vary widely around an average class size figure.

It is possible to expand the above analysis to take into account the diversity of teachers' status (for example, full-time, part-time and hourly) and the structure of salary scales, including the effects of qualifications and seniority. For the purpose here, it is useful to express average teacher salary as a function of base salary in addition to indicators representing average qualifications and seniority.

The formula given above is only one example of an expression of unit expenditures on teaching staff as a function of significant indicators. It should in fact be adjusted in each country to reflect characteristics of the organization of teaching, curriculum, status, and conditions of remuneration of teachers. It may be used to make comparisons between geographical areas or over time.

ANALYSIS OF THE CONSEQUENCES OF RESOURCE ALLOCATION

The studies undertaken within the framework of the institute's research involved calculation of total and unit current expenditures, by type, by purpose (education, administration, and boarding), and by source of financing. Therefore, the ultimate results of the processes of allocation and mobilization of resources are available. What conclusions may be drawn about the processes themselves?

If resources are distributed to institutions offering the same level and type of education in an equitable way and in conformity with set criteria, then (1) total expenditure will be well explained by a small number of indicators expressing the needs of the institution (essentially its size), and (2) variation in *unit* expenditure for institutions of the same size will be limited.

However, important disparities may exist in the distribution of resources to institutions of the same size for the following reasons:

1. The intervention of various actors in the public resource allocation process may favor certain regions and types of institutions;

2. Local administration may have limited and unreliable information about the needs of institutions or may not be able to dis-

tribute resources as a function of needs identified (such as difficulty of access to schools and refusal of teachers to work in backward areas);

3. Institutions may be able to directly mobilize resources whose amounts vary widely according to location and level of income of pupils' parents;

4. The price of certain inputs (particularly those of teachers) may vary significantly according to their status, qualification, and seniority.

The location of the institution (region, district or area, urban/rural) may therefore be taken as an explanatory variable, if territorial disparities exist in the allocation of resources or if the contributions of parents vary according to the schools' situation.

Regression analyses were carried out wherein the dependent variable was either total expenditure or unit expenditure and the independent variables included size, various transformations of size,[6] and dummy variables capturing the location of the establishment. The independent variables were introduced successively. Because size can be a function of location, the introduction of location after size reveals the impact of location after taking into account the effect of size. In countries where parents make contributions to institutions, separate regression models were estimated for public and private resources. Finally, attention was paid to expenditures on the boarding school sector in countries where these data are available.

Analysis of Total Expenditure

The Role of Size. The results reported in Table 4–2 lead to the following conclusions: First, the number of class sections explains variation in total expenditures at least as well as the total number of pupils. It therefore appears that the allocation of resources, and in particular those for teachers, is more a function of the number of classes than the number of students. Often in developing countries, resources allocated to an institution are insufficient to meet the needs expressed by the director. The number of sections is then typically reduced, increasing the number of pupils per class. It is worth noting that in all cases where size offers little explanation for variation in total expenditure, enrollment constitutes a better explanatory variable than the number of classes.

Table 4-2. Proportion of Variance in Total Expenditures Explained by Size (enrollments and number of sections or classes).

	ETS		ENTS		ENS		ET	
	Enroll	Sections or Classes	Enroll	Sections or Classes	Enroll	Sections or Classes	Enroll	Sections or Classes
Primary Education								
Congo	0.819	0.929	0.569	0.700	0.387	0.348	0.828	0.933
Sudan	0.577	0.528	0.225	0.278	0.019	0.009	0.182	0.142
Nepal	0.703	—	0.441	—	0.171	—	0.673	—
Venezuela (1976–77)	0.911	0.935	0.752	0.753	0.039	0.061	0.906	0.927
Venezuela (1978–79)	0.937	0.952	0.831	0.834	0.105	0.098	0.917	0.929
Secondary Education								
Algeria	0.876	0.882	0.621	0.615	0.578	0.583	0.782	0.780
Colombia	0.789	—	0.342	—	0.478	—	0.784	—
Congo	0.860	0.938	0.629	0.694	0.282	0.362	0.832	0.906
Indonesia (1st cycle public)	0.550	0.517	0.039	0.051	0.033	0.040	0.258	0.156
Indonesia (1st cycle private)	0.273	0.195	0.217	0.243	0.014	0.017	0.151	0.159
Indonesia (2nd cycle public)	0.373	0.290	0.125	0.055	0.073	0.041	0.185	0.115
Indonesia (2nd cycle private)	0.345	0.280	0.139	0.127	0.135	0.146	0.305	0.298
Morocco	0.957	0.971	0.735	0.718	0.089	0.151	0.955	0.968
Nepal	0.157	—	0.195	—	0.895	—	0.579	—
Sudan (intermed)	0.761	0.704	0.441	0.409	0.190	0.166	0.739	0.683
Sudan (second)	0.691	0.730	0.328	0.351	0.710	0.746	0.839	0.888
Venezuela (1976–77)	0.818	0.909	0.602	0.703	0.084	0.446	0.769	0.894
Venezuela (1978–79)	0.851	0.895	0.708	0.698	0.141	0.166	0.839	0.876

ETS = Total expenditure on teaching staff   FNS = Total expenditures on nonsalary current inputs

Second, in a majority of countries, from 75 percent to more than 95 percent of the variation in total expenditures is explained by size. These results are similar to those obtained in other studies.[7] The explanatory power is lower for institutions in Nepal and quite low (less than 30 percent) in Indonesia and the primary schools of Sudan. In these two countries, total expenditure appears to vary widely in institutions offering the same education, belonging to the same network, and operating at the same size.

All countries with exclusively public financing are among those where size explains at least 75 percent of variation in total expenditures. In contrast, only countries with mixed financing can be found in the other group where size is a poor predictor. Secondary schools of Colombia and the Sudan constitute atypical cases. Here, parents' contributions concern only nonsalary expenditures and are low in comparison to total resources.

When possible, public and private resources were analyzed separately as a function of size (see Table 4–3). In each case (except for the secondary schools of Nepal), private resources are less well explained by size than public resources. This supports the hypothesis that the mobilization of private resources tends to increase disparities in the provision of educational services. In several cases (primary schools in the Sudan, secondary schools in Nepal, second-cycle secondary schools in Indonesia), variation in the level of public resources

Table 4-3. Proportion of Variance in Public and Private Resources Explained by Size (*enrollments*).

	Public Resources	Private Resources	Total Expenditures
Primary Education			
Nepal	0.695	0.266	0.673
Sudan	0.190	0.022	0.182
Secondary Education			
Colombia	0.820	0.464	0.784
Indonesia (1st cycle public)	0.630	0.096	0.258
Indonesia (2nd cycle public)	0.435	0.139	0.185
Nepal	0.257	0.631	0.432
Sudan (intermediate)	0.715	0.130	0.739
Sudan (secondary)	0.904	0.311	0.839

is only poorly explained by size. This raises questions about the role played by public administration in these countries and the criteria used for distribution.

Third, the data show that the explanatory power of size variables varies widely even among countries with public financing. Comparison of Algeria and Morocco, two neighboring countries whose administrative structures and financing mechanisms are the same, is significant in the context. Central administrative control of resource allocation processes appears to be stricter in Morocco, probably because financial constraints are stronger and have existed for many years.

Fourth, generally the explanatory power of the size variable is higher for expenditures on teachers than for nonteaching staff. It is also higher for nonteaching staff relative to nonsalary expenditures. The only exceptions are secondary institutions in Nepal and Sudan. In many countries, total nonsalary expenditures are practically not explained at all by size. This reveals an instance of wide disparities in expenditure levels among comparable institutions.

The Role of Location. Table 4–4 indicates the gain in explained variation of total expenditures associated with the addition of location variables to a regression model already containing size variables. According to these results, once the effects of size have been taken into account, location does not improve the explanation of total expenditures except in a small number of cases (second-cycle secondary public and private schools in Indonesia, secondary schools in the Sudan, and general colleges of education in the Congo). The effect of location is somewhat more marked with certain indicators (urban/rural environment, size of conglomeration) that probably correspond to more precise socioeconomic differences than others (region, for example). The same analysis was carried out for each component of total expenditure, and revealed that location is more important for both nonteaching staff expenditures and nonsalary expenditures.

In order to discriminate among hypotheses explaining the role of location, its effects on public and private revenue levels were analyzed separately in countries with mixed financing (see Table 4–5). Explanations are different according to country. For example, in second-cycle secondary schools in the public sectors of Indonesia, the role of location is linked to the mobilization of private resources as well as to variation in the proportion of part-time teachers em-

Table 4-4. Gain in Variance of Total Expenditures Explained Following the Addition of Location Variables (*percentage*).

	Region/Province	*Environment*
Primary Education		
Congo	—	—
Nepal	0.8%	—
Sudan	—	0.9%
Venezuela		
1976–77	—	—
1978–79	—	—
Secondary Education		
Algeria	1.3	—
Colombia	—	—
Congo	0.7	1.9
Indonesia		
(1st cycle public)	—	—
(1st cycle private)	1.3	—
(2nd cycle public)	8.1	—
(2nd cycle private)	4.9	—
Morocco	—	—
Nepal	37.7	—
Sudan		
(Intermediate)	—	—
(Secondary)	2.0	2.5
Venezuela		
1976–77	—	—
1978–79	—	—

— = Not applicable.
Environment = Urban versus rural except for Morocco, where environment relates to the size of the conglomeration (small versus large).

ployed within a province.[8] In the Sudan, it is both the allocation of public resources and the mobilization of private resources that depend on location for secondary schools.

Analysis of Total Boarding Expenditures. The following three types of explanatory variables were adopted and introduced in order into a regression model designed to reveal determinants of expenditures in

Table 4-5. Gain in Variance of Total Public and Private Resources Explained Following Addition of Location Variables (*percentage*).

	Public Resources	Private Resources	Total Expenditures
Primary Education			
Nepal	—	6.2%	0.8%
Sudan	0.8%	—	0.9
Secondary Education			
Colombia	—	1.3	—
Indonesia			
1st cycle public	0.7	0.7	—
2nd cycle public	—	10.8	8.1
Nepal	58.9	14.4	37.7
Sudan			
Intermediate	—	—	—
Secondary	4.0	2.4	2.5

boarding institutions: the number of boarding students, the region, or environment, and the number of class sections. Table 4-6 reports these results. With the exception of Algeria,[9] variation in total expenditure was explained to a large extent by the number of boarding students. Depending on the country, the explanation is better for salary expenditures (Morocco, Sudan, primary and secondary schools), or for nonsalary expenditure (Algeria, Tunisia, Sudan, intermediate schools).

The introduction of the number of class sections improves the explanation for salary expenditures in all countries, except Morocco and the Sudan (primary schools only). It therefore seems that large-size institutions benefit by more administrative personnel than the smallest and that a part of this "supplementary" staff serves the boarding school because the effect of the number of class sections remains significant even after taking account of the effect of the number of boarders.

Analysis of Unit Expenditures

The Magnitude of Variation in Unit Expenditures. Before analyzing the role of size in explaining unit expenditure variation, it is interesting to show the magnitude of variation in both unit expenditures and a series of indicators measuring how resources are utilized within schooling institutions (see Table 4–7). Several results are particularly striking. First, the coefficients of variation of total unit expenditure (and of its components) differ greatly according to country. At one extreme is Morocco where unit expenditures, especially those for teaching staff, vary minimally and where disparities in resources among institutions are therefore quite small. At the other extreme is Indonesia where the coefficients of variation of unit expenditures and indicators are very high, indicating the diversity of local situations in this country. Contributing factors include variation in the density of population, difficulty of access to school, level of income of parents, and levels of school fees. The results in Indonesia may also be explained by the presence of more limited control by central administration on the public resource allocation process.

Second, coefficients of variation of the utilization indicators also differ very much according to country and reveal sometimes large disparities in teaching conditions (as measured by the average number of pupils per class, the average length of classes, and the average number of teaching hours per teacher) among otherwise similar schooling institutions within nations.

Third, in general, the coefficients of variation for unit expenditures on teaching staff are smaller than those for unit expenditures on nonteaching staff. In turn, the coefficients for unit expenditures on nonteaching staff are smaller than those of expenditures for nonsalary inputs.

Size and Expenditure. Attention turns now to the relationship between size and unit expenditures. These analyses are reported in Table 4–8 and lead to the following conclusions.

First, in a majority of countries, less than one-third of the variation in total unit expenditure (and often less than 10 percent) is explained by size. Only three exceptions can be found in the table (institutions in Nepal, secondary schools in the Congo, and secondary schools in the Sudan). One may then say that in certain countries

Table 4-6. Proportion of Variance in Total Expenditures Explained by the Size and Location of Boarding Institutions.

	Salary Expenditures				Nonsalary Expenditures			
	1 *No. of* *Boarders*	*2* *No. of* *Boarders* *and* *Region*	*3* *No. of* *Boarders* *and* *Environment*	*4* *No. of* *Boarders* *and* *No. of* *Class* *Sections*	*1* *No. of* *Boarders*	*2* *No. of* *Boarders* *and* *Region*	*3* *No. of* *Boarders* *and* *Environment*	*4* *No. of* *Boarders* *and* *No. of* *Class* *Sections*
Algeria	0.831	0.833	0.840	0.860	0.894	0.899	0.900	0.895
Morocco	0.914	0.914	0.914	0.915	0.729	0.745	0.729	0.731
Sudan								
Primary	0.809	0.809	0.809	0.809	0.721	0.721	0.724	0.723
Intermediate	0.679	0.679	0.724	0.735	0.744	0.744	0.745	0.744
Secondary	0.798	0.799	0.811	0.828	0.696	0.712	0.709	0.699
Tunisia	0.733	0.756	—	0.795	0.903	0.904	—	0.903

Total Expenditures

	1 *No. of Boarders*	2 *No. of Boarders and Region*	3 *No. of Boarders and Environment*	4 *No. of Boarders and No. of Class Sections*
Algeria	0.679	0.679	0.686	0.682
Morocco	0.860	0.866	0.861	0.862
Sudan				
Primary	0.782	0.782	0.784	0.783
Intermediate	0.783	0.783	0.786	0.784
Secondary	0.796	0.806	0.802	0.803
Tunisia	0.883	0.891	—	0.902

No. of Boarders = Number of boarding students.
Environment = Urban versus rural except for Morocco, where environment relates to the size of the conglomeration (small versus large).

Table 4-7. Unit Expenditures and Teacher Utilization Indicators: Coefficients of Variation in a Sample of Countries (*nonprimary education only*).

	Colombia		Indonesia		Morocco	Sudan	
	1st Cycle General	2nd Cycle Comprehensive	1st Cycle Public	2nd Cycle Public		Intermediate	Secondary
Unit Expenditures							
Total current unit expenditures for teaching staff	0.36	0.40	0.45	0.52	0.10	0.28	0.25
Total current unit for nonteaching staff	1.72	0.51	1.40	1.00	0.34	0.49	0.47
Total current unit expenditures on non-salary items	0.83	0.70	2.10	1.97	0.81	0.85	0.30
Total current unit	0.51	0.35	0.72	0.69	0.09	0.30	0.21
Teacher Utilization Indicators							
Average number of pupils per class	0.29	0.19	0.37	0.27	0.07	0.15	0.12
Weekly average number of periods per class	0.21	0.30	—	—	0.03	0.12	0.15
Weekly average teaching load	0.14	0.25	0.54	0.68	0.05	0.17	0.20
Average teacher's salary	0.22	0.19	0.42	0.32	0.06	0.28	0.28

	Teaching Staff		Nonteaching Staff		Nonsalary Expenditure		Total Expenditure	
	T	U	T	U	T	U	T	U
Primary Education								
Congo	0.819	0.089	0.569	0.794	0.387	0.015	0.828	0.325
Nepal	0.703	0.939	0.441	0.301	0.171	0.138	0.673	0.912
Sudan	0.577	0.077	0.225	0.178	0.019	0.045	0.182	0.063
Venezuela (1976–77)	0.911	0.126	0.752	0.179	0.039	0.045	0.906	0.081
Venezuela (1978–79)	0.937	0.058	0.831	0.143	0.105	0.036	0.917	0.043
Secondary Education								
Algeria	0.876	0.087	0.621	0.207	0.578	0.213	0.782	0.087
Colombia	0.789	0.063	0.342	0.071	0.478	0.045	0.784	0.096
Congo	0.860	0.604	0.629	0.392	0.282	0.819	0.832	0.603
Indonesia								
(1st cycle public)	0.550	0.077	0.039	0.255	0.033	0.211	0.258	0.297
(2nd cycle public)	0.373	0.070	0.125	0.119	0.073	0.245	0.185	0.293
(1st cycle private)	0.273	0.029	0.217	0.141	0.014	0.008	0.151	0.045
(2nd cycle private)	0.345	0.051	0.139	0.175	0.135	0.135	0.305	0.070
Morocco	0.957	0.048	0.735	0.801	0.089	0.190	0.955	0.338
Nepal	0.157	0.843	0.195	0.932	0.895	0.810	0.579	0.889
Sudan								
Intermediate	0.761	0.190	0.441	0.045	0.190	0.098	0.739	0.242
Secondary	0.691	0.291	0.328	0.515	0.710	0.295	0.839	0.524
Venezuela (1976–77)	0.818	0.089	0.702	0.228	0.084	0.063	0.769	0.113
Venezuela (1978–79)	0.851	0.116	0.708	0.123	0.141	0.058	0.839	0.049

T = total expenditure.   U = unit expenditure.

(Algeria, Indonesia private first- and second-cycle secondary schools, primary schools in the Sudan, and primary and secondary schools in Venezuela) total unit expenditures do not vary significantly as a function of the size of the institution. In other cases (primary schools in the Congo, first- and second-cycle public institutions in Indonesia, first-cycle secondary schools in Morocco, and intermediate schools in the Sudan), the relationship is more significant but size does not constitute an important explanatory factor. In other words, for any given size, total unit expenditures vary widely.

Second, unit expenditures for teaching staff (and nonsalary unit expenditures) are less well explained in general than total unit expenditures. Moreover, the relationship between nonteaching staff unit expenditure and size is, as a general rule, stronger than the relationship between total unit expenditure and size.

The Direction of Relationships between Unit Expenditure and Size. In general, unit expenditures tend to diminish as the size of an institution increases. However, as indicated above, this trend is not always strong. Although determinants of this evolution differ according to country, the following general tendencies are revealed by the available data.

First, an increase in the number of pupils per class is the strongest and most general factor in decreasing unit expenditure on teaching staff. Second, with the exception of Indonesia, the use of teaching staff does not vary much above a certain minimum size. (This minimum size appears to be in the neighborhood of a low enrollment of 200 to 300 pupils per school.)

In fact, the use of teachers[10] depends on a large number of factors that are not necessarily linked to the size of the schooling institution. These include the global relationship between supply and demand for teachers; guarantees of employment and the inertia of the teaching stock in periods of diminishing enrollments; preferences of teachers for work in towns and urban areas; possible constraints on the transfer of teachers employed in an institution when there is a surplus of staff; and finally, decisions made by the head of the institution regarding the internal deployment of staff.

The following examples of these influences on the utilization of teachers are quite instructive in this context. Consider Mexico where all teachers graduating from public and even private colleges have been offered until very recently a teaching post regardless of the actual real need for new teachers. In Togo, school enrollments in the

Table 4-9. Gain in Variance of Unit Expenditure Explained Following the Addition of Location Variables (*percentage*).

	Region/Province	Environment
Primary Education		
Congo	1.9%	0.6%
Nepal	—	—
Sudan	—	1.8
Venezuela		
(1976-77)	16.5[a]	7.7
(1978-79)	13.8[a]	0.9
Secondary Education		
Algeria	0.9	4.3[b]
Colombia	2.5	—
Congo	1.4	—
Indonesia		
1st cycle public	0.6	—
1st cycle private	3.2	—
2nd cycle public	3.9	—
2nd cycle private	5.8	—
Morocco	2.2	6.5[c]
Nepal	9.9	—
Sudan		
Intermediate	1.2	0.6
Secondary	4.0	6.4
Venezuela		
1976-77	—	—
1978-79	—	—

— = Not applicable.

a. Type of school (*planteles graduados; unitarios; concentrados*). A characteristic strongly associated with the location of primary schools.

b. Two geographical distributions east/center/west, north/center/south.

c. Size of the conglomeration.

first and second cycles of secondary education have diminished by one-third since 1981–82 while the number of teachers employed has remained constant. More generally, there are countries where teachers cannot be posted elsewhere if they are not in agreement. Moreover, there are countries where central administration has more power in theory than it is able or willing to exercise.

On average, the use of teaching staff is not very satisfactory in many countries. Although in North Africa their rate of use is between 90 and 95 percent according to country, it is much lower elsewhere and falls to 70 percent in Indonesia; moreover, as a general rule, unit expenditure on nonteaching staff diminishes as a function of size. The number of nonteaching staff does not increase proportionally with the number of pupils.

Role of Location. After taking account of the effects of size, it appears that location of an institution plays a limited but significant role explaining variation in unit expenditures. The results reported in Table 4–9 are analogous to those reported earlier in Table 4–4.

Unit Expenditures for Boarding. Regression analyses of unit expenditures for boarding institutions were carried out only as a function of the number of boarding students (see Table 4–10). The portion of variance in boarding institution unit expenditures explained

Table 4-10. Proportion of Variance in Total Expenditure and Unit Expenditure of Boarding Institutions Explained by the Number of Boarding Students.

	Salary Expenditure		Nonsalary Expenditure		Total Expenditure	
	T	*U*	*T*	*U*	*T*	*U*
Algeria	0.831	0.474	0.894	0.717	0.679	0.277
Morocco	0.914	0.520	0.729	0.392	0.860	0.511
Sudan[a]	0.809	0.787	0.721	0.787	0.782	0.817
Sudan[b]	0.679	0.605	0.744	0.801	0.783	0.844
Sudan[c]	0.798	0.495	0.696	0.771	0.796	0.829
Tunisia	0.733	0.260	0.903	0.630	0.883	0.693

a = primary; b = intermediate; c = secondary.
T = total expenditure; U = unit expenditure.

by the number of boarders is in general quite high. With the exception of Algeria, one may see a definite and sometimes very close link between unit expenditures for boarding institutions and the number of boarders. The relationships shown are much more significant than those concerning unit expenditure in nonboarding settings.

CONCLUSIONS

The diversity of financing mechanisms for primary and secondary education and of internal resource allocation processes is one of the most striking findings of this comparative analysis. The research carried out by the Institute has been able to highlight several consequences for current unit expenditures and, more generally, has demonstrated disparities in resource levels among institutions within nations as well as in the internal utilization of these resources. The results support the general thesis that even in nations with what appear at first glance to have highly centralized educational governance structures, considerable variation can exist at the local level in the distribution and utilization of financial resources.

The following conclusions can be drawn. First, for any given size, disparities in resources among institutions are in general more marked in countries where several sources of finance coexist. This variation is most clear in countries where parents contribute revenues directly to the educational system in the form of fees. In contrast, where financing is entirely the responsibility of the central government, less internal variation is present.

Second, these disparities in resource levels are the most acute for nonsalary expenditures, less for nonteaching staff, and finally least for expenditures on teaching staff. Third, in different countries there are significant geographical disparities in public resource allocation that are not only the result of variation in salaries or qualifications of teachers according to the location of the institution. In countries with mixed financing, disparities in the supply of private resources are generally more marked than those of public resources.

Fourth, unit expenditures vary to a surprisingly limited extent as a function of size. In most countries, less than 30 percent and sometimes even less than 10 percent of the variance of unit expenditures can be explained by size. Fifth, to the limited extent that there is a relationship between unit expenditures and size, unit expenditures tend to diminish as a function of size mainly because the large institutions are also those where the number of pupils per class is higher. Use of teachers, while not very satisfactory in small institutions, tends to improve up to the point where a minimum size is reached (of the order of 200 to 300 pupils for secondary institutions). Above this number, larger numbers of pupils have little effect on teacher utilization.

Finally, numerous factors not linked to size influence the average use of teachers. These factors include but are not limited to the relationship between supply and demand for teachers both globally and by subject, constraints in the posting and transferring of staff, and decisions made by the director of the institution.

At a time when the level of resources devoted to education is stagnating or even diminishing in real terms in many developing countries, the research results discussed in this chapter will provide useful baseline information for administrators at a variety of decision-making levels within educational systems.

NOTES

1. Algeria, Brazil, Colombia, Congo, Indonesia, Morocco, Nepal, Philippines, Sudan, Thailand, Tunisia, and Venezuela.
2. A network is a set of institutions as determined by the source of control and mechanisms of financing. For example, the term *private network* will be used to designate all private institutions having the same financing mechanisms, even though there may be varying sources of control.
3. Kenya and Mexico were not covered by the research, but their financing mechanisms have been presented to show the diversity more clearly.
4. A more detailed analysis should also take into account the nature and characteristics of the intergovernmental fiscal mechanisms for education, if relevant, and mechanisms for the distribution of public resources between networks, when several networks receive resources from the same level of government.
5. That is, 2.5 percent of total salaries paid in the private sector.
6. Depending on the dependent variable these included size squared, size cubed, and the inverse of size.
7. See, for example, Hough (1981).
8. The cost per teaching hour of part-time teachers is half that of full-time teachers. The use of part-time teachers varies widely among provinces.

9. Data on salary expenditures for boarding were missing for a certain number of institutions.
10. The rate of use of a teacher is defined as the actual number of teaching hours per week divided by the number of teaching hours required by regulations.

REFERENCES

Hough, J. R. 1981. "A Study of School Costs." Windsor, United Kingdom: NFER, Nelson Publishing Co.

5 INCENTIVES, OUTCOME-BASED INSTRUCTION, AND SCHOOL EFFICIENCY

Stephen A. Hoenack

Changes in incentives for students and teachers are necessary if the nation's schools are to increase their productivity. This chapter proposes criteria for a model system of incentives and suggests how a system that combines incentives with outcome-based instruction can meet these criteria. Incentives are the rewards and penalties that attach to uses of resources and are present whether or not they are intentionally established. Incentives can favorably or unfavorably affect what students are taught, how well they learn, how efficiently students' time and school resources are utilized, and whether the education sector of the economy will experience productivity growth. They can be altered to improve all of these outcomes and can increase the likelihood that proposed innovations in schools will be adopted and succeed. Consequently, incentives represent more than simple rewards for individual teachers who accomplish parts of the important educational outcomes under their control. A good system of incentives also can affect other important educational outcomes,

My first experience with outcome-based instruction occurred in North Yemen while serving on a USAID project design team. Many of the ideas in this chapter were developed as a result of lengthy discussions with my co-team members Mona Habib, Wade Robinson, and Andrea Rugh and with the USAID resident education specialist, Karl Schwartz. The chapter also benefited from discussions with Suzanne and William Becker. Melissa Anderson and David H. Monk made many excellent comments on earlier drafts. Colleen T. Davidson did much of the bibliographic research for the project, and Darrell R. Lewis spent a great deal of time sharing insights that helped me correct numerous weaknesses in the argument. Only I am responsible for the chapter's remaining deficiencies.

the choices of methods used to achieve them including the appropriate degree of cooperation among teachers, and they can motivate students as well as teachers.

An appropriately established incentive system can additionally assist a community in deciding the desirable relative emphasis to place on different possible outcomes of the educational process, and it can encourage resource usage within schools so as to enhance efficiency. The term *efficiency* refers to the level of desired learning outcomes that are accomplished with the resources available to schools. Incentives can encourage teachers to learn about new instructional methods and to experiment on their own to raise efficiency. I shall refer to an incentive system that accomplishes all of the ends mentioned above as one that is successful or that improves school efficiency.

The kind of incentives that can reliably increase school efficiency requires costly information, and these costs may not always be justified by the resulting benefits. Incentives should be uniquely designed and thoughtfully applied to the particular situation so that they direct the activities of teachers and students toward educational accomplishments that are important to the community. Desirable incentives must also be based on appropriate evaluation procedures. Simplistic approaches to applying monetary incentives, such as recent "merit pay" proposals for teachers,[1] are unlikely to be successful.

The traditional ways in which incentives are placed on teachers and students are also unsatisfactory.[2] Schools are complex enterprises whose specific activities cannot be economically influenced directly by administrators or outsiders in ways that improve efficiency. It is costly for administrators, politicians, and the public to learn about the most educationally significant activities of students and teachers and to ensure that they are carried out. Influences directed at teachers' activities therefore do not always reliably reward or penalize the most important characteristics of their performance, many of which are intangible and difficult to evaluate. Instead, they tend to relate to the most observable aspects of work, such as being in the classroom during required hours, handling or avoiding discipline problems, attending meetings, and avoiding negative remarks from parents and other teachers. These attributes of performance correlate imperfectly with teachers' efficiency in helping students learn.

Teachers need a considerable amount of discretion over their activities in order to use available resources to maximize their pupils' achievement. The pace of the learning process is not precisely predictable, and it is not always possible to anticipate the right examples and emphases to introduce at particular times. Heavy-handed administrative controls such as requirements to spend time in particular ways and to cover subjects in exact sequences diminish teachers' capability to use their own judgment to take advantage of opportunities created by students' interests and the directions that discussions take. (For more on these points, see Chapter 2.) Another unproductive diminution of teachers' discretion occurs when teachers are so occupied with discipline problems that there is relatively little time to devote to learning of any kind.

The degree to which teacher discretion contributes to the most valued learning outcomes depends on the ways in which it is used. It will be more or less automatically employed to bring about desired achievement when teachers are capable and motivated and when their objectives for students' learning tend to coincide with those of parents and the broader community. However, that this is often not the case is reflected in numerous highly publicized criticisms of schools by professional educators, government commissions, parents, and the general public. Teachers lacking the desirable characteristics mentioned above are not necessarily required to develop them, nor are they always encouraged to leave the profession.

This is the context in which incentives are a potentially useful policy tool.[3] The success of a system of incentives depends on the way it is designed and implemented (as is discussed in the next section). Because it can be costly to introduce an effective system of incentives, it is not a generally applicable policy tool in all organizational settings. However, a recent well-known innovation in schools, outcome-based instructional systems, can provide as part of the educational process much of the costly information needed for an incentive system that increases efficiency in these institutions. Consequently, it may well be that a successful system of school incentives can be introduced in conjunction with an outcome-based instructional system. The possibility is explored in this chapter.

Nonetheless, this chapter is not really about outcome-based instruction but about incentives. That is, the merits and demerits of outcome-based instruction are not discussed, although the author confesses to a belief that the former outweigh the latter. The main focus here is on the incentives that outcome-based instruction makes relatively economical to apply.

Outcome-based instructional systems sometimes[4] go by other names, including "mastery learning" and "competency-based instruction," and although there are variants on the basic theme, these innovations have several key elements in common. They include the establishment of detailed definitions of learning milestones or competencies; the determination of learning objectives for each student based on his or her present state of knowledge and understanding; and the regular assessment of the student's learning progress and correction or redirection of learning efforts when appropriate.

The assessment of each student's learning is based on "criterion referenced" testing, which measures his or her accomplishment according to the learning objectives and defined competencies. This is in contrast to "norm referenced" tests that compare different students' relative knowledge of subject matter, and are not necessarily fully representative of the curriculum employed in the school. An outcome-based instructional system thus can contain a considerable amount of information about the educational goals being accomplished by the educational system and about the ongoing success of teachers and students in accomplishing these goals. (The discussion will deal with aspects of learning that are often regarded as difficult to measure.) We shall see that such data on outcomes do not constitute all of the information needed for a successful incentive system. However, valid and comprehensive measures of educational outcomes are the most costly required information, and the discussion will deal with the aspects of learning that are difficult to measure. Weighing against these costs and perhaps generously offsetting them would be the joint contribution of the outcome-based instruction system employed and the incentives. It is possible that the benefits of one of these mutually supporting policies taken alone would not justify its costs, while the two together could constitute an extremely worthwhile investment.

The proponents of outcome-based instructional systems have presented evidence that this innovation can produce dramatic increases in students' learning (Bloom 1984; Jones and Spady 1985).[5] Future research is needed to determine the general conditions under which this innovation produces superior learning gains. However, those who have created outcome-based instruction have given relatively little attention to the incentives for teachers and students that could enhance its success where employed and make its implementation more widespread. Spady (1982: 125–26) has noted the "formidable institutional obstacles" to the required underlying institutional changes including those in teacher attitudes, redefinition of their roles and responsibilities, and "the system of power and incentives governing the conditions of staff service, performance, and influence" (Spady 1982: 126–27).

There is so far relatively little successful experience with outcome-based instructional systems in large urban schools where problems of educational productivity are perhaps the most serious. Two institutional problems are noted by Jones and Spady (1985: 32) with implementation in such schools, one of which has been the relative neglect of low achieving students. The other problem was the failure to cope adequately with the managerial issues raised by diverse groups of students having different rates of learning. Incentives hold the promise of being able to direct teachers' attention and creative efforts to the particular needs of slower learning students, and they can encourage the types of coordination necessary to provide specialized instruction at a variety of levels. For example, premium rewards can be given for raising the learning of the slowest students while still raising the learning of others, and incentives can be shared by groups of teachers so that they are rewarded for coordinating their activities. The absence of appropriate incentives may help explain why a promising innovation like outcome-based instructional systems is not more widely used.

There are objectionable ways of implementing an outcome-based instructional system, such as when faster learning students have to wait while slower learning students catch up or when teachers lack sufficient discretion to experiment with alternative means of increasing students' learning progress. The usefulness of incentives created in connection with outcome-based instruction is highly contingent on the nature of this innovation's implementation.

The following section presents an overview of different types of incentives in any organization along with criteria for an incentive system that would improve school efficiency. The next section describes a model incentive system employing an outcome-based instructional system combined with organizational procedures under which teachers are rewarded for increased productivity. The final sections discuss possible problems with the suggested incentive system and describe how it could be initially established.

TWO TYPES OF INCENTIVES AND
ELEMENTS OF AN IDEAL INCENTIVE
SYSTEM FOR SCHOOLS

Teachers have decisionmaking influence over their own time, the time of students, classroom space, a certain amount of supplies and equipment, and sometimes the time of supporting personnel. Valuable educational outputs can be produced with these resources. I have suggested elsewhere (Hoenack 1983) that there are two means by which the productivity of an employee's uses of the resources delegated to him or her can be influenced. One of these, the "specific" method is to impose requirements vis-à-vis the particular activities that are most economical for those imposing accountability to observe. An example is that, as noted in the introduction, it is not difficult to keep track of such observable aspects of work as a teacher's actual time on the job. The disadvantage of this accountability method is that the most readily observed attributes of an employee's performance are often not the most important ones.

The alternative "overall value" method of accountability for productivity is to assess the value of an employee's productive contribution in relation to the value of the resources delegated to him or her. When the employee is rewarded according to the difference between these two values, there are incentives to employ resources efficiently even when the employee's specific uses of resources are not observed. That is, not only will a teacher be led to comply with the easily observed aspects of work such as being in class but, most important, will focus on the more substantive dimensions of performance in order to accomplish the ends being evaluated. A teacher working under overall value incentives could be encouraged to give the appropriate weight to each educational outcome and would also gain from using each resource that contributes to these outcomes in a cost-effective manner.

For example, if an estimated value is placed on each important educational contribution of a teacher (or teacher group), and if each resource employed, including the teacher's and students' time, is also valued, it might be possible to establish rewards for the teacher or group based on the accomplished "value added." This value added is the total estimated value of the teacher's productive contributions minus the total estimated value of resources employed by him or her. The inputs and productive contributions can be explicitly priced, but implicit valuations can also be effective as incentives. For instance, teachers' ongoing discussions with administrators and their experience with previous rewards for their activities can give them a good idea of their relative valuations of different educational outcomes achieved. That is, when school administrators do not explicitly state that a particular dimension of performance, such as specific learning achievements of students with learning disabilities, is worth a certain amount of money or recognition, teachers can observe the rewards given to teachers with different accomplishments and then infer the relative weight or implicit price attached to each. Likewise, the rewards themselves can be in cash or in increased status, official recognition, or other nonmonetary benefits that weigh heavily with teachers.

Similarly, the resources delegated to teachers can be explicitly priced, as when teachers are given budgets to purchase teaching materials or auxiliary equipment, but these resources can also be implicitly priced where teachers infer their values to administrators.

A teacher would gain under the overall value method of accountability from adding emphasis to more valued educational contributions when they are not proportionately more costly to achieve. For example, there would be an incentive to emphasize more rewarded topics or categories of students whose learning is placed at a premium. Similarly, teachers can benefit from finding and experimenting with relatively economical methods of achieving each output. The overall value method of accountability could induce teachers to learn about and try methods such as cooperating with each other to substitute small group help sessions for some lecture periods or to try new teaching materials to see if they are more cost effective. As a result, the overall value method can provide a general incentive for efficiency even when the teacher's activities are not observed and specifically influenced by administrators or others. Overall value incentives lead teachers to learn about the most cost-effective resources not currently available to them and to pressure administrators to allow their use even though the expense of these resources is weighed against the teachers' productivity. Because they reward experimentation aimed at more efficient utilization of educational resources, overall value incentives have the potential to introduce productivity growth into the educational sector of an economy.

Students often are given specific incentives for fulfilling attendance requirements, turning in assignments, and avoiding the most serious discipline problems. For some students these incentives are complemented by overall incentives imparted by parents to use their time wisely to acquire valuable learning and skills. Those students lacking these additional incentives may learn considerably less. The lack of appropriate incentives facing students may help explain the discipline and motivational problems that are so often noted in large urban schools but that occur in other schools as well.

Whichever of the two means by which teachers are held accountable by administrators, parents, or funding agencies, they can have a measure of discretion to use resources according to their own preferences when they do not have overwhelming discipline and student motivation problems, which, of course, can absorb most of any teacher's time. The most capable and internally motivated teachers often use whatever discretion they have to do a much better job than required. Unfortunately, others can use discretion in less desirable ways. If all teachers used whatever discretion is available to them to pursue the learning objectives of students, parents, and the community, there would be little need for improved incentives.

Overall value incentives are preferable to specific incentives, but they can be designed in different ways with varying effects on school efficiency. In fact, if improperly established, even these incentives could have undesirable impacts. Seven criteria for a system of school incentives are presented below, followed by an explanation of their significance.

Seven Criteria for a System of School Incentives

1. Incentives should give shared responsibility for educational outcomes to groups of teachers when their productivity is enhanced by joint decisionmaking and coordinated actions.

2. Teachers should be rewarded for all educational contributions that they make and that are desired by students, parents, and the broader community.

3. The motivation of students, as well as that of teachers, should be addressed in a system of school incentives.

4. Teachers should personally benefit from the residual gain when there is an increase in the value of educational outcomes over the value of resources used to accomplish these outcomes.

5. It is necessary for teachers to be confident that an incentive system's procedures and rewards will remain in place over a long period of time.

6. Incentives should encourage and foster innovation.

7. The gains from the incentive system should represent a justifiable return on the costs of implementing it.

The first criterion of shared responsibility requires overall value incentives to be placed on groups of teachers rather than solely on individuals because cooperation can facilitate teachers' experimenting with shared instructional roles, taking advantage of possible specializations, and mutual decisionmaking.[6] For example, all of a school's teachers on a particular topic may find that many students' learning is much improved with small group tutorial sessions for students grouped by level of accomplishment where each teacher specializes in a particular level. Teachers would thus share students, switching them among the tutorial groups as their accomplishment changes or specialized needs arise. Strictly individualized incentives could discourage such cooperation.

The significance of the second criterion that all important educational contributions be rewarded can readily be seen. If some are not, they will tend to be underemphasized by teachers. For example, one of the criticisms of "merit pay" proposals is that the achievement tests on which merit pay is sometimes based may not encompass all of the important attributes of student learning and development. One reason that school principals are often regarded as crucial for effective schools is that they are in a position to give recognition to and otherwise reward unmeasured but significant educational contributions. Of course, not all administrators will use their discretion to carry out this role unless they have incentives to do so.

Students' motivation, the object of the third criterion, is often overlooked in discussions of incentives. This is in spite of evidence that the pupil's family background, which is a key determinant of motivation, is a significant influence on his or her learning success.[7] The ultimate labor market rewards from learning difficult subjects can have small motivational effects, especially for students whose parents have not themselves gained these benefits from education. When students come from families that do not encourage learning and have not had successful educational experiences, introducing appropriate learning incentives is a higher priority than it is when students have received these benefits. Immediate rewards may help offset the differences in learning between these students and those from advantaged backgrounds.

The fourth criterion that teachers should gain from increases in the benefits over costs from their activities is the key characteristic of overall value incentives. Aside from the rewards for benefits, this incentive, by giving teachers responsibility for the resources they use, makes them sensitive to costs. However, when resources used by teachers are not readily available to teachers at their cost to the school they will tend to be underutilized. For example, visual aids, recording equipment, computers, and software cannot be employed in the appropriate uses unless they are readily purchasable.

Aside from avoiding the need to influence the details of teachers' performance, overall value incentives encourage experimentation with improved techniques. Such experimentation is requisite to increases in instructional productivity. Because these activities are time consuming and costly, criterion five states that teachers need assurance that the gains from successful changes will occur over a long enough time to justify the investment.

The sixth criterion that incentives should encourage and foster innovation partially overlaps with the fourth and fifth criteria. However, there is the additional requirement that information about successful changes in instructional techniques should flow readily among teachers within and between schools. It is desirable for the widespread adoption of these techniques not only that information be disseminated but that the focus of attention be on the methods employed as well as on the personal qualities of the teachers involved.

The significance of the seventh criterion of cost efficiency is obvious. If an incentive system is so expensive to implement in relation to its benefits that it represents a poor investment, the system should not be put in place.

A MODEL INCENTIVE SYSTEM THAT INCLUDES ELEMENTS OF AN OUTCOME-BASED INSTRUCTIONAL SYSTEM

The model incentive system described here makes use of an outcome-based instructional system's specificity of learning objectives and its regular assessment of students' progress to measure the instructional performance of teacher groups within primary or secondary schools. In this incentive system teacher groups gain both from raising their students' instructional achievement and from reducing costs. All of a school's instructors are placed in groups according to subject matter of the curriculum (such as English or mathematics).[8]

To some extent, the model incentive system brings the concept of "school site budgeting" down to a more disaggregated level within the school. Under a school site budget, a school receives unrestricted revenues and is required to provide information about the costs of its students' achieving milestones that could include specified learning objectives. Accountability comes through the information on achievement and costs that can be used to pressure schools to be more cost effective. (See Garms, Guthrie, and Pierce 1978: 282–84.) However, a significant difference other than disaggregation between school site budgeting and the model incentive system is that in the latter teacher groups are explicitly funded on the basis of students' achievement. Also, in the model system the budgetary carryovers can be used to supplement teachers' incomes, a degree of flexibility in expenditures that may not be envisaged in all school site budgeting proposals.

Each group's budget for any given time period varies with the number of students who achieve particular competencies in the group's subject. With this budget the group must pay its teachers and other expenses, and it is responsible for budgetary carryovers. Each group has wide latitude in how it may spend its budget.

The schools using the model incentive system employ two key elements of an outcome-based instructional system: detailed learning objectives in each subject with specified competency milestones based on these objectives; and a procedure for assessing every student's learning progress toward the next milestone. Although graduation can be based on the student's age as well as on his or her achieving certain minimum competency milestones, traditional grades based on age would have no educational role although they could continue to serve social purposes. The faster learning students move on for a higher competency goal in any subject as soon as each lower one is mastered.[9] Students of a given age group will differ in the competencies they have mastered, and many students will not have reached the highest competencies when they graduate.[10]

The first criterion for a successful incentive system described in the previous section requires jointly productive employees to have shared accountability. Teachers under outcome-based instructional systems are especially involved in mutually reinforcing activities.

Murphy (1984: 11) mentions "the feeling of cohesion among staff members since all teachers are part of the *same* system rather than being artificially divided into grades and/or ability tracks. Teachers freely shared materials and ideas with each other." In the model incentive system, teacher groups would include all faculty in each subject field because of the required high degree of coordination among them.[11] This coordination includes having individual teachers specialize in working with students at particular learning levels or speeds, often on an ad hoc basis, and requires all teachers to regularly refer students to the appropriate specialized groups. In addition, the assessments for students within these milestones may indicate a need for different instructional approaches taken by individual teachers within the group. The larger the number of teachers who share teaching responsibilities, the greater the potential gains from specializations. However, larger groups can also gain from supplementing the incentives on the group as a whole with incentives on individual teachers based on their own measured performance using the assessment data for students at each stage.

By developing learning objectives for each important subject area and regularly assessing students' learning progress under an outcome-based instructional system, it would be possible to satisfy the second criterion that all of the important educational outcomes are measured and that teacher groups are rewarded for their roles in achieving these outcomes. Under the outcome-based instructional system that accompanies the incentive system, students achieve competency levels in the subjects and the teacher groups are rewarded as these competencies are reached. Although the learning objectives in principle should reflect the preferences of parents and the community, in practice this is in large part a technical task that should be carried out by teachers and consultant specialists paid by the school district. An oversight committee of parents, school board representatives, and members of the larger community can ensure that community goals are reflected in the learning objectives to the extent that these individuals desire to become involved. Establishing learning objectives represents the largest start-up cost of an outcome-based system, including one combined with incentives. Ideally this cost could be funded in part by foundations or governments.

Another key task is that of attaching valuations to different learning outcomes in such a way that teacher groups can be rewarded for students' achieving them. Such valuations are inherent in any educational system; the only difference in the model incentive system is that they are made explicit. The importance currently attached to different learning outcomes in most schools is determined by individual teachers, school district staff, subject requirements, teacher assignments, and parents and teacher groups. For example, teachers often have wide latitude in deciding how to emphasize different subjects, and school- or districtwide curriculum can substitute more centrally determined weights. There are time requirements for coverage of subjects, decisions to hire teachers with different specialty interests, and parents can encourage schools to cover particular subjects. Teachers in particular subject areas can urge greater coverage of their fields, and teacher groups sometimes even succeed in obtaining legislation requiring time in their specialties.

In the model incentive system the relative weights or importance attached to learning outcomes are cash valuations applied as incentives for teacher groups. They represent per student payments to teacher groups for students' achieving each substantial competency milestone. Aside from their roles as incentives on teacher groups, these valuations can be readily observed by everyone. That is, it would not be costly for any parent or other constituent of a school system to know the relative importance attached by the school system to each major learning outcome.

A first step in establishing these prices is to calculate reasonably accurately the current per student cost[12] of each subject specialty and to estimate the numbers of students achieving competencies roughly comparable to those that would be offered in the model incentive system. The resulting crude estimate of per student costs of achieving competencies can serve as baselines, from which changes can be made to reflect deliberate choices about the relative importance of different subjects and competencies within them.

One way to adjust these approximate values is simply to allow political pressures to influence them over a brief period. The difference between the effects of political pressures under existing educational systems and under the model incentive system is that, as noted above, the costs of information about the valuations would be much lower than at present for most participants. A more client-oriented approach is to allow parents and students to adjust the weights. For example, each parent could be allowed to place weights on a set of major learning outcomes in a questionnaire and these responses could be aggregated to adjust the baseline values.

The incomes of teacher units would be determined by the prices attached to the major learning outcomes they cover and the number of students achieving each such outcome. It would be possible but not necessary to allow parents and students a certain range of choice of required competency outcomes, giving teacher groups an incentive to attract students to the outcomes they cover.

The payments to teacher groups create incentives to raise instructional productivity by moving students more promptly through the competencey milestones. At the same time, the regular assessment of students' learning progress by independent testing and evaluation personnel helps ensure that quality standards are maintained or increased. The second criterion for a successful incentive system of rewarding all important educational outcomes will be satisfied to the extent that quality is ensured and the payments to teacher groups represent rewards for these outcomes.

Testing personnel are not to be members of the teacher groups and must be placed under independent incentives.[13] Tests specifically examine students' accomplishment of learning objectives and reveal the possible need for corrective action. Some aspects of learning are, of course, more difficult to assess than others. In the context of using learning outcomes as incentives, Berk (1984) pointed out the relative difficulty of inferring abstract reasoning capabilities and the student's development of attitudes and values. To the extent that valued competency milestones include these attributes of students, the learning assessment function cannot rely solely on relatively economical written tests. Regular discussions with and oral examinations of students are necessary, and close communication between the assessment and instructional personnel is required. The expense of this kind of assessment in subjects where needed is a necessary condition for an incentive system to improve school efficiency in all important dimensions.

Another measurement is needed in order to make the combined cost of the per student payments remain within the available budget. It is necessary in implementing the incentive system to anticipate the numbers of students who will reach each competency within a time period (such as an academic year.) Data from other schools with outcome-based instructional systems can be used for this purpose after making allowances for the effects of the incentives. Initially, extra funds should be allotted for higher than anticipated achievement.

Another desirable incentive is for the responsible teacher groups to make the higher competencies, which are not required for graduation, as attractive as possible to students. One key means for teacher groups to accomplish this end is to build their reputations for effective teaching by doing as good a job as possible teaching the required competencies.

As part of the model incentive system, students would also receive rewards when they achieve important competency milestones, thus meeting the third criterion for a desirable incentive system. As noted in the previous section, these incentives are necessary because study and rigorous thought are often not enjoyable to children, and the prospect of resulting future labor market gains may not sufficiently motivate many students to carry out these learning activities to the extent necessary to achieve their learning potential. Student motivation is no less important under outcome-based instructional systems. Spady and Mitchell (1977: 12) note that "Unless the students adopt the goals, all that the renewed emphasis on goal achievement as the basis for behavior control can hope to accomplish is to make student role expectations more demanding and less exciting."

The rewards for students can be cash or in kind, perhaps with the former incentive being more prevalent for older students. In addition, the teacher groups could reward faster learning students who act as tutors and part-time instructors; these students would undoubtedly gain further learning benefits from this role. Larger incentives for students could be provided in schools with many students from backgrounds where parents typically do not provide motivation to learn.

Each teacher group would ultimately have considerable flexibility in spending its revenues. Initially this may not be the case; however, as retirements and resignations occur, budgetary flexibility would rise. Within broad guidelines departing teachers may be replaced with auxiliary personnel and the released funds could also be employed in purchasing supplies and equipment and even used to supplement the incomes of remaining teachers. After a short time with a group a newly hired teacher will become crucial for the group's success. Hence, even though groups may be able to hire teachers at salaries below the earnings of current group members, newcomers would probably soon share fully in the group's income. As a result, the most successful teacher groups will have the highest quality applicants for teaching posts. Administrators need to become involved in groups' hiring practices only when weak groups have difficulty adding able new instructors; in such cases, pay supplements may be required for capable new hires until the groups become more successful.

Flexibility on the expenditure side, combined with the groups' gain from budgetary surpluses, creates overall value incentives for efficient resource uses and for productivity growth via teachers' investments in learning about new instructional techniques. These incentives provide the residual gain from increased productivity, which is the fourth criterion for incentives that improve school efficiency. The requirement to pay out of the group's own funds for each resource used for instruction provides teachers with an interest in learning about every item's relative efficiency in producing rewarded educational outcomes. In conventional schools, teachers lack a strong incentive to acquire this information about each possible resource used in instruction, and, as a result, key variables such as the numbers of teachers, class sizes, uses of teaching aids, and the applications of new methodologies may not be efficient. Because the payoffs from teachers' investments in learning about improved methods can grow over time, the groups would be given assurance that the model incentive system will remain in place for a lengthy period. This assurance would satisfy the fifth criterion for an incentive system.

The incentive for teacher groups to innovate could be augmented by having a demonstration school with the same incentives but where extra funding is provided for instructional experimentation. Data on the relative performance of teacher groups in this and each other school could be made readily available to all interested parties. This would help meet the sixth criterion for an incentive system by ensuring that promising new teaching techniques get attention and by creating information for parents and communities to use in influencing schools for adoption. Further incentives would result if students were allowed to have free choice among schools. However, success of the model incentive system does not depend on this option.

The accrued budgetary surpluses of the teacher groups would probably grow enough over time so that the compensation of those instructors who choose to remain in the groups would increase well above their initial salaries. These surpluses could be directly paid to teachers in the groups or credited to their retirement accounts, and the groups would have an incentive to reinvest funds in improved instructional methods when expected returns are competitive. The initially established rules of the incentive scheme can also specify that part of these funds are to be "taxed" to compensate risks taken by the school district and community in providing start up funding.

We now turn to the issue of whether the model incentive system would satisfy the seventh criterion of justifying its costs. One of the expenses of this system would be the establishment of procedures for assessing student learning. Many of these would be new to the school unless an outcome-based instructional system were already in place. As noted before, learning assessment personnel would not be members of the teacher groups. Independent incentives ensuring quality performance and cost-effective resource utilitzation by these personnel could be achieved by using independent contractors rather than permanent school staff for the learning assessment function, and by periodically taking competitive bids from contractors other than those currently being used. It should be noted, however, that even with these incentives, learning assessment would represent a costly element of the model incentive system if the schools in which it is implemented did not already have an outcome-based instructional system. Other increases in ongoing expenses would result from the per student payments to teacher groups, which would rise by agreement as students' learning accomplishments increase, and from providing rewards to students as they reach competency milestones.

Implementation of the model incentive system would additionally require substantial start up costs if an outcome-based instructional system were not already in place. These costs would include the expense of deciding on learning objectives and defining the competency milestones. Other important costs incurred even if an outcome-based system is already utilized include establishing the payments to students when they achieve learning competencies. Another worthwhile cost would be to provide initial "venture capital" funding to teacher groups for curriculum development, for some of the costs of false steps in the teacher groups' early experimentation with instructional techniques, and to help cover the expenses of searching for or creating new teaching materials. The experiments proposed below would provide schools with information on the likely start up costs of implementing the model incentive system. These costs would decline with the number of schools already using this system.

The total expense of the education of students in the school under the model incentive system would rise significantly in the initial implementation of the system. Depending on what is learned from this system about the degree to which teacher groups achieve major efficiencies, it may turn out that the payment schedules of teacher groups in subsequent incentive systems in other schools could be adjusted so that the learning could be accomplished at substantially lower cost.

In any event, a likely outcome of establishing and fully funding the model incentive system is that students' learning achievements will demonstrably rise by such a substantial amount that the public will be willing to provide the extra funding for subsequent uses of the incentive system. Added to the effects of outcome-based instructional systems lacking the new incentives will be the additional perhaps very substantial effects of incentives on student accomplishment. This advance will be measured in terms of numbers of students achieving subject matter competencies that are important to the community. Perhaps the greatest contribution of incentives would be in the large urban schools with many students from disadvantaged backgrounds where improved learning is crucial for social mobility.

POSSIBLE CRITICISMS OF THE MODEL INCENTIVE SYSTEM

The nature of the model system may attract criticisms that certain of its components will adversely affect the educational process. These criticisms could pertain to (1) the effects of rewards for students and teachers on student learning and teachers' efficiency; (2) the progress of slower learning[14] students; (3) impacts for disadvantaged students and those in inner city schools; (4) the possibility of foreclosing opportunities for cooperative learning; (5) problems in scheduling teachers' workloads; and (6) diminished control on the part of teachers. Each of these will be discussed in turn.

The Effects of Rewards for Students and Teachers on Student Learning and Teacher Efficiency

There is a body of research suggesting that immediate rewards to teachers or to students tied specifically to learning outcomes can actually diminish students' accomplishment. Some work (Garbarino 1975) suggests that teachers are less helpful when they receive such rewards—that they place excessive pressure on students while failing to explain concepts properly. Other work provides evidence that students under immediate extrinsic rewards give more wrong answers to questions and take longer to do some tasks. Negative effects are noted by McGraw (1978) and Condry and Chambers (1978) on tasks that require insight, creativity, and concept "discrimination." The studies that show negative effects of rewards tied to students' learning are largely offset by other studies that give opposite results. Kazdin (1977) discusses at least as substantial a body of research that contradicts the negative findings mentioned above. He states (1977: 105) that "Reinforcement has been used to alter a wide variety of academic skills including accuracy in reading, arithmetic, handwriting, and spelling assignments, completing in-class homework assignments, creative writing, and developing vocabulary." Opposing researchers acknowledge the importance of the work by Kazdin and others (Lepper and Greene 1978: 225).

Unfortunately, much of the research both positive and negative is only partially relevant to the model incentive system. The research, including that of Garbarino on teacher incentives, deals with experimental situations in which rewards are meted out for solving particular problems involving less than a day of time, and often much less.[15] The image of a game show comes to mind where contestants can become so anxious that their minds fail to function as well as normally. In the model incentive system, teachers and students would be rewarded for mastery of substantial learning competencies or groups of them; such milestones might typically be reached by a student two to four times a year.[16] Perhaps nearer-term incentives would speed up these accomplishments; however, they are not essential for the model incentive system.

Considering how closely overall value incentives and successful inventive and entrepreneurial activity have been historically,[17] it would be most surprising if these relationships did not hold in education.

The Progress of Slower Learning Students

Under the model incentive system teachers would have incentives to experiment with alternative ways of taking corrective actions to increase the achievement of slower learning students. Undoubtedly this would include specialized sessions according to the student's assessed learning needs, which conjures up the image of "tracking." Actually, such sessions would be temporary and flexible for many students who have transient difficulties with particular material. Nonetheless, it is the case that students would systematically differ in the speed of movement through competencies.

Much research suggests that slower learning students benefit from being included in the same classroom with faster learning students, and some research suggests that separate groupings within classrooms can be detrimental. The problem with this research is that it fails to control properly for the behavior of teachers or for the curriculum. Hiebert (1983: 236–39) presents numerous research findings in regard to reading instruction that teachers spend a higher proportion of time with slower learning students on procedural and behavioral matters, take more actions that are not conducive to learning, and respond more negatively to the same errors that faster students make.

Unlike the research situations in which teachers are not rewarded for success with slower learning students, rewards are present in the model incentive system. Indeed, it would not be difficult and it would perhaps be highly desirable to provide teacher groups with substantially larger rewards for the initially slower students' accomplishment. Similarly, reward premiums can be provided for teacher groups in urban districts where behavior problems are serious. It appears that self-esteem is important for any learning situation and teacher behaviors are crucial for a student's feeling of confidence. With appropriate incentives teachers would devote the necessary efforts to create good learning situations for students that are less enjoyable for some to work with. There also would be incentives for flexibility of teachers' workloads so those who gain relatively more enjoyment from working with particular categories of students will be assigned to them.

Impacts for Disadvantaged Students and Those in Inner-City Schools

One possible criticism is that the model incentive system is appropriate only for wealthy school districts where much of the implementation of outcome-based instruction has occurred. In fact, the model incentive system is flexible in terms of sizes of rewards for different categories of students and is particularly adaptable to the needs of inner city schools. Incentives can be tailored to offset the relatively lesser satisfaction that teachers may receive from working in such schools, and they can at least indirectly assist with discipline problems. Kazdin (1977: 105) cites many studies that support the hypothesis that better learning achievement tends to reduce disruptive behavior. To the extent that this relationship holds, incentives that increase learning outcomes would thus also bring about improvements in discipline.

Substantial evidence appears to support the proposition that separate learning sessions for disadvantaged or slower learning students reduce their learning. For example, Persell (1977: 90) points out that "a tracking program highly related to social class contains differential options within the tracks. In short, available evidence shows that students in different tracks receive different instructional styles, teacher effort, educational content and options, with the alternatives more highly valued by educators and students consistently going to those in higher tracks." Oakes (1985: 76–77) states that "Teachers of the high-track classes . . . had students do activities that demanded critical thinking, problem solving, drawing conclusions, making generalizations, or evaluating or synthesizing knowledge. The learnings in low-track classes, in nearly all cases, required only simple memory tasks or comprehension." Thus, the issue of "tracking" is not reduced learning due to separate sessions but reduced learning due to different and inferior educational inputs.

The Possibility of Foreclosing Opportunities for Cooperative Learning

Some research (see Johnson and Johnson 1974) implies that students learn more of certain types of material, such as that involving problemsolving, when they are placed in cooperative learning situations. Cooperative learning would be necessarily precluded as an option under the model incentive system only if incentives were established in such a way that students perceived that their rewards for learning were at the expense of those going to others. This can be avoided by paying rewards out of pools of funds dedicated to entire schools rather than to individual classes and allowing these pools to fluctuate from year to year. Teachers under incentives would have every interest in experimenting with promising techniques, including cooperative arrangements where students work together in groups or more advanced students teach less advanced ones.

Possible Problems in Scheduling Teachers' Workloads

Teachers often specialize in teaching particular grades, and it may seem that under the model incentive system they would specialize in particular competencies or categories of students according to progress in achieving competencies. However, teacher assignments in any time period (perhaps as often as every week) would have to be regularly adjusted. That is, given the changing numbers of students who are at each stage of learning, it would be necessary to ensure that individual instructors are regularly assigned workloads that can change from period to period to avoid under- or overutilizing particular teachers. There would be no technical difficulty in carrying out this scheduling task since student progress would be carefully monitored anyway. It does require flexibility on the part of teachers.

Diminished Teachers' Control

Outcome-based instruction has been criticized on the grounds that teachers have reduced control over learning objectives and diminished authority over students (because evaluation is based on the defined learning objectives rather than the teacher's personal learning objectives and other issues such as students' deportment). The addition of incentives would not augment teachers' control over these variables, although it was noted earlier that as a practical matter teachers should be heavily involved in the definition of detailed learning objectives. The model incentive system would open up new areas for teachers' discretion in the techniques and resources used to help students achieve the learning objectives. In many ways, teachers would have greatly enhanced control over their daily activities and work environments. It is therefore not at all clear that teacher satisfaction would be lessened under the model incentive system. Indeed, after time is allowed for teachers to adjust to the combination of incentives and outcome-based instruction, there may be a substantial rise in many teachers' morale.

In Murphy (1984: 11) one teacher using outcome-based instruction without incentives says the following:

> Since I gained security by this organized and highly structured approach and I felt I had command of the subject, I could turn my attention away from the books and papers, *and to the students*. . . . I also had . . . freedom . . . [to do] a whole class or small group board lesson if it seemed appropriate . . . give a presentation . . . have students working individually or in small groups . . . have students play a math game or do some other concept-enriching activity . . . have several of these activities occurring simultaneously, meeting a variety of needs at the same time. . . . I could tailor the class to accommodate a bright fourth grader or a slower sixth grader who were doing the same work. . . . I could manage to "touch base" many times per class with a slower student who needed a lot of attention.

Because the model incentive system would give teachers added control over budgets, teachers would have even more flexibility than in an outcome-based system without the incentives. In addition to giving flexibility to teachers, the model incentive system would strongly encourage collegial activity and provide significant rewards to teacher groups who excel by being creative in finding ways of raising educational productivity.

INITIAL FUNDING AND EARLY IMPLEMENTATION OF THE MODEL INCENTIVE SYSTEM

The model incentive system described in this chapter holds sufficient promise to make implementation worthwhile on an experimental basis. Local communities cannot be expected to provide the necessary funding. There would be sizable start up costs, and the system's ongoing costs would be at least initially higher than is presently the case. Communities may be unwilling to provide tax support to cover these added expenses unless they have evidence of the benefits likely to be gained from doing so. Moreover, teacher groups would be apprehensive about a change that not only significantly alters their regular routines but also may give them less financial security. One use of the externally provided funds would be for advisors to assist teachers as they adjust to the system. These funds could also be used to guarantee the previous salaries of teachers involved in the incentive system's early implementation.

It is inevitable that there would be missteps during the early years of the new system, both in the ways in which its procedures and incentives are established and in the management of teacher groups and their uses of resources. Although these missteps are by-products of the learning process induced by incentives, they will ultimately improve school efficiency. However, because these mistakes can be personally costly to school personnel, they may be inhibited from making the trial and error actions necessary to determine what will be the best ways of managing the incentive system. Providing funding for advisors can mitigate the most costly errors, and other funds could be used to absorb portions of teacher groups' early losses.

The gains to the funders of the experiment would be information that could help ensure that the incentive system has a chance to be implemented successfully. This information about student achievement and about the best ways to generate the system could be made readily available to school districts and communities considering the system for their schools. In addition, it has been suggested (Pincus et al. 1980) that political decisionmakers desire more information in evaluations of educational innovations than just that pertaining to learning outcomes and internal school variables. This is because of the interests of the groups to which political decisionmakers must be responsive. Hence, the experiment could also provide information about phenomena such as the socialization effects of not using the traditional grade structure for educational purposes and impacts on teacher satisfaction and the characteristics of those teachers who are most and least satisfied with the system. Another example is to provide information when the incentive system is implemented in urban schools on the possibly reduced numbers of parents who choose to move to suburban school districts.

Urban schools with many students from disadvantaged backgrounds are likely to be the largest potential gainers from the incentive system. There the rewards to teacher groups and to students themselves for achieving learning competencies may substitute in part for parental influences on student learning that are smaller in these schools than in more prosperous communities. Varying amounts of these rewards can be attempted, and they can be made larger for students in especially deprived circumstances.

There should be two separate control groups of schools. In one group traditional schools lacking outcome-based instruction would have no change other than the regular assessment of students' achievement of learning competencies (even though the schools lack this designation of learning). In the other control group an outcome-based instructional system would be implemented without the overall value incentives. With these control groups it would be possible to monitor the impacts of outcome-based instruction in the group of schools without the incentive system, as well as to evaluate the incremental impacts of the incentives. Differentials in each group's instructional costs could also be measured.

It would be desirable to employ the new incentive system in two categories of schools. In one set of schools, the ongoing expense of the incentive system would be allowed to rise above the school's previous level of costs, while in another group this expense would be held to the same amount. It would then be possible to evaluate the differences in types and amounts of resources used by teacher groups and monitor the differences in students' learning achievement.

If the experiment were conducted only at either the primary or secondary level, it would probably be necessary to include fifteen or so schools in the experiment: There would be three or four rural schools and perhaps six or seven large urban schools to experiment with student incentives. The remaining schools would act as controls.

CONCLUSION

A combination of outcome-based instruction and overall value incentives on groups of teachers holds the promise of significantly enhancing the amount of innovative activity on the part of teachers and thereby raising productivity in schools. Incentives also have potential for motivating students who, after all, are usually very young and often not yet concerned with the importance of their future careers. The model incentive system presented here is not just another merit pay proposal. This proposal is designed to satisfy seven key criteria for a successful system of school incentives, none of which is met by most of the widely discussed or attempted merit pay schemes.

It is unlikely that productivity in schools will ever increase appreciably in the absence of appropriate incentives for teachers and students. The promise of the model incentive system discussed in this chapter suggests that the cost of a carefully implemented experiment would be well justified.

NOTES

1. Oversimplified merit pay proposals are criticized in Bacharach, Lipsky, and Shedd (1984). Another discussion is provided by Murnane and Cohen (1986), who explain why such proposals are rarely implemented successfully. Benson (1968: 10) remains one of the best discussions of the deficiencies in prevailing teacher compensation policies.

2. An example of recent criticism of schools is expressed in the National Commission on Excellence in Education, *A Nation at Risk: The Imperative for Educational Reform* (1983). The Gallup polls (Elam 1984; Gallup and Clark 1987) indicate that public dissatisfaction with local public education has been high at least since 1974, when a new question asked those surveyed to assign grades to their schools. In 1974, 32 percent of those interviewed said they would give their local public schools grades of C, D, or fail. The comparable figure for 1987 was 43 percent. Hanushek (1981: Table 1, 1986: Table 5) presents data showing that over much of the same period there have been rising per student expenditures in schools.

3. Parents may face lower costs than administrators of obtaining information about which school activities directly affect their children. When this is the case, parents can be a force for school effectiveness when they possess the necessary understanding of their childrens' learning needs to make correct inferences from this information and are willing to devote time to deal with teachers and, if necessary, pressure school officials and boards. When parental influences do not occur or are counterproductive, there is a greater need for a system of improved incentives within schools than otherwise.

4. Two excellent summaries of the elements of outcome-based instructional systems are provided in Spady (1982) and Jones and Spady (1985).

5. The findings of "two sigma" learning improvements have recently been questioned (Slavin 1987), and it has been suggested that actual learning improvements were smaller, although still substantial. However, the studies that challenged the original "two sigma" results employed standardized tests rather than criterion referenced exams based on the actual learning objectives that were employed in the schools using outcome-based instruction. There are other findings related to the effects of criterion-referenced testing on learning (see Popham 1987). However, Bracey (1987a) argues that because such testing is almost always in the multiple choice format, the kinds of learning that can be assessed are very limited.

6. The limitations of individualized incentives when such coordination is required have been noted by Bacharach et al. (1984: 19).

7. In a survey article, Hanushek (1986: 1163) points out that "family background is clearly very important in explaining differences in achievement. Virtually regardless of how measured, more educated and wealthy parents have children who perform better on average." In an earlier study Murnane, Maynard, and Ohls (1981) focus specifically on the mother's education as a positive influence on children's achievement.

8. The most important criterion in defining groups is the desirable degree of coordination among their members. Groups should also not be so large that members have trouble keeping track of each others' productivity. Coordination is particularly significant in subject matter specialties under an outcome-based instructional system where each student is regularly placed at learning levels according to his or her assessed needs. As noted below traditional grades are (or should be) given reduced importance under outcome-based instruction. If learning-based incentives were attempted while retaining traditional grades in a large school, the grouping of teachers by grade could encourage some of the same adjusting of students placements among learning levels. There is no reason why "matrix" groupings both according to grade levels and subject matter specialties could not be employed. With any grouping smaller than the entire school there will be a lack of incentives for teachers to participate in responsibilities such as assisting with students' activities. Additional incentives or personnel need to be provided for these functions.

9. This avoids the problem of holding back the faster learning students while the slower learners catch up, which occurs when an outcome-based system is implemented with a rigid grade structure. This problem has been referred to as the "Robin Hood effect" (Bracey 1987b). Rubin and Spady (1984) discuss how faster learning students' progress can be maintained in an outcome-based instructional system.

10. Each student's diploma could specify the competencies achieved, or, alternatively, these could be described in transcripts. For discussion, see Frith and Clark (1984).

11. In smaller schools, the teacher groups responsible for specialized subjects (such as languages) could be small. Monk (1987) presents evidence for schools in New York State showing how the size of the school affects the numbers of teachers in each subject area. In the largest schools there could be separate competing groups covering all levels of instruction in the same subject.

12. A school's teacher salaries can be straightforwardly allocated to subjects taught, and other costs such as supplies and equipment can be readily, although somewhat arbitrarily, assigned to subjects based on enrollments when there do not appear to be large differences between the subjects' per student usage of these items. When these differences are large, the cost of the resources can be separately assigned to the subject in question. If the schools employing the model incentive system did not previously use the

same competency milestones in every subject, it will be difficult to assign the costs allocated to each subject to their competencies. However, this task can be facilitated by obtaining information on the relative costs of different subject competencies from schools where outcome-based instruction has been employed.

13. Benoist (1981) provides a discussion of the relative advantages and costs of in-course and external assessment of students' learning under outcome-based instructional systems. He points out (1981: 235) that "An assessment system that uses in-course evaluation can provide [a] close linkage of outcomes, assessment, curriculum and instruction." On the side of external assessment, he remarks that "When teacher-made tests are . . . not subjected to any kind of validity/reliability check, then in-course assessment is improper. A more general . . . criticism of the in-course method is that quality control of assessment is much more difficult to achieve."

14. In the literature on student grouping (for example, the review article by Dawson 1987) the terms *low ability* and *low achievement* are frequently used interchangeably.

15. These individual tasks can be part of research projects in which the subjects are dealt with for lengthy periods, even exceeding a year. However, the rewards are attached to the component tasks which usually take very little time.

16. An example of a long-term incentive is the famous one created by Eugene Lang in 1980 for the sixth-grade class of P.S. 121 in Harlem (*Time* 1985). This example, where Lang offered college tuition funds to each student on graduation from high school, also illustrates how special treatment of students can usefully accompany incentives.

17. Perhaps the most interesting available discussion is in Schumpeter's classic book, *Capitalism, Socialism and Democracy*. The author argues that the historically most important role of market incentives has not been to achieve efficiency but to foster innovative activity.

REFERENCES

Bacharach, Samuel B., David B. Lipsky, and Joseph B. Shedd. 1984. *Paying for Better Teaching: Merit Pay and Its Alternatives.* Ithaca, N.Y.: OAP, Inc.

Benoist, Howard. 1981. "Assessment of Outcome-Oriented Learning: External or In-Course?" *Alternative Higher Education: The Journal of Nontraditional Studies* 5 (Summer): 231–41.

Benson, Charles S. 1968. *The Economics of Public Education*, 2d ed. Boston: Houghton Mifflin.

Berk, Ronald A. 1984. "The Use of Student Achievement Test Scores as Criteria for Allocation of Teacher Merit Pay." Paper presented at the National Conference on Merit Pay for Teachers, Sarasota, Florida, March 22–23.

Bloom, B. S. 1984. "The Search for Methods of Whole Group Instruction as Effective as One-to-One Tutoring." *Educational Leadership* 8: 4–18.

Bracey, Gerald W. 1987a. "Measurement-Driven Instruction: Catchy Phrase, Dangerous Practice." *Phi Delta Kappan* 68 (May): 683–86.

———. 1987b. "Robin Hood and His Merry Band of Sigmas." *Phi Delta Kappan* 69 (September): 75–76.

Condry, John, and James Chambers. 1978. "Intrinsic Motivation and the Process of Learning." In *The Hidden Costs of Reward*, edited by Mark R. Lepper and David Greene, pp. 61–84. Hillsdale, N.J.: Lawrence Erlbaum Associates.

Dawson, Margaret M. 1987. "Beyond Ability Grouping: A Review of the Effectiveness of Ability Grouping and Its Alternatives." *School Psychology Review* 16: 348–69.

Elam, S. M., ed. 1984. *Gallup Polls of Attitudes toward Education 1969–1984: A Topical Summary.* Bloomington, Ind.: Phi Delta Kappa.

Frith, Greg H., and Reba Clark. 1984. "Differentiated Diplomas or Competency Based Transcripts? Let's Not Fail to Cummunicate." *NASSP Bulletin* 68 (May): 104–07.

Gallup, Alec M., and David L. Clark. 1987. "The 19th Annual Gallup Poll of the Public's Attitudes towards the Public Schools." *Phi Delta Kappan* 69 (September): 17–30.

Garbarino, James. 1975. "The Impact of Anticipated Reward upon Cross-Age Tutoring." *Journal of Personality and Social Psychology* 32: 421–28.

Garms, Walter J., James W. Guthrie, and Lawrence C. Pierce. 1978. *School Finance: The Economics and Politics of Public Education.* Englewood Cliffs, N.J.: Prentice-Hall.

Hanushek, Eric A. 1986. "The Economics of Schooling: Production and Efficiency in Public Schools." *Journal of Economic Literature* 24 (September): 1141–77.

———. 1981. "Throwing Money at Schools." *Journal of Policy Analysis and Management* 1: 19–41.

Hiebert, Elfrieda H. 1983. "An Examination of Ability Grouping for Reading Instruction." *Reading Research Quarterly* 18: 231–55.

Hoenack, Stephen A. 1983. *Economic Behavior within Organizations.* New York: Cambridge University Press.

Jones, Beau Fly, and William G. Spady. 1985. "Enhanced Mastery Learning and Quality of Instruction." In *Improving Student Achievement through Mastery Learning Programs*, edited by D. U. Levine, pp. 11–43. San Francisco: Jossey-Bass.

Johnson, David W., and Roger T. Johnson. 1974. "Instructional Goal Structure: Cooperative, Competitive, or Individualistic." *Review of Educational Research* 44: 213–40.

Kazdin, Alan E. 1977. *The Token Economy.* New York: Plenum Press.

Lepper, Mark R., and David Greene. 1978. "Divergent Approaches to the Study of Rewards." In *The Hidden Costs of Reward*, edited by Mark R. Lepper and David Greene, pp. 217–44. Hillsdale, N.J.: Lawrence Erlbaum Associates.

McGraw, Kenneth O. 1978. "The Detrimental Effects of Reward on Performance: A Literature Review and a Prediction Model." In *The Hidden Costs of Reward*, edited by Mark R. Lepper and David Greene, pp. 33–60. Hillsdale, N.J.: Lawrence Erlbaum Associates.

Monk, David H. 1987. "Secondary School Size and Curriculum Comprehensiveness." *Economics of Education Review* 6: 137–50.

Murnane, Richard J., and Cohen, David K. 1986. "Merit Pay and the Evaluation Problem: Why Most Merit Pay Plans Fail and a Few Survive." *Harvard Educational Review* 56 (February): 1–17.

Murnane, Richard J., Rebecca A. Maynard, and James C. Ohls. 1981. "Home Resources and Children's Achievement." *Review of Economics and Statistics* 3 (August): 69–77.

Murphy, Carol, ed. 1984. *Outcome-Based Instructional Systems: Primer and Practice*. San Francisco: Far West Laboratory for Educational Research and Development.

National Commission on Excellence in Education. 1983. *A Nation at Risk: The Imperative for Educational Reform*. Washington, D.C.: U.S. Government Printing Office.

Oakes, Jeannie. 1985. *Keeping Track: How Schools Structure Inequality*. New Haven: Yale University Press.

Persell, Caroline Hodges. 1977. *Education and Inequality*. New York: Free Press.

Pincus, J., S. E. Berryman, T. K. Glennan, Jr., P. T. Hill, M. W. McLaughlin, M. Stearns, and D. Weiler. 1980. *Educational Evaluation in the Public Policy Setting*. Publication R-2502-RC. Santa Monica: RAND Corporation.

Popham, W. James. 1987. "The Merits of Measurement-Driven Instruction." *Phi Delta Kappan* 68 (May): 679–82.

Rubin, S. E., and William G. Spady. 1984. "Achieving Excellence through Outcome-Based Instructional Delivery." *Educational Leadership* 8 (May): 27–44.

Schumpeter, Joseph A. 1950. *Capitalism, Socialism and Democracy*, 3d ed. New York: Harper & Row.

Slavin, Robert E. 1987. "Mastery Learning Reconsidered." *Review of Educational Research* 57 (Summer): 175–213.

Spady, William G. 1982. "Outcome-Based Instructional Management: A Sociological Perspective." *Australian Journal of Education* 26 (1982): 123–43.

Spady, William G., and Douglas E. Mitchell. 1977. "Competency Based Education: Organizational Issues and Implications." *Educational Researcher* 6 (February): 9–15.

Time. 1985. "'I Will Keep My Promise'" (November 25): 96.

6 THE ETHICS OF RESOURCE ALLOCATION IN EDUCATION
Questions of Democracy and Justice

Kenneth Strike

This chapter addresses two normative issues about how educational resources ought to be allocated: the question of process and the question of justice.[1] The question of process concerns the nature of legitimate authority and ways to decide how to allocate resources. The question of justice concerns what is to count as a fair result of some allocation of resources.

The crucial issue that must be resolved in deciding the ethical status of a given allocation of resources is not the goodness of the outcome. It is important that the process whereby the allocative decision is reached be legitimate and that the result of the allocation be just. Some decisions about the allocation of resources are justified solely because they are legitimately made. If the process is fair and legitimate the result of the process is justified for that reason alone. In other cases, to be fully justified a decision must not only be fairly made, but its outcome must conform with certain standards of justice. Thus an adequate consideration of the ethics of resource allocation requires an integration of questions of process and questions of justice.

Imagine a particular issue of resource allocation. Suppose that Mr. Primrose, the superintendent of schools of the Briar Patch Manor School District, has available a sum of money to be spent for the support of extracurricular activities. He decides to give the money to

George Toothorn, the band director, for the purchase of new trombones. Having made this decision he is confronted by Rocky Buldgemuscle, the football coach. Rocky offers several objections to the decision. First, Rocky argues that it was improper for Mr. Primrose to make this decision without consulting the faculty. Second, he argues that football is more important than band. Finally, he claims that the football team consists disproportionately of poor and minority students who cannot afford to subsidize their extracurricular activities and who need special encouragement to study and to stay in school. However, the band consists of middle-class children whose parents could afford a trombone and who are not at risk academically. Mr. Buldgemuscle wonders if the decision might not have been motivated by considerations of race or class.

Three strains of argument can be distilled here. First, there are claims of educational worth. Some policies may be argued for by holding that the values they realize are more worthy than competing values. The claim that football is more important than music is such a claim. I shall call such claims *goodness* claims. Second, there are claims about the legitimacy of the decisionmaking process. The charge that Mr. Primrose's decision was undemocratic is a claim about the process of decisionmaking. I shall call such claims *process* claims. Finally, Mr. Bulgemuscle argues that the resulting distribution of resources is unjust. His final comments about the composition of the band and the football team and about the comparative claims of the advantaged and the disadvantaged on resources presuppose that standards concerning the nature of a just allocation have been violated. I shall call such claims *justice* claims.

Thus, three types of questions can be asked about the ethics of resource allocation:

1. Are the results or objectives of a given resource allocation a worthwhile, or the most worthwhile, use of that resource?
2. Is the decisionmaking process for the allocation of a given resource fair and legitimate?
3. Is the resulting allocation just?

This chapter is concerned chiefly with the last two of these questions. I note the first, however, because the questions of its relevance for the second and third questions cannot be avoided.

It has been common in those traditions in ethics that are heavily influenced by Kant to distinguish between the right and the good.

Questions about the good are questions about the nature of objects or activities that are intrinsically worthwhile. The claim that Bach is better than the Beatles is a claim about the good. Issues about the right concern the moral principles that ought to regulate conduct. Moral principles are about rights, duties, and obligations. Two points should be made.

First, questions of process and questions of justice are questions about the nature of the right. They form part of what philosophers refer to as questions of distributive justice.

Second, this distinction generates questions about the nature of the connection between the right and the good. One common viewpoint, *consequentialism*, understands the right (or justice) as what maximizes the good. Nonconsequentialist theories, by contrast, hold that there are considerations beyond the maximization of the good that are relevant to determining what counts as justice. Generally, nonconsequentialists will hold that claims about rights or justice are neither fully justified nor surmounted by the requirements of social efficiency.[2]

Some issues about resource allocation should be considered settled *if* they are achieved as the result of a morally satisfactory decisionmaking process. Suppose that Mr. Primrose is able to counter Mr. Buldgemuscle's claim that the decision was made unfairly. Mr. Primrose circulated a memo (that Mr. Buldgemuscle failed to read) requesting suggestions about how the funds in question were to be spent. Mr. Primrose also presented the suggestions received to the school board that held a hearing on the issue and decided the matter only after an enthusiastic debate. Thus, all objections against the fairness of the decision process have been removed. The issues of the good and of justice still remain.

The legitimacy of the decisionmaking process tends to trump claims about what is educationally worthwhile, but not claims about justice. That is, the decision continues to be a valid decision even if Mr. Bulgemuscle's views about the comparative merits of music and football are true. Normally, the legitimacy of a decision that results from a legitimate democratic process is not defeated simply by showing that it is wrong. A belief in democracy requires the willingness to accept incorrect decisions as long as they are democratically achieved (Gutmann 1987).

Thus, *goodness claims generally do not trump process claims, but process claims do trump goodness claims.*

This is not true with justice claims. If a certain distribution of resources is required by justice, then I have a right to my share under that distribution. Moreover, valid rights claims defeat valid process claims. If I have a right not to be discriminated against on account of my race, then my school district may not democratically decide to allocate resources on racially discriminatory criteria. Thus, *justice claims trump both goodness claims and process claims.*[3]

This view of the relationship between goodness claims, process claims, and justice claims is enshrined in American law by means of the distinction between the division of powers between the judiciary and the legislature. To claim that the legislature has erred concerning the good does not serve to remove the issue to another forum. Bad decisions by duly constituted legislatures survive goodness challenges, but they may not survive justice claims. Thus, we need to be clear about what rights people have concerning resource allocation because democratic decisionmaking is constrained by rights.

PROCESS

Educational philosophers from Plato on have tended to assume the following view of what an argument for an educational policy should be like. Educational decisions begin in a view of the good. At the most abstract level, what is required is a view of the nature of a worthwhile human existence. This vision of the good must then be transformed into a view of a desirable society and then into a view of desirable educational outcomes. We will ultimately need to know the kinds of characteristics that people capable of fulfilling this vision of the good should have. Having answered these questions, we may then move on to the details of an educational program designed to produce these characteristics (Cornford 1941; Frankena 1965).

This view is elitist and undemocratic in character. Plato was clear on the matter. Authority, especially over the education of the young, must reside with those who possess the knowledge required to make educational decisions correctly. Those who know should rule. Because the type of knowledge required is knowledge of the good, philosophers should be kings.

This way of thinking assumes that whoever has power over schools is entitled to determine the educational goods that shall be pursued by others. Liberal societies, however, have commonly assumed that individuals have a right to their own conception of their own good and, within limits imposed by justice, the right to pursue this conception without interference from others. I shall refer to this idea as the ideal of liberal neutrality or simply as neutrality.

Why should one accept this doctrine? A variety of assumptions are possible (Gutmann 1987). We might believe that the good is unknowable in any general way. Perhaps what is good for people is simply a matter of taste. Perhaps each individual is normally the best judge of his or her own good. Certainly there is no general agreement among people about what is good. It is possible to argue that one of the defining characteristics of a free society is that these differences are respected. Liberals have often argued that people are by nature sovereign over their own lives (Locke 1960) and that this natural sovereignty includes the right to one's own conception of one's good.

That people have a right to their own conception of their own good argues for democratic decisionmaking in two ways. First, it undermines elitist views of decisionmaking. Neither philosopher kings nor professional educators who claim to know what is good for people are consistent with the proposition that people are entitled to their own conception of their own good. Second, the proposition that people have a natural right to self-governance has been a major piece of theoretical support for democracy (Locke 1960; Benn and Peters 1959). People who are naturally free can surrender this natural freedom only voluntarily and to a government that rests on their consent. Moreover, this surrender of freedom is always both tentative and partial. People surrender their right to self-governance only over specified areas of life where collective choice seems required. Moreover, people's continual participation in political institutions that affect their welfare is seen as a requirement of a government that has the consent of those over whom it exercises its authority (Benn and Peters 1959). Governments that encroach on the individual's private sphere or that deny democratic participation are illegitimate.

Democratic decisionmaking, including democratic decisionmaking about the allocation of educational resources, has strong roots in our political heritage. Claims to any inherent right to make decisions based on expert knowledge about what is educationally worthwhile must be treated with the utmost suspicion within this tradition. However, there must also be limits to what can be democratically decided. There is no right to democratically decide what is good for people. In a democracy people continue to have the right to their own conception of their own good even if they must enter into cooperative and democratically governed relationships with others in order to pursue their good effectively.

This formulation poses crucial problems for those allocating educational resources. It suggests that neither educators nor democratically elected legislative bodies have the right to structure education based on some particular vision about what is educationally worthwhile. The right of people to their own sense of their own good turns out to be both a reason that decisions must be made democratically when collective decisions are justified and also a reason that some matters should not be the object of collective decisions at all. Public schools must somehow do justice to diverse conceptions of the good and to the right of individuals to their own conception of their own good. It is thus of considerable importance to a theory of resource allocation to know the boundaries of legitimate democratic decision-making. The following sections review the views of John Stuart Mill, Bruce Ackerman, and Amy Gutmann on how this boundary might be drawn.

John Stuart Mill

Mill (1956) holds that government of society may interfere with the liberty of an individual only when that individual's acts harm others. Individuals may not, however, be interfered with solely for their own good. Mill's formulation makes the right to interfere in someone's life contingent on the consequences of that person's act. A government may interfere in someone else's behavior to the degree that the behavior affects the welfare of others.

The view is fraught with problems. The distinction between what harms others and what affects only one's self is notoriously vague (Wolff 1968). For example, if A is devoted to his religion so that he finds B's rejection of his faith deeply painful, has B harmed A? Moreover, Mill's way of drawing this line does not do justice to the grounds for treating many acts as private. Sex, for example, might be thought to be a private matter, not because it affects only those who engage in it but because it is deeply personal. Finally, Mill claims that his defense of his principle of liberty is a utilitarian one (Mill 1956: 14). Mill's intent is to argue that the social consequences of respecting his principle are desirable. At the same time, this type of argument for liberty makes liberty contingent. The rights we have depend on the consequences of our having them, and, presumably, they may be suspended or altered when these consequences are deemed undesirable.

Nevertheless, the range and magnitude of the consequences of an action must provide some part of our sense of when a government may act to regulate behavior. That ignorance harms not only the ignorant but the society in which they live is part of the justification of compulsory education and most other forms of educational coercion. If not, then public schools are built on a foundation of governmental paternalism instead of social interest.

Bruce Ackerman

A second approach to the question is provided by Bruce Ackerman (1980). Ackerman's starting point is that a liberal society is one in which claims to power over social resources must be justified by discussion and argument (conversations). However, not any argument will do. One constraint on conversations that can be used to justify social authority is that they must be neutral. Neutral justifications have two primary characteristics. First, they must avoid any presumption that some individuals are intrinsically superior to others. Any argument that claimed that As should receive more resources than Bs because As are inherently more worthy than Bs would be rejected on this criterion. Second, neutrality requires that arguments justifying social authority may not presume that someone's conception of the good is inherently superior to that of others. This criterion precludes people from successfully arguing for resources or power because they have some privileged conception of a good life.

The application of these standards is complex. Nevertheless, it is clear that neutrality places severe restrictions on how claims about educational resources can be justified. It will rule out most of the arguments given by philosophers or educators that a certain vision of a good education should be pursued in public schools because it is intrinsically superior to others. Mr. Buldgemuscle's argument about the superiority of football to music will be ruled out.

There are a variety of ways of making claims on public resources that are compatible with neutrality. We may justify public expenditures on the grounds that they are required to secure justice (Strike 1984). Thus, claims on educational resources in pursuit of citizenship or a more just distribution of wealth are consistent with neutrality. Moreover, it seems possible to argue for some distributions of public educational resources to individuals with differing conceptions of their educational good that meet neutrality requirements. We might, for example, prorate such resources. A system of elective courses and extracurricular activities, together with a funding scheme supporting them roughly in line with participation (perhaps with some allowance for differing costs), might satisfy neutrality. The demand for neutrality, then, tends to generate a view of schooling and of resource allocation where schools may expend public resources where required to fulfill some demand of justice, but where other activities may be supported only where they are voluntary and a neutral funding scheme can be devised.

Consider two objections to this formulation of liberal neutrality. First, it might be overly restrictive. It may be difficult to see how a society can function or how a school can provide an education if it cannot make assumptions about what is good. Second, it may be argued that the conception of neutrality is objectionably individualistic. To view schools as aggregates of individuals with conflicting conceptions of their own good bound together only by a common view of justice denies the educational benefits of initiating human beings into a community united by common purposes and a shared outlook. The next conception of the limits on democratic decision-making is sensitive to these objections.

Amy Gutmann

Amy Gutmann (1987) develops a view about the constraints on democratic decisionmaking that she claims follows from the nature of the democratic ideal itself. First, in democratic education the central goal that must be satisfied is the development of democratic character. Democratic character is that set of capacities, character traits, knowledge, and skills that enables one to participate in the life of a democratic community. Second, other goals of a democratic education may be chosen democratically as long as these goals respect what Gutmann calls the principle of nondiscrimination and the principle of nonrepression. The principle of nondiscrimination requires that all children be educated. The principle of nonrepression, in Gutmann's (1987: 44) words,

> prevents the state, and any group within it, from using education to restrict rational deliberation of competing conceptions of the good life and the good society. Nonrepression is not a principle of negative freedom. It secures freedom from interference only to the extent that it forbids using education to restrict *rational* deliberation or consideration of different ways of life.

The principles of nonrepression and nondiscrimination, although similar in form to neutrality, have a different justification and a different scope. Gutmann's principles are *for the sake of* the long-term maintenance of the democratic community. They are not seen as the residue in civil society of the individual's natural right to self-governance. Also, the scope of Gutmann's principles is different from neutrality. On Gutmann's view, school boards can democratically decide to pursue goals whose justification would violate neutrality. The principle of nonrepression is formulated as a restriction on interference with rational deliberation. It does not prohibit a democratic choice to pursue goals whose justification violates neutrality as long as those who would have chosen otherwise are free to continue to advocate opposing views. For example, Gutmann (1987: 232–55) is willing to subsidize, at public expense, cultural activities that are democratically chosen. Moreover, Gutmann's position seems capable of denying a voice to viewpoints if their advancement is seen as inconsistent with the long-term maintenance of democratic institutions.[4]

Gutmann appears to have a communitarian view of democracy wherein democracy is seen as a form of human association that has its own distinct values that are intrinsically worthwhile and where acceptance of these values is required of community members. Gutmann (1987: 286), to use a Dewey phrase, sees democracy as "a way of life." Consider the following:

> The primacy of political education reorients our expectations of primary [elementary and secondary] schooling away from the distributive goals set by standard interpretations of equal opportunity (such as educating every child for choice among the widest range of good lives) and toward the goal of giving every child an education adequate to participate in the political process by which choices among good lives are socially structured.

Advocates of neutrality may agree with the primacy of political education (Ackerman 1980). But they are not likely to see initiation into a political community as a good in itself (or at least not one that is anything more than one among other possible goods), nor are they going to be willing to agree that the choices among good lives should be socially structured if that means collectively chosen.

Gutmann's views thus represent a significantly different approach to the question of what can be democratically decided than that of liberal neutrality. Gutmann's position permits considerable latitude for collective democratic choice of educational goals as long as the principles of nondiscrimination and nonrepression are respected. It does so because it rejects the individualistic picture presented by traditional liberalism wherein the right to select one's own goods is part of one's liberty. Gutmann substitutes for the liberal vision one in which associated living in democratic communities is the chief good and in which individuals must choose and pursue their own goods within the bounds set by the democratic community. Visions of the good may not be handed down by philosopher kings or by inspired educators, but they may be democratically chosen and collectively pursued, even if liberal neutrality is violated, as long as nonrepression and nondiscrimination are not violated.

Implications for Decisionmaking Levels

These three differing views of what can be democratically decided have implications for the level at which decisions about resource allocation should be made. Insofar as each view values diversity and insofar as local decisionmaking actually promotes diversity, each view includes a general presumption in favor of allocating resources at the local level (Bull 1984). However, the views differ about why this is a good thing and about the conditions for overriding the imperative for local decisionmaking.

Mill's view will tend to attach most importance to the range of effects of a decision. If it is the fact that a given decision affects people that entitles them to some say about it, then it seems reasonable that a given educational decision should be made in such a way as to allow participation by those who are affected by it. This means that decisions will be appropriately made by local districts to the extent that their effects are confined to that district. When the consequences of decisions flow over district borders, higher democratic bodies should make them; otherwise local districts will be able to impose the consequences of their decisions on others who have not had the opportunity to participate in making them.

Gutmann's position may provide an additional reason to prefer local decisionmaking. Local politics may have desirable educational consequences for the development of democratic communities. It may have these consequences insofar as its smaller scale permits a higher level of direct participation and insofar as it permits discussion and debate to be face to face.

Gutmann's views also have implications for who should be considered to be members of a democratic community. In conventional reasoning about democracy (Haller and Strike 1986), it is easy to assume that the members of the community are the citizens who live in a district. These people are represented by a properly elected school board that is empowered to make decisions about educational policy. Such a view may also see teachers and administrators as employees of the district who exist to implement democratically made decisions. According to this view, attempts by teachers to gain a share of power over educational decisionmaking will be seen as a usurpation of democratic authority. Claims of teachers to be professionals and thus to be entitled to a measure of self-governance of their profession will lead us to see them as so many aspirant philosopher kings attempting to impose their vision of what is educationally worthwhile against that of the people.

Gutmann's more communitarian vision of democracy can support a different view. What is most important about democracy is that educational goals be chosen by the community as the result of a process of face-to-face discussion of issues and aspirations. This view does not give power to teachers because of their superior expertise, but it does make it difficult to exclude them from the community's conversation and to treat them as employees whose duty is to do the will of the people. As participants in the process of education, teachers should be participants in the community's conversations as teachers, not simply as citizens who happen to work in the school. Gutmann approaches the question about the membership of the community not so much as a problem of working out the details of a theory of representation, but as a matter of identifying the groups of people who, because they have a stake, something to contribute or because they are members of the school community, should be in-

volved in the conversation. In this matter, too, Gutmann's more communitarian vision of democracy offers a different way of posing the
issues than do more conventional liberal approaches.

Summary

One element of an ethical allocation of educational resources is that
the allocation must be the result of a legitimate process. The view
that individuals have a right to their own conception of their own
good leads to two important observations about the nature of such a
legitimate process. First, claims to authority over resource allocation
decisions rooted in a presumption of expertise are suspect. Instead,
resources must be allocated democratically. Second, the scope of
democratic decisionmaking must be constrained. I have explored
three views on how and why the scope of decisionmaking should be
constrained. Although I have not argued a position on this issue, it
should be clear that having a defensible view is required if one is
to have a responsible position on how local boards and local administrators may act in allocating resources.

JUSTICE

The inquiry into issues about what justice may require for the distribution of educational resources is divided into two parts: first,
views of equal opportunity; next, views about what counts as a just
view of the distribution of social resources.

Equal Opportunity

Consider the normative model of the school's role in providing equal
opportunity shown in Figure 6-1. This diagram suggests several
points about equal opportunity. First, it indicates that equal opportunity can be thought about as a relationship between individual
characteristics, school resources, and proximate and remote measures
of school success, achievement, and appropriate socially relevant outcomes. The latter two are commonly measured by test scores and
income, although these measures do not exhaust their meaning. Second, the diagram suggests that educational resources ought to be dis-

Figure 6-1. A Model of Equal Educational Opportunity.

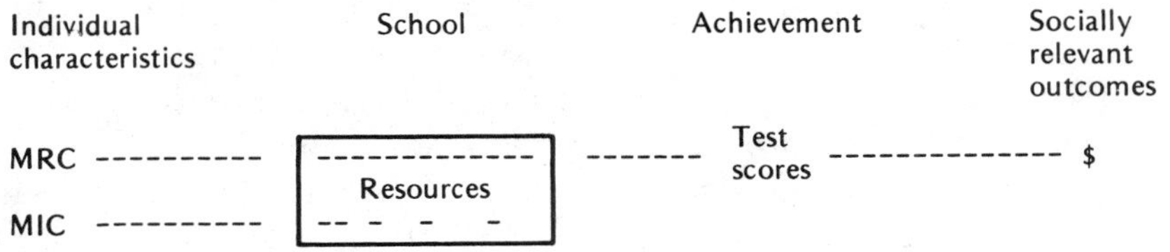

Individual characteristics	School	Achievement	Socially relevant outcomes
MRC ----------	┌─────────────┐ │ Resources │	------- Test scores	------------ $
MIC ----------	└─ -- - - - ─┘		

MRC = morally relevant characteristics; MIC = morally irrelevant characteristics.

tributed so that achievement and socially relevant outcomes depend only on morally relevant characteristics.

The model makes both moral and empirical assumptions. The central moral assumptions are: first, that unequal results are morally acceptable as long as they result from fair competition and, second, that fair competition exists only when results are affected exclusively by morally relevant characteristics (MRC). This last claim is a tautology. A morally relevant characteristic is one that may permissibly affect the distribution of relevant outcomes. Morally irrelevant characteristics (MIC) are those that should not affect the distribution of relevant outcomes.

To apply the model we need to have a principled view of what counts as morally relevant and morally irrelevant characteristics. Assume, for the moment, that such things as ability, aspirations, and effort normally[5] count as morally relevant characteristics, and that such things as race, sex, religion, and socioeconomic class normally do not.

The empirical assumptions required by the model are largely that the causal connections represented by the lines can be specified in a plausible way. The most ovious way to represent these connections is to hold that (1) the main determinate of socially relevant outcomes is cognitive achievement and (2) cognitive achievement is largely a product of schooling. Note, however, that the model assumes more than that schools substantially affect cognitive achievement. It also assumes that (3) schools can affect relative differences between people's achievement. Certainly if schools do not and cannot be made to have an appreciable effect on the relative distribution of achievement and relevant social outcomes, the model has no application to the world. The "schools don't make a difference" literature of the late 1960s and 1970s (Jencks et al. 1972; Coleman et al. 1966) does not undercut the moral force of the concept of equality of opportunity, but it does cast doubt on its achievability through schooling.

The concept of equal opportunity does not speak to all issues of equality that can arise about the distribution of educational resources. Its force is to insist that it is morally inappropriate for one's life chances to depend on morally irrelevant characteristics, but it does not inform us about how we may attach resources to morally relevant characteristics. For example, ability is a morally relevant characteristic, but knowing this does not tell whether (or when) more resources should be expended on high-ability or on low-ability children. Answers to such questions require additional principles. These are not a part of the concept of equal opportunity, nor does the doctrine of equal opportunity tell how much economic inequality we should tolerate in society. It does insist that whatever degree of inequality we do tolerate should not be inherited. The answer to these larger questions of equality requires a more comprehensive theory of justice of the sort discussed below.

Given this, what shall count as a fair measure of having achieved equality of opportunity? In my view, what we should expect as a result of having achieved equality of opportunity is parity in the distribution of achievement and relevant social outcomes between groups defined by morally irrelevant characteristics. Take two groups, A and B. Assume that these groups are defined by some morally irrelevant characteristic such as race or socioeconomic class and that they have the same distribution of morally relevant characteristics.

Of what are relevant social outcomes a product? Assume that they are a product of individual characteristics, morally relevant and morally irrelevant, and opportunity. I want to understand the terms of this formulation broadly enough so that it must be true. All individual characteristics can be divided into morally relevant and morally irrelevant ones. A person's opportunities consist of the entire set of environmental factors that interact with individual characteristics. This exhausts the universe of discourse. We might then express the determinates of outcomes as follows:

$$\text{Outcomes} = f(MIC, MRC, \text{opportunity})$$

If opportunities are distributed in a way that eliminates the effects of morally irrelevant characteristics, then outcomes can only be the product of morally relevant characteristics and opportunity. Nothing else remains for them to be a product of. Conversely we also know that if the distribution of outcomes between group A and group B differ, that must be a result of some inequality of opportunity. (*Ex hypothesi* As and Bs differ only on irrelevant characteristics.) We can thus treat parity in the distribution of relevant social outcomes between groups distinguished solely by morally irrelevant characteristics as a measure of the achievement of equality of opportunity.

This argument for an outcome measure of equal opportunity may be attacked in two ways. It may be argued, first, that I have unreasonably assumed that morally relevant and morally irrelevant characteristics are independent and, second, that there are reasons that we should not use the sort of expanded conception of opportunity that appears in the formulation.

The premise of the first objection is true. The formulation does assume the independence of morally relevant and morally irrelevant characteristics. It does not refute the basic view, however, if morally relevant and morally irrelevant characteristics are not independent. It does require that we make it more complicated.

The required approach to development of the model is easily stated. We must identify any systematic associations between morally relevant and morally irrelevant characteristics. We must then control for this association in a way that allows us to demonstrate that any departures from parity result from the association between morally relevant and morally irrelevant characteristics.

The execution of this simple suggestion is enormously complex. Associations between morally relevant and morally irrelevant characteristics might be of two sorts, natural and social. Any genetically based association between race and intelligence would be a natural connection. Obviously, claims about such associations are highly controversial and enormously difficult to demonstrate. An example of a social connection between a morally relevant and a morally irrelevant characteristic would be a connection between educational aspirations and religious convictions. Here there is an additional problem beyond ascertaining the facts. We must also decide if such social associations are themselves morally acceptable. We might suppose that people may legitimately differ in their educational aspirations because of their religious convictions and that departures from parity traceable to such differences are not unjust. If men and women differ in educational aspirations, however, it is less clear that such differences are morally acceptable. They may result from insidious forms of socialization. If so, they will not justify departure from parity.

Given the complexity introduced by such possible associations between morally relevant and morally irrelevant characteristics, the best course may be to treat any departure from parity as prima facie evidence of unequal opportunity and to invest a burden of proof on those who claim that such departures from parity result from an association between morally relevant and morally irrelevant characteristics to demonstrate this.

The second objection will be to the expanded notion of what counts as an opportunity. Here I have identified opportunity with the set of environmental influences that affect relevant outcomes. Obviously this definition of opportunity includes far more than schools.

It is not conceptually odd to identify a person's opportunities with the set of environmental influences that affect relevant social outcomes. That is what opportunities are. The objection will be to the policies the definition invites. It is likely to lead the state, in the name of equality of opportunity, to invade the home and the community in ways that violate family privacy and community autonomy (Coleman 1974).

This is not inevitable. Insofar as the effects of family or community on individual characteristics have a just history, the fact that they affect relevant social outcomes is not a reason for state intervention. There is no injustice to remedy. Insofar as the state is likely to reach into the family in order to redress inequalities of opportunity, it is likely to want to deal with such things as the effects of poverty, unemployment, or inadequate health care. Poverty, unemployment, and poor health are rarely among those values that families and communities prize. In contrast, those values associated with a family's religion or an ethnic group's cultural heritage are not likely to be the target of state remedies.

Also there is nothing about the conception of equality of opportunity that requires environmental inequalities to be remedied at the site of their occurrence. That some inequalities result from differences in families' abilities to educate their children does not require that the state seek to equalize family educational capacity. It requires that the state respond to the resulting inequality with a program designed to redress it. What determines the point of state intervention is not the site of the original inequality. Instead, the site of intervention should be determined by considerations both of intrusiveness and effectiveness. The state should intervene at those points that are least likely to intrude into family or community life in offensive ways and are most likely to make a difference. Equality of opportunity does not require that the opportunities of As and Bs be equal at every point, but that the mix of opportunities available to As and Bs be roughly equivalent in their effects on life chances.

One implication of this position is that schools will be called on to remedy inequalities of which they are not the cause. Moreover, in order to do so, they may have to spend a disproportionate share of resources on the education of those whose preschool and extra-school environments are educationally disadvantaged. Insofar as home and community do affect the capacity to profit from schooling, equality of opportunity requires schools to use their resources in a way that compensates for resulting inequalities. A common curriculum and/or nondiscriminatory placement will be insufficient.[6]

Some may argue that schools have no moral obligation to cure inequalities of which they are not the cause. This response is like arguing that government has no responsibility to provide for the security of citizens except when government agents threaten that security. Governments exist to secure the rights of their citizens. If there is a right to equal opportunity, then government should remedy inequality even if it is not the source of inequality (when this is true). Thus, the view of equality of opportunity sketched here presents a strong case for having schools compensate for inequalities that they do not cause by spending a suitably disproportionate share of resources on the educationally disadvantaged.

Another view of educational equality is put forth by Amy Gutmann. First, Gutmann (1987: 131) provides several objections to a view that is something like the view I have described above, a view she labels "equalization":

> According to equalization, the educational attainment of children should not differ in any systematic and significant manner with their natural or environmentally determined characteristics. Rightly distributed, education should be used to overcome all environmental and natural causes of differential educational attainment, since these causes of social inequalities are beyond people's control, and therefore "arbitrary from a moral perspective."

Gutmann explores several objections to this view, including the claim that it would result in unwarranted intrusion into family life.

Her basic objection, however, is that the demands of "equalization" are too extreme (Gutmann 1987: 132–33):

> Completely realized, equalization requires the state to devote all its educational resources to educationally less able children until they reach either the same level of educational attainment as the more able or the highest level they are capable of attaining. Given limited educational resources and unlimited capacity for educational innovation, this time may never come, in which case the state would provide no educational resources to the more able.

I do not believe that such conclusions follow from the view of equality of educational opportunity I have sketched. Moreover, there is a key difference between Gutmann's characterization of "equalization" and the view of equality of opportunity I have argued for. That difference concerns what is to count as morally relevant and morally irrelevant characteristics. Gutmann's view of morally irrelevant is what is beyond people's control and therefore "arbitrary from a moral perspective." She also notes that both natural and environmental influences on achievement are beyond an individual's control. They are therefore morally irrelevant.

Natural and environmental influences on achievement seem to exhaust the possibilities. Thus the effect of Gutmann's conception is that all factors that influence achievement are morally irrelevant. It follows that all differences in achievement violate equality of opportunity. Given this conception of what is morally irrelevant, the demand for equal opportunity leads to a demand for educational parity, not between groups characterized by morally irrelevant characteristics but between individuals. A similar line of argument would also lead to a demand for parity between individuals on all measures of social welfare. Clearly such demands are impossible to realize.

Why identify the morally irrelevant with that over which one has no control? Gutmann does not say. The underlining assumption must be that what should determine the welfare of individuals in society is virtue or morally praiseworthy behavior. Because behavior is morally praiseworthy only when it is freely engaged in, individuals cannot be held responsible for or rewarded for actions or achievements that depend on characteristics that simply happen to them. Achievement is not morally praiseworthy if it depends on heredity and environment, two characteristics that merely happen to people and are not therefore morally praiseworthy. If achievement depends on heredity and environment, two characteristics that are "morally arbitrary," there are no morally relevant reasons why people should rightly differ in achievement or why they should be rewarded for such differences as occur. We are thus led to a view of equal opportunity—parity in achievement between individuals—that is impossible to fulfill.

To accept such a characterization of what is morally irrelevant confuses distributive justice with retributive justice. It is to assume that social benefits should be distributed according to moral desert (Rawls 1971: 310–15). Why assume this? Other options are available. We might argue that one factor that defines what is to count as morally relevant is the tendency to promote efficient use of resources. Presumably, it is reasonable to admit people to medical school because they have the capacity for profiting from a medical education. We attach resources to the ability to profit because we all are better off if the people we train to be physicians can profit from the training. We are not attempting to reward applicants for morally praiseworthy characteristics. Similarly, race is morally irrelevant to getting a medical education, not because it is an accident of birth and therefore reflects no moral merit on anyone, but because race has no connection to the ability to profit from a medical education. It may then be that characteristics such as ability, aspirations, or effort are morally relevant for the distribution of educational resources despite the fact that the possession of them reflects no moral desert on the possessors. If we accept this view and can generate a suitable list of such characteristics, we need not conclude that equal opportunity generates a requirement of parity in achievement between individuals.

Gutmann (1987) provides an alternative to equal opportunity. That alternative is roughly this. First, we should distribute educational resources in a way that ensures that everyone has at least those minimal capacities required for democratic participation. This is called the *democratic threshold principle.* Second, having achieved such a distribution, further allocations of educational resources can be made democratically. This is called the *democratic authorization principle.*

I reject the democratic authorization principle, but accept the democratic threshold principle. I reject the democratic authorization principle because it requires the rejection of equal opportunity. It permits distributions of resources incompatible with equal opportunity as long as they are the product of democratic decisions. I do, however, accept the democratic threshold principle. Moreover, I claim that it takes precedence over equal opportunity. Equal opportunity does not come into play until the democratic threshold principle has been satisfied.

I cannot fully argue the case for the democratic threshold principle. My acceptance of it is motivated by two assumptions. First, the demands of citizenship take precedence over economic demands when they conflict. One difficulty with the model of equal opportunity I described earlier is that it sees relevant social outcomes as largely economic in their character. It identifies them with income, wealth, or status. It omits goals such as citizenship. Public schools, however, also have political objectives. A basic purpose for their existence is to create citizens for a democratic society. This goal takes precedence over the economic purposes of schooling.[7]

Second, equal opportunity is not an adequate principle for the distribution of those resources on which citizenship depends. Equal opportunity does not preclude significant inequalities in the distribution of relevant outcomes. It merely precludes these outcomes from being a consequence of morally irrelevant characteristics. It is therefore logically possible for equality of opportunity to be fully realized and still have some who fail to reach the threshold of democratic participation. However, every person capable of achieving the threshold of democratic citizenship has a right to an education that permits at least this threshold to be achieved. Thus, if a distribution of educational resources to slow learners beyond what is required by equal opportunity is needed to bring all above the threshold required for democratic citizenship, there is a strong moral case for providing it.[8]

Finally, note that my view on these matters is more restrictive of democratic decisionmaking than is Gutmann's. On Gutmann's view it is impermissible to decide democratically to distribute resources in such a way that the democratic threshold is not satisfied. Beyond this, resources may be distributed democratically. Once the threshold principle is satisfied, justice constrains democracy no further. I, however, would also constrain democratic decisionmaking by the principle of equal opportunity. Thus, someone who can show that some decision to allocate resources in a certain way violates equal opportunity has a claim against that decision even if it was achieved democratically.

Justice in Distribution

Equal opportunity, even supplemented by the democratic threshold principle, is not a sufficient account of justice. Indeed, it assumes some more general account of justice that legitimates, at least to a degree, a competitive market allocation of economic rewards. Equality of opportunity is part of a theory of fair competition. It makes little sense in a view of justice that regards competitive allocation of social benefits as inherently unjust. A Marxist society would not value equality of opportunity.[9] This section reviews comprehensive theories of distributive justice and then sketches the details of two competing views for resource allocation in education.

Robert Nozick (1974), in *Anarchy State and Utopia*, distinguishes among *historical, patterned,* and *end state* theories of justice. These are distinguished as follows:

Historical: A historical theory holds that an entitlement is justified when it is a product of a just history. That is, whether a given distribution is just depends on how it came about (Nozick 1974: 152). Nozick, for example, holds that entitlements are justified (assuming an initial just distribution) when they are a result of voluntary transactions.

Patterned: Patterned principles of distributive justice hold that a distribution is just when it varies according to a certain criterion. Patterned principles thus have the form "To each according to his _____ ," where the blank may be filled in by some characteristic that serves as the criterion according to which just distributions vary. "To each according to his virtue" or "To each according to the value of his marginal productivity" are examples.

End state: End state principles hold that a given distribution is just when the end result (a certain specified time slice) of that distribution accords with a rule that describes the structure of a just distribution. The claim that a just distribution provides the greatest good for the greatest number is such a theory. Justice is characterized as some global property of the resulting distribution.

These views are not mutually exclusive. For example, one might argue for a certain patterned theory of distribution because it leads to a desired end state. One might, for example, hold that "To each according to the value of his marginal productivity" is a principle to be followed because it leads to the greatest good for the greatest number. If, however, one regards these views as expressing a classification of ultimate principles of distributive justice, then they become mutually exclusive.

Whatever the merits of these different views, there are reasons to suppose that historical theories and patterned theories, or at least some common instances of them, are not very interesting for the ethics of resource allocation in public schools. On Nozick's views, it is doubtful whether there would be public schools because it is unlikely that a system of tax supported and compulsory education is consistent with a view of justice that sees just distributions resulting solely from voluntary transactions.

Patterned theories may have more potential for application, but there are other problems. Consider that patterned theories are often linked to some notion of desert. That is, people are held to be entitled to a given benefit or resource because they deserve it. "To each according to his virtue" treats economic goods as merited in that they are seen as rewards for virtuous conduct. "To each according to the value of his marginal productivity" (unless this principle is subservient to, perhaps, a desire to maximize the average welfare) assumes that people deserve what they earn where earnings are defined by the market.

Such views have two distinct liabilities. First, it is difficult to conceive of children as deserving or as having earned anything. Indeed, it seems that education of some sort is a precondition for children to grow into the kinds of individuals who might be held to be responsible for either virtuous or productive behavior and, thus, rewarded for them. It is difficult to treat an elementary education as deserved or earned.

Second, historical and patterned principles of justice seem to disassociate thinking about the justice of a distribution of educational resources from considerations of the public welfare or the public interest. In order to connect questions of the distribution of resources to questions of the public welfare, we need to have some conception of what counts as a desired outcome. One of the merits of end state principles of justice is that they help form a conception of desired outcomes.

I have already appealed to these considerations in objecting to Gutmann's conception of what was to count as a morally relevant criterion. She assumed that "morally relevant" was to be identified with morally praiseworthy behavior. She rightly noted that most of the characteristics that affect learning reflect no moral merit on the individuals who possess them. She thus concluded that there are no morally relevant characteristics that permit some to learn more than others and held that equity required parity of outcomes between individuals, a result impossible to achieve. The fault here lies in the attempt to determine what is to count as morally relevant in the context of a patterned theory rather than in terms of an end state theory of justice. The latter allows us to connect what is to count as morally relevant to notions of public welfare.

In what follows, I examine two end state theories. These theories represent what may be the two dominate strains of thought on the nature of justice in western political thought. The first, utilitarianism, is the philosophy of Jeremy Bentham (1961) and John Stuart Mill. This theory constitutes the philosophical backing of much modern economic theory. The second, justice as fairness, is the view of philosopher John Rawls (1971). It is a rights-based theory and is an heir to the social contract theory of Locke (1960).

I shall develop these views as answers to two questions. The first concerns what is to be distributed. Societies distribute all sorts of things: cars, dollars, and drivers' licenses. A view of distributive justice must decide which among the plethora of goods and services that a society distributes matters so fundamentally that their distribution may be taken as a measure of justice. It must have a view about what counts as basic goods. Second, a view of distributive justice must have a view about what counts as a just distribution of those goods.

Utilitarianism

Utilitarianism's answer to these two questions is alarmingly simple. We should fundamentally be concerned with the distribution of happiness, and the most just society is the society that produces the greatest happiness for the greatest number of people.

Why happiness? Utilitarians are interested in happiness because they believe happiness to be the basic good and the goal (together with the avoidance of pain) toward which all human action aims. Other social goods have value because of the happiness they produce.

Happiness is the common currency of distributive justice. If we can determine the effects of social institutions on human happiness, we can thereby measure their worth.

Just institutions are those that maximize the good. Utilitarians generally refer to their measure of social welfare as the "average utility." The average utility of a given society is determined by summing the total happiness of the members of that society, subtracting the total pain of its members, and dividing by the number of persons in that society.

Happiness is not an easy thing to measure. After a few futile attempts to develop a "hedonist calculus" (Bentham 1961), utilitarians have generally preferred to look at indirect measures. For example, if one assumes that the amount people are willing to spend for something is a reflection of the satisfaction it would bring them, it becomes possible to treat wealth as a surrogate for happiness and the gross national product as a surrogate for the average utility. Modern-day utilitarians are likely to look at the production and distribution of wealth rather than happiness.

Given this viewpoint, utilitarians are also likely to see just institutions as those that tend to maximize production of goods and services. This is not to say that they do not value social institutions that enhance freedom or equality. It is to say that they value them as means to an efficient and productive society. They maximize the prospects that as many of us will get as much of what we want as is possible.

Utilitarianism has several implications for the distribution of educational resources. First, utilitarians value equality of opportunity. They understand it as a means to productive efficiency. A productive society requires the development of the productive capacity of its members. Education is an investment in human capital. Just as any rational business person will invest his or her resources in the most productive way available, educators should invest educational resources where they will achieve the maximum return on investment.

To use irrelevant characteristics such as race, sex, or national origin as criteria for deciding who is to get what educational resource is to invest inefficiently. A decision to allocate some educational resource on the basis of race, for example, is a decision to neglect to develop the productive capacity of the able members of the group discriminated against and, instead, to invest in development of the capacities of less able members of the favored group.

This view of equality of educational opportunity does not require that we distribute educational resources equally. That is, it does not require that everyone get the same amount of educational dollars, teacher time, or facilities. What it requires is that educational resources be distributed based on ability to profit in a way that maximizes productivity. Ability to profit is the relevant criterion because it (along with motivation and interest) determines who is most able to make productive use of educational resources. Thus from the utilitarian view, educational resources are likely to flow to the people who are most able. This does not mean that the less able should be neglected. Having a tiny, well-educated elite and a poorly educated mass would probably not maximize society's overall welfare. The actual distribution of available resources between the able and the less able will be decided by asking what distribution will produce the maximum gain in productivity or overall social welfare.

These arguments suggest that in evaluating the commitment of educational resources to various programs for various groups, the essential questions to ask are those that concern the rate of return on our investment. In evaluating the merits of some educational program, we will want to ask such questions as, "How much must be invested in the education of a given person in order to increase that person's lifetime earnings by a given amount?" and "Is there an alternative program that will generate a more favorable rate of return on our educational investment?"[10] In asking such questions, we assume that a person's earnings are a measure of his or her productivity and that a person's productivity is a measure of his or her contribution to the satisfaction of members of society. In short, to express an interest in the rate of return on our educational investment is to express a concern for maximizing the average utility. It is to seek the greatest good for the greatest number and as a consequence to seek justice.[11]

Objections to Utilitarianism

There are several related criticisms of utilitarianism that have become common in the philosophical literature. First, utilitarianism makes rights contingent things that can be overturned for the sake of the average welfare or traded for economic benefits. Suppose, for example, that we can imagine a certain economic state of affairs in which slavery was economically efficient. Utilitarianism under such circumstances seems to require slavery because slavery satisfies the average utility. Here the issue is not whether there are conditions under which slavery might actually satisfy the requirements of the average utility. The point is that were there such circumstances, utilitarianism would produce results that run strongly against basic notions of human rights. Utilitarianism thus holds fundamental rights hostage to the average utility.

Second, utilitarianism is concerned only with the average welfare in society, but not with the actual distribution of happiness. It will thus prefer a society in which the distribution of happiness is highly unequal to one where the distribution is equal but where the average is lower. The failure to consider the distribution of happiness as well as the average may be a defect.

Third, utilitarianism may require unfair trades among the welfare of individuals. Utilitarianism will require arrangements in which some people benefit at the expense of others as long as the average welfare is enhanced thereby.

All of these objections revolve around a common focus. One of our central moral convictions is that human beings are persons and as such are objects of value entitled to dignity and worth and possessed of equal rights. As persons they must be treated as ends, not means. The arguments against utilitarianism given above are all instances in which utilitarianism fails to treat individuals with equal respect or to grant them equal rights. Instead, by countenancing, indeed, requiring trades that violate the rights of some or disregard the needs of some for the sake of the welfare of others, it can treat some people as means to the welfare of others. If so, it is inadequate as a theory of distributive justice.

Justice as Fairness

Justice as fairness is a modern version of a social contract theory.[12] It was developed by John Rawls (1971) in his now classic *A Theory of Justice.* Rawls often presents his view in opposition to utilitarianism and as a corrective to the problems noted above.

The first question that we asked of utilitarianism was, "What are we distributing?" The utilitarian response is happiness. Rawls finds the response too subjective. How are we to measure happiness? How are we to know what sorts of institutions promote it? He suggests that we should focus on a set of goods that everyone will find important to their lives, no matter what sort of lives they live. These goods, which Rawls calls primary goods, are universal instrumentalities; they are useful for getting what we want in life, no matter what we want. Primary goods are things that reasonable people want, whatever else they want.

One example of a primary good is wealth or income. Different individuals in our society may legitimately have very different views about how they wish to live and what sort of life is good for them. However, it is difficult to imagine a way of life that does not require income of some sort. Any reasonable person wants some income, no matter what else he or she wants. Income is a primary good.

There are other primary goods in addition to income. Various liberties and rights of political participation are primary goods. For example, any reasonable person will want the right to act on fundamental personal convictions, whatever they happen to be. Thus liberties such as freedom of religion and freedom of conscience are primary goods. Likewise, reasonable people will want the right to participate in decisions that affect their welfare. They will also want opportunities to learn and to work because education and economic opportunity are also universal instrumentalities.

Administrators who wished to apply this view to decisionmaking might conclude that it is not really their concern to determine how education affects overall happiness. Instead, they should ask themselves how schools distribute primary goods or things that determine the value of primary goods.

We might reason as follows: The central purpose of public school education is to transmit basic skills such as reading, writing, and computation. What makes these valuable and central is that they are connected with various primary goods. For example, although various political liberties are protected by the U.S. Constitution, the value of these liberties to any individual depends on the possession of certain skills. The value of the right to vote, for example, depends on our ability to decide which candidate best supports our interests. The rights of free speech or a free press are valuable to the extent that one has something to say and the ability to say it. In short, a prerequisite to the value of one's fundamental rights is the ability to obtain and use ideas and information. Literacy is central to meaningful citizenship.

Basic skills are also important for access to the economic system. It is apparent enough that reasonable proficiency in reading, writing, and computation is a prerequisite for access to or success in further education, which is, in turn, essential for access to many jobs.

One might then reason that we need not be concerned with the consequences of education for the long-term happiness of students. Rather, we need to be concerned more directly with providing the opportunity to acquire a basic education (Strike 1982). An elementary education provides an opportunity to acquire certain skills that are crucial because they are essential for effective participation in the political and economic institutions of our society.[13]

However, this determines only what goods we should emphasize as far as distributive justice is concerned. It does not tell us what counts as a just distribution. Thus we need to return to Rawls and ask what principles define fairness in the distribution of primary goods.

Rawls (1971: 302) addresses this question by providing the following two principles:

First Principle
Each person is to have an equal right to the most extensive total system of equal basic liberties compatible with a similar system of liberty for all.

Second Principle
Social and economic inequalities are to be arranged so that they are both: (a) to the greatest benefit of the least advantaged . . . and (b) attached to offices and positions open to all under conditions of fair equality of opportunity.

The first principle is concerned with political rights such as free speech, a free press, and freedom of religion. Here Rawls insists that a just society provides everyone with the greatest extent of such liberties consistent with similar liberties for all. Our right of free speech, for example, is limited only when we employ speech to limit the rights of others. Similarly, people are to have freedom of religion or conscience, but they may not act on religious convictions that would compel others to accept their views.

The first principle, can be realized in two general ways. A just society must, first of all, have a just constitution. That is, it must provide legal protection for rights such as free speech, freedom of assembly, and the right to vote. Second, a just society must provide for the fair value of these rights to individuals. Among other things, this requires an education for everyone such that everyone has the skills necessary to exercise his or her rights meaningfully. (This provides a justification for Gutmann's democratic threshold principle.)

The second principle has two parts. The second part demands that economic opportunity be available to all on the basis of their ability and that equal opportunity be provided. The general idea is that a society's economic positions must be assigned on relevant criteria and that a fair opportunity must be available to acquire the skills required for economic participation. Rawls assumes that this requirement is fulfilled when people with similar aspirations and abilities have equal life prospects.[14]

The first part of the second principle is referred to as the difference principle. It requires that any equalities in the distribution of primary goods be justified so that such inequalities are to the benefit of all, particularly to the least advantaged members of society. The difference principle is perhaps both most important and most difficult. Some additional comment is required.

Consider Figure 6-2, three diagrams of the distribution of some social good (income, perhaps) among a four-person society. In these diagrams, the size of the circles indicates the total amount of income being distributed. The size of the wedges indicates both the amount and the proportion available to each individual. Note that an underlying assumption is that the proportion of the distribution affects the amount to be distributed. That is, inequalities in the distribution of goods affect the amount of goods available. One reason for this is that incentives are required to stimulate productivity. People are

Figure 6-2. Comparative Distribution.

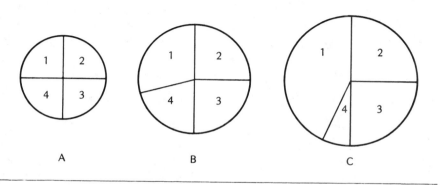

unlikely to put forth effort in their jobs or undergo extensive training for a difficult position if doing so has no effect on their reward. Thus some inequality in the distribution of goods is required if people are to be motivated to be productive.

Rawls insists, however, that such inequalities are just only if they benefit everyone. We can see what this means by looking at the diagrams. Circle A represents an equal division. It is also the smallest of the three. Circle B has some inequality but is also larger. Circle C has more inequality and is larger still.

The key person for Rawls is person 4 because this person has the smallest share in the unequal distributions of B and C. The crucial difference for Rawls between B and C is that under the distribution in B, person 4, the least advantaged person, is better off than under the distribution in A, whereas under C, person 4 is worse off. Thus Rawls prefers B to C even though C is larger because only in B are the inequalities to everyone's advantage. That is, in B, but not C, everyone is better off than in A.

We should note that since its average is higher, C is the distribution that would be preferred by a utilitarian. Moreover, Rawls's objection to C is precisely the one we explored concerning utilitarianism. In C there has been an unfair trade. The welfare of person 4 has been traded for an increase in the average. It is just such trades that Rawls argues are unfair. The rejection of such trades suggests a key feature of Rawls's view and of his argument for his two principles. One may regard Rawls's principles as an attempt to express something of what it means to show respect for the equal dignity and worth of persons. Rawls is, in effect, saying that when we respect persons' worth, we do so by respecting their freedom of choice, by granting them a fair chance to earn their living, and by securing for them a fair share of available social goods. In understanding this system of rights, it is important in each case that respecting people's rights does not permit us to exchange their right for some increase in the average welfare. To have a right is to have it even if having it is inconsistent with some increment in the average welfare.

Applications of Justice as Fairness

To see how justice as fairness applies to the allocation of educational resources, we must first reaffirm that the point of justice as fairness is not to maximize happiness but is to promote fairness in life prospects.[15] Generally, the aspiration is to promote an equitable distribution of those social resources that are required by individuals, each of whom is pursuing his or her own conception of a good life. Departures from an equal division of these basic resources (primary goods) are justified only when such inequalities are to the benefit of those receiving the lesser share.

Educational resources either are primary goods or affect primary goods. Thus justice as fairness will have direct implications for how educational resources are allocated.

Consider the kind of distribution of educational resources that would satisfy the demands of equal liberty. An appropriate distribution might have four features. First, it will seek to achieve a level of education for everyone that guarantees access to a meaningful participation in the fundamental political institutions of a democratic society. In short, it will seek a wide dispersion of basic skills where what counts as basic is defined in terms of a connection with political competence. This is to say that it must first satisfy Gutmann's threshold principle.

Second, insofar as society aspires to provide a level of politically relevant skills beyond the minimum, it will continue to seek as even a distribution of these skills as possible. To put the point negatively, efforts should be made to prevent educational results that generate significant disparities in the ability to use political institutions to pursue one's interests.

Third, insofar as disparities in political competence are likely to result, the educational system should seek to distribute them in such a way that groups of individuals characterized by common interests do not lack for effective advocates. The disadvantageous consequences of political incompetence may be mitigated if people who lack political skills share common interests with those who possess them. To use an obvious example, the rights and interests of the handicapped, even the mentally handicapped, are better protected and pursued when some portion of handicapped persons become effective advocates for themselves.

Finally, such disparities in political competence as are likely to result from differences in individual capacity will be more morally acceptable to the extent that those who possess them are inclined to use them for the benefit of all. Such inequalities in political competence as are inevitable will be more acceptable to the extent that those who possess them are motivated by the public interest instead of personal gain.

The second principle applies most directly to those kinds of educational resources that affect income. It requires equal opportunity. However, the difference principle may set an even more demanding equity standard in that it may require us to be especially attentive to the educational needs of those whose levels of educational attainment are likely to put them among society's most disadvantaged.

Recall again that the difference principle requires us to strive to equalize life prospects unless inequalities benefit those with the lesser share. Applied to those kinds of educational resources that generate the capacity to produce income, this will mean that we must give preference to the educational requirements of less able students unless it can be shown that less able students will ultimately benefit more if resources are expended on the most able. There is, of course, no absolute requirement to prefer academic need to academic ability. There is, however, a requirement to promote equal life prospects unless those who are less well off gain from the increased productivity of those who are made better off.

Justice as fairness then leads to the following generalization about the allocation of educational resources. First, schools should emphasize basic skills. Basic skills, in fact, might be defined as those skills that are associated with primary goods. Generally this will mean that schools should emphasize the acquisition of skills required for political and economic participation. Second, justice as fairness will judge the fairness of a given allocation of resources largely by its results. The central goal is to equalize life prospects. Third, given that the point is to equalize life prospects, justice as fairness will emphasize educational need as a central criterion for allocating resources. Those who are less able as a rule will get a disproportionate share. Finally, justice as fairness permits inequalities in life prospects when everyone, especially the least advantaged, benefit.

Comparing Utilitarianism and Justice as Fairness

To recapitulate, I have been contrasting two general ways of thinking about justice in the allocation of educational resources—utilitarianism and justice as fairness. The general structure of these views is summarized in Table 6-1, which clarifies but oversimplifies matters considerably. It may, however, be helpful to attempt to distill the essential issues. Two matters are of great importance.

The first concerns what it means to have a right. Utilitarianism argues for rights in terms of their consequences. Rights are viewed as social arrangements that must be justified by showing that they promote the general welfare. This view of rights means that rights are seen as tentative things in that their availability depends on their consequences. Rights may be altered or suspended if they do not serve the general welfare. In this sense, rights may be traded for other benefits if the average welfare is enhanced thereby.

Justice as fairness, however, tends to see rights as inalienable in the sense that people are understood to have their rights simply by virtue of their being persons. Their possession of rights is not dependent on the consequences of their possessing these rights. Nor may people be deprived of their rights if their exercise or possession of them does not serve the general welfare.

Second, utilitarianism understands justice in a way that permits some people to benefit at the expense of others as long as the average welfare is enhanced. Justice as fairness does not. Inequalities are permissible only when everyone benefits as a consequence.

These issues may be expressed more simply as a single issue. Many central moral concepts are captured in the notion that human beings

Table 6-1. Utilitarianism versus Justice as Fairness.

	Utilitarianism	Justice as Fairness
What is distributed	Happiness	Primary goods
Central concept of justice	Justice requires promoting average welfare	Inequalities are justified only if they benefit those receiving the lesser share
Focus of distribution of educational resources	Invest to maximize productivity	Invest to promote equality of relevant political and economic skills
Favored criterion for resource allocation	Ability to profit	Need
Typical result	Disproportionate concentration of resources on high-ability students	Disproportionate concentration of resources on disadvantaged students

are objects of intrinsic value and, as such, are entitled to equal respect. The issue is, then, the extent to which the value of equal respect of persons permits trades between the welfare of individuals in order to promote the average welfare. To what extent can equality be traded for productivity? Utilitarianism can be regarded as holding that the value of equal respect for persons is consistent with such trades. Justice as fairness denies it.

Common practice in educational resource allocation seems to be utilitarian in its structure. It seems common to judge educational programs primarily on their effects on economic productivity in a way that is concerned more with maximizing production than with the distribution of the results of production. For example, the argument of *A Nation at Risk* (1983), a document that has received unparalleled attention among educators, seems largely utilitarian in its assumptions. The results of this chapter should suggest at least that utilitarian ways of thinking about educational resources are not self-evidently true and that a moral case can be made for patterns of resource allocation that are far more attentive to the needs of the disadvantaged.

SUMMARY

The principle that individuals have a right to their own conception of their own good constrains decisionmaking about resource allocation in two ways. First, collective decisions must be democratic rather than elitist. Democratic societies do not have experts in what is good for others. Second, even democratic decisionmaking must respect people's right to their own conception of their own good. Democratic choices cannot be motivated by the assumption that some vision of the good is to be preferred to some other.

A conception of equality of opportunity requires that parity of outcomes between groups be characterized by morally irrelevant criteria and that equal opportunity needs to be supplemented with the democratic threshold principle. Two general views of distributive justice—utilitarianism and justice as fairness—differ, as far as the allocation of educational resources is concerned, in that utilitarianism is most attentive to ability to profit whereas justice as fairness is more attentive to need. This chapter has not argued the merits of justice as fairness over utilitarianism but suggests that it should be treated as viable alternative to utilitarianism as the moral basis for the allocation of scarce productive resources.

NOTES

1. This volume's chief concern is resource allocation at the district level, but it is not clear that there are ethical issues that are unique to the district level. Moreover, it is clear that many issues of justice are interdistrict issues. That is especially true of issues of justice that are linked to taxation and the allocation of state resources to districts. Nevertheless, districts must allocate available resources among students and programs. They must do so in a just and fair way. Thus district administrators must have a concern for intradistrict fairness. In this chapter I will discuss a variety of problems, most of which have interdistrict application; I will, however, emphasize their intradistrict applications.

2. Of the views of justice reviewed below, utilitarianism is a consequentialist theory and justice as fairness is a nonconsequentialist theory.

3. This assertion raises a number of perplexing issues that I shall not discuss. One is the obligation to obey an unjust law. A law that produces an unjust consequence cannot be rendered morally acceptable merely because it was legitimately promulgated. It does not follow that we are not bound to obey it because it is morally defective. Second, there is a question about the nature of rights and whether the view that justice claims trump process claims extends to anything we might reasonably call a right. Here it is useful to distinguish between rights that might be created by some democratic process (such as the right to a driver's license) and rights that might be seen as fundamental in the sense that they are not created by any democratic process and might be held to express normative standards by means of which democratic decisions can be judged.

4. She is, for example, willing to exclude scientific creationism from public schools on the grounds that its commitment to faith instead of reason is inconsistent with the requirements of the long-term maintenance of democratic institutions. See Gutmann (1987: 103).

5. The distinction between morally relevant and morally irrelevant characteristics can be contextual. Religion, for example, may generally be irrelevant to how educational resources should be distributed, but it is surely not an irrelevant consideration if the educational resource is a theological education.

6. Suppose that the resources required for schools to succeed in promoting equal opportunity were finite but very large. Are schools or the society that supports them required to expend these resources? A full response to this question requires a fully developed view of justice. However, gener-

ally I suppose that the answer to this question is that there must be limits on the moral requirement to expend resources to promote equality. A resource-exhausting attempt to succeed in realizing one aspect of justice may lead to a withdrawal of resources from some program designed to realize some other moral principle that also has a claim on us. One of the roles of a comprehensive theory of justice is to order such competing claims.

7. See Gutmann (1987) for a variety of applications of this view.

8. This is an application of Rawls's principle of equal liberty described below. The caveat expressed in note 6 applies here as well.

9. See Strike (in press) for a Marxist view of equality of opportunity.

10. The fact that we are interested in intradistrict allocation of resources will mean that we need not consider noneducational uses for these resources.

11. For a philosophical appraisal of cost benefit analysis, see Bowie 1981: 143–217.

12. Portions of the final section of this chapter are adapted with permission from the Haller and Strike's (1986: 166–207) chapter on resource allocation and school achievement.

13. Note that a justification of a curriculum that emphasizes primary goods is neutral, in Ackerman's sense. Because primary goods are universal instrumentalities, no one's vision of a good life is affirmed or rejected.

14. The following remarks suggest that Rawls's view of equal opportunity are consistent with the view that I argued above. However, the reader should note that the applications of equal opportunity that follow assume not only Rawls's account but my development of it.

15. Rawls insists that his principles are to be applied to the basic structure of society (Rawls 1971: 7–10). They are not principles governing relations among individuals and are not generally to be used to analyze individual institutions apart from the rest. Nevertheless, if the basic structure of society is to be just, individual institutions must behave in certain ways. Thus I do not believe that it is inconsistent with Rawls's views to apply his principles to judge the justice of the allocative behavior of school districts. I believe that this would also be the case for other views of justice. It is important, however, to be clear that the fact that there are local applications of theories of justice does not mean that one may restrict one's reasoning to the evaluation of the local consequences of decisions. For example, someone who wishes to make a local decision on utilitarian standards will have to consider the consequences of that decision for everyone, not just for the individuals in that person's district. That theories of justice have microapplications is not a reason for preferring the interests of locals over the interests of others. To state the point more broadly, the microapplication of a principle of justice must take into account its full range of consequences and cannot be inconsistent with the macro application of the

same principle. Political subdivisions do not mark the bounds of moral responsibility.

REFERENCES

Ackerman, B. 1980. *Social Justice in the Liberal State*. New Haven, Conn.: Yale University Press.

Benn, S. I., and R. S. Peters. 1959. *The Principles of Political Thought*. New York: Free Press.

Bentham, Jeremy. 1961. *An Introduction to the Principles of Morals and Legislation*. Garden City, N.Y.: Doubleday.

Bowie, Norman E. 1981. "The Adequacy of Cost Benefit Analysis." In *Ethical Issues in Government*, edited by N. E. Bowie, pp. 143–217. Philadelphia: Temple University Press.

Bull, B. 1984. "Liberty and the New Localism: Toward an Evaluation of the Trade-Off between Educational Equity and Local Control of Schools." *Educational Theory* 34 (1): 75–94.

Coleman, James. 1974. "Inequality, Sociology, and Moral Philosophy." *American Journal of Sociology* 80 (November): 739–64.

Coleman, J. S., E. Q. Campbell, C. J. Hobson, J. McPartland, A. M. Mood, F. C. Weinfield, and R. L. York. 1966. *Equality of Educational Opportunity*. Washington, D.C.: U.S. Government Printing Office.

Cornford, Francis M. (translator). 1941. 1962. *The Republic of Plato*. New York: Oxford University Press.

Frankena, William K. 1965. *Three Historical Philosophies of Education: Aristotle, Kant and Dewey*. Chicago: Scott, Foresman.

Gutmann, Amy. 1987. *Democratic Education*. Princeton, N.J.: Princeton University Press.

Haller, Emil J., and Kenneth A. Strike. 1986. *An Introduction to Education Administration*. New York: Longman.

Jencks, C. S., M. Smith, H. Acland, M. Bane, D. Cohen, H. Gintis, B. Heyns, and S. Michelson. 1972. *Inequality: A Reassessment of the Effect of Family and Schooling in America*. New York: Harper & Row.

Locke, John. 1960. *Two Treatises of Government*, rev. ed. New York: Cambridge University Press.

Mill, J. S. 1956. *On Liberty*. New York: Bobbs-Merrill.

National Commission on Excellence in Education. 1983. *A Nation at Risk: The Imperative for Educational Reform*. Washington, D.C.: U.S. Government Printing Office.

Nozick, R. 1974. *Anarchy, State, and Utopia*. New York: Basic Books.

Rawls, John. 1971. *A Theory of Justice*. Cambridge, Mass.: Harvard University Press.

Smart, J.J.C., and Bernard Williams. 1973. *Utilitarianism: For and Against*, New York: Cambridge University Press.

Strike, Kenneth A. 1982. *Educational Policy and the Just Society*. Urbana: University of Illinois Press.

_____. 1984. "Fiscal Justice and Judicial Sovereignty: Plotting the Logic of a Slippery Slope." *Educational Theory* 34 (1) (Winter): 5–21.

Strike, K.A. In press. *Liberal Justice and the Marxist Critique of Education.* London: Routledge & Kegan Paul.

Wolff, R. 1968. *The Poverty of Liberalism.* Boston: Beacon Press.

II MICROLEVEL EDUCATIONAL PRODUCTIVITY

7 THE MICROECONOMICS OF LEARNING
Students, Teachers, and Classrooms

Byron W. Brown

The microeconomics of schooling is concerned with theoretical and empirical aspects of resource allocation at the level of the student, classroom, and school.[1] As with all economic analyses, it emphasizes the conflict between limited resources and unlimited desires. We know that classrooms have a limited amount of a teacher's time, a given number of computer terminals, only so many teacher's aides, books, and so on. Yet we want to maximize each child's learning potential. The scarcity of resources forces us to make difficult choices about which children in a school get the greatest amounts of resources and services. Therefore, spending another fifteen minutes a day on math means spending less time on reading, social studies, or recess. Decisions about these tradeoffs determine who gets what in classrooms and consequently dictate the distribution of learning outcomes across students.

The microeconomics of schooling can also be a valuable aid in thinking about controversial issues. For example, what is the likely effect of having more computers in schools, what is the effect of increasing the length of the school day or year, and under what circumstances would merit pay for teachers improve our schools?

Microeconomic theory analyzes classrooms and schools as if they were firms using scarce resource inputs in the production of a variety of educational outputs. The branch of economics known as the theory of the firm seems ready made to help us understand the rules of optimal school resource allocation and distribution. What makes using the theory of the firm to understand schools an interesting exercise, however, is that schools do not conform in many ways to the standard notion of the "firm."

For example, firms usually are assumed to try to maximize profits. Schools, at least those publicly operated, do not. Firms usually produce a well-defined product or service and sell it on the open market. Schools produce many services, some difficult to measure, and they are not financed by market sales. Many firms produce their products or services in assembly-line fashion, and the standard version of economic theory seems to incorporate this as an assumption. An example is an automobile production assembly line. Schools, on the other hand, are more like job shops, firms in which each item has different operations or treatments performed on it. An example is an automobile repair shop. As we shall see in what follows, a sensible analysis of schools as firms requires accounting for a multitude of public schooling's unique features.

The plan of this chapter is first to present the theoretical outline of the economics of students and classrooms. Then a small series of policy issues will be taken up by reviewing recent research. These topics include instructional time, ability grouping, computers, and effective schools. We turn first to the basic theoretical model used to explore the issues.

MICROECONOMIC THEORY OF SCHOOLS: THE STUDENT

Education in the United States has prided itself on its concern for the development of the individual student's learning potential. The student as the focus of education has become so ingrained in our thinking about schools that we take it for granted. That individuals matter, after all, is what the arguments concerning equity in education are all about. If individual students did not matter, we would not be so concerned about the distribution of schooling among them. It is not surprising, then, for an economic analysis of schooling to begin with the student.

Each student is presumed to have a learning curve that will determine the level of learning as a function of that student's characteristics and the resources devoted to the learning process. The notion of the learning curve is directly analogous to the production function in the microeconomic analysis of the firm, and I use the terms interchangeably. The production function describes relationships between inputs and outputs. In addition to its listing the inputs or resources used in production, the production function tells us the maximum amount of output associated with any input combination. A key objective in empirical research has been to estimate the learning curve—that is, to find factors that affect learning and estimate the magnitudes of their effects. The production function itself is a black box into which flow inputs and out of which issue educational outputs. Generally, more inputs lead to more output, and substitution among inputs is possible. The learning curve is simply assumed to exist, and neither teachers nor economists need to know the molecular biology of how inputs end up as learning.

Studies measuring the learning curve have often used results of standardized test scores as output measures. For example, Summers and Wolfe (1977) used the Iowa Test of Basic Skills (composite) to measure sixth-grade and third-grade achievement. Brown and Saks (1975) used the Michigan Educational Assessment Program data, and Brown and Saks (1987) used the Beginning Teacher Evaluation Study (Fisher et al. 1978), which measured reading and mathematics skills of some California grade schoolers. SAT scores and ACT scores are widely used as output assessment measures, both for individual students and in the aggregate.

Measures other than test scores have sometimes been used as schooling outcomes. Among them are student attitudes, socialization measures (Bowles and Gintis 1976), and school dropout rates. These measures have been especially popular in studies linking school performance to subsequent labor market performance (Saks 1986).

Even though achievement scores are often incomplete and imperfect measures of schooling outcomes, they do have the advantage of being easily quantifiable. They are usually also the first thing people think about when assessing school performance. In what follows, schooling outcomes are usually identified with achievement scores, in most cases simply as a convenience to aid thinking about the production problem. The benefits from using economics in thinking about schools do not depend on the particular definition of output the analyst has in mind. Indeed, it is the multiplicity of outputs that makes the study of schools economically interesting.

The independent variables in the learning curve include all factors affecting a student's achievement. Among these are the student's prior achievement level and other characteristics that affect the ability to learn, and the amounts of resources devoted to learning over the period being studied.

Just as with outputs, controversy has emerged over the nature of schooling inputs and their measurement. The controversy had its origin in the inability of many studies to demonstrate a significant, stable relationship between output (usually achievement scores) and any school inputs. Published studies have found positive effects on learning for some input variables some of the time, but as Hanushek (1986: 1162) has noted: "The results are startlingly consistent in finding no strong evidence that teacher-student ratios, teacher education, or teacher experience have an expected positive effect on student achievement."

The lack of an observed relationship between achievement and schooling inputs in a variety of studies has been explained in two related ways: faulty input data specification and faulty modeling of the schooling process.

As an example of faulty data specification, consider the relationship between student achievement and the number of days the student attended school during the year. The number of days attending is likely to be a poor proxy for time spent learning or other school resources more directly related to the student's learning. There is simply too much variation across schools in how time is used to be able to tell much from attendance about how time affects learning. If we believe that time devoted to learning is an important input, then better measures than attendance can, at a cost, be obtained. We should not, however, reject the hypothesis that learning time is an important input because of a weak or absent relation between attendance and achievement.

Another example of faulty input specification is the use of measures of teacher qualifications as input variables in the learning curve. These could include whether teachers have master's degrees or how many years of experience they possess. These variables are probably included to measure the teacher's competence and ability in organizing classroom resources. Because these variables are not direct measures of the actual learning resources received by the student, however, the statistical relationship between these measures and learning may be weak or absent. The studies in Hanushek's (1986) survey confirm that teachers' education and experience seem unrelated to their students' achievement.

Students in Classrooms

One of the principal difficulties in interpreting the results of empirical studies of input effectiveness has been the use of poorly or incorrectly specified models of learning (Brown and Saks 1981). Somewhat surprisingly, many of the modeling defects derive from a failure to recognize that students are most often taught in classes. In many cases the analysis of student learning has proceeded on the assumption, sometimes implicit, that students are always tutored or that all students in a class are treated in exactly the same way by the teacher. The assumption turns out not to be an innocuous one for understanding the production of learning for real students in real schools. We know that classes have a complex organizational structure under the managerial supervision of a teacher. Students must learn several subjects; they have different prior learning levels and abilities to learn; teachers may employ a variety of scheduling and grouping strategies for dealing with these complications.

The heterogeneity of student abilities and the diversity of learning outcomes imply that it is erroneous to treat the class as a homogeneous unit. Yet this is what is usually done in the analysis of classroom or school level data, and in many cases at the individual student level. When students are taught in classes, a correct specification and estimation of a student's learning curve requires that the group nature of instruction be taken into account. In the first place, we should be careful to recognize that in classrooms the effect of a minute of instruction depends on the context in which it is provided. A student receiving instruction in, say, mathematics would probably learn a different amount if the student were part of a group than if the student were tutored individually. In the second place, the classroom provides opportunities for teachers to be innovative resource managers in grouping students and subjects. There will be complex interdependence both between the students in a class and between learning in different subjects. This has led to excellent research on the effect of ability groupings and on the integration of subject matter teaching. Some of the current research on ability grouping will be discussed later. The point here is that the microeconomic theory of classroom recourse allocation suggests this is an important issue.

To illustrate these ideas, and to see how a study of the microeconomics of the problem can assist our understanding, take the stylized example of two students being taught as a class under the supervision of a teacher. The teacher has only so much time available for instruction. In the simplest case, the teacher may tutor each student in a subject (say, math) but not teach both together as a class. While one student is tutored, the other is assumed to be engaged in "seatwork." If the teacher's total time to allocate is limited, the results of the instruction for this stylized classroom can be summarized as a production possibilities (or product transformation) curve in the students' scores.

Figure 7-1 illustrates the analysis. Point M shows the achievement levels of the students before instruction. Student 1 began with math skills at M_1, more than student 2, who had M_2. These prior achievement levels are the combined results of the students' abilities and the instruction they have received both at home and in school. With tutoring instruction over a period of time the entire range of final outcomes along ZZ' is available. The shape and position of the curve representing final outcomes depends on total available time and on the underlying learning curves for the two students.[2] If tutoring time is more productive with student 1, for example, that student's maximum potential achievement will be greater. Where the students will end up in relative achievement along ZZ' is a function of the time allocation between them, which will be determined by the goals of the teacher and others. The conclusion is that a particular student's learning is as much the result of teacher choices about how to allocate resources within a class as it is on the total resources available to a class.

Because resources place limits on learning and because resource substitution among students is possible, teachers have at least two important roles to play. One is to use resources efficiently to get on the production possibilities curve, instead of being stuck inside it. In Figure 7-1, points inside the curve, such as C, involve wasted classroom resources because more learning is possible for both students. Economists usually assume that this sort of inefficiency does not occur and that learning takes place along ZZ'. This may be a poor assumption in the case of schools, and later on I offer an interpreta-

Figure 7-1. Learning Limits and Trade-off Possibilities When Students Are Taught in Classes.

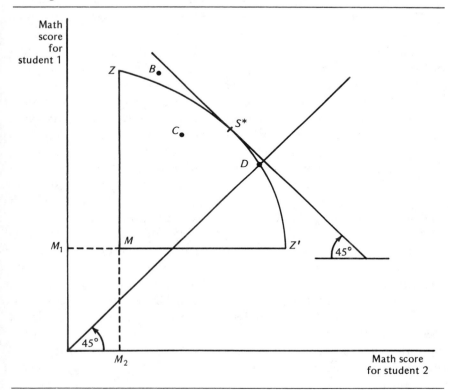

tion of the effective schools literature that relies on this idea. The second role for teachers is to decide how unequal the distribution of learning will be in a class. The most egalitarian outcome of instruction in Figure 7–1, point D, and the most unequal outcome, point Z, are only two of the possibilities. Teacher preferences, shaped by the pressures from principals, parents, and schools of education, will determine the result.

Comparing average test scores across schools and school districts has become common practice in some states, the idea being that better schools have higher mean scores. We can use Figure 7–1 to show that this is a highly questionable process. There is no reason to believe that the best distribution of scores coincides with maximizing the mean. Despite the rhetoric, the mean would be a strange thing to want to maximize because that would boil down to giving an equal weight to score gains by all students, regardless of their levels of prior achievement or other characteristics. In Figure 7–1, the average score in the class is maximized only by allocating time so that the students end up at point S^*. This is only one of the multitude of possible outcomes along ZZ' that might be judged best by the school authorities. Comparisons of mean achievement scores across classes or even school districts are in general not meaningful simply because school authorities and teachers do not allocate resources to maximize the mean. Evidence reported later is consistent with teachers' not maximizing the average and giving more weight to improving the scores of lower-ability students.

The basic microeconomic model also helps explore the effects of having more classroom resources. Expanding the time devoted to instruction, for example, will move the production possibilities curve farther from the origin so that more learning is possible for both students. But as the total time grows, we will experience diminishing *marginal* returns, and the extra learning from more time spent learning may be small, even though the total amount learned may be large. A failure to distinguish between the *total* and *marginal* returns to a schooling input would give a misleading impression of the worth of a resource. Smaller marginal returns are the inevitable result of more intensive use of an input and should not be used to judge the "importance" of the input. The reader should be aware that it is just these *marginal* returns that are measured in production function or input/output studies of schooling.[3]

What if the students whose learning outcomes are shown in Figure 7–1 are grouped and taught together as a class? The effects are complicated. If the combined tutoring time is used instead in whole class instruction, the production possibilities curve is reduced to a point. No learning tradeoff across students is possible because each is the mutual recipient of the class time, but each student will get more time from the teacher with grouped instruction than with tutoring. The question is whether that extra time more than makes up for the inability to individualize the instruction. The point in Figure 7–1 representing the result of whole class instruction may, as a result of these conflicting effects, lie either inside (point C) or outside (point B) the learning possibilities for tutoring.

Some insights into measuring the relation between schooling inputs and learning can be gleaned from even this simple and idealized analysis. One is that when the individual student is the focus, we can hope to measure the learning curve only by observing the inputs applied to that student, not simply the aggregate available to the whole class or school. In Figure 7-1 the same total amount of instructional time can yield quite different outcomes depending on how it is applied. Another is that even when the student is the focus we cannot ignore the classroom context in which instruction takes place. How students are grouped and the characteristics of classmates are important. Finally, schooling outcomes that do not maximize the average scores of students may be preferred by school authorities. Comparisons of mean achievement scores across classes or even school districts are, in general, not meaningful exercises in measuring efficiency.

CLASSROOM ORGANIZATION AND ESTIMATING LEARNING CURVES

A correct estimation of students' learning curves must take into account the fact that students are taught in classes. The shape and position of each student's learning curve will vary with the number, ability, and other characteristics of classmates. The possibility of whole class instruction or ability grouping, in addition to tutoring, creates management options for teachers to exploit the possibilities of grouping.

The next sections report on two kinds of studies that have examined student learning curves, in the context of the classroom, using resource measures that directly impinge on the students. The first reports the results of a study of the effects of time allocations on reading and math scores of elementary school students. The second reports the results of two studies of the effects of ability grouping on student learning.

Time Allocation and Learning

Brown and Saks (1987) have estimated learning curves for individual students taught in classrooms using data from the Beginning Teacher Evaluation Study (BTES). The BTES collected math and reading test scores at three points in a school year on about a half dozen pupils in each of twenty-one fifth- and twenty-five second-grade classrooms. Detailed information was also gathered on the amounts of time allocated to each of the pupils in each subject, as well as on how the time was used (whether the student was working alone or in a group, whether the lesson was self-paced or other-paced, and so forth).

One of Brown and Saks' objectives was to explore the extent to which additional instructional time increased learning, and whether this varied by subject, grade level, and how the time was used in the classroom. The authors reported that total allocated time had significant positive effects on learning in both grades in both subjects. They found that there was significant variation across teachers in the effectiveness of time spent on mathematics, but not in reading. This may reflect less agreement among teachers on how math should be taught or simply some teachers' dislike for teaching math.

On average, each 1 percent increase in time increased reading scores by about .13 percent in grade two and by .07 percent in grade five. There is a similar drop for mathematics with the results of a 1 percent increase in time dropping from .24 percent in grade two to near zero in grade five. The decreased effectiveness of time in fifth grade compared to second grade may reflect the increasing difficulty of the material.

Time was consistently more productive with low-ability than high-ability students. With the exception of fifth-grade mathematics, the context in which students received instructional time did not seem to matter for learning. Grouping students for math instruction in fifth grade seemed to have significant positive effects on learning.

Brown and Saks also examined teachers' preferences for increasing or reducing the variance of student achievement within classes as revealed by teacher time allocations. Most of the teachers in the sample used compensating strategies. That is, the teachers consistently allocated more time to slower students and thus reduced the spread of achievement.

Ability Grouping and Learning

One of the most common instructional strategies used by teachers is the formation of ability groups. Economic theory suggests that whether to form ability groups is a complex decision with the factors of class size, the degree of heterogeneity of student abilities, and other student characteristics coming into play. Two issues raised by the practice of grouping are why teachers form groups at all, and how grouping affects the level and distribution of learning outcomes in a class. Both class size and heterogeneity in student abilities are primary factors in understanding the issues.[4]

Changing class size affects achievement even if the distribution of student abilities is constant, and teachers may deal with the undesirable effects of larger class sizes by forming smaller groups for instruction. When class size increases, certain kinds of management problems confronting the teacher are exacerbated. In larger classes the mere mechanics of distributing and collecting papers means there will be less time available for instruction. In larger classes teachers find it more difficult to hold students' attention or control behavior so that a given amount of whole class instructional time will tend to be less effective because of lower student engagement rates.

The microeconomic model developed by Monk (1984) suggests that the switch point at which forming small groups becomes worthwhile is determined both by the relative productivity of classroom resources in the large and small groups and by the preferences of teachers for certain outcome distributions. Productivity enters the decision to form groups because the declining effectiveness of whole class instruction as size increases makes it beneficial to bear the trouble of forming and monitoring groups. That is, the net gain from having groups must be greater than the net gain from the extra time the students get in whole class instruction. Grouping may occur even in relatively small classes if the teacher prefers a distribution of learning outcomes very different from what would occur with whole class instruction. For example, if the teacher valued highly a great variance in learning outcomes, this could be accomplished by forming a subgroup to receive most of the instructional resources.

In their study of class size and achievement Hallinan and Sørensen (1985) argue that class size affects two aspects of the inputs a student receives. The first is the length of instruction and the second is the quality of instruction. Larger classes shorten the length of instruction, as we stated above, by increasing the administrative burden of running a class and leaving less time available to teach. With a larger class the quality of instruction will fall because the teacher will be less able to adapt feedback and instruction to student learning styles.

What are their results on the effects on achievement of class size and ability grouping? They find, after controlling for race, prior ability, and gender, that it is ability group size rather than class size that affects achievement. In classes in which the teacher used only whole class instruction, no class size effects were found. Thus it seems to be through instructional subgrouping that size affects achievement.

Consider now the consequences of varying degrees of heterogeneity among students in whole class instruction. If students in a class tend to be similar in background, learning levels, and ability to learn, then it is more likely that a teacher, in tailoring instruction to one of the students, will find it unnecessary to readapt instruction to others. Because one teaching tactic or explanation is effective for many students at once, there is an obvious economy in the use of the teacher's time. The teacher does not need to make three different explanations of a lesson to adapt it to three different abilities of heterogeneous students when the class is already homogeneous.[5]

Sørensen and Hallinan (1986) expanded their research on classrooms using an elaborate and clever theory of individual student learning to explore the effects of ability grouping on reading achievement. They suggest that grouping affects what is taught and emphasize the importance of "opportunities for learning," a concept they intend to capture the variety of content covered. Of the material to which students are exposed, different students will learn different amounts, depending on ability and effort. The authors point out that one possible effect of ability grouping is increased homogeneity of students in a group with the result that the teacher can cover more material. Thus there may be more opportunities for learning in homogeneous groups. As was pointed out above, however, the presence of grouping may mean less instructional time for the students in a group compared to the amount a student would get in whole class instruction.

Sørensen and Hallinan (1986) found, somewhat counterintuitively, that students in grouped classes are exposed to fewer opportunities for learning. It seems that less is taught or covered in subgroups compared to whole class instruction. Moreover, it appears in their data that grouped students have either higher ability and/or effort and therefore learn more of what is taught.[6] On balance it appears that these two effects offset each other and that the grouped and ungrouped students end up learning about the same amount. Thus, there is no net effect of grouping.

Sørensen and Hallinan explored another important aspect of ability grouping that is suggested by the microeconomic theory of schooling. They asked whether the formation of groups leads to larger differentials among students in learning outcomes. They found that inequality in achievement across students is increased by grouping. In particular, there was evidence that more opportunities for learning were provided for high-ability groups and that high-ability students were taught more.

COMPUTERS IN SCHOOLS

Historians of education tell us that school technology is remarkably stable and unchanging, and this in the face of a technological revolution in the workplace and the home. Transportation, agricultural production, and communications have changed dramatically over the last fifty years thanks to technological development. Yet society has chosen continually to organize the production of elementary and secondary schooling by collecting students together in classes of modest size (less than thirty or forty students), usually segregated by age, and under the supervision of a teacher.

Now comes the computer into the classroom. It is heralded by some (for example, Papert 1980) as a device that can change the role of the teacher, help students learn more efficiently, and even change the way students think. It has received more advance notice of revolutionary promise than any teaching tool since instructional television in the 1950s. It is sobering to be reminded (see Cuban 1986) of the unfulfilled promise of ITV and to see how little it has, over a quarter of a century, changed how we teach in schools. Of course, television has had social impacts. It has, for example, been a prime candidate to take the blame for a declining trend in SAT scores. In the classroom, however, the extent of its use is a faint shadow of its promise. Will the computer revolutionize education? Or will it become one of the changes that will modestly affect how teachers teach, still in the context of traditional classrooms?

The microeconomics of schooling can assist us in understanding the nature of computers' likely impact. It provides the structure within which we can see the variety of changes likely to be brought about by technology. Because computers change the resource base of the classroom, their presence will expand the production possibilities curve outward. More learning will be possible for the students in a class. Moreover, the presence of computers may not only affect learning in terms of traditional outcomes but also create new kinds of learning.

Analyses of the impact of computer use have identified at least two effects on student learning. The first is the impact on learning in traditional subject areas such as math and language skills. Here the computer is an instrument of instruction. Computers have been used in this way as drill and practice aids in math and as electronic textbooks for teaching new material. Word processing software makes the revision and printing of written work quicker and easier, which can improve writing skills. These effects are brought about by an expansion of the resource base in the classroom. In terms of the microeconomics of classrooms, computers are expected to shift outward the production possibilities curve of students' achievement levels or test scores. If the potential of the computers as a successful innovation is to be met, then they must expand significantly the range of obtainable learning outcomes.

This kind of computer use in traditional subjects may have complex effects on classroom organization. Just as variations in the relative productivities of tutoring versus grouped instruction can give rise to a variety of classroom organizations, the productivity of computers will ultimately determine how classrooms look as productive organizations. Traditional classrooms may disappear for some subjects, and the number and kind of teachers may change.

In addition to being an instrument of instruction, the computer also may be the object of instruction. This second effect of the presence of computers on learning is the creation of a new kind of educational outcome: knowing about computers and computer programming. To the extent that schools use their computers to teach computer use and programming to students, the worth of those skills needs to be evaluated separately from the effects on reading, writing, or math. The extra outputs do not show up as an outward shift in the production possibilities curve for students' reading scores, say, but as a new dimension in output space. This has implications for evaluating the cost effectiveness of computers. Unless we include all outputs, we will undervalue the benefits derived from using computers.

It is worthwhile at this point to review the facts about how computers are used in schools. Two national surveys of computer use in schools were undertaken in 1983 and 1985 and have been analyzed by Becker (1983, 1983–84, 1984a, 1984b, 1984c, 1984–85, 1987). There were far more computers in schools in 1985 than there were in 1983. The number of students and time use doubled, and the number of computers quadrupled. Although it is now true that the "typical high school has more than 20 computers, and the typical elementary school has 6" (Becker 1987: 149), there are still not enough in use to provide a substantial degree of computer use by students, either in programming instruction or in word processing or computer-assisted instruction (CAI).

The microeconomics of schooling predicts significant differences in resource productivity and use across students. Becker's report on the computer survey confirms wide variation in who uses computers and how they are used.

The proportion of students using computers falls significantly from elementary to high school. Less than one-half of elementary students and only about one-third of high school students use a computer *at all* in school. Use in elementary schools is generally spotty, it is characterized by short time use, and often days or weeks go by between uses. In high school the use is more intensive, and it is dominated by juniors and seniors.

Significant variation exists in how computers are used in instruction as students progress through the grades. More than half the time in elementary schools is used in CAI, while high school students spend only 16 percent of their computer time on CAI and about 50 percent on programming. In high school, the computer is more often the object of instruction rather than the "medium of instruction or a productivity tool."

Perhaps not surprisingly, computer use varied across student ability levels. The 1985 survey showed that at all grade levels high-ability students use computers more than low-ability students. Within this pattern there are variations in how the students in varying ability levels use computers. Low-ability students use computers in elementary school for instruction primarily, while the distinguishing feature of high-ability students is their propensity to do computer programming. It is also interesting to note that high- and low-ability students are affected differently by computer use. Low-ability students using computers improve motivation, confidence, and self-discipline. This may be a reflection of the ways students with different ability levels use computers. At lower ability levels the emphasis is on CAI for basic math and language arts skills. At higher ability levels there is more emphasis on higher-order thinking skills, programming, science, and writing. These effects are compounded by the fact that higher-ability students are more likely to have a computer in the home.

Overall it appears that so far computers have had only a limited impact on instruction. High-ability students have had a dramatic increase in programming instruction. Word processing has become more important in high school, but it is still not the regular means by which students prepare papers, essays, and reports. Computers are not predominant tools in the teaching of math and science.

What can microeconomics contribute to our understanding of the current pattern of computer use in schools? Suppose that teachers' preferences with respect to the distribution of learning outcomes across students have been relatively constant over time. There is no evidence to suggest that preferences have changed over time, at least with respect to the traditional subject matter, so the stability of preferences is probably a reasonable assumption. In this case, the use of computers with lower-ability students in elementary schools is strong evidence that they are relatively more productive with those students than with higher-ability students.[7] That is not to say that there are not significant benefits to high-ability students, for the computers may free up some of the teacher's time, which can then be devoted to the higher-ability students. Indeed, computers may be an example of a change in technology that is biased in favor of low-ability students but also benefits higher-ability students. We would not expect computer time to be allocated equally in a well-run classroom any more than we would expect equal use across students of other resources.

The use of computers mostly by high-ability students in the teaching of programming (the computer as *object* of instruction) is quite another case. This represents a new output of schooling and not a simple expansion of production possibilities in traditional subjects. That high-ability students in high school use computers more in programming may reflect either the greater productivity of computers with those students in that application or the greater preferences of teachers to have those students have those particular kinds of skills. The current pattern of use increases the variance in educational outcomes. But this may be the result of the high value of that kind of knowledge for high-ability students because it may be highly complementary with the high school subjects those students traditionally study (math and science), not that such students are in some sense better at programming. All we really know at this point is that the current way in which computers are used to teach programming makes educational outcomes more unequal.

This discussion illustrates a crucial point of the microeconomic theory of schooling. When the individual student matters, we must pay attention to the differential effects of resource use. First, this involves discovering differences among students in the productivity of a resource, which in turn sets the shape and position of the production possibilities curve. Second, it compels us to examine how the resource is distributed across students as well as how it is used by students. With this knowledge in hand, it becomes possible to determine the learning outcomes of students along the relevant production possibilities curve.

EFFECTIVE SCHOOLS

One branch of the research studying the determinants of student achievement has approached the problem by finding schools that are outliers in producing achievement and then subjecting these to intense scrutiny to find the secrets of their success. The schools in question are invariably inner-city schools, schools that face the problem of recruitment and retention of good teachers. Why some of the schools attain a remarkable degree of success in promoting student achievement is the subject of the effective schools research. The purpose of this section is to review a few highpoints of the effective schools research and to show its relation to the microeconomic theory of schooling.

Rosenholz (1985) has done an extensive evaluation of the effective schools literature. Although she uncovers several serious problems with the research in the area, she finds some common, strong findings that seem to hold up across the studies. She reports finding within the research (1) that schools that were described as "turnaround" schools became so because of changes in organizational conditions and (2) that about a third of the between school variations in achievement can be accounted for by differences in organizational characteristics.

In Rosenholz's view, good inner-city schools all center on the principal. Although the teacher is the person directly involved in delivering the resources of the classroom to students, the principal plays a crucial role. Successful schools have principals who have the mission of improved student achievement and an absolute certainty that achievement goals can be met. The principals recruit teachers who have similar goals, and the principal manages to imbue in teachers the spirit that they will succeed. The principals and teachers in effective schools form team bonds that assist in communicating ideas and other forms of help in achieving their goals. This all sounds very simple, but the skills required in a successful principal cannot, in this view, be overestimated. The effective principal is a master of recruitment, teaching strategy, organizational and motivational tools, and a monitor of the complexities of school organization.

The existence of effective schools and educational researchers' analyses of them presents a significant challenge to the microeconomic theory of schooling on two fronts. The first is that the existence of effective schools as an *exception* makes the presence of inefficiency the *rule*. Yet economists almost always interpret the choices made by people and firms to be the efficient result of careful calculation and optimizing behavior. Underlying this challenge is the idea that market prices and costs provide the discipline for efficient behavior, and it is the absence of market information in schools that makes them inefficient. How can the economic analysis of efficiency based on markets be a useful tool in understanding inefficiency in a nonmarket setting?

The second challenge is that effective schools seem based on maximizing the efforts of teachers and students. Yet economic theories seem to neglect the idea of effort. When workers are used in production, those workers are assumed to be inert and used to maximum effect, the way machines or raw materials would enter the process. There is a one-to-one relationship between the quantities of inputs and output, so the production possibilities curve is well defined. What can be the meaning of the production possibilities curve setting limits to output if we can get more output from the same inputs by simply getting people to work harder?

Understanding the response of economists to these challenges lies first in realizing that their theories of behavior in fact do not rely on the existence of markets, but rather on the presence of scarcity and on the desires of people to do the best they can under the circumstances. Markets, when they exist, only provide the constraints under which people and firms must make choices. A nonmarket environment, such as the internal organization of a school, creates its own incentives and restraints within which people optimize choices. The usefulness of economic analysis is not restricted to market settings. That the incentives and restraints within a school are not externally imposed but arise with the organization itself in no way changes the essence of the resource allocation problem.

Recall that it was nonmarket forces, the optimization of teachers' preferences, that provided the incentives for efficient production of learning and the allocation of resources within classrooms. The microeconomics of learning does not rely exclusively on market prices and costs, or indeed on a market setting, to define efficient outcomes. One important lesson of the economic model of classrooms is that, even in a nonmarket setting, changing the structure of rewards (teacher utility) and constraints (learning curves) will change behavior.

On the other hand, it is true that economists have usually assumed away the concept of worker effort as an aspect of production, with the result that a manager's problem is reduced simply to determining the best combination of inputs. For teachers and schools this amounts to assuming that learning always takes place on the production possibilities curve and not "inside" it. But certainly our conception of decisionmaking within schools need not be so simplistic.

Consideration of the analysis of effort incorporates the theoretical framework erected earlier but must also go beyond it. Economist Harvey Leibenstein (1980) has constructed a theory of the firm that includes effort. His work is linked in many respects to that of Herbert Simon (1957). Parts of Leibenstein's model can be applied directly to understanding teachers and schooling, and the model is consistent with the evidence on effective schools. As applied to teachers, Leibenstein's theory would have us focus on effort by looking at the pace of their activities and the quality with which teaching activities are done. Because teachers can choose the pace of work and quality with which tasks are performed, this theory incorporates our earlier assumption that teachers have a good deal of control over the work environment in which they operate and that they are decisionmakers in their own right.

Pace and the quality of work—the two components of effort that affect student learning—matter both to the teacher expending effort and to the school in which the teacher is employed. The objective for a school, perhaps through its agent the principal, is to find the set of rewards and incentives to manage teacher effort that will ultimately maximize the outputs of the school. Note that we do not necessarily wish to maximize teacher effort. High levels of teacher effort may be associated with high levels of pace (speed) or intensity, which in turn may be associated with low levels of work quality (sloppiness).

In this conception, the components of effort are simply additional inputs to be managed effectively. They should be used in optimal amounts (not necessarily maximized), and the amount of effort we observe in a given classroom or school is the result of the rewards and constraints constructed in that setting. In no sense can good management repeal the fact of scarce resources. Good management organizes resources efficiently; it moves learning outcomes toward the possibilities curve. But good principals and teachers cannot realize ever improving results with fixed resources.

CONCLUSION

The microeconomics of learning focuses on the scarcity and efficient allocation of educational resources. Through the choice of a few examples, this essay emphasizes primarily the role of teachers and principals as decisionmakers and examines the implications of their resource allocation decisions for individual students' learning. More than anything else the economics of learning is one way of looking at the consequences of schooling alternatives: better ways of allocating time or organizing classrooms, using more computers in instruction, or finding schemes to optimize the work efforts of teachers.

The analysis of time allocation points out the nature of the trade-offs teachers confront in choosing grouped or whole class instruction. It emphasizes the role of class size and heterogeneity in trying to organize teaching and elevates the question of the distribution of learning among students in a class to a central position.

Computers, the economic analysis tells us, can be expected to influence the output possibilities of schools in complex ways. Computers create new kinds of learning outcomes such as programming, but they also expand the set of traditional outcomes such as writing. It is certainly too early to tell whether computers will revolutionize schooling. Not enough computers are currently in schools, not enough teachers know how to use them effectively in instruction, and not enough software exists to enable us to see clearly their long-run potential. Microeconomics tells us that for computers to fulfill the promise of their optimistic proponents they must improve the learning outcomes in traditional subjects and/or create sufficiently valuable new kinds of learning. In addition, they must do this more cheaply than alternative modes of instruction.

The effective schools literature emphasizes the crucial role of managerial resources. These resources, while scarce, are not, the economic analysis suggests, in the exclusive domain of principals. The organization of production in schools does not conform to the usually assumed private-sector dichotomy in which workers, the actual producers, are overseen and monitored by managers. The microeconomic theory developed in this chapter sees teachers, the actual producers in schools, as having important managerial functions. Principals and teachers interact in a nonmarket setting, making choices about teacher effort and other inputs that in the end determine learning outcomes.

NOTES

1. Microeconomics, theoretical and applied, focuses on the smallest decision-making unit in an economic world. The standard units are "firms" and "consumers," but those are symbolic. Some aggregations of the basic units are usually analyzed in micro theory ("firms" are grouped into "industries"), but the locus of decisionmaking power at the smallest level is never lost to sight. Macroeconomics looks only at relations among aggregates. National income theory, for example, explores the relationships among national consumption, employment income, prices, and so forth. If there were a macroeconomics of schooling (the term has never been used as far as I know), it would examine issues such as the rate of return to schooling and aggregative relations among spending, achievement, and revenues in the school finance literature. *Economics* in this chapter means *microeconomics*.

2. I am assuming that the students are passive recipients of instructional inputs. By taking the learning curves as given and known to the teacher, I am abstracting from student effort and incentives to manipulate it. For a discussion of the role of rewards for effort see Brown and Saks (1981: 241–47).

3. The idea of the total return to a *single* input does not have a sensible meaning when there are many inputs. Many resources are combined to produce learning in a complex way, and the total effect of one of them cannot be isolated. Six men and six shovels move thirty yards of earth an hour. It is ridiculous to say, for example, that the men moved fifteen and the shovels fifteen.

4. Note that increasing student heterogeneity and increasing class size are quite different phenomena, and the existence of one does not imply the other.

5. On the other hand, if the classroom is heterogeneous in ability, the teacher may try to make an explanation of a lesson directed to an average student in the class, or the teacher may set the pace of instruction to accommodate a particular level of ability. This phenomenon has been investigated in the education literature (see Dahllof 1971), and researchers have found that teachers set the pace of instruction so that students in the tenth to twenty-fifth percentiles in the class are just able to keep up. Teachers, in this notion, identify "steering groups" that serve to guide the instructional efforts and presentation.

6. The authors maintain there is some ambiguity in this result because it depends on a statistical procedure to control for sample selection bias.

7. This may be the result of currently available software and not an inherent characteristic of computer use. Development of new kinds of software may change this conclusion.

REFERENCES

Becker, Henry Jay. 1983. "School Uses of Microcomputers: Report #1 from a National Survey." *Journal of Computers in Mathematics and Science Teaching* 3 (1) (Fall): 29–33.

_____ . 1983–84. "School Uses of Microcomputers: Report #2 from a National Survey." *Journal of Computers in Mathematics and Science Teaching* 3 (2) (Winter): 16–21.

_____ . 1984a. "School Uses of Microcomputers: Report #3 from a National Survey." *Journal of Computers in Mathematics and Science Teaching* 3 (3) (Spring): 26–32.

_____ . 1984b. "School Uses of Microcomputers: Report #4 from a National Survey." *Journal of Computers in Mathematics and Science Teaching* 3 (4) (Summer): 24–33.

_____ . 1984c. "School Uses of Microcomputers: Report #5 from a National Survey." *Journal of Computers in Mathematics and Science Teaching* 4 (1) (Fall): 38–42.

_____ . 1984–85. "School Uses of Microcomputers: Report #6 from a National Survey." *Journal of Computers in Mathematics and Science Teaching* 4 (2) (Winter): 42–49.

_____ . 1987. "Using Computers for Instruction." *Byte* 12 (2) (February): 149–62.

Bowles, Samuel, and Herbert Gintis. 1976. *Schooling in Capitalist America.* New York: Basic Books.

Brown, Byron W., and Daniel H. Saks. 1975. "The Production and Distribution of Cognitive Skills within Schools." *Journal of Political Economy* 83 (3) (May–June): 571–93.

_____. 1981. "The Microeconomics of Schooling." *Review of Research in Education* 9: 217–54.

_____. 1987. "The Microeconomics of the Allocation of Teacher's Time and Student Learning." *Economics of Education Review* 6 (4): 319–32.

Cuban, Larry. 1986. *Teachers and Machines.* New York: Teachers College Press, Columbia University.

Dahllof, U. S. 1971. *Ability Grouping, Content Validity and Curriculum Process Analysis.* New York: Teachers College Press.

Fisher, Charles W., N. Filby, R. Marliave, L. Cahen, M. Dishaw, J. Moore, and D. Berliner. 1978. "Teaching Behaviors, Academic Learning Time and Student Achievement: Final Report of Phase III-B, Beginning Teacher Evaluation Study." (Technical Report V-I). Sacramento: California State Commission for Teacher Preparation and Licensing.

Hallinan, Maureen T., and Aage B. Sørensen. 1985. "Class Size, Ability Group Size, and Student Achievement." *American Journal of Education* 94 (1) (November): 71–89.

Hanushek, Eric. 1986. "The Economics of Schooling: Production and Efficiency in the Public Schools." *Journal of Economic Literature* 24 (3) (September): 1141–77.

Leibenstein, Harvey. 1980. *Beyond Economic Man: A New Foundation for Microeconomics.* Cambridge, Mass.: Harvard University Press.

Monk, David H. 1984. "Interdependencies among Educational Inputs and Resource Allocation in Classrooms." *Economics of Education Review* 3 (1): 65–73.

Murnane, Richard J. 1981. "New Evidence on the Relationship between Mother's Education and Children's Cognitive Skills." *Economics of Education Review* 1 (2) (Spring): 245–52.

Papert, Seymour. 1980. *Mindstorms.* New York: Basic Books.

Rosenholtz, Susan J. 1985. "Effective Schools: Interpreting the Evidence." *American Journal of Education* 93 (3) (Mau): 352–88.

Saks, Daniel H. 1986. "A Legacy for the 21st Century: Investment Opportunities in Our Children's Schooling." *Peabody Journal of Education* 63 (2): 27–69.

Simon, Herbert. 1957. *Models of Man.* New York: Wiley.

Sørensen, Aage B., and Maureen T. Hallinan. 1986. "Effects of Ability Grouping on Growth in Academic Achievement." *American Educational Research Journal* 23 (4) (Winter): 519–42.

Summers, Anita A., and Barbara L. Wolfe. 1977. "Do Schools Make a Difference?" *American Economic Review* 67 (4) (September): 639–52.

8 RESOURCE ALLOCATION AND THE EFFECTS OF SCHOOLING
A Sociological Perspective

Adam Gamoran

This chapter discusses the importance of resource allocation in the production of school achievement. Its argument rests on an organizational view of school systems that focuses on technology—the knowledge, materials, and operational processes of classroom instruction—as the key conveyor of new information and skills to students. According to this formulation, resource allocation both influences and constitutes the technology of school systems.[1] This perspective represents a significant departure from earlier sociological work on the prediction of schooling outcomes.

The major early contribution of sociologists to the study of achievement was to document the large impact of nonschool conditions, especially student family background characteristics (such as Coleman et al. 1966; Jencks et al. 1972). Through the end of the 1970s, sociological research had made relatively little headway in discovering equally powerful school-related influences on achievement.

The author is grateful for the collaboration of Martin Nystrand and for the research assistance of Mark Berends and John Knapp, each of whom also provided helpful comments on this chapter. Useful suggestions were also offered by Robert Dreeben, David Monk, and Fred Newmann. Research reported in this chapter was supported by the National Center on Effective Secondary Schools at the Wisconsin Center for Education Research, Madison, Wisconsin, which is supported in part by a grant from the U.S. Office of Educational Research and Improvement (Grant No. G–008690007). Any opinions, findings, and conclusions are those of the author and do not necessarily reflect the views of this agency or the U.S. Department of Education.

It had not ignored the possibility that resources in schools may be related to outcomes. On the contrary, these studies examined a long list of resources for their possible impact, including per pupil expenditures, school laboratories, books in the school library, school average teacher verbal ability, and so on. This focus had two serious flaws. First, the resources examined were not chosen as the result of a thorough conceptualization of what was most likely to influence achievement. Instead, studies considered resources that were, in principle, relatively easy to manipulate, such as expenditures. Although this approach might have produced information of practical value had it revealed important predictors of achievement, it was not destined to do so because the resources studied generally lacked a compelling theoretical connection to achievement.

The second problem with sociologists' early focus on resources was that data were gathered only on the availability of resources, not on their use. For example, researchers noted how many books were in the school library, but not whether any students actually read them. Obviously it is the use of resources that has a direct effect on outcomes; resource availability may or may not contribute an indirect effect, by constraining the use of resources. This point has been noted by researchers in educational administration as well (Monk 1981; Rossmiller 1986).

An organizational view of school systems leads to a very different approach to examining educational resources. Rather than starting with the resources most easily manipulated, it considers first what resources are most likely to influence outcomes. Instead of noting solely the availability of resources, it points toward tracing the availability of resources at the district level to their allocation in schools and classrooms and their application with students. The central question of this perspective is not, "Why do some students learn more than others?" but "How is school achievement produced?" (see Barr and Dreeben 1983). The former question involves examining only the direct contributors to achievement, whereas the latter requires one to study the distribution of resources through the layers of school system organization, as well as their eventual impact on student outcomes.

SCHOOL SYSTEM ORGANIZATION AND
THE ALLOCATION OF RESOURCES

Parsons (1960) held that three qualitatively different levels exist in complex organizations. Activities of legitimation, procurement, and administration take place at the institutional and managerial levels, but the actual work of the organization occurs at the technical level. Building on this insight, subsequent writers described the efforts of organizations to shield their technical cores from environmental fluctuation (such as Thompson 1967; for a review see Scott 1987: Ch. 8). Among other needs, a stable and adequate supply of resources is required for successful operation at the technical level. Hickson, Pugh, and Pheysey (1969) offered an elaborated conception of organizational technology, describing its three dimensions as (1) the knowledge required for carrying out tasks; (2) the materials used in organizational work, including both raw materials and workplace equipment; and (3) the operations carried out with the available knowledge and materials. According to this view, the distribution of resources has a crucial impact on organizational technology: as knowledge and materials, resources constitute aspects of technology in themselves, and moreover they play a large role in determining the nature and success of operational processes.

As Parsons (1960) himself noted, classrooms constitute the technical level of educational organizations. The technology of school systems consists of "the conduct of classes by the teacher" (Parsons 1960: 60). What are the elements of this technology? Following Hickson, Pugh, and Pheysey's (1969) categories, educational technology may be seen as (1) teachers' knowledge and skills; (2) the characteristics of curricular materials, other classroom equipment and supplies, and students;[2] (3) the instructional activities that take place in classrooms. These core elements of educational organizations are the direct producers of student achievement, and they must be examined to discover how the outcomes of schooling are fashioned. Identifying the technology of school systems also shows where to seek district and school influences on the outcomes of schooling. According to this perspective, decisions about resource allocation are the most likely source of administrative influence on student achievement. These influences are believed to occur indirectly, operating through effects on what goes on inside classrooms.

What empirical support exists for this general formulation? By the mid-1970s, researchers had begun to show that despite the lack of powerful between-school effects on achievement, variation in within-school conditions did have notable effects (Summers and Wolfe 1974, 1977; Murnane 1975; Brown and Saks 1975, 1980). Barr and Dreeben (1983) argued that these findings reflected differences within schools in the availability of resources such as teacher and student competencies. They extended the argument by pointing out that such resources had effects because they influenced classroom activities (see further Gamoran and Dreeben 1986). Analyses of first-grade reading showed that the availability of time, curricular materials, and students' competencies had important influences on the introduction of new words and phonics concepts (Barr and Dreeben 1983).

Although earlier writers had uncovered the importance of resource availability, Barr and Dreeben (1983) showed that it was the *use* of resources in classroom activities that had a direct impact on achievement. Similarly, Rowan and Miracle (1983) linked classroom events to student outcomes by showing that standardized achievement scores rose more when students proceeded faster through the reading curriculum. Thus it was not the curriculum *per se* but its implementation that mattered for achievement. Arguing that resource allocation made it possible to coordinate work in school systems, Gamoran and Dreeben (1986) discovered strong ties between resource allocation and resource use, on the one hand, and resource use and student achievement, on the other.

According to Kostakis (1987), different technologies are required for teaching different subject matters. Consequently, school subjects vary in their dependence on particular resources. An analysis of physics and literature achievement in Greece revealed that the former was more sensitive to school-level variation in physical resources, while the latter depended more on the composition and organization of the student body. This occurs, she suggested, because physics instruction relies more on the availability of materials whereas literature instruction benefits more from an able student population. The effects of teacher experience also varied across subjects, with a linear effect in literature but a curvilinear relation in physics, and Kostakis proposed a technological explanation for this as well: Over time, physics teachers' knowledge may become obsolete, rendering them less effective teachers.

These studies support the notion that administrative decisions about resource allocation influence teaching by constraining the choices of teachers as they carry out their work in classrooms. The technology of school systems consists of teachers using resources provided by districts and schools. At the same time, learning that occurs among students is greatly influenced by these classroom processes.

LIMITATIONS ON THE EFFECTS OF RESOURCE ALLOCATION

Thus far I have stressed the importance of resource allocation in establishing the conditions under which teachers carry out their work, but there are important constraints that limit the influence of resource availability. First, teachers take steps to make independent decisions about classroom instruction, sometimes irrespective of the presence of resources. Second, structural constraints inherent in school and classroom organization may limit the ways teachers can use resources.

The spatial isolation of teachers within schools, coupled with norms of professional autonomy, means that teachers have great latitude in how they use resources distributed from higher levels of organization (Bidwell 1965). Teachers are rarely supervised, and they receive few directives specifying exactly what they must do in class (Lortie 1975). Resources such as time, curricular materials, and student capacities set important constraints on instruction (Gamoran and Dreeben 1986), but within those constraints teachers have considerable discretion.

Variation across subject matters in the impact of resources on teachers' work depends not only on the technological requirements of teaching different subjects, as shown by Kostakis (1987), but also on the preferences of individual teachers. The availability of resources is likely to have its greatest impact on teaching when there is a consensus throughout the school system on the importance of a particular program of study. For example, reading instruction constitutes the main educational agenda of first-grade classes. Teachers, principals, and community leaders share in this belief. Consequently, teachers tend to make great use of the resources they have for read-

Table 8-1.   Use of Scheduled Time in Eleven First-Grade Classrooms.

Subject	Minutes Scheduled[a]	Minutes Spent[b]	Percentage
Reading and language arts	148.45	147.00	99.0
Mathematics	39.64	30.07	75.9
Other subjects (social studies, science, and health combined)	37.27	20.73	55.6

a. Average daily minutes on the schedule teachers handed in to administrators.
b. Average daily minutes actually spent as recorded over twelve full-day observations.

ing instruction, but to be more selective in other subjects. Data collected from eleven first-grade classes by Dreeben and Barr (1985) show that when it came to reading, teachers used virtually all the time that had been scheduled, but they used smaller proportions of scheduled time in other subjects (see Table 8-1). Teachers appear more free to exercise preferences for other topics, so the availability of resources would constitute a less salient consideration.

Teachers also lessen the impact of resource allocation by reorganizing students. The formulation presented above suggests that the capacities of students allocated to teachers constitutes a resource with which teachers must work to carry out the technology of teaching, but the impact of this resource depends in part on how teachers arrange students within classrooms. For example, when teachers divide students into within-class ability groups, they change the nature of the linkage between student abilities and instruction. Instead of being tied to the capacities of the class as a whole, instructional processes would now be connected to the aptitudes of the groups (Barr and Dreeben 1983). Despite such reorganization, Gamoran and Dreeben (1986) showed that the aptitude levels of small reading groups were closely related to the average aptitude level of the class, so that instruction in groups was still constrained by the type of students allocated to classrooms. At the same time, however, ability grouping weakened the tie between the curricular materials made available by districts and schools and teachers' coverage of materials. Teachers appeared compelled to complete the texts with high groups, but less constrained with middle- and low-ability groups. Consequently, the impact of materials on the pace of instructional coverage was felt primarily in high groups and not elsewhere.

The relation between teacher discretion and the impact of resources is bilateral: Resource availability constrains what teachers can do, even as teachers take steps to reduce their dependence on resources. As I noted above, even though teachers form their own reading groups and thus reorganize the class distribution of student aptitudes, the groups they create are still tied to the overall class composition. Moreover, the amount of time available, the adequacy of instructional materials, and the physical layout of the classroom all limit the size and number of small groups teachers can form (Hallinan and Sørensen 1983, 1986).

Besides teacher discretion, structural constraints in classroom organization can also limit the impact of resource allocation on instructional technology and its effects. The tension between treating the class as a whole and dealing with students as individuals is one such structural difficulty. Because of this tension, teachers may arrange and instruct students in their customary fashion, even with increased space, time, and materials. Hallinan and Sørensen (1983, 1986) suggested that among other considerations, the need to maintain order in the classroom leads teachers to form three groups of similar size, irrespective of the class aptitude distribution. In addition, teachers' concerns with the diverse needs of individual students might cause them to devote any additional time or materials to particular students. This would reduce the impact of resource allocation on instruction and on outcomes for the class as a whole.

As in the case of resource allocation and teacher discretion, the availability and use of resources modifies the impact of structural constraints at the same time as structure limits the effects of resources. Given more time for classroom instruction, for example, the one-teacher/many-students configuration of classrooms may be less limiting. This tension could also be alleviated by providing more teachers per class (that is, team teaching) or fewer students per teacher (reducing class size). These measures involve varying the district's or school's allocation of resources to the classroom. With team teaching or smaller classes, an increase in other resources such as time and materials might have greater impact on student learning.

DISTRIBUTION OF RESOURCES BETWEEN
AND WITHIN SCHOOLS

The availability and application of resources varies between and within schools. In both cases, it is important to recognize that resources are not distributed randomly but often correspond to well-known bases of inequality. Residential determination of school attendance has meant that disadvantaged youth attend school with a disproportionate number of other disadvantaged students, and students from wealthier families are more likely to attend school with others from positions of privilege. Consequently, poor and minority youth have, on average, less access to one of the few resources that appears to bear between-school effects on achievement: high-SES, racial majority peers (Coleman et al. 1966).

School-level sociodemographic conditions are likely to be associated with student outcomes for a number of reasons. First, because socioeconomic status, race, and ethnicity are correlated with achievement, schools with high concentrations of disadvantaged youth are likely to contain a disproportionate number of low-achieving students (Brookover et al. 1979). Student competencies are one kind of resource with which teachers work: the availability of student aptitude or prior knowledge has an impact on instruction (Dahllof 1971; Barr and Dreeben 1983). Concentrations of low achievers may hinder students' academic progress, net of their own aptitude levels. Second, low-SES schools may be considered less desirable locations for teachers. Experienced and successful teachers have more say in their job placements, and many avoid the schools considered most difficult when given a chance (Lortie 1975). Consequently low-SES schools may contain less teacher competence on the average. Third, schools may vary in physical resources (such as labs and libraries) according to their socioeconomic surroundings (Coleman et al. 1966). Thus, both the availability and the use of resources may vary across schools along socioeconomic, racial, and ethnic lines.

It is worth recalling, though, that past research has been unable to ascribe much of the variation in outcomes to variation in physical resources (for a review, see Averch et al. 1972). Furthermore, Gamoran's (1987) analysis of between-school effects on high school achievement found that neither school composition nor course offerings had consistent effects. However, a study of first graders showed that racial differences in reading achievement could be explained by differences between schools attended by whites and those attended by blacks in the use of time and curricular materials (Dreeben and Gamoran 1986).

More evidence is available on the structure and significance of within-school resource distributions. Many studies have shown that resource allocation in secondary schools varies by ability group and curricular track. Students in high-ability classes and college-bound programs take more academic courses (Gamoran 1987), cover academic topics more thoroughly (Metz 1978; Page 1984; Oakes 1985), and are exposed to more high-status knowledge (Keddie 1971; Ball 1981; Oakes 1985). They have more college-bound friends and receive more encouragement from teachers and guidance counselors to attend college (Heyns 1974; Rehberg and Rosenthal 1978; Alexander and Cook 1982). Consequently, both the academic and affective environments favor high-track students (Vanfossen, Jones, and Spade 1987).

Studies at the elementary level have also shown that resources and their use vary by ability-group level. Barr and Dreeben (1983) found that teachers proceeded through the curriculum faster with high-ability groups, producing greater learning (see also Gamoran 1986). According to Eder (1981), instruction in low groups is characterized by more frequent interruptions, due to the shorter attention spans of students assigned to those groups. In contrast to the findings for secondary schools, however, the differential allocation of resources does not always appear to favor high-ability students at the expense of others. By varying instruction, teachers believe they are meeting the needs of different groups of students. Some evidence appears to support this belief. Rowan and Miracle (1983) found that by proceeding at a faster pace with low-ability groups, teachers sometimes use grouping in a compensatory fashion, narrowing the achievement gap with higher groups. Weinstein (1976) observed teachers who gave more praise to low-ability students and who, by creating smaller low-ability groups, gave more time to low-group students. A recent review of ability-grouping research suggested that students learn more in certain types of grouped classes than they do in ungrouped ones (Slavin 1987). In sum, observing a differential allocation of resources still leaves open the question of whether or not such resources are distributed equitably.

EMPIRICAL ILLUSTRATION

I will use data from a recent study of ninth-grade English instruction to illustrate the perspective outlined above. The analysis will give evidence on three points: (1) the importance of resource allocation in creating a technology of teaching and in producing the outcomes of schooling; (2) the role of teacher discretion in limiting the impact of resource allocation; and (3) within-school differences in resource allocation and use, and their impact on student achievement.

The data were collected in a pilot study whose goal was to develop techniques for measuring instruction in the context of varied tracks and ability groups. Two English classes in each of two schools in a midsized midwestern city participated in the study. Each class was observed on four occasions during the spring of 1987. In addition, teachers and students filled out questionnaires, and students took tests of writing and of literature achievement. Finally, school officials provided standardized test scores from school records. The present analysis relies largely on the test and observational data.

The measurement of instructional practices was guided by the notion that effective teaching involves reciprocal interaction between teacher and students. Students are expected to learn more when they have more input and greater investment in the flow of classroom activities (see Nystrand 1987 for elaboration of this view). One indicator of instruction that derives from this perspective is the locus of control of classroom activities—for example, the extent to which students ask questions as well as teachers. Another is the "authenticity" of teacher questions—whether they require students to contribute new knowledge to the discussion or merely ask students to recite information that the teacher already knows and wants to check whether the student also knows.[3] The levels of these instructional conditions depend in part on the availability of resources and on the teacher's skill at using them.

High-quality instruction involves activities that are not only engaging but that refer to meaningful content (Barr 1987). Thus the curricular content of instruction (which depends partly on the availability of resources) was also scrutinized.

Although resource allocation was not the primary focus of the study, information from the observations and questionnaires reveals the importance of resources for instruction and achievement, and thus provides support for the formulation I have presented. Because of the limited number of classes, I will use a case-study approach to illustrate the argument. My conclusions from this analysis may be seen as hypotheses that could be tested with quantitative data from a larger sample of classes.

School A, Class 1: Instruction as the Application of Available Resources

The two participating classes in School A were taught by Mrs. Timm, who had worked at School A for eleven of her twelve years as a teacher.[4] Class 1 was a "regular" English class, but students were very bright on the whole; they averaged in the seventy-eighth percentile on the reading section of the California Achievement Test (CAT) (see Table 8-2). This level of aptitude was characteristic of School A, which draws a large proportion of children whose parents are highly educated and hold professional and managerial occupations.

Table 8-2. Description of Four Ninth-Grade English Classes, Test Score Means (*in parentheses, standard error of difference from class 1*).

School	Class	Rank Description	Class Size	CAT[a]	Literature Achievement[b]	Adjusted[c] Literature Achievement
A	1	"Regular"	25	78.05	16.37	16.69
A	2	"Academically talented"	30	90.88 (4.28)	18.17 (.99)	17.90 (1.14)
B	3	"High ability"	21	80.39 (3.12)	18.22 (1.08)	18.30 (1.16)
B	4	"Low ability"	15	41.28 (4.20)	12.70 (1.29)	13.17 (1.73)
F-value (*$*p < .01$, **$**p < .001$)				32.43**	7.86**	5.34*

a. National percentile ranking on the reading section of the California Achievement Test, administered by the school district in spring 1986 when students were in eighth grade. For some students in school B, scores were estimated from the Nelson-Denny test administered in fall 1986.

b. Test administered by researchers in spring 1987. See text and note 5 for description.

c. Adjusted for CAT scores (see note 6).

All four classes in the study had the same amount of daily time available: fifty minutes. This amount was reduced by assemblies and special programs that sometimes were held during class time, but we were unable to obtain estimates of how the classes might have varied along this dimension. The curricular materials used in Class 1 were chosen by Mrs. Timm, in collaboration with the head of the English department and other faculty, from a list approved by the district. Over the course of the school year, students were assigned to read one play (*Romeo and Juliet*), two novels (*Of Mice and Men* and *Animal Farm*), three short story units, and one poetry unit. These readings were supplemented by numerous worksheets that asked questions about the texts. In sum, the resources available consisted of a high-achieving group of students, a set of texts and accompanying materials, and fifty minutes per day in which to use them.

Each day, Mrs. Timm combined these resources to carry out instruction. She usually managed to spend about forty of the available fifty minutes on instructional tasks, with the rest of the time used for routine procedures. Typically, Mrs. Timm mixed lecture and discussion to convey to students the points she believed important about the readings. Around one-fifth of the time used for instruction was usually spent in lecture, while about half was devoted to discussion (see Table 8–3).

After spending a few minutes on routine procedures, Mrs. Timm typically began instruction with an introductory lecture about the topic for the day. The remainder of the period was spent discussing the reading, using a worksheet that students were supposed to have filled out as a springboard to discussion. It is important to recognize that what I am calling "discussion" was heavily dominated by the teacher. Periods of lecturing were interspersed throughout the discussion, as Mrs. Timm elaborated on related points. Moreover, in this class the teacher asked an average of 87 percent of the questions. Most of the questions required students to recall a point of fact from the stories. Only 13 percent of her questions were "authentic" and asked students to make an original contribution to the discussion. Thus the relatively large amount of discussion time actually consisted of a great deal of talk by the teacher, a finding that is consistent with other recent studies (Goodlad 1984; Powell, Farrar, and Cohen 1985).

Instruction in this class focused on the meanings of the texts mainly at a surface level, with occasional attention to broader or deeper

Table 8-3. Instruction in Four Ninth-Grade English Classes.

School	Class	Daily Time Available	Percentage Used for Instruction	Daily Minutes Spent On:			Locus[b] of Questioning	Authenticity[c] of Teacher Questions
				Lecture	Discussion	Mixture[a]		
A	1	50 minutes	81.5%	6.50	18.50	2.00	.83	.13
A	2	50 minutes	72.0	3.75	1.00	8.50	.58	.25
B	3	50 minutes	85.5	0.00	4.25	26.00	.92	.49
B	4	50 minutes	90.0	12.25	1.00	25.25	.99	.13

a. Intermingling of lecture and discussion. Activities not listed here were noninstructional management, student presentation, small group work, seatwork, tests and quizzes.
b. Average proportion of teacher questions out of total number of questions asked.
c. Average proportion of teacher questions that were authentic (see text).

implications. Mrs. Timm appeared to have a detailed plan for how to proceed, including the questions she intended to ask. Her approach allowed little room for students to influence the direction of discussions. This pattern characterized three of the four periods we observed in Class 1. In the fourth, students spent nearly half the period working in small groups planning to present scenes from plays. This activity obviously gave more latitude to students, but it did not appear to be a common occurrence in Class 1. Instruction generally consisted of the following pattern: For homework, students read the assigned text and completed worksheets designed to ensure their reading and check their comprehension. The teacher's lecture and class discussion further clarified the surface meanings of the reading, and students were subsequently tested on their recall and understanding.

This description reveals the technology of instruction in Class 1. It shows how the teacher applied available time and materials to students in order to impart knowledge. In this case, there was little place for student input, although students contributed more than in some classes (see Powell, Farrar, and Cohen 1985). Discovering what produces student achievement would require one to examine these technological elements, focusing on variation across classrooms. What are the unique contributions of time, materials, and the pattern of instructional activities to achievement? The sample of classes in this study is too small to permit an adequate test of the hypothesis that variation in resources and their use produces achievement, but the point can be illustrated through qualitative comparisons with the availability and use of resources in other classes.

School A, Class 2: Student Participation in the Conduct of Classes

Although the teacher and the amount of time available were the same in Class 2 as in Class 1, the collection of students was significantly different. Class 2 was called an "academically talented" class, the only one in the school for ninth-grade English. Students were admitted to Class 2 on the basis of their CAT scores and recommendations by their eighth-grade teachers. Table 8-2 shows that on the average, Class 2 students scored in the ninety-first percentile on the CAT. Another difference in resources was the selection of materials made by the teacher along with the English department chair. In addition to reading all the texts assigned to Class 1, Class 2 students read three more novels (*The Pearl, A Tale of Two Cities*, and *To Kill a Mockingbird*). Mrs. Timm covered the texts more quickly in Class 2 so that she could include more of them.

There were other significant differences in the application of resources. Mrs. Timm allowed students in Class 2 to play a larger role in directing the flow of instruction. She used less straight lecture and instead punctuated her introductory remarks with questions for students. More than 40 percent of the questions asked in Class 2 were posed by students. One-quarter of the teacher's questions were authentic ones, almost twice the proportion in Class 1 (see Table 8-3).

These comparisons reveal some important technological differences, including faster and broader coverage of literary texts, and more student input into the activities of instruction. The differences resulted in part from variation in a key resource: student competencies. More able students presumably allowed Mrs. Timm to cover more ground and to let students speculate and draw conclusions more. In addition, Mrs. Timm was encouraged and expected by the department head to cover more novels with this "academically talented" class. The technological differences also result from choices made by the teacher to modify instruction in this fashion. It was her decision to pose more genuine questions in this class, for example. Students clearly took advantage of the opportunity to participate, asking nearly twice as many questions as students in any of the other three classes we observed. This evidence highlights the fact that although student competencies are a resource with which teachers work, they are not the passive "raw material" used in the technology of manufacturing organizations. Instead, they play an active role in shaping the operational processes of instruction.

Table 8-2 shows that student achievement in literature was somewhat higher in Class 2 than in Class 1. The literature test consisted of questions ranging from simple recall to the nature of the theme and conflict in a random sample of the novels, plays, and stories students had read in class. The questions were the same for each class, but they concerned different texts. Thus, the test scores reflect what students learned out of the literature curriculum in their own class.[5] The last column in Table 8-2 reveals that the difference in literature achievement remains even after scores are adjusted for students'

Table 8-4. Instructional Effects on Literature Achievement.

Independent Variables	Dependent Variable: Literature Achievement		
	Unstandardized b	Standard Error	T
CAT score	.038	(.027)	1.398
Locus of questions	-4.443	(3.339)	-1.331
Teacher authenticity	7.319	(3.268)	2.240
	$R^2 = .223$		

N = 76 students.

eighth-grade CAT rankings.[6] Note further that because of differences in curricular materials, the higher scores in Class 2 reflect greater knowledge about more literary texts.

This achievement gap may have resulted in part from the greater authenticity of teacher questions and the increased opportunity for students to ask questions. Table 8-4 shows that controlling for CAT scores, students in classes with greater authenticity and more student locus of questioning scored higher on the achievement test. According to these results, the difference between none and all of a teachers' questions being authentic would be about seven points on the tests; the difference of .12 between Classes 1 and 2 would be worth about nine-tenths of a point. Similarly, the observed .25 difference in locus of questioning would lead to an achievement difference of 1.11 points. Because it is based on only four classes and lacks adequate controls for selection biases, this analysis must be regarded as exploratory and speculative. Still, it is consistent with the argument that the activities of instruction—which were influenced by the allocation of resources—have an important impact on student achievement.

School B, Class 3: Authentic Discussion in a High-Ability Class

The link between resources, technology, and achievement can be further illustrated with descriptions of classes in another school in the same district. Class 3 in School B was formed as a high-ability class (although it did not have the "academically talented" label as in

School A). The average student in Class 3 scored in the eightieth percentile on the CAT. This achievement level is not as high as the highest-ranked class in School A; in fact it is closer to the "regular" class there (see Table 8-2). This occurred, first, because School B students come from a population that is more diverse socioeconomically, in which achievement is not as high on the average. Second, the high-ability class in School B was one of several at that rank, whereas the academically talented class in School A was unique and thus more selective.

Despite the difference in student aptitude, Class 3 revealed certain technological similarities to Class 2. Lessons were discussion-oriented. We observed no pure lectures; the teacher, Mrs. Carson (a twenty-year veteran), always involved students by asking questions even when presenting new material. Although the teacher asked the large majority of the questions, nearly half were authentic. The total amount of reading required of students in this class—two mystery novels, two other novels (*Of Mice and Men, Great Expectations*), one play (*Romeo and Juliet*), and numerous short stories—was slightly less than that assigned in Class 2, so the similar level of literature achievement (see Table 8-2, column 2) reflects comparable learning of less material. However, after adjusting the achievement differences for prior CAT scores (column 3), Class 3's average appears highest.

The achievement findings may reflect a tradeoff between greater breadth in Class 2 (more reading assigned) and greater depth in Class 3 (more authentic discussion about the readings). The tradeoff results from differences in the use of available resources of time, materials, and student competencies. Two processes may have brought about the observed differences: greater administrative pressures for coverage in School A or varying teacher decisions in how to use resources. Available data do not permit us to distinguish between these two possibilities. Comparing Class 3 with Class 1 suggests another inference: Student competencies were high enough in Class 1 for more genuine discussion, if not more reading, had the teacher elected to do so.

School B, Class 4: Pseudodiscourse and Pseudotexts

Class 4 provides the sharpest contrast with the others. The amount of time available is the only resource that was the same for this class as the others. Taught by Mrs. Rogers, who had nineteen years' experience at School B and twenty-seven years' experience overall, the class was designated a "low-ability" one. As expected, student competencies were low relative to other classes in the school; the average CAT score was in the forty-first national percentile. The size of the class, fifteen students, was the smallest in the sample (and among the smallest in the school for English). Students in this class read fewer literary texts: They were assigned two short story units and two novels (*The Contender* and *Shane*). They also read an edited version of *Romeo and Juliet* and excerpts from *To Kill a Mockingbird*. Class 4 was the only one to use the modified version of Shakespeare in place of the regular text, and the only one in which a novel was excerpted instead of being read in its entirety. To compensate, Mrs. Rogers showed the movie version of *Mockingbird*.

Given these resources, it is not surprising that the instructional approach was unlike the other classes in the study. Mrs. Rogers made efficient use of time, spending an average of 90 percent on instruction. The smaller class size may well have contributed to this efficiency. At the same time, though, instruction was highly regimented. More time was spent on lecture here (see Table 8–3); during one observation Mrs. Rogers lectured for almost the whole period. Like other observers of low-ability classes, we found a greater amount of structured seatwork in this class (Metz 1978; Page 1984). The discussion that did occur was almost completely dominated by the teacher: She asked 99 percent of the questions, and only 13 percent of them were authentic (see Table 8–3). The study of *To Kill a Mockingbird*, which we observed, appeared fragmented and superficial, similar to what has been reported for low-ability classes elsewhere (see Page 1987). Chiefly through worksheets and lecture, Mrs. Rogers taught the setting and characters to the students—but students read only the scenes featuring certain characters.

The literature test results show that students in Class 4 scored lowest on the average, even after the means are adjusted for eighth-grade CAT reading scores (Table 8–2, last column). In other words, with prior skills statistically held constant, students in Class 4 learned the least in literature. Table 8–4 suggests that the teacher dominance of questioning and the low authenticity of her questions may have contributed to the widening gap. Moreover, it is important to note that the lower scores occurred in combination with less total reading.

Summary

The description of the four classes illustrates the view that the technology of educational organizations consists of teachers using resources in classrooms. The work of teachers is constrained in several ways by the availability of resources. In these examples, all four teachers were limited to an inflexible structure of fifty minutes per day. Mrs. Rogers was constrained by the low level of student competencies in Class 4; Mrs. Timm, possibly by pressures for coverage in Class 2.

At the same time, teacher discretion played a role in how the resources were applied. For example, the similarities between Classes 1 and 3 in student aptitude and in quantity and types of materials suggests that Mrs. Timm could have created more opportunities for students in Class 1 to become engaged, as did Mrs. Carson in Class 3 and as Mrs. Timm herself did in Class 2. Although an equivalent comparison is lacking, one can speculate that Mrs. Rogers did not need to substitute literary fragments for texts in Class 4. A tentative quantitative analysis (Table 8–4) suggests that between-class differences in how teachers presented material to students may have contributed to variation in student achievement in literature.

The observations are largely consistent with previous research showing a differential allocation of resources across ability levels. Class 2, with the highest relative rank of the four, read the most literature; Class 4, the lowest-ranked, read the least. Classes also varied systematically in instructional activities: We saw more student involvement in the "regular" class than in the low, and more in the two higher-ranked classes than in the regular. Although I argued earlier that differential allocation does not automatically imply inequities, these observations support the contrary, in that the low-ability class was exposed to literary fragments and substitutes.

CONCLUSIONS: IMPLICATIONS FOR EDUCATIONAL ADMINISTRATION

Among sociologists who study educational organizations, the view that school districts are "loosely coupled systems" (Weick 1976) has become widely accepted (see further Bidwell 1965; Meyer and

Rowan 1978; Meyer et al. 1978; Weick 1982; Tyler 1985). According to this position, schools do not operate like conventional bureaucracies characterized by commands, adherence to rules, supervision, and evaluation. Instead, the spatial isolation, limited supervision, and professional discretion of teachers allows them to proceed largely independently of bureaucratic authority. Consequently, this position holds that decisions and activities occurring at one level of the organization—for example, in district or school administration—have little impact on activities taking place elsewhere—such as in classrooms.

This description of school systems appears to deny much possibility for administrative intervention into classroom instruction and student achievement. How can administrators work to improve the outcomes of schooling, if their decisions lack influence on classroom events? What are the chances for successful intervention in a loosely coupled system?

The view expressed in this chapter is somewhat different. Without denying the attenuation of bureaucratic authority in school systems, I have suggested that administrative effects on teaching and learning occur primarily through the distribution of resources, which begins at the district level and flows to schools and classes and affects the work of teachers (see further Gamoran and Dreeben 1986). If student achievement results from the technical activities of instruction, and if instruction is constrained by the allocation of resources, then resource allocation would seem to offer an opportunity for administrators to have an impact on teaching and learning. For example, school leaders might be able to improve classroom instruction (and consequently student achievement) by providing more time for teaching and better curricular materials (Gamoran and Dreeben 1986).

The problem with this straightforward conclusion, however, is that it does not take account of teachers' wide latitude in making use of resources. Although resource availability invariably *constrains* teaching—in the extreme, teachers could hardly teach without any time or materials—additional resources are no guarantee of *improved* teaching. Improving the allocation of resources will only have a positive effect on teaching and learning if teachers make good use of the added resources they receive.

How can administrators bring teachers to use resources in the ways they intend? A systemwide consensus on academic goals may be a precondition for success in this effort. As Purkey and Smith (1983) argued, administrative leadership has little impact when the goals espoused by managers are not shared elsewhere in the school system. Several studies have argued that administrators, especially principals, can play a key role in establishing a school climate that emphasizes academic achievement (Bentzen 1974; Goodlad 1975; Neale, Bailey, and Ross 1981; Purkey and Smith 1983). Others have noted that this kind of positive climate is conducive to higher achievement (Brookover et al. 1979; Rutter et al. 1979). The notion that goal consensus facilitates an effective allocation of resources is consistent with Gamoran and Dreeben's (1986) findings that resource allocation had large impacts on teaching and learning in first grade reading. Consensus on the primacy of reading in first grade is virtually universal, so it is not surprising that available resources were used for reading instruction. Had the authors studied a different subject or grade level, the findings might have been different (see Table 8-1).

Researchers adopting the "loose coupling" perspective have also suggested that the main task for school managers is to establish a positive atmosphere in the school (Meyer and Rowan 1978; Weick 1982). These writers argued that although the loose structure of school systems prevents administrators from managing technical activities, leadership is provided through influence over the school's symbolic environment. According to this view, administrative leadership consists of establishing a vision or theme that guides teachers, who are the ones who carry out the actual work of educational organizations (see especially Weick 1982).

Although I do not dispute the role of administrators in articulating and promoting unifying themes and goals, I have argued in this chapter that by making decisions about the allocation of resources, administrators have a hand in managing the school's technical activities as well. Administrators who wish to improve teaching and learning thus need to focus on two areas of leadership: (1) the allocation of resources and (2) the school's academic climate, which, among other things, affects how those resources are used. Alone, neither of these elements may suffice to influence the work of teachers.

This chapter's approach centers on the classroom, the organizational level at which teaching and learning occur. I have argued that external influences on student outcomes, particularly those involving resource allocation, operate indirectly, by affecting the teacher's use of resources, which in turn produces achievement. As one moves out from the classroom, effects on teaching and learning tend to become more and more indirect. Consequently this chapter's implications for state-level educational administration are more ambiguous than they are for management at the district and school levels. On the one hand, state assistance in the allocation of resources, and guidance in their use, would appear reasonable sources of potential influence on classroom instruction. On the other hand, broad variation in local needs would make it difficult to establish a statewide program that would be effective across all districts. At a minimum, state efforts to improve the allocation and use of resources would require a high degree of sensitivity to district and school-level differences in such local conditions as student and teacher competences and community demands.

Finally, the findings of this chapter imply a dual responsibility for researchers: We must learn more about what resources have significant effects on teaching and learning; and we need to provide information on how administrators can foster consensus in their schools. Both of these areas are subjects of current research. The first is being examined by a growing number of writers who adopt the view that achievement is produced when teachers use resources to instruct students in classrooms (Barr and Dreeben 1983). The second is the subject of much interest on the part of writers in the "effective schools" tradition (Purkey and Smith 1983). The findings of these studies may be of real benefit if the viewpoint expressed in this chapter is correct.

NOTES

1. Throughout this chapter, I use the word *technology* in the organizational sense, to refer to the knowledge, materials, and processes of organizational work (Hickson, Pugh, and Pheysey 1969). Hence, the term *educational technology* does *not* mean simply the use of computers in school systems.

2. As the "raw materials" that educators attempt to "transform," students constitute one of the important resources provided to teachers. However, it is important to recognize that students differ from the raw materials used in manufacturing organizations. They do not wait passively to be transformed but play an active role in the transformation process. This point will become clearer in the empirical illustration that follows.

3. Examples of authentic questions were:

> How do you like Orlack?
> From your point of view, is the forge a positive symbol?
> Good question. What do you think?
> Is it possible for a sister to treat a brother that badly?

Examples of inauthentic questions were:

> What was Joe's wife doing?
> What did she do next?
> "Joe is a Hercules in strength and weakness." What does that mean?

4. All names are pseudonyms.
5. All questions on the test were open-ended. Examples were:

> For as many stories as you can remember, briefly explain how each story ended. Write no more than two sentences for each story. [Followed by a list of stories with spaces for answers.]

> For each story that had a conflict you can remember, briefly explain what this conflict was. [Followed by a list of stories with spaces for answers.]

Tests were scored holistically on student's success at recalling the ending, describing the conflict, and so on. Each test was scored by two raters, and the marks averaged. The interrater reliability correlation was computed as .86.

6. Literature achievement was adjusted for CAT scores using a regression of literature achievement on CAT scores and on dummy variables for the classes. An adjusted class mean can then be computed by summing the product of the coefficient for CAT scores times its mean, plus the constant, plus the coefficient for a given class. The F-value comes from this regression as well.

REFERENCES

Alexander, Karl L., and Martha A. Cook. 1982. "Curricula and Coursework: A Surprise Ending to a Familiar Story." *American Sociological Review* 47: 626–40.

Averch, H., S. J. Carroll, T. S. Donaldson, H. J. Kiesling, and J. Pincus. 1972. *How Effective Is Schooling?* Santa Monica, Calif.: RAND Corporation.

Ball, Stephen J. 1981. *Beachside Comprehensive: A Case-Study of Secondary Schooling.* Cambridge: Cambridge University Press.

Barr, Rebecca. 1987. "Classroom Interaction and Curriculum Content." In *Literacy and Schooling*, edited by David Bloome, pp. 150–68. Norwood, N.J.: Ablex.

Barr, Rebecca, and Robert Dreeben. 1983. *How Schools Work.* Chicago: University of Chicago Press.

Bentzen, M. M. 1974. *Changing Schools: The Magic Feather Principle.* New York: McGraw-Hill.

Bidwell, Charles E. 1965. "The School as a Formal Organization." In *Handbook of Organizations*, edited by James G. March, pp. 972–1018. Chicago: Rand-McNally.

Brookover, W., C. Beady, P. Flood, J. Schweitzer, and J. Wisenbaker. 1979. *School Social Systems and Student Achievement.* New York: Praeger.

Brown, Byron W., and Daniel H. Saks. 1975. "The Production and Distribution of Cognitive Skills within Classrooms. *Journal of Political Economy* 83: 571–93.

_____. 1980. "Production Technologies and Resource Allocations within Classrooms and Schools: Theory and Measurement." In *The Analysis of Educational Productivity, Volume 1: Issues in Microanalysis*, edited by Robert Dreeben and J. Alan Thomas, pp. 53–117. Cambridge, Mass.: Ballinger.

Coleman, J., E. Campbell, C. Hobson, J. McPartland, A. Mood, F. Weinfield, and R. York. 1966. *Equality of Educational Opportunity.* Washington, D.C.: U.S. Government Printing Office.

Dreeben, Robert, and Rebecca Barr. 1985. "Technical Report for the Project on Classroom Organization, Instruction, and Learning." Unpublished manuscript, University of Chicago.

Dreeben, Robert, and Adam Gamoran. 1986. "Race, Instruction, and Learning." *American Sociological Review* 51: 660–69.

Eder, Donna. 1981. "Ability Grouping as a Self-Fulfilling Prophecy: A Microanalysis of Teacher-Student Interaction." *Sociology of Education* 54: 151–61.

Gamoran, Adam. 1987. "The Stratification of High School Learning Opportunities." *Sociology of Education* 60: 135–55.

Gamoran, Adam, and Robert Dreeben. 1986. "Coupling and Control in Educational Organizations." *Administrative Science Quarterly* 31: 612–32.

Goodlad, John I. 1975. *The Dynamics of Educational Change.* New York: McGraw-Hill.

_____. 1984. *A Place Called School.* New York: McGraw-Hill.

Hallinan, Maureen T., and Aage B. Sørensen. 1983. "The Formation and Stability of Instructional Groups." *American Sociological Review* 48: 838–61.

_____. 1986. "Student Characteristics and Assignment to Ability Groups: Two Conceptual Formulations." *Sociological Quarterly* 27: 1–13.

Heyns, Barbara. 1974. "Social Selection and Stratification within Schools." *American Journal of Sociology* 79: 1434–51.

Hickson, David J., D. S. Pugh, Diana C. Pheysey. 1969. "Operations Technology and Organization Structure: An Empirical Reappraisal." *Administrative Science Quarterly* 14: 378–97.

Jencks, C. L., M. Smith, H. Acland, M. J. Bane, D. K. Cohen, H. Gintis, B. Heyns, and S. Michaelson. 1972. *Inequality: A Reassessment of the Effects of Family and Schooling in America.* New York: Basic Books.

Keddie, N. 1971. "Classroom Knowledge." In *Knowledge and Control*, edited by Michael F. D. Young, pp. 133–60. London: Collier-Macmillan.

Kostakis, Anastasia. 1987. "Differences among School Outputs and Educational Production Functions." *Sociology of Education* 60: 232–41.

Lortie, Dan. 1975. *Schoolteacher*. Chicago: University of Chicago Press.

Metz, Mary Haywood. 1978. *Classrooms and Corridors: The Crisis of Authority in Desegregated Secondary Schools*. Berkeley, Calif.: University of California Press.

Meyer, John W., and Brian Rowan. 1978. "The Structure of Educational Organizations." In *Environments and Organizations*, edited by Marshall Meyer and associates, pp. 78–109. San Francisco: Jossey-Bass.

Meyer, John W., W. R. Scott, S. Cole, and J. Intili. 1978. "Instructional Dissensus and Institutional Consensus in Schools." In *Environments and Organizations*, edited by Marshall Meyer and associates, pp. 233–63. San Francisco: Jossey-Bass.

Monk, David H. 1981. "Toward a Multilevel Perspective on the Allocation of Educational Resources." *Review of Educational Research* 51: 215–36.

Murnane, Richard J. 1975. *The Impact of School Resources on the Learning of Inner City Children*. Cambridge, Mass.: Ballinger.

Neale, D. C., W. J. Bailey, and B. E. Ross. 1981. *Strategies for School Improvement: Cooperative Planning and Organization Development*. Boston: Allyn and Bacon.

Nystrand, Martin. 1987. "A Framework for Assessing the Role of Instructional Discourse in High School English and Social Studies." Paper presented at the annual meetings of the American Educational Research Association, Washington, D.C., April 1987.

Oakes, Jeannie. 1985. *Keeping Track: How Schools Structure Inequality*. New Haven, Conn.: Yale University Press.

Page, Reba N. 1984. *Perspectives and Processes: The Negotiation of Educational Meaning in High School Classes for Academically Unsuccessful Students*. Unpublished Ph.D. dissertation, University of Wisconsin-Madison.

_____. 1986. "The Social Construction of the Curriculum in Lower-Track High School Classrooms." Paper presented at the annual meeting of the American Educational Research Association, San Francisco.

Parsons, Talcott. 1960. "Some Ingredients of a General Theory of Formal Organization." In *Structure and Process in Modern Societies*, pp. 59–96. Glencoe, Ill.: Free Press.

Powell, Arthur, Eleanor Farrar, and David K. Cohen. 1985. *The Shopping Mall High School*. Boston: Houghton-Mifflin.

Purkey, Stewart C., and Marshall S. Smith. 1983. "Effective Schools: A Review." *Elementary School Journal* 83: 427–52.

Rehberg, Richard A., and Evelyn R. Rosenthal. 1978. *Class and Merit in the American High School*. New York: Longman.

Rossmiller, Richard A. 1986. *Resource Utilitization in Schools and Classrooms: Final Report*. Program Report 86-7. Madison, Wis.: Wisconsin Center for Education Research.

Rowan, Brian, and Andrew W. Miracle, Jr. 1983. "Systems of Ability Grouping and the Stratification of Achievement in Elementary Schools." *Sociology of Education* 56: 133-44.

Rutter, M., B. Maugham, P. Mortimore, J. Ousten, and A. Smith. *Fifteen Thousand Hours: Secondary Schools and Their Effects on Children*. Cambridge, Mass.: Harvard University Press, 1979.

Scott, W. Richard. 1987. *Organizations: Rational, Natural, and Open Systems*, 2d ed. Englewood Cliffs, N.J.: Prentice-Hall.

Slavin, Robert E. 1987. "Ability Grouping and Student Achievement in Elementary Schools: A 'Best-Evidence' Synthesis." *Review of Educational Research* 57: 293-336.

Summers, Anita A., and Barbara L. Wolfe. 1974. *Equality of Educational Opportunity Quantified: A Production Function Approach*. Philadelphia: Federal Reserve Bank of Philadelphia.

_____. 1977. "Do Schools Make a Difference?" *American Economic Review* 67: 639-52.

Thompson, James D. 1967. *Organizations in Action*. New York: McGraw-Hill.

Tyler, William B. 1985. "The Organizational Structure of the School." *Annual Review of Sociology* 11: 49-73.

Vanfossen, Beth E., James D. Jones, and Joan Z. Spade. 1987. "Curriculum Tracking and Status Maintenance." *Sociology of Education* 60: 104-22.

Weick, Karl E. 1976. "Educational Organizations as Loosely Coupled Systems." *Administrative Science Quarterly* 21: 1-19.

_____. 1982. "Administering Education in Loosely Coupled Systems." *Phi Delta Kappan* 63: 673-76.

Weinstein, Rhona S. 1976. "Reading Group Membership in First Grade: Teacher Behaviors and Pupil Experience over Time." *Journal of Educational Psychology* 68: 103-16.

9 MOTIVATION, SATISFACTION, AND PRODUCTIVITY
A Psychological Perspective on Resource Allocation in Education

Bettye MacPhail-Wilcox

Economic and psychological perspectives on schooling are not the unlikely companions they might seem to be. They are disciplines with similar goals, kindred concepts, and related propositions. Economists investigage ways that resources are allocated to satisfy human wants, and motivation scholars identify the needs undergirding wants and the processes that activate and sustain behavior. Both seek to explain how these phenomena affect satisfaction, behavior, and productivity.

Economic and psychological assumptions underpin career ladder, merit pay, loan-forgiveness, performance bonus, and testing programs for students and teachers. The reform rhetoric associated with them promises to improve the productivity of schools while simultaneously upgrading the job satisfaction of teachers, increasing the education labor pool, and reducing public dissatisfaction with schools.

From a more practical perspective, it is necessary to attract and retain qualified employees, an adequate client base, and school outcomes that are supported by the public in order to "have school." Macro- and microeconomic education researchers seek the unique stocks and flows of resources that will accomplish these ends. They search for important relations between resources, technologies, and a variety of performance outcomes. Their goals, especially those concerned with explaining satisfaction and performance, are similar to those that guide the work of motivation scholars. This chapter assumes that combining economic and psychological perspectives offers insights into pressing educational technology problems that are unavailable to those using either discipline in isolation from the other.

The chapter begins with a brief summary of the resource allocation literature, emphasizing the more recent microeconomic perspectives. Because the economic perspective is discussed in the chapter by Brown, only a brief overview is included here. This is followed by selected content and process theories of motivation and a representative review of research pertaining to each. The reviews of content and process motivation close with an integrated and interpretive set of implications for further consideration and investigation.

RESOURCE ALLOCATION IN SCHOOLS

In order to make sense of school production processes, it is essential to understand that resource decisions at each level of the educational hierarchy constrain resource allocation practices at the next level. Moreover, it is necessary to disentangle fiscal, education, and technological resources from one another and from educational production processes (technologies) conceptually.

The term *technology*, as used in this chapter, refers to all knowledge, processes, arrangements, and resources used to produce learning. It essentially describes "how things are done in schools," in terms of both administrative and instructional practices. Basic technological resources are human energy, knowledge, affect, skill, information, and time. These resources are allocated and configured in recognizable patterns described as educational technologies.

From a rational perspective, schools seek fiscal resources in order to acquire technological resources needed to attain their goals. These resources arrive in "bundles" that are called educational resources. They are tangible and concrete, including things like personnel, curriculum guides, books, supplies, equipment, and facilities. But these educational resources are significant theoretically only in the sense that they embody the energy, information, skill, affect, and time to influence the work accomplished in schools. Conceptually, then, fiscal resources are transformed into educational resources that employ educational technologies. By means of these practices and arrangements important technological resources are distributed to students. Through this resource chain, school goals are pursued.

Of the technological resources, only one has received explicit and recent attention by finance scholars at the classroom level. Time has been the subject of conceptual and empirical work (Dreeben and Thomas 1980; Monk 1982; Rossmiller 1983, 1986). Findings indicate that the ways students and teachers allocate and use time vary substantially and that this variance is related to certain achievement outcomes.

It is possible to identify educational technologies that are primary concerns at different levels of the organization. Scheduling, salary allocation based on experience, education, and tenure, and the allocation of personnel and supply money on a per-pupil basis, for example, are technologies that result in measures like pupil-teacher ratios, expenditures per pupil, percentage of professional personnel teaching out of field, average teacher salary, and proportion of students in a track. These are examples of proxy measures for educational technologies commonly associated with macroperspectives of schooling and have been the subjects of numerous investigations in school finance (MacPhail-Wilcox and King 1986a, 1986b).

Microperspective technologies include a wide range of things like classroom grouping arrangements, instructional formats (such as direct, inquiry, discovery, and independent instruction), instructional delivery strategies (such as audio, visual, and kinesthetic modes), student incentive systems (teacher praise, reinforcement, and feedback practices), the use of time (allocated, engaged, and wait time), questioning strategies (divergent and convergent), and so on. Of these technologies, only one has emerged clearly in the theoretical and empirical literature of school finance at the classroom level. It is termed *classroom structure* (Thomas, Kemmerer, and Monk 1982; Barr and Dreeben 1983) but might be more appropriately called *organization of work groups in the classroom* because it seems to incorporate only two aspects of structure: the division of labor and the distribution of work. Nonetheless, variations in grouping technologies used seem to occur across grade levels, curriculum content, and student aptitude (Rossmiller 1983, 1986), and these differences correlate well with the pace and difficulty of work assignments in the classroom (Barr and Dreeben 1983). Variations in grouping technologies seem to be causally linked to teachers' perceptions of student needs, as measured by the range of aptitudes among students assigned to the teacher (Barr and Dreeben 1983).

Resource allocation and production function studies are germane to improving the satisfaction and productivity of students and teachers. The former describe the quality and quantity of resources obtained by educational organizations, while the latter investigate relations between stocks of resources and various outcomes. Until recently, these studies were macro in scope, focusing on aggregated stocks of resources and stock-productivity relations at federal, state, school district, and school levels. Early in this decade, the scope, focus, and conceptual design began to change.

Scholars began to shift the level of analysis to classroom units, to acknowledge the independent effects of values and technological biases on student performance, to focus on resource flows rather than stocks, and to disentangle the effects of resource allocation practices throughout the school hierarchy. Studies based on these considerations have been dubbed microeconomic resource allocation investigations (Brown and Saks 1975; Monk 1981; Kirst 1983; Barr and Dreeben 1983).

Both the macro- and microeconomic lines of research have implications for improving teacher and student motivation. The macroperspective illuminates the organizational context of production, while the microperspective attempts to open the "black boxes" mediating input-output relations.

Macroeconomic Resource Allocation and Production Function Studies

A recent review of resource allocation studies observes substantial differences in the quantity and quality of fiscal and educational resources among states, districts, schools, and classrooms (MacPhail-Wilcox and King 1986a). There are important disparities in line-item expenditures, discretionary spending, pupil-teacher ratios, salary levels, teacher verbal abilities, attitudes, years of education, and experience. In general, these conditions are systematically related to the wealth, demographic, ethnic, educational attainment, and socioeconomic characteristics of populations in an educational unit. These patterns continue to be reported in the literature (Scheuer 1986).

Macrolevel production function studies document similar differences in resource stocks among educational units, but these differences are investigaged relative to various performance indicators. Teacher attributes—especially verbal ability, experience, educational attainments, turnover, and job satisfaction—are often correlated with aggregated student performance measures (MacPhail-Wilcox and King 1986b), but interpretations of these relations differ somewhat (Hanushek 1986).

The findings of these studies are optimistic. Despite many conceptual, design, and methodological problems, they identify some moderate to strong correlations between the resources over which administrators and teachers enjoy some discretion and student performance. For example, teacher span of control, often operationalized as pupil-teacher ratio, class size, and presence of paraprofessional assistance, is one of the most investigated administrative arrangements over which policymakers and educators have control. Others include the number of teacher preparations, tracking, and grouping practices.

Findings from macrostudies of relations between facilities, fiscal characteristics, and performance indexes are more ambiguous. This is not discouraging because these variables exert an indirect and distant influence on performance. Not surprisingly, the ambiguity regarding the direction and strength of correlated conditions decreases as studies shift from more abstract and distant measures of school technologies to more concrete measures of educational resources (teacher verbal ability), technological resources (grouping practices) and student levels of analysis (MacPhail-Wilcox and King 1986a, 1986b; Childs and Shakeshaft 1986).

These findings do not diminish the importance of macrolevel studies. They are essential because they illuminate the organizational context in which instruction and learning occur. It is likely that this context influences satisfaction and productivity by constraining instructional practices, which subsequently restricts the flow of technological resources to students. These are powerful reasons to expect studies that combine macro- and microeconomic perspectives to produce less ambiguous knowledge about school production.

Microeconomic Investigations of Resource Allocation Practices

Microeconomic studies of resource allocation also indicate that the levels and qualities of tangible resources vary among and within schools, classrooms, instructional groups, and individual students (MacPhail-Wilcox and King 1986a; Dreeben and Thomas 1980; Monk 1982; Barr and Dreeben 1983; Cohen 1983; Rossmiller 1983, 1986) and between types of schools (Coleman, Hoffer and Kilgore 1982; Murnane 1981). These variations are related to community and student population attributes, particularly socioeconomic status, educational need, ethnicity, income levels, size of unit, gender, prior educational attainment, and subject matter.

Microeconomic resource allocation studies are, in a sense, the precursors of microeconomic production functions in classrooms. By identifying the flows of technological resources inherent in production technologies, they provide the basis for determining correlated and causal relations with attitudinal and performance outcomes for different groups of teachers and students in different learning contexts. But there are no pure microproduction function studies from which to generalize at this time. Because microeconomic resource allocation studies are so central to the advancement of knowledge about school production, a very brief chronology of this work follows.

After Coleman's (1966) pronouncement that school inputs were relatively unproductive, Brown and Saks (1975) argued that variance was as important a measure of school effects as mean test performance. They argued that schools are multiproduct firms in which the development of each pupil is a matter of consequence.

Using a large Michigan database, Brown and Saks (1975) demonstrated that all school inputs were productive in suburban, rural, and city school districts. That is, educational resources (such as teacher experience and training) and organizational technologies (such as teacher-student ratios) were associated with either increased mean outputs or reduced variance in outputs.

Dreeben and Thomas (1980) urged scholars to reconceptualize school effect studies. They proposed longitudinal, rather than cross-sectional studies; data disaggregation to classroom, instructional group, and individual student levels; the use of multiple outcome measures; and a focus on flows rather than stocks of resources.

Brown and Saks (1980) observed different resource flows and effects for different pupils. Among the technologies and educational resources showing differential effects were class size, teacher experience, and peer group influences. Student attributes mediating the differential use of educational technologies were ethnicity, socioeconomic status, and prior achievement levels. These attributes influenced teachers' decisions about instructional technologies, thereby affecting the ways in which students used time.

Thus, Brown and Saks (1980) argued that the job shop was a more appropriate model of school production than the assembly line. The similarities between schools and job shops included multiple inputs, multiple outputs, and the use of streaming technologies (small batch processes used when production materials are more homogeneous and desired outputs are identical). Grouping and tracking were identified as instances of streaming at classroom and school levels, with student attributes serving as one operational link to classroom streaming decisions.

Brown and Saks (1980) also addressed the active role of the student in learning, particularly the influences of aptitude (acquired ability) and motivation (effort) on student use of time and learning. They suggested that student effort (motivation) is a function of preferences for rewards, particularly those imposed by teachers' incentive systems, pace, and difficulty of curriculum work. They raised the question of whether it is better to reward learning processes or attainments, a question that is widely investigated in motivation studies seeking the differential effects of intrinsic and extrinsic rewards.

Thomas, Kemmerer, and Monk (1982) and Monk (1982) investigated the flow of teacher resources to individual students based on the cost of an hour of teacher labor and under assumptions of joint or separable resources. Among the findings were substantial variation in the flow of human resources to pupils within and between classrooms, with greater flows to higher achieving students. Dispersions of test scores and family socioeconomic status were related to differences observed in classroom resource flows, with differences among classrooms exceeding those within. These findings supported earlier contentions that teachers allocate scarce resources to pupils through different production technologies and their selection of instructional technologies is influenced by the socioeconomic and aptitude dispersions characterizing the class.

In 1983, Barr and Dreeben conducted a secondary data analysis for six first-grade classrooms, investigating relations among reading aptitude, learning outcomes, class size, student background, reading group membership, instructional materials, content difficulty, content coverage, multiple measures of instructional time, and teacher experience. Using three levels of data analysis—individual students, instructional groups, and classes, they partitioned aptitude variation into five scores. Their findings indicated that the range of aptitude in a class operates on student outcomes through resource allocation decisions reflected in teacher decisions about production technologies. Because aptitude-outcome relations were significant at group levels, grouping seemed to be one example of a school production technology.

Their findings also indicated that teachers' instructional grouping decisions were most constrained by larger numbers of low-aptitude students. This finding illustrates how schoolwide student assignment practices (organizational technologies) subsequently influence teachers' use of instructional technologies. The resource flows inherent in these technologies then influence student performance outcomes. There were similarly strong relations between pace of instruction, content coverage, and learning outcomes at the instructional group level. Teachers used standard curricula materials provided by the district, but made them more appropriate for groups of students by changing the time alloted for instruction as well as the amount and difficulty of the content assigned according to student aptitude.

In a longitudinal study, Rossmiller (1983, 1986) investigated relations between classroom technologies, time, and student outcomes in classrooms of different grade levels in four Wisconsin elementary schools. He observed declining allocations of time to academic subject areas, a predominant use of independent and whole group instructional modes, and patterned shifts in the amount of time that specific instructional modes were used in grade levels and by students with particular achievement levels.

An analysis of the extent to which student time on task accounted for variance in academic performance produced statistical significance, but the small portion of variance accounted for indicated that there were other important variables not included in the analysis. Rossmiller concluded that time on task was an important classroom consideration, but not the panacea that many hoped it would be. Rather, there are many complex resource decisions made by both teachers and students, and these influence congnitive and affective performance in very individualistic ways.

Brown and Saks (1984) stressed the importance of understanding what a teacher is trying to accomplish in the classroom. They suggest that teachers' goals are to maximize personal satisfaction with their work. They implicitly acknowledge the potential impact of motivation on teachers' efforts, behaviors, and use of particular production technologies. Thus teacher motivation, an affective state, is posited as another link in the production process—the flow of resources to individual and groups of students in the classroom. They suggest that student achievement is a source of teacher job satisfaction, and this important inducement may be limited by the effects of other resource allocation decisions throughout the educational hierarchy.

The next sections of this chapter link teacher and student motivation to resource allocation issues in education. What follows is a set of introductory statements and a brief overview of selected content and process theories of motivation. Each theoretical overview is followed by a representative review of research, and an integrated interpretation of the resource allocation and motivation literatures.

THEORIES OF MOTIVATION

Motivation is a process in which environmental stimuli and individual attributes interact to produce states of arousal, attitudes, intentions to act, and purposive behaviors. This definition is consistent with the notion of shared responsibility for learning outcomes (Brown and Saks 1980) between education policymakers, administrators, and teachers, as well as parents and students. The environmental stimuli are the responsibility of the former, while the individual attributes are the responsibility of the parent and student.

It is widely assumed that motivation influences work attitudes (job satisfaction, commitment, burnout, and sense of efficacy), work behaviors (particularly turnover, absenteeism, tardiness, involvement, and effort), and work outcomes (efficiency and effectiveness in goal attainment). Thus, motivation is a partial determinant of organizational effectiveness via labor supplies, personnel costs, and productivity. In education, this is most visible in the flight of teachers from the profession and the anticipated consequences of this exodus for the nation (MacPhail-Wilcox 1981; Carnegie Corporation 1986).

Studies of motivation are conducted within numerous theoretical frameworks in psychology (such as the psychoanalytic, behavioral, psychosocial, and cognitive domains). Some are primarily concerned with "what" motivates people, while others focus predominantly on "how" motivation occurs. This content-process classification is neither exhaustive, exclusive, nor independent (MacPhail-Wilcox and Hyler 1985), but it is a useful scheme for organizing knowledge about teacher and student motivation.

Content Theories of Motivation and Educational Research

Content theories of motivation assume that people have unlimited wants, an axiom shared by economic theories. The driving forces of motivation have been defined as instincts, drives, needs, various forms of intrapsychic energy and conflict, ego states, cognitive and psychosocial developmental stages, and learned behavior resulting from external reinforcements (Arkes and Garske 1982; MacPhail-Wilcox and Hyler 1985). Those who view motivation as intrinsic contend that internal stimuli press behavior into the willful service of human growth and purpose. Proponents of extrinsic motivation argue that behavior is the result of external stimulus-reward relations. Interactionists believe that behavior results from a complex interplay of internal and external stimuli and that this behavior subsequently exerts a reciprocal influence on the environment (Weiner 1980; Steers and Porter 1983). Although all individuals are presumed to exhibit motivated behavior, the primacy and expression of motivating forces is unstable across time, places, and persons. That is, what is motivating at one point may not be at another.

Assuming, then, the hypothetical construct of human needs, it is important to know what they are. Needs are numerous and there are many taxonomies available. Murray (1938) detailed an important list of twenty that included dominance, nurturance, exhibition, achievement, and affiliation. In the context of work motivation, achievement, affiliation, and, most recently, power needs have been emphasized. These have been investigated extensively in business settings (McClelland, Clark, and Lowell 1963; Atkinson 1954; Stahl 1983;

Sorrentino and Field 1986; Reuman, Alwin, and Veroff 1984) with findings indicating that the level of achievement and power needs is a strong predictor of performance. Studies of achievement needs in education are recent, focusing only on administrators and students (Castenell 1983; Sorrentino and Field 1986; Farmer 1987).

Maslow (1954) developed another content theory of motivation. His general theory of human motivation is based on a concise hierarchy of five prepotent needs (physiological, safety, security, belonging, esteem, and self-actualization) that has enjoyed wide appeal, even in the area of work motivation. This taxonomy has been contemporized by deleting physiological and adding autonomy needs (Porter 1961; Lawler 1973) and by distinguishing between factors that promote satisfaction (motivators) and those that promote dissatisfaction (hygienes) (Herzberg 1966) to yield a more parsimonious hierarchy that clearly provides for behavioral regression under need-frustrating circumstances (Alderfer 1971). Despite these modifications, the content of each taxonomy does not seem conceptually distinct from Maslow's (MacPhail-Wilcox and Hyler 1985).

Human needs are culturally embedded (Porter 1961), and all needs can be expressed, frustrated, and satisfied in a variety of ways. From the interactionist perspective, motivation is the result of the interplay of individual and environmental circumstances. Thus, it is possible for different conditions to satisfy or frustrate individuals who express similar needs. It is also possible for the same conditions to satisfy different needs. This may be one reason that Herzberg's theory fails to distinguish unambiguously between hygiene factors and motivators (MacPhail-Wilcox and Hyler 1985).

Research about what motivates behavior is primarily descriptive or relational, but neither research is particularly well developed in education. Some studies describe self-reported motives and motivational deficiencies among teachers. Findings indicate generalized differences between people who pursue teaching careers and those who do not. Thus, they offer some guidance in designing reforms and organizational improvement plans that will attract, retain, and satisfy teachers.

Persons who pursue education careers are more strongly motivated by particular needs than are some other groups. Gould (1954), Sergiovanni (1967), Lortie (1969, 1975), and Bruno (1986) report that teachers are particularly motivated by nonpecuniary or psychic benefits, including "the work itself" and opportunities for self-improvement. These are wants that seem to fit within esteem, autonomy, achievement, and self-actualization need classifications. Gould (1954) reports that students not entering teaching placed stronger emphasis on motives pertaining to salary, work conditions, and advancement opportunities. Bruno (1986) estimated that it would require a very large pecuniary benefit to offset the absence of psychic benefits among teachers, and Murnane's investigation (1981) of teacher mobility patterns suggests that teachers have lost one important means of obtaining these psychic benefits (transfers to other schools).

Other descriptive studies give cause for concern about the degree to which veteran teachers find their work motivating and satisfying. Teachers report serious deficits in esteem, autonomy, and self-actualization needs (Sergiovanni and Carver 1973), the same factors that attracted them to the profession (Gould 1954; Lortie 1975; Bruno 1986). These perceived need deficiencies seem to be systematically related to teachers' age and gender, and perhaps ethnicity as suggested by a study in another sector (Bartel 1981).

Younger teachers report the greatest deficiencies in esteem needs; middle-aged teachers reported the most unmet higher order needs; and teachers older than age forty-five report the fewest unmet needs. Rather than meaning that schools satisfy these needs, Sergiovanni and Carver (1973) believe these data suggest that older teachers have become resigned to their work situations. Resignation seems to reduce expectations of need satisfaction.

A recent regression analysis of teacher motivation and burnout offers supporting evidence (Anderson and Iwanicki 1984). Teachers' perceptions of needs and level of burnout (feelings of exhaustion, depersonalization, and perceptions of personal accomplishment) were analyzed using a regression model with controls for age, gender, level of teaching, and years of teaching experience. When compared with previous findings, results indicated that teachers' needs for security and belonging were increasing, but they reported larger need deficiencies in esteem, autonomy, and self-actualization.

A secondary analysis using background variables to partition the data set indicated that gender, age, and experience moderated perceived need deficiencies. Male teachers reported larger need deficiencies then females, and younger, more inexperienced teachers reported significantly higher levels of burnout than older, more experienced teachers. Regressions also indicated that self-actualization and esteem need deficiencies were significant predictors of burnout, more so for emotional exhaustion than depersonalization or negative perceptions of personal accomplishments. Similar findings were obtained in a qualitative investigation (Blase 1982). It seems likely that gender, age, and experience may be proxies for underlying life and work conditions that influence teachers' perceived needs.

Because the level of need satisfaction is presumed to influence job attitudes, behaviors, and work outcomes, relational studies are important considerations. In general, studies linking job satisfaction, commitment, and productivity have produced consistent, albeit weak to moderate, correlations (Brayfield and Crockett 1955; Vroom 1964; Curry et al. 1986). Similar findings have been reported for relationships between job satisfaction, absenteeism, turnover, and employee mental and physical health (Steers and Porter 1983; Anderson and Iwanicki 1984; Scott and Taylor 1985). Other studies contest these findings (Clegg 1983; Bridges 1980), and attempts to specify the causal ordering among variables have been frustrating (Curry et al. 1986; Bridges 1980).

A more detailed analysis of these studies reveals that the most widely investigated job attitude is satisfaction. Investigations either employ molar or molecular measures of job satisfaction (Lawler 1973; Herzberg 1966). Molar measures assess general job or life satisfaction, while molecular measures tap satisfaction with particular job dimensions and conditions. Some studies employ both.

Early studies, based on molar job satisfaction measures, were not particularly illuminating. Steers and Porter (1983) observed that satisfaction with pay, work itself, and supervision make the largest contributions to global measures of satisfaction in the private sector. Herzberg's (1966) two-factor model and Lawler's (1973) job facet model are more informative. Rather than assessing overall job satisfaction, they tease out relationships between particular aspects of work and employee attitudes. While the content of Herzberg's model corresponds to Maslow's need hierarchy, the content of Lawler's job facet model is broader and contains more concrete descriptors of work conditions.

Replications of Herzberg's interview research in education conclude that teacher satisfaction is affected by job conditions that influence achievement, recognition, challenges intrinsic to teaching, responsibility, advancement, and professional growth opportunities (Sergiovanni 1967). Teacher dissatisfaction is influenced by job conditions, including salary, fringe benefits, type of supervision, working

conditions, administrative behaviors and practices, interpersonal relations, job security, and the impact of the job on their personal lives
(Sergiovanni 1967; Savage 1967; Wickstrom 1971; Holdaway 1978).
Specific aspects of work that are dissatisfying include housekeeping,
attendance, paperwork, lunch duty responsibilities, insensitive administrative practices and policies, and poor relationships with parents
and colleagues (Sergiovanni and Carter 1973). But the distinction
between satisfying and dissatisfying factors is ambiguous.

More recent studies of teacher motivation are based on the facet
model of job satisfaction. These studies are grounded in social systems theory in as much as they attempt to assess the fit between personal (idiographic) needs and organizational (nomothetic) expectations. Employees are asked how much of something, like pay or
autonomy, a job should provide and how much the job does provide.
The direction and size of the response discrepancy is taken as a measure of job facet satisfaction or dissatisfaction. Discrepancy measures
can then be used as independent variables to investigate other attitudes, behaviors, and performance outcomes. Job facet studies yield
stronger relations with other job attitudes and particular behaviors
(Fisher 1980; Bridges 1980), than do overall assessments of job satisfaction (Fisher 1980).

The job facet method has not been widely used in education research (Miskel, Glasnapp, and Hartley 1975; Bridges 1980), despite
the existence of reasonably good instruments (Smith, Kendall, and
Hulin 1969; Porter 1961; Holdaway 1978; Miskel 1974). Miskel,
Glasnapp, and Hartley (1975) report that teachers' satisfaction is significantly related to the discrepancy between desired and available
rewards. An investigation of school climate that used the discrepancy
methodology found important relations between student preferences
for particular classroom environments and their cognitive attainments (Rentoul and Fraser 1979, 1980). Fraser (1982) reports that
both teachers and students prefer classrooms with more personaliza-
tion, participation, investigation, differentiation, and independence
than is actually available. Further, student perceptions of these conditions in classrooms are different from teachers' perceptions, with
actual levels, as perceived by students, being lower.

Comprehensive studies of relations between teacher needs, satisfaction, other job attitudes, and behaviors are sparse. Spuck (1974),
Bridges (1980), and Bruno (1986) report that teacher perceived motivational conditions are correlated with certain withdrawal behaviors,
particularly absenteeism, turnover, and transfers, although the coef-

ficients and explained variance are not large. Bridges's study of elementary teachers suggests that relations between job facet satisfaction and absenteeism are mediated by job characteristics, particularly the amount of interdependence required by the job. Both Bridges and Bruno acknowledge the high cost of absenteeism and turnover to educational organizations, which in the private sector is estimated at $30 billion per year (Johns 1987).

Relations between teachers' motivational needs and productivity have not been investigated. In other sectors, such studies produce ambiguous findings (Likert 1958; Brayfield and Crockett 1955; Vroom 1964; Petty, McGee, and Cavender 1984). Some have argued that this is because performance produces satisfaction, rather than satisfaction producing performance, and that linkages between performance and organizational reward systems are imperfect (Lawler and Porter 1967). However, the strong evidence of an inverse relationship between satisfaction, turnover, and absenteeism (Ross and Zander 1957; Vroom 1964) suggests that relations between satisfaction and performance may be indirect and very complex.

Studies of student motivation from a content perspective are even less common than those pertaining to teachers. Achievement motivation is the most prominent motive investigated. It is inferred from student behaviors deemed to demonstrate concern for the quantity and quality of their work, like planning, striving, and competing. In general, students with high achievement motivation prefer to participate in setting performance goals, and they take personal responsibility for the results of their efforts. They are more future oriented than students with low achievement motivation and value intrinsically motivating tasks more than extrinsically rewarded tasks (Wlodkowski 1977; Stipek and Weisz 1981).

Recent reviews and investigations (Castenell 1983; Nolen-Hoeksema, Seligman, and Geigus 1986) indicate that student achievement motivation is a partial function of race, gender, social class, attribution biases, and the functional area of task involvement. These differences suggest that the utility of particular instructional, reward, and reinforcement processes will vary depending on the values of these mediating variables. In other words, one incentive would not be expected to motivate all students in a class to invest their resources in learning.

Farmer (1987) illustrated the differential strength of background, personal, and environmental influences on aspiration, mastery, and career commitment for children and adults. In general, aspiration motivation is most influenced by background factors, while mastery motivation and career commitment were most influenced by personal variables. However, in each model, all three sets of variables were significant, and the influence of each was mediated by ethnicity and gender.

The findings for student achievement motivation are hopeful. It is influenced by personal attributes, such as attribution biases, learned helplessness, self-esteem, persistence, and learned abilities, which are subject to treatment, and there are environmental circumstances, such as level of support, that are amenable to change. However, the specification of treatments and environments that will improve student motivation depend on the ability to determine and acquire the necessary resources and educational technologies that will accomplish these ends. This is a task that has only just begun under the rubric of microeconomic resource allocation studies.

Implications of Content Theories for Resource Allocation Studies

Content motivation literature indicates that teachers, more than some other populations, want jobs that will provide for esteem, autonomy, achievement, and self-actualization needs. However, the realities of teaching are disappointing. Need deficiencies in the same areas are related to burnout indexes, absenteeism, turnover, transfers, and attitudinal and behavioral changes (Veenman 1984). This disparity between what teaching jobs offer and what teachers want from their work deserves further investigation. It is important to determine what conditions teachers believe will enhance their satisfaction, enthusiasm, commitment, and productivity.

It seems reasonable to suspect that much teacher dissatisfaction springs from the undifferentiated structure, overregulation (Ratsoy 1973; Miskel, Fevurly, and Stewart 1979), and rigid resource configurations that characterize public education. These practices seem devoid of concern for esteem, autonomy, achievement, or self-actualization needs. Teachers are severely limited in opportunities to take on new professional functions and to obtain promotions. Accountability regulations that result in tighter controls on curriculum, pedagogy, testing, and appraisal reduce latitude for discovering and using improved production technologies in classrooms. Teachers' work responsibilities have become increasingly unwieldy as school purposes, curricula, span of student needs, and demands for paper accountability trails have increased. Yet neither fiscal resources nor structural and technological changes that would accommodate these changes have been forthcoming. Given these circumstances, the reports of burnout and reduced labor pools among teachers are not surprising.

Because the relational literature pertaining to teacher motivation is so underdeveloped, it is impossible to give a full empirical account of how perceived need deficiencies influence work attitudes, behaviors, and productivity. However, the emphasis teachers place on "the work itself" is worthy of substantial additional investigation. Job characteristics and job enrichment literatures offer one means by which this construct can be understood. Studies conducted within these frameworks report strong relations between job attributes, employee satisfaction and performance (Brass 1981; Oldham and Hackman 1981; and Ranson, Hinings, and Greenwood 1980; Ferris and Aranya 1983; LaRocco 1985).

Job characteristics are technical and interpersonal attributes of particular jobs. For example, jobs differ technically in their task variety, significance, and feedback. They also differ in the amount of autonomy, challenge, skill, and monotony. Jobs also have different interpersonal attributes. Some require significant interaction with and interdependence among other persons, while other jobs are accomplished in isolation.

Job characteristics scholars view work in a societal and organizational context, both of which influence job characteristics. Hence, job characteristics mediate relations between context and worker motivation, satisfaction, and productivity. The societal context of work is described in terms of its turbulence and velocity of change. For example, when the public is disturbed by economic, national defense, or social matters, schools are often the targets of blame as well as the agents of repair. Societal turbulence can lead to the dissolution, replacement, or improvement of schools and affects resources and resource allocation practices in schools.

The organizational context of work is described by its technologies (complexity, uncertainty, routine), anatomical structure (size, hierarchy, division of labor, span of control), and operational structure (centralization, formalization, standardization). Note that these organizational context factors influence the structural, technological, and regulatory attributes of schools and classrooms. Hence, organizational context encompasses the idea of hierarchical constraints on resource allocation described in the school finance literature. Furthermore, the concepts of technologies, anatomical, and operational structure can be used to identify and clarify constraints on satisfaction and productivity at each level of the organization.

Business studies indicate that these contextual conditions influence worker attitudes and behaviors through the task and interpersonal characteristics of a job. Task-related job characteristics include span of control, scope of responsibility, authority, variety, autonomy, challenge, significance, routine, monotony, and level of skill demanded. Of task attributes, span of control, scope of responsibility, and autonomy seem critically important to resource allocation issues in education. They concern the number and range of differences among students assigned to a teacher, the scope and depth of curriculum mandates and other responsibilities, and the degree to which technologies are constrained by hierarchial resource decisions, policies, and rules.

Interpersonal job characteristics include supervisory practices (task feedback), task support from others, degree of interdependent and collaborative relationships required, and status (Brass 1981; Oldham and Hackman 1981; and Ranson, Hinings, and Greenwood 1980; Ferris and Aranya 1983; LaRocco 1985).

It is important to note that perceptions of job characteristics are, in part, a function of individual attributes (Seligman and Schulman 1986; Weiner 1980; Pearce-McCall and Newman 1986; Ferris and Aranya 1983; Lopez 1982; Barrett, O'Connor, and Alexander 1980). Level of skill and knowledge, attribution biases, self-esteem, intelligence, and gender seem to moderate relations between job attitudes, turnover, termination, and performance.

The job characteristics literature (Brass 1981; Oldham and Hackman 1981; LaRocco 1985) seems especially useful for extending knowledge of relations between motivation, resource allocation, job attitudes, and productivity in public schools. It can help to identify and conceptualize hierarchical constraints on classroom production resulting from technologies as well as the anatomical and operational structures at each level.

It can be used also as a basis for determining how specific task and interpersonal job characteristics relate to teachers' work attitudes, behaviors, and productivity. It seems certain that the attributes inherent in anatomical and operational structures will influence teachers' decisions to use or not use particular classroom technologies for control and instruction. By combining this knowledge with information about how different classroom technologies influence the flow of resources to students, it will be possible to trace the effects of resource allocation decisions on student attitudes and productivity. In fact, logic suggests that student attitudes and productivity will be, in part, mediated by teacher attitudes and productivity.

The discrepancy model for studying need deficiencies provides a useful method for studying some of these issues. By investigating teacher perceptions of discrepancies between optimal and actual job characteristics (especially educational resources and pupil assignment practices) relative to particular tasks, changes that might enhance satisfaction with work and productivity could be identified. Similar investigations with students can elicit their perceptions of classroom conditions and instructional technologies that would increase their learning satisfaction and productivity. Both sets of discrepancies could be used to investigate other job attitudes, behaviors, and performance outcomes.

However, both the content motivation and resource allocation literatures warn that studies should attend to aptitude-treatment interactions. Recall the differences in findings associated with teacher age, gender, experience, and level of education. For students, important motivation differences are linked to aptitude, gender, ethnicity, socioeconomic status, attribution biases, and subject matter. These would seem to mediate perceived needs, need deficiencies, preferred stocks and flows of resources, desires for particular technologies, attitudes, and productivity.

Process Theories of Motivation, Research, and Resource Allocation

Process theories of motivation attempt to explain how motivation occurs and what factors influence the level of motivation. Only process theories of motivation that assume an information-processing view will be presented here. Goal, expectancy, and equity theories of motivation are described briefly and followed by a summary review

of research. The section closes with implications for resource allocation investigations based on an integrated interpretation of process
theories of motivation and the resource allocation literature.

Goal Theories of Motivation.   Goal theories of motivation assume
that human behavior is purposive and goal driven. Goals are viewed
as differentially attractive to individuals, and goal attainment is a
function of the number and difficulty of obstacles along a path to
the goal. Studies based on goal theories attempt to determine the
effects of goal setting on energizing and sustaining work satisfaction
and performance (Locke 1968; House 1971; Georgopoulos, Mahoney,
and Jones 1957).

Laboratory and field investigations of goal theory have been supported in noneducational settings (Lathan and Yukl 1975; Mento,
Cartledge, and Locke 1980; Ivancevich and McMahon 1982; Erez and
Kanfer 1983; Miller and Monge 1986; Erez, Earley, and Hulin 1985).
Findings suggest that explicit, difficult goals that are accepted by the
employee, participative goal setting, and formal performance feedback yield higher levels of satisfaction, organizational commitment,
efficiency (as measured by reduced costs and overtime), and effectiveness (as measured by quality control citations and proficiency
ratings).

However, these relations are complex, and conclusions often
depend on the particular dependent variables used in the study (Ivancevich and McMahon 1982; Shalley and Oldham 1985; Harackiewicz
and Larson 1986). For example, the degree to which feedback is controlling, the amount of task competence information contained in
the feedback, the source of feedback, and success in attaining difficult goals were observed to influence both attitudes and productivity
in studies of specific populations.

Unfortunately, goal theories of motivation are little more than
normative statements in the educational literature. There are no comprehensive investigations of goal theory for teachers or students reported in the literature reviewed. However, Blase (1982) conducted
a study of teacher burnout that is pertinent.

He proposed a teacher performance-motivation theory in which
teachers' perceptions of their effectiveness were based on attaining
instructional, moral, and counseling goals with students. His study
revealed that teacher burnout was a function of perceived failure to
overcome aspects of the job that interfered with attaining the three

types of goals. Further, burnout indexes correlated with reduced effort and reduced capacity to cope with job difficulties. Whether this means that burnout is an important job attitude influencing performance or that goal frustration leads to burnout is a matter of debate. Nonetheless, the study supports the contention that goal obstacles influence job attitudes and performance.

McConnell and Sosin (1984) report that despite inconclusive relations between class size and student performance on standardized tests, students are happier and learn to think more critically in smaller classes. This suggests that class size may be an important goal obstacle for students, and a survey of student perceptions in large economics and business classes seems supportive (McConnell and Sosin 1984). Here, student motivation, attention, and satisfaction with instructor interaction and instructional technologies seemed to be influenced by class size.

Expectancy Theory. Expectancy theory originated with Vroom (1964) and was later modified by Galbraith and Cummings (1967), Porter and Lawler (1968) and Lawler (1973). Like goal theory, it assumes that people react somewhat systematically to external stimuli, and these responses are a function of values (needs and wants), prior learnings, cognitive estimations, and anticipations.

Expectancy theory posits that people have approach-avoidance reactions to a variety of goals, such that each goal or outcome can be assigned a positive, neutral, or negative valence. It also assumes that people recognize "means-ends chains" (Simon 1957), such that the immediate outcomes of actions (direct outcomes) are more or less helpful (instrumental) in attaining or avoiding more remote outcomes (indirect outcomes). Further, the theory posits that people estimate the probability that they can perform the actions necessary to attain the direct outcomes. This probability estimate is called an expectancy, and it is influenced by an individual's ability, role perceptions, and attribution biases. Weiner (1980) explains that causal attributions (beliefs by which persons explain success and failure based on luck, ability, effort, or the gratuitious nature of others) result in emotive states that directly influence low and high achievement behaviors.

Research based on expectancy theory indicates that motivational force is positively correlated with job attitudes, effort, and some measures of productivity in noneducational settings (Mitchell 1974;

Arnold 1981). Others dispute these contentions on the basis of theoretical and methodological shortcomings (Campbell and Pritchard 1976; Schwab, Olian-Gottlieb, and Heneman 1979).

Tests of expectancy theory in education are recent, scant, but supportive (Mowday 1978; Miskel, Defrain, and Wilcox 1980) for administrators and teachers. The force of motivation seems to be a significant predictor of teacher job satisfaction and job performance (measured by administrative appraisals), but the overall variance explained is low. Instrumentality demonstrates the strongest relationship with job attitude and performance.

Because expectancy theory places substantial emphasis on external stimuli that may be perceived as rewards, and because teachers are strongly motivated by "the work itself," it is important to consider research pertaining to intrinsic and extrinsic motivation.

There is substantial evidence that people respond differently to intrinsic and extrinsic rewards. Extrinsic rewards that are administered contingent to good performance of an intrinsically motivating task will reduce subsequent intrinsic motivation for the same task and the effects of intrinsic and extrinsic rewards are not additive (de Charms 1968; Deci 1972; Morgan 1984). However, noncontingent monetary payments, verbal reinforcement, and the administration of rewards on the basis of an output criterion of excellence rather than a process criterion either have no effect or enhance intrinsic motivation (Deci 1972; Morgan 1984; Harackiewicz and Larson 1986; Hughes, Sullivan, and Beaird 1986).

The differential effects of these stimuli are explained in terms of an individual's self-perception as the origin of performance and their sense of competence. Extrinsic rewards cause behaviors once judged the result of private initiative or pleasure to develop an external locus of origin. This seems to precipitate feelings of increased dependency, reduced choice, diminished commitment, and loss of personal efficacy.

Recent work (Brass 1981; Hughes, Sullivan, and Beaird 1986; Gottfried 1986) indicates that the specific domain of the work task, task difficulty, performance evaluator, gender, perceptions of competence, and task anxiety may particularize the level of intrinsic motivation and response to extrinsic or intrinsic rewards. Despite the more extensive research in this area, relations between contingent reward strategies, work attitudes, and productivity await investigation.

Given the scant attention to expectancy theory among teacher populations, it is not surprising to find that the theory has not been applied to analyses of student motivation. This may be due, in part, to the fairly recent reconceptualization of students as workers in educational organizations. Nonetheless, expectancy theory, especially the concepts of valence, instrumentality, and expectancy seem useful tools for investigating the efficacy of resource allocation practices in education. Some utilities will be described in the closing section of this chapter.

Equity Theory. Equity theory is a social cognitive comparison framework for explaining and predicting motivation and behavior. It assumes an exchange process between individuals and between organizations and individuals. It was derived by integrating the concepts of deprivation, gratification, and distributive justice (Adams 1965) to explain human perception of and judgments about equity. The theory relies heavily on an economic model of costs and benefits, which are described as the inputs and outputs of exchange partners and comparison others.

Teachers and students are involved in an exchange process, albeit one is less freely choosen than the other. Teachers are hired by school districts in order to obtain their informational and energy resources. For this, they receive certain economic, psychological, and social benefits and disbenefits. Similarly, students are required to invest their resources (time, energy, forgone opportunities, knowledge, and skill) in schools in order to obtain technological resources that will enhance their human capital and later lead to additional social and economic benefits.

Each partner in an exchange expects personal contributions to be met by a just return. However, what one party perceives as a relevant input or benefit may not be isomorphic with others' perceptions of the same, and even undesirable receipts must be included in analyses of "benefits" associated with an exchange.

Within the equity framework, motivation and behavior are functions of perceived discrepancies between what people believe their returns should be and what they actually are relative to comparison with others, alternative opportunities, and their own inputs (such as time, abilities, effort, sacrifices, training, skills, job behaviors, and the like) (Adams 1965). Inputs and rewards are assumed to be weighted differentially by individuals. Morale and satisfaction are lower when the probability of obtaining a reward is estimated high but subsequently not obtained than when the perceived probability of obtaining the reward is low. The theory also posits that if the reward is not perceived to be what it should be relative to comparison others, those who are underrewarded experience a keen sense of injustice, hostility toward those who were rewarded, and diminished productivity.

More specifically, if rewards exceed what the employee thinks they should be and what similar others who put forth the same or more inputs received, guilt and other forms of discomfort will result, but not lowered morale and dissatisfaction. If returns are lower than the individual thinks they should be or lower than what others who put forth the same or less effort received, dissatisfaction and lowered productivity will result. When all these factors are congruent, the individual has the potential to experience high morale and satisfaction and to be more productive (Adams 1965).

Recent work suggests that people's perceptions of what their returns should be are a function of perceived job demands, especially job difficulty, level of responsibility, and job level in the hierarchy. When rewards do not parallel increases in these conditions, dissatisfaction will result. Despite the appearance of parsimony, the determination of satisfaction within this theoretical framework is complicated by the fact that people make qualitatively different attributions about the roles of effort, ability, and luck in obtaining particular outcomes (Jones 1976; Bradley 1978; Weiner 1980).

Adams (1965) found that perceived inequity influences a number of affective states and behavioral outcomes. Affective outcomes include morale and degree of satisfaction or dissatisfaction. Chief among the behavioral outcomes are distorted cognitions that seem to reduce perceived inequity, withdrawal from the exchange, hostile acts toward others, and lowered efficiency.

Recent extensions of this theoretical work and empirical studies have adopted a contingency perspective of distributive justice in organizations (Lansberg 1984). Within this framework, alternative distributive justice values guide resource allocation decisions and perceptions. These include equity, equality, winner-takes-all, and need, each of which may be appropriate depending on other institutional, situational, and individual factors. Relevant institutional and situational factors are the competitive or cooperative nature of the work situation, the level of risk associated with work, degree of impersonality or socioemotional emphasis in the situation, and hierarchical position of the employee.

There are laboratory and field tests of contingencies included in this extended equity framework. In general, variable preferences for different distributive justice values have been supported by research and the hierarchical level of the employee seems to moderate emphasis on organizational or unit equity concerns (Lansberg 1984).

Research based on equity theories of motivation in education is practically nonexistent. It is a theoretical base ripe with opportunity for the investigation of resource allocation and it is highly compatible with economic models (McClintock, Kramer, and Keil 1984). The linkage with economics is apparent in assertions that individuals attempt to maximize personal economic utilities and outcomes. Indifference curves, maps of preferences for combinations of inputs, offer one method of identifying differences in preferences for social, physical, and temporal resources among teachers and students with different life circumstances and with qualitatively or quantitatively different clients and educational needs (MacPhail-Wilcox and Hyler 1985; McClintock, Kramer, and Keil 1984). These indifference curves could then be linked to affective, behavioral, and performance outcomes for students and teachers.

Implications of Process Theories for Resource Allocation

Goal, expectancy, and equity theories of motivation are useful frameworks for exploring and analyzing the effects of resource allocation arrangements in education. They seem especially suited to analyses of organizational incentive plans and resource configurations that may influence satisfaction and productivity. Collectively, they suggest that higher salaries may be necessary but insufficient motivators for teachers.

Organizational incentives for teachers have been dominated by monetary rewards, promotion to scarce administrative positions, and assignment tradeoffs, such as exchanging one class assignment for bus duty or club sponsorship. Furthermore, professional development activities (such as conference participation, staff development, and new role assignments) and important organizational maintenance tasks (such as curriculum development and program and personnel assessment) are often whole group activities treated as add-on teacher duties. When these activities are not suited to the individual teachers' needs, they will contribute little to satisfaction or productivity. When they must be undertaken gratuitously either during summer months, on weekends, or after long and tedious workdays during the school year, they can hardly be viewed as incentives. Rather, they are demoralizing conditions that will affect teacher satisfaction and productivity negatively. It is little wonder that such practices do not prevail in private-sector jobs.

This narrow view of teacher incentives has prevailed despite the fact that content motivation research indicates that it is insufficient. Content and process theories of motivation suggest that organizational incentive systems must be broader in scope and more carefully conceptualized, if they are to address the range of needs characterizing human beings. They must extend beyond salary and test performance to incorporate the goals and incentives that are attractive to teachers and students. Only recently (Sizer 1985; Carnegie Corporation 1986) have modifications in teaching jobs that provide reasonable opportunities to improve student outcomes and assume new professional challenges received serious consideration.

Goal theories of motivation also serve as a reminder that other organizational practices, particularly student assignment plans, resource allocation practices, and politically prescribed technologies can be obstacles to goal attainment for both teachers and students. When these practices and policies interfere with teachers' ability to derive satisfaction from "the work itself," they will decrease work satisfaction and productivity. The job characteristics literature provides one framework for investigating the degree to which task and interpersonal aspects of work are perceived as goal obstacles by teachers.

For example, assume that "work itself" means helping students to change in important academic and social ways. If teachers perceive the span of control (class size and distribution of student aptitude) and scope of responsibilities (mandated curriculum, number of teaching assignments, and the like) to interfere with this, then these job characteristics will likely be sources of dissatisfaction and reduced productivity.

This proposition suggests a series of microeconomic investigations to determine the influence of job characteristics on the use of specific educational technologies, the subsequent flow of technological resources to students, and resulting student outcomes. Findings from such studies could lead to the identification of modified educational resource and student assignment arrangements that can improve the flow of resources to students and subsequently influence their attainments. This would also enhance teacher satisfaction and productivity.

Changing the job characteristics of teachers has implications for macroeconomic investigations also. Modifying job characteristics so that they are appropriate relative to the goals to be accomplished, the technologies available, and the particulars of the client base will either require additional resources, the reallocation of existing resources, or both. Thus, changing teacher job characteristics will alter organizational technologies and the stocks of educational and fiscal resources needed.

In assessing the degree to which resources and student assignment practices are perceived as goal obstacles, it is important to recall that satisfaction and productivity are specific to context. Consequently, it is necessary to determine which resource and student configurations are perceived to foster or obstruct the attainment of specific goals in clearly defined circumstances. Minimally, these circumstances include particular subject matter, range of student aptitude, achievement, and degree of socialized behavior. The degree to which resources and student assignment plans interact to influence the attainment of specific instructional goals should be assessed. If the obtained and desired outcomes are discrepant, organizational policies and practices that foster the discrepancy should be identified and altered. Such inquiries will aid the search for educational technologies appropriate for particular clientele and circumstances.

Expectancy theory extends goal theory by providing a mathematical model for measuring many of the aforementioned variables and computing the force of motivation. Research based on this theory indicates that it predicts work attitudes and some measures of productivity, albeit weakly in some cases. When expectancy theory is used within a microeconomic resource allocation study, both mean and dispersion measures of student performance should be used as productivity indexes.

Expectancy theory also can be used to address resource allocation questions at the organizational and classroom level. At the organizational level, expectancy models can be used to assess teachers' valences for rewards and opportunities included in the incentive system (indirect outcomes) and for causal conditions that lead to the attainment of organizational rewards (direct outcomes such as using particular teaching processes, student behavioral and cognitive performance indexes, and the like). These can be combined with instrumentality and expectancy measures in the usual ways (Lawler 1973) to compute the force of teacher motivation to attain particular organizational incentives. Teacher-perceived instrumentalities between direct and indirect outcomes can identify loose linkages in the incentive system, while teacher expectancy measures will reflect perceived abilities to produce the direct outcomes. Relations between and among each of these measures and other job attitudes, withdrawal behaviors, and productivity will produce a rich knowledge base to guide teacher recruitment and retention plans.

At individual and classroom levels, expectancy theory can be especially useful when combined with microeconomic findings regarding the flow of resources to students. It could be used to identify tacit teacher theories about (1) appropriate instructional technologies for obtaining varied student outcomes within particular contexts and for particular students; (2) resource flows that make these technologies more or less appropriate; and (3) how student assignment and resource allocation practices at the organizational level affect teachers' decisions to use particular technologies. This might be accomplished by asking teachers to assess the instrumentality between (1) particular technologies and student attainments for certain groups of students; (2) the use of a particular technology and the level of technological resources students receive; and (3) job characteristics (especially scope and span of control as reflected in student assignment practices, assigned responsibilities as reflected in mandated curriculum goals, educational and technological resources) and their subsequent ability to employ certain educational technologies (grouping arrangements, pedagogical techniques, and the like).

By combining this information with observed relations between resource flows inherent in particular technologies and various student performance indicators, it is possible to identify invalid pedagogical theories, inappropriate technologies, and organizational constraints on attitudes and performance.

Expectancy theory indicates that it is equally important to assess teacher expectancy. Given a particular set of teaching circumstances, how likely is it that the teacher could employ particular instructional technologies and why? Because this estimate encompasses ability approximations as well as contextual limitations, it could be used to identify suspect organizational constraints and staff development needs. If limiting factors were primarily contextual, organizational inquiries and adjustments are indicated; if they arise primarily from teacher ability, staff development and improved teacher selection are indicated. By combining expectancy theory and microeconomic resource allocation knowledge, it will be possible to identify organizational, technological, and teacher constraints on work satisfaction and productivity.

Similar studies with students would be instructive. To clarify the effect of classroom incentive systems, it would be helpful to know whether students perceive indirect and direct outcome relations in classroom reward systems. If so, what are they, and what valences do particular groups of students hold for these indirect and direct outcomes?

To further illuminate microeconomic issues, students might be asked about the usefulness (instrumentality) of different classroom student assignment practices and instructional technologies on their satisfaction and productivity. This information, when compared with microeconomic data describing resource flows associated with different instructional technologies and subsequent student performance outcomes, can identify technological and educational resource levels that students believe to influence their motivation to learn.

Given the significant emphasis on extrinsic rewards in goal and expectancy theories of motivation, a note of caution seems in order. Assuming the importance of "life long" and "continuous self-directed" learning, it seems essential to ensure that educational incentive systems foster intrinsic motivation for teaching and learning. Current research suggests this is possible when nonprecuniary and interpersonal reward strategies are emphasized and output rather than process criteria of excellence are used to assess performance. It is noteworthy that explicit output criteria of performance enable both students and teachers to assess their own productivity.

Equity theories of motivation can also illuminate resource allocation issues pertaining to incentive systems and productivity. Despite the fact that supporters of merit pay reforms point to teacher perceived inequities in traditional incentive systems, particularly salary plans, serious investigations of this assumption have yet to be undertaken. Furthermore, although equity theory is most often associated with notions of unjust compensation, it provides a framework for investigating perceived inequities in the distribution of resources and the use of particular technologies and student assignment plans.

For example, teachers assigned students with a wide dispersion of aptitude will likely perceive the assignment of an instructional aide to another teacher whose class has a more homogeneous aptitude as unfair. In the framework of equity theory, this will reduce the teacher's satisfaction and productivity. Similarly, students with less aptitude—say, in mathematics—may perceive the amount of time that teachers allocate to more able students as unfair, thus reducing their motivation to learn. To the degree that work tasks are perceived to vary in difficulty by teachers and students, logic seems to indicate different resource configurations and flows in order to attain equity.

In summary, content and process motivation theories offer rich and numerous frameworks for clarifying resource allocation questions. These theories are compatible with many economic assumptions and methods, and they offer unique methods and perspectives for explaining satisfaction and performance differences among teachers and students. It seems reasonable to expect motivation literature to help school finance scholars estimate and map the effects of resource allocation practices on both teachers and students. It is equally probable that resource allocation studies will inform the work of motivation scholars. Psychology and school finance are indeed powerful allies in the pursuit of more effective schools.

REFERENCES

Adams, J. S. 1965. "Injustice in Social Exchange." In *Advances in Experimental Social Psychology*, vol. 2, edited by L. Berkowitz, pp. 267–99. New York: Academic Press.

Alderfer, C. P. 1971. *Human Needs in Organizational Settings*. New York: Free Press.

Anderson, M. B., and E. Iwanicki. 1984. "Teacher Motivation and Its Relationship to Burnout." *Educational Administration Quarterly* 20 (2) (Spring): 109–32.

Arkes, Hal R., and John P. Garske. 1982. *Psychological Theories of Motivation*, 2d ed. Monterey, Calif.: Brooks/Cole.

Arnold, H. 1981. "A Test of the Validity of the Multiplicative Hypothesis of Expectancy-Valence Theories of Work Motivation." *Academy of Management Journal* 24: 128–41.

Atkinson, John. 1954. "The Achievement Motive and Recall of Interrupted and Completed Tasks." *Journal of Experimental Psychology* 46: 381–90.

Barr, Rebecca, and Robert Dreeben. 1983. *How Schools Work.* Chicago: University of Chicago Press.

Barrett, Gerald, Forbes O'Connor, and R. Alexander. 1980. "Ability-Satisfaction Relationship: Field and Laboratory Studies." *Academy of Management Journal* 23 (3): 550–55.

Bartel, A. 1981. "Race Differences in Job Satisfaction: A Reappraisal." *Journal of Human Resources* 16 (2): 294–303.

Blase, Joseph. 1982. "A Social-Psychological Grounded Theory of Teacher Stress and Burnout." *Educational Administration Quarterly* 18 (4) (Fall): 60–80.

Bradley, G. 1978. "Self-Serving Biases in the Attribution Process: A Reexamination of the Fact or Fiction Question." *Journal of Personality and Social Psychology* 36: 56–71.

Brass, D. 1981. "Structural Relationships, Job Characteristics, and Worker Satisfaction and Performance." *Administrative Science Quarterly* 26: 331–48.

Brayfield, A., and W. Crockett. 1955. "Employee Attitudes and Employee Performance." *Psychological Bulletin* 52: 396–424.

Bridges, E. 1980. "Job Satisfaction and Teacher Absenteeism." *Educational Administration Quarterly* 16 (2): 41–56.

Brown, Byron, and Daniel Saks. 1975. "The Production and Distribution of Cognitive Skills in Schools." *Journal of Political Economy* 83 (3): 571–93.

_____. 1980. "Production Technologies and Resource Allocations within Classrooms and Schools: Theory and Measurement." In *The Analysis of Educational Productivity*, edited by R. Dreeben and J. Thomas, pp. 53–117. Cambridge, Mass.: Ballinger.

_____. 1984. "An Economic View of the Acquisition of Reasoning Skills: Agenda for Research in the Information Age." *Review of Educational Research* 54 (4) (Winter): 560–76.

Bruno, James. 1986. "Supply-Demand Model of Teacher Shortage in Large Urban School Districts." *Journal of Education Finance* 11 (4): 447–59.

Campbell, J., and R. Pritchard. 1976. "Motivation Theory in Industrial and Organizational Psychology." In *Handbook of Industrial and Organizational Psychology*, edited by Marvin Dunnette, pp. 63–130. Chicago: Rand-McNally.

Carnegie Corporation. 1986. *A Nation Prepared: Teachers for the 21st Century.* New York: Carnegie Forum on Educational and the Economy.

Castenell, Louis. 1983. "Achievement Motivation: An Investigation of Adolescents' Achievement Patterns." *American Educational Research Journal* 20 (4) (Winter): 503–10.

Childs, Stephen, and Charol Shakeshaft. 1986. "A Meta-Analysis of Research on the Relationship between Educational Expenditures and Student Achievement." *Journal of Education Finance* 12 (2) (Fall): 249–63.

Clegg, C. 1983. "Psychology of Employee Lateness, Absence, and Turnover: A Methodological Critique and an Empirical Study." *Journal of Applied Psychology* 68 (1): 88-101.

Cohen, M. 1983. "Instructional, Management, and Social Conditions in Effective Schools." In *School Finance Improvement Linkages for the 1980s*, edited by A. Odden and L. D. Webb, pp. 17-50. Cambridge, Mass.: Ballinger.

Coleman, James, T. Hoffer, and S. Kilgore. 1982. *High School Achievement: Public, Catholic, and Private Schools.* New York: Basic Books.

Coleman, James, E. Campbell, D. Hobson, J. McParland, A. Mood, F. Weinfeld, and R. York. 1966. *Equality of Educational Opportunity.* Washington, D.C.: U.S. Department of Health, Education and Welfare.

Curry, J., D. Wakefield, J. Price, and C. Mueller. 1986. "On the Causal Ordering of Job Satisfaction and Organizational Commitment." *Academy of Management Journal* 29 (4): 847-58.

de Charms, R. 1968. *Personal Causation: The Internal Affective Determinants of Behavior.* New York: Academic Press.

Deci, Edward. 1972. "The Effects of Contingent and Noncontingent Rewards and Controls on Intrinsic Motivation." *Organizational Behavior and Human Performance* 8: 217-29.

Dreeben, R., and J. A. Thomas. 1980. *The Analysis of Educational Productivity, Vol. I: Issues in Microanalysis.* Cambridge, Mass.: Ballinger.

Erez, Miriam, and Frederick Kanfer. 1983. "The Role of Goal Acceptance in Goal Setting and Task Performance." *Academy of Management Review* 8 (3): 454-63.

Erez, Miriam, P. Earley, and C. Hulin. 1985. "The Impact of Participation on Goal Acceptance and Performance: A Two Step Model." *Academy of Management Journal* 28 (1): 50-66.

Farmer, Helen. 1987. "A Multivariate Model for Explaining Gender Differences in Career and Achievement Motivation." *Educational Researcher* 16 (2): 5-9.

Ferris, Kenneth, and Nission Aranya. 1983. "A Comparison of Two Organizational Commitment Goals." *Personnel Psychology* 36 (1): 87-98.

Fisher, Cynthia. 1980. "On the Dubious Wisdom of Expecting Job Satisfaction to Correlate with Performance." *Academy of Management Review* 5: 607-12.

Fraser, B. 1982. "Differences between Student and Teacher Perceptions of Actual and Preferred Classroom Learning Environment." *Educational Evaluation and Policy Analysis* 4 (4): 511-19.

Galbraith, J., and L. Cummings. 1967. "An Empirical Investigation of the Motivational Determinants of Task Performance." *Organizational Behavior and Human Performance* 2: 237-57.

Georgopoulos, B., G. Mahoney, and M. Jones, 1957. "A Path-Goal Approach to Productivity." *Journal of Applied Psychology* 41: 345-53.

Gottfried, A. 1986. "Academic Intrinsic Motivation in Elementary and Junior High School Students." *Journal of Educational Psychology* 77 (6): 631-45.

Gould, G. 1954. *The Teacher and His Work*. New York: Ronald Press.

Hanushek, Eric. 1986. "The Economics of Schooling: Production and Efficiency in Public Schools." *Journal of Economic Literature* 25 (September): 1141-77.

Harackiewicz, J., and J. R. Larson. 1986. "Managing Motivation: The Impact of Supervisor Feedback on Subordinate Task Interest." *Journal of Personality and Social Psychology* 51 (3): 547-56.

Herzberg, F. 1966. *Work and the Nature of Man*. Cleveland, Ohio: World.

Holdaway, E. A. 1978. "Facet and Overall Satisfaction of Teachers." *Educational Administration Quarterly* 14: 30-47.

House, R. J. 1971. "A Path-Goal Theory of Leader Effectiveness." *Administrative Science Quarterly* 16: 321-38.

Hughes, Billie, Howard Sullivan, and James Beaird. 1986. "Continuing Motivation of Boys and Girls under Differing Evaluation Conditions and Achievement Levels." *American Educational Research Journal* 23 (4) (Winter): 660-67.

Ivancevich, J., and J. McMahon. 1982. "The Effects of Goal Setting, External Feedback, and Self-Generated Feedback on Outcome Variables: A Field Experiment." *Academy of Management Journal* 25 (2) 359-72.

Johns, Gary. 1987. "The Great Escape." *Psychology Today* (October): 30-33.

Jones, E. 1976. "How Do People Perceive the Causes of Behavior?" *American Scientist* 64: 300-05.

Kirst, M. 1983. "A New School Finance for and Era of Fiscal Constraint." In *School Finance Improvement Linkages for the 1980s*, edited by A. Odden and L. D. Webb, pp. 1-15. Cambridge, Mass.: Ballinger.

Lansberg, I. 1984. "Hierarchy as a Mediator of Fairness: A Contingency Approach to Distributive Justice in Organizations." *Journal of Applied Social Psychology* 14 (2): 124-35.

LaRocco, James. 1985. "Effects of Job Conditions on Worker Perceptions: Ambient Stimuli vs. Group Influence." *Journal of Applied Social Psychology* 15 (8): 735-57.

Lathan, G., and G. Yukl. 1975. "A Review of Research on the Application of Goal Setting in Organizations." *Academy of Management Journal* 18: 824-45.

Lawler, Edward. 1973. *Motivation in Work Organizations*. Monterey, Calif.: Brooks/Cole.

Lawler, E., and L. Porter. 1967. "The Effect of Performance on Job Satisfaction." *Industrial Relations* 7: 20-28.

Likert, Renis. 1958. *The Human Organization*. New York: Wiley.

Locke, E. 1968. "Toward a Theory of Task Motivation and Incentives." *Organizational Behavior and Human Performance* 3: 157-89.

Lopez, Elsa. 1982. "A Test of the Self-Consistency Theory of the Job Performance-Job Satisfaction Relationship." *Academy of Management Journal* 25 (2): 335-48.

Lortie, Dan. 1969. "The Balance of Control and Autonomy in Elementary School Teaching." In *The Semi-Professions and Their Organization: Teachers, Nurses, Social Workers*, edited by Amatai Etzioni, pp. 1-53. New York: Free Press.

_____. 1975. *School Teacher: A Sociological Study*. Chicago: University of Chicago Press.

MacPhail-Wilcox, Bettye. 1981. "An Analysis of Investment in Teacher Education: The Texas Case, 1978-79." *Journal of Education Finance* 7 (4) (Spring): 462-72.

MacPhail-Wilcox, Bettye, and Linda Hyler. 1985. "Improving the Quality of Worklife for Teachers." *Journal of Research and Development in Education* 18 (3) (Spring): 16-23.

MacPhail-Wilcox, Bettye, and Richard King. 1986a. "Resource Allocation Studies: Implications for School Improvement and School Finance Research." *Journal of Education Finance* 11 (4): 416-32.

_____. 1986b. "Production Functions Revisited in the Context of Educational Reform." *Journal of Education Finance* 12 (2) (Fall): 191-222.

Maslow, A. 1954. *Motivation and Personality*. New York: Harper.

McConnell, C. R., and K. Sosin. 1984. "Some Determinants of Student Attitudes toward Large Classes." *Journal of Economic Education* (Summer): 181-90.

McClelland, David, R. Clark, and E. Lowell. 1953. *The Achievement Motive*. New York: Appleton-Century-Crofts.

McClintock, Charles, Roderick Kramer, and Linda Keil. 1984. "Equity and Social Exchange in Human Relationships." In *Advances in Experimental Psychology*, vol. 17, edited by Leonard Berkowitz, pp. 184-222. New York: Academic Press.

Mento, A., N. Cartledge, and E. Locke. 1980. "Maryland vs. Michigan vs. Minnesota: Another Look at the Relationship of Expectancy and Goal Difficulty to Task Performance." *Organizational Behavior and Human Performance* 25: 419-40.

Miskel, Cecil. 1974. "Intrinsic, Extrinsic, and Risk Propensity Factors in the Work Attitudes of Teachers, Educational Administrators, and Business Managers." *Journal of Applied Psychology* 59 339-43.

Miskel, C., D. Glasnapp, and R. Hartley. 1975. "A Test of the Inequity Theory for Job Satisfaction Using Educators Attitudes toward Work Motivation and Work Incentives." *Educational Administration Quarterly* 11: 38-54.

Miskel, Cecil, Robert Fevurly, and John Stewart. 1979. "Organizational Structures and Processes, Perceived School Effectiveness, Loyalty, and Job Satisfaction." *Educational Administration Quarterly* 9: 97-118.

Miskel, Cecil, J. DeFrain, and K. Wilcox. 1980. "A Test of Expectancy Motivation Theory in Educational Organizations." *Educational Administration Quarterly* 16 (Winter): 70-92.

Mitchell, R. 1974. "Expectancy Models of Job Satisfaction, Occupational Preference, and Effort: A Theoretical, Methodological, and Empirical Appraisal." *Psychological Bulletin* 81: 1053-77.

Monk, David. 1981. "Toward a Multilevel Perspective on the Allocation of Educational Resources." *Review of Educational Research* 51: 215-36.

_____. 1982. "Alternative Perceptions of Cost and the Resource Allocation Behavior of Teachers." *Educational Administration Quarterly* 18 (2) (Spring): 60-80.

Morgan, Mark. 1984. "Reward-Induced Decrements and Increments in Intrinsic Motivation." *Review of Educational Research* 54 (1) (Spring): 5-30.

Mowday, R. T. 1978. "The Exercise of Upward Influence in Organizations." *Administrative Science Quarterly* 23: 137-56.

Murnane, Richard. 1981. "Teacher Mobility Revisited." *Journal of Human Resources* 16: 3-19.

_____. 1984. "A Review Essay—Comparisons of Public and Private Schools: Lessons from the Uproar." *Journal of Human Resources* 19: 263-77.

Murray, Henry. 1938. *Explorations in Personality.* New York: Oxford University Press.

Nolen-Hoeksema, Susan, M. Seligman, Joan Geigus. 1986. "Learned Helplessness in Children: A Longitudinal Study of Depression, Achievement, and Explanatory Style." *Journal of Personality and Social Psychology* 51 (2): 435-42.

Oldham, G., and J. R. Hackman. 1981. "Relationships between Organizational Structure and Employee Reactions: Comparing Alternative Frameworks." *Administrative Science Quarterly* 26: 66-83.

Pearce-McCall, D., and Joseph Newman. 1986. "Expectation of Success Following Non-Contingent Punishment in Introverts and Extraverts." *Journal of Personality and Social Psychology* 50 (2): 439-46.

Petty, M. M., G. McGee, and J. Cavender. 1984. "A Meta-Analysis of Relationships between Individual Job Satisfaction and Individual Performance." *Academy of Management Review* 9 (4) 712-21.

Porter, Lyman. 1961. "A Study of Perceived Need Satisfaction in Bottom and Middle Management Jobs." *Journal of Applied Psychology* 45: 1-10.

Porter, Lyman, and Edward Lawler III. 1968. *Managerial Attitudes and Performance.* Homewood, Ill.: Richard D. Irvin.

Ranson, S., B. Hinings, and R. Greenwood. 1980. "The Structuring of Organizational Structures." *Administrative Science Quarterly* 25: 1-17.

Ratsoy, E. W. 1973. "Participative and Hierarchical Management of Schools: Some Emerging Generalizations." *Journal of Educational Administration* 11: 161-70.

Rentoul, A., and B. Fraser. 1979. "Conceptualization of Inquiry-Based or Open Classroom Learning Environments." *Journal of Curriculum Studies* 11: 233-45.

_____. 1980. "Predicting Learning from Classroom Individualization and Actual-Preferred Congruence." *Studies in Educational Evaluation* 6: 265–77.

Reuman, David, Duane Alwin, and Joseph Veroff. 1984. "Assessing the Validity of the Achievement Motive in the Presence of Random Measurement Error." *Journal of Personality and Social Psychology* 47 (6): 1347–62.

Ross, I., and A. Zander. 1957. "Need Satisfaction and Employee Turnover." *Personnel Psychology* 10: 327–38.

Rossmiller, Richard. 1983. "Resource Allocation and Achievement: A Classroom Analysis." In *School Finance and School Improvement: Linkages for the 1980s*, edited by A. Odden and L. Dean Webb, pp. 171–92. Cambridge, Mass.: Ballinger.

_____. 1986. "Resource Utilization in Schools and Classrooms: Final Report." University of Wisconsin-Madison: Wisconsin Center for Educational Research.

Savage, Ralph. 1967. "A Study of Teacher Satisfaction and Attitudes: Causes and Effects." Unpublished doctoral dissertation, Auburn University.

Scheuer, J. 1986. "The Distribution of Staff in New York State Schools 1984–1985." *Journal of Education Finance* 12 (1): 97–121.

Scott, K. D., and G. Taylor. 1985. "An Examination of Conflicting Findings on the Relationship between Job Satisfaction and Absenteeism: A Meta-Analysis." *Academy of Management Journal* 28 (3): 599–612.

Seligman, Martin, and Peter Schulman. 1986. "Explanatory Styles as a Predictor of Productivity and Quitting among Life Insurance Agents." *Journal of Personality and Social Psychology* 50 (4): 832–38.

Sergiovanni, Thomas. 1967. "Factors Which Affect Satisfaction and Dissatisfaction of Teachers." *Journal of Educational Administration* 5 (1) (May): 66–82.

Sergiovanni, Thomas, and Fred Carver. 1973. *The New School Executive: A Theory of Administration*. New York: Dodd, Mead.

Shalley, C., and G. Oldham. 1985. "Effects of Goal Difficulty and Expected External Evaluation on Intrinsic Motivation: A Laboratory Study." *Academy of Management Journal* 28 (3): 628–40.

Simon, H. A. 1957. *Administrative Behavior*. New York: The Free Press.

Sizer, Theodore. 1985. *Horace's Compromise: The Dilemma of the American High School*. Boston: Houghton Mifflin.

Smith, P., I. Kendall, and C. Hulin. 1969. *The Measurement of Satisfaction in Work and Retirement*. Chicago: Rand-McNally.

Sorrentino, Richard, and Nigel Field. 1986. "Emergent Leadership over Time: The Functional Value of Positive Motivation." *Journal of Personality and Social Psychology* 50 (6): 1091–99.

Spuck, D. 1974. "Reward Structures in the Public High School." *Education Administration Quarterly* 10 (1) (Winter): 18–34.

Stahl, Michael. 1983. "Achievement, Power, and Managerial Motivation: Selecting Managerial Talent with the Job Choice Exercise." *Personnel Psychology* 36: 775–89.

Steers, Richard, and Lyman Porter. 1983. *Motivation and Work Behavior*, 3d ed. New York: McGraw-Hill.

Stipek, Deborah, and John Weisz. 1981. "Perceived Personal Control and Academic Achievement." *Review of Educational Research* 51 (1): 101–37.

Thomas, J. Alan, Frances Kemmerer, and David Monk. 1982. "Efficiency in Educational Finance: The Classroom Perspective." In *Financing Education: Overcoming Inefficiency and Inequity*, edited by W. W. McMahon and T. Geske, pp. 100–18. Urbana: University of Illinois Press.

Veenman, Simon. 1984. "Perceived Problems of Beginning Teachers." *Review of Educational Research* 54 (2): 143–78.

Vroom, Victor. 1964. *Work and Motivation*. New York: Wiley.

Weiner, Bernard. 1980. "The Role of Affect in Rational (Attributional) Approaches to Human Motivation." *Educational Researcher* (July-August): 4–11.

Wickstrom, Rodney. 1971. "An Investigation into Job Satisfaction Among Teachers." Unpublished dissertation. University of Oregon.

Wlodkowski, Raymond. 1977. *Motivation*. Washington, D.C.: National Education Association.

10 THE POLITICS OF EDUCATIONAL PRODUCTIVITY

William Lowe Boyd
William T. Hartman

Until recently, educational productivity was a bit like the weather; everybody talked about it, but nobody did anything about it. Increasingly, however, people actually are trying to do something about improving educational productivity, in large part because of mounting public pressure for significant action. Despite few signs of increasing productivity, the costs of operating schools and colleges have been soaring. As Peter Brimelow (1987:199), senior editor of *Forbes* magazine sees it,

> The issue is not complicated. First, you look at the input versus the output. In the U.S. since 1945, spending per K–12 pupil, when adjusted for inflation, has virtually quadrupled. This represents a productivity collapse of 75 percent, completely without parallel in any other industry. *And this is before any consideration of output quality* — the apparent deterioration of which has been the focus of national debate typified by the *A Nation at Risk* report [emphasis in original].[1]

Indeed, on top of cost considerations, public concern about both the performance of our schools and our nation's economic "competitiveness" has become acute (Magnet 1988). Influential business leaders, such as David Kearns (1988), chief executive officer of the Xerox Corporation, now call our public schools "a failed monopoly," and many share Brimelow's (1986, 1987) dismal view of this domain.[2]

Consequently, businesspersons, politicians, and the public have embraced the proposition that a key to improving our "competitiveness" is to improve the efficiency and effectiveness of our system of education.[3]

Thus, the educational "excellence" reform movement, as Secretary of Education William Bennett often reminded us, is committed to improving the *results* of schooling.[4] Bennett and the Reagan administration also popularized the notion that we *know* how to do this, that we know *What Works* (U.S. Department of Education 1987a, 1987b). Moreover, they spread the idea that *what works does not require additional dollars*. What is needed, they argued—with support from an increasing number of scholars (Kirst 1983; Mann and Inman 1984; Rossmiller 1987; Walberg and Fowler 1987)—is more productive use of existing resources. Greater educational effectiveness, they proclaimed, can be achieved through greater efficiency in the management and operation of U.S. schools.

At the same time, the educational "excellence" movement has raised, in a new way, perennial questions about equity and adequacy in the provision of educational services to all sectors of our diverse population. Many observers and participants have grave concerns about current school reform policies that tend to divorce excellence from equity considerations and also try to build improvements on top of underfunded, inadequate schools (Bastian et al. 1985; Fowler 1988). Thus, the politics of educational productivity revolves around the contest over whose conceptions of efficiency and equity in schooling will prevail and, consequently, who will benefit and who will lose in resource allocation and decisionmaking in the structure, operation, and outcomes of the educational process.

If, as Secretary Bennett has claimed, we know "what works," why aren't we doing more of it? Bennett believes educators have been slow to apply what works because there is too little accountability of educators for producing desirable results.[5] Consequently, he championed a campaign to increase accountability. Despite occasional efforts in this regard in the past, real efforts to increase accountability have been just as rare as real efforts to increase productivity. Many in the public may agree with Secretary Bennett's view that the main impediments here are political ones, that teachers unions—and perhaps also school administrators (Rodman 1988)—are the villains blocking real improvement of schooling.[6] Such rhetoric is common, but there is little systematic analysis of such assertions. To what extent, really, are our problems with educational productivity *political* ones, rather than *technical* ones associated with insufficient knowledge of what works? Beyond these considerations, may *organizational* and *financial* factors also contribute significantly to the problem? These questions provide the point of departure for this exploratory chapter into this largely uncharted terrain.

To begin with, we need to deal at the outset with the scholarly view that we really know almost nothing about the educational production function—that is, "the relationship among the different inputs into and outcomes of the educational process" (Hanushek 1986: 1148). Although one can make a case for this view in the precise technical terms of economists, the models economists have used to explore this matter have been gross oversimplifications of the complexities of the schooling process. Thus, in a incisive critique, economists Byron Brown and Daniel Saks (1980: 112) conclude that the models of the education production function "most used are also most useless." The difficulties lie in the assumptions underlying the production function concept and their questionable validity in education. Problems abound with respect to the conception and measurement of outputs, inputs, and the relationships among them (see, for example, Brown and Saks 1980, 1981; Levin 1974; Hanushek 1972, 1979, 1986). This is not the place to delve into the specifics of these difficulties, but one example may convey a sense of the problems: Education production function studies typically use aggregate test scores or test score gains in which a single or average education production function is calculated for a group of students that is assumed to apply to all students equally. Yet if children learn in different ways and at different rates—as they in fact do—then the application of a single educational production for all students is inappropriate. This problem led Katzman (1971) to conclude, as Bickel (1986: 185) put it, "that it was no more reasonable to conceptualize *the* educational production function than *the* agricultural production function abstracted from crop or geography."

However, it should be noted that economists such as Eric Hanushek (1986) emphasize that public school educators generally are operating in disregard of what economists believe we *do* know. Consequently, for the purposes of this chapter we shall take the position that, while we are far from having the technical command of the education production function implied by Secretary Bennett's rhetoric about what works, we do have useful and important knowledge, gleaned from research on instruction and effective schools (Bossert 1988; Purkey and Smith 1983; Rossmiller 1987; Walberg 1984), that makes it impossible for educators to avoid responsibility for the practices they choose. In short, the burden of educational success no longer can be placed solely on the backs of children and their families.[7]

Thus, the central question of this chapter is why, until recently, has there been so little systematic effort by educators to improve educational productivity? Answers to this question help us understand why progress in improving school performance is so difficult, even now when pressure for better results is forcing attention to the issue. The roots of the educational productivity problem, we believe, are to be found in a complex tangle of technical, sociological, economic, and political factors. The result, we shall argue, is a political economy of public schooling that makes improvement in this arena difficult, but not impossible. In laying out our analysis, we first consider why educational productivity has become such an issue recently. Next, we review what is known about administrative efforts to increase educational productivity. In light of this discussion, we turn to our central issue—explanations for why so little usually is done to promote productivity. Finally, we consider forces and strategies likely to change this state of affairs.

THE EMERGENCE OF CONCERNS FOR EDUCATIONAL PRODUCTIVITY

The perennial concern of public educators has been the problem of securing adequate resources and facilities to provide access to schooling for all, regardless of their family background or geographic location. Thus, until the late 1960s equality in education was understood not in terms of educational *outcomes*, but in terms of *access* to favorable combinations of desirable inputs and recommended educational processes. The quest for "equal educational opportunity" in fact began from this point of view, based on a widespread belief that most poor and minority children were attending schools that were below average in staffing, resources, and facilities. When James S. Coleman's (1966) *Equality of Educational Opportunity* report appeared, however, it created an immediate furor because it contradicted this belief. Indeed, its finding that educational services generally were provided rather equally (in terms of gross input categories), and that student achievement varied primarily according to social class background, led to the popular, but erroneous, idea that schooling "doesn't make a difference." Not surprisingly, this touched off an extended scholarly debate and numerous reanalyses of the original data set (Jencks et al. 1972; Levine and Bane 1975). The Coleman report transformed the policy debate by redefining educational opportunity in terms of the *outcomes* of schooling. Further, it set in motion an urgent search for "effective schools" and instructional practices effective with disadvantaged children.

By the late 1970s, public concern was mounting over newspaper stories highlighting the declining average performance of U.S. students on standardized tests and invidious comparisons with the test performance of students in other countries. Although the latter often were confounded by comparing "apples and oranges"—the students of elite European secondary school systems versus the wider band of students gaining access in our comprehensive high school system (Kirst 1984: 73-93)—concern has continued to grow over unfavorable comparisons of the math and science performance of the middle band of students in the United States versus their counterparts in other countries. Moreover, contrary to widespread opinion, it is not clear that our top students compare well with the top students of other nations. As Magnet (1988: 86) notes, "The top 5 percent of the U.S. 12th-graders who took international calculus and algebra tests in 1982 came in dead last among the top 12th-graders of nine developed countries."

By the spring of 1981 a growing sense of crisis was manifested by the release of another controversial Coleman report, *Public and Private Schools* (Coleman, Hoffer, and Kilgore 1981) and by the appearance of the first installment of an "unprecedented" three-part series in *Newsweek* magazine entitled "Why Public Schools Fail" (*Newsweek* 1981). It is not surprising, then, that following the Republican victory in the presidential election of 1980, equity in education increasingly was defined by the Reagan administration in terms of competence or even "excellence" in student achievement outcomes. Indeed, with the release of the enormously influential *A Nation at Risk* report in 1983, achieving "excellence in education" was linked to national economic sruvival. Rather than fading into the obscurity most reports soon find, the rhetoric of *A Nation at Risk* caught on. With the increasing sense of a productivity crisis in U.S. industry, in competition with foreign producers—and above all Japan—the "excellence" school reform movement has continued long beyond the brief "window of opportunity" forecast for it in 1983. In fact, as Jennings (1987) has argued, the "competitiveness" crisis linked to schooling has become "the Sputnik of the eighties."

On top of the "competitiveness" crisis, other forces have reinforced pressures for improved student performance and school productivity. Demographic trends pose the dual challenge of a rapidly expanding body of retired, senior citizens and a growing body of at-risk minority students, soon to constitute one-third of all U.S. students. Because we will have moved from seventeen workers for every retired person in 1952 to three workers for every retired person by 1992, we no longer can afford high failure rates—if we ever could—among our increasing number of minority students, most of whom will need to become productive citizens if we are to maintain our standard of living (Hodgkinson 1985). Economic trends and constraints also have generated pressures for greater productivity in education. At the same time that evidence has mounted that more dollars spent do not necessarily produce better student outcomes (Hanushek 1981; P. Coleman 1986; Walberg and Fowler 1987), effective schools practices requiring few or no extra dollars have been documented that are associated with better outcomes (Mann and Inman 1984). Obviously, these developments lead to greater concern for cost-effectiveness and accountability. Despite frequent use of the rhetoric of cost-effectiveness, however, the rare use of actual cost-effectiveness techniques in educational decisionmaking is symptomatic of the strong tendency to neglect productivity concerns in education (Levin 1983, 1988).

Skillful and aggressive use of the federal "bully pulpit" to propagate the idea that we now know "what works" and its corollary, that greater accountability should be demanded, have been a key part of the contemporary politics of educational productivity. An important element of the federal effort has been the "Wall Chart" comparing the educational performance of the fifty states. Ginsburg, Noell, and Plisko (1988) assert that "the impact of the wall chart can be seen as completing the shift started by the Coleman Report to assess education primarily in terms of outcomes rather than inputs." The keen interest of the educational research community in the "effective schools" research (Purkey and Smith 1983), widespread attempts by school districts and even states to foster adoption of prescriptions coming out of this body of research, and occasional judicial attention to "minimally adequate" educational programs (van Geel 1987: 261–313) have lent credibility and legitimacy to the whole productivity movement.

Some significant milestones in this development are worth noting. First, the 1979 *Pauley v. Kelly* decision in West Virginia provided a detailed definition, largely in terms of educational outcomes to be efficiently achieved, of the meaning of the state's constitutionally guaranteed "thorough and efficient" system of public education (see van Geel 1987: 272). Then in the *Pauley v. Bailey* decision in 1982, Judge Arthur Recht provided a massive 244-page opinion elaborating the ways in which the state fell far short of providing this guaranteed "thorough and efficient" system (Sirkin 1985).

Second, although "most courts have avoided declaring that the state has a constitutional duty to educate effectively" and have been unwilling "to permit the schools to be sued for educational malpractice" (van Geel 1987: 261), the idea of a "right" to an effective education has been spreading. In a *Texas Law Review* article, Gershon Ratner (1985: 777, 781) has argued that state and federal constitutional law, and also the state common law of negligence, should be interpreted to impose a legal duty on public schools requiring them "to educate successfully in basic skills the vast majority of [their] students, regardless of the proportions of poor and minority students." Although legal scholars doubt Ratner's claim that the "effective schools" research could be used to convince the judiciary to accept this argument (van Geel 1987: 300), there are signs that educational leaders are beginning to adopt it. The most dramatic illustration has been the acceptance by the Council of Chief State School Officers of a plan embodying eleven *guarantees* of a high-quality secondary education for those students deemed least likely to finish high school (Olson 1987a, 1987b). These state guarantees (Olson 1987a: 17) include such bold provisions as

1. An education program "of the quality available" to students who attend schools with high graduation rates;
2. Enrollment in a school that demonstrates "substantial and sustained" student progress;
3. Enrollment in a school with "systematically designed and delivered instruction of demonstrable effectiveness" and with "adequate and up-to-date learning technologies and materials of proven value";

4. Information that would help identify at-risk students and report on school conditions and performance. The information must be "sufficient to let one know whether the guarantees are being met";

5. Procedures that enable students, their parents, or their representatives to ensure that these guarantees are met.

Thus, it seems that the "genie" of educational performance has gotten "out of the bottle." The upshot of these developments is that it is now clear that we are on the brink of what Murphy and Hallinger (forthcoming) call a "third generation" concept of equity in education. The first and second generation concepts of equity in education focused, respectively, on access to schooling and on equality of aggregated resources. The third generation concept holds that state of the art educational processes should be in place—and accessible to all, regardless of social class, tracking arrangements, and so forth—even if we still lack the knowledge about the education production function to be able to guarantee equity in outcomes. Agreeing with Murphy and Hallinger, Rossmiller (1987: 567) concludes that "most of the variables [found to be associated with school effectiveness] relate much more to the way in which resources are used—the processes of the school and classroom—than to the level of resources per se, thus lending support to the view that adequate resources are necessary, but not sufficient, to insure increased student achievement, and lending credence to the third generation equity issues."

WHAT DO SCHOOL ADMINISTRATORS DO ABOUT PRODUCTIVITY?

In light of this background, we now can examine the evidence about what school administrators typically do about productivity. School administrators usually feel a strong sense of dual responsibility for both the maintenance and improvement of their organizations. They try to foster improvement at the same time as they discharge their inescapable responsibilities for maintaining the day-to-day operation of their organizations. But, research shows that the latter dominate their activities. Indeed, systematic attention and concerted efforts toward the improvement of instruction and student achievement usually are conspicuous by their absence. In an extensive review of the literature, Boyd and Crowson (1981: 357–58) conclude that

> Research on what school administrators actually do has shown that they spend nearly all of the time on organizational maintenance and pupil control activities despite rhetoric about the importance of instructional leadership. ... [Thus] what may be most important is what school building principals *don't* do or do very little. ... [T]hey spend little time on the instructional program and entrepreneurship and much more time on disturbance handling. They do little by way of external public liaison activity and maintain a pronounced "inside" focus. Their resource allocation activity lacks economic muscle because they have little influence over the reward schedule for teachers.[8]

Similarly, in their thoughtful review of the literature, Leithwood and Montgomery (1982: 309, 331) found that research suggests that *less than half* of elementary school principals actually attempt to improve their schools' instructional effectiveness. Instead, the emphasis for typical principals usually is on maintaining a smooth-running organization, with harmonious staff relationships, and on assuming that teachers are competent and "leaving teachers alone to teach." By contrast, effective principals are quite achievement and task-oriented (Leithwood and Montgomery 1982: 320–23).

Studies in the Mintzberg (1973) mode that focus on how school administrators use their time document the common neglect of instructional improvement and student achievement. For example, Martin's five high school principals spent almost 80 percent of their time on organizational maintenance tasks (53.9 percent) and pupil control tasks (23.8 percent). By contrast, only 17.4 percent of their time was spent on the school's academic program (Martin and Willower 1981). Moreover, Peterson (1978: 3) found that neither of the two elementary principals he studied spent more than 6 percent of his time planning and coordinating the school program, curriculum, or materials. Although Peterson and Martin categorize activities differently, neither produced encouraging findings. As Peterson (1978: 3) noted, the time spent by principals on tasks associated with the technical or instructional core of the school "take[s] up less than 25 minutes in a six-hour day."

It is vital to recognize, of course, that the Mintzberg-type studies overlook the importance of indirect leadership techniques, strategic

280 MICROLEVEL EDUCATIONAL PRODUCTIVITY

actions, and one-time only activities, such as assignments in grouping teachers and students, which may be quite significant for the effectiveness of the educational program (Bossert 1988; Murphy forthcoming). Moreover, serious concerns have been raised about the ability of the Mintzberg methodology to capture the reality of school leadership (Gron 1982). Nevertheless, these studies still raise some serious questions about the priorities of school administrators.

If school principals seldom spend much time on improving the curriculum and instruction, may they be exerting substantial leadership and influence via their role in evaluating teachers? Here, again, the research findings are disturbing. Principals generally view supervision and evaluation of teachers as ticklish and even risky matters; consequently, they tend to minimize their activity in this domain (Shapiro and Crowson 1985). Rosenholtz (1985) presents similar findings in her review of the evidence on "effective schools." She notes "an NEA survey in which fewer than 50 percent of the randomly sampled principals reported sufficient time for the accurate assessment of teachers" and cites "an even gloomier picture" presented by Natriello and Dornbush (1980–81). "In their sample, teachers reported receiving formal evaluations from their supervisors only once in every three years" (Rosenholtz 1985: 368).

If routine supervision and evaluation are often minimized, what about the remediation or removal of incompetent teachers? Here, it appears that action often is postponed or avoided altogether—at least until the situation is so flagrant that it both demands and facilitates administrative intervention. The fact that Bridges' (1986) book on this subject filled a void in the literature is evidence in itself of the extent of this problem.

Could it be that district-level administrators or other supervisory personnel are filling the frequent gap in supervision and instructional leadership on the part of principals? Research in this area is thinner than on the principalship, but what we do know is far from encouraging (Wimpelberg 1988). Although successful school improvement efforts generally have—and probably require—sustained support from the central office (Fullan 1982; Clark, Lotto, and Astuto 1984; Jones and Leithwood 1988; LaRocque and Coleman 1985; Leithwood 1988; Purkey and Smith 1985), studies of central office activities suggest this occurs infrequently. As Wimpelberg (1988) summarizes this literature:

Salley (1979–80) reported that curriculum and instruction are low on super-intendents' lists of job priorities, regardless of the kinds of school districts they serve. In the same vein, Hannaway and Sproull (1978–79) found that chief and assistant superintendents spend an average of less than 1 percent of their time on instruction in schools and classrooms. Research by Pitner and Ogawa (1981) corroborates these findings. This literature appears to confirm a trend that Griffiths (1977: 102) had spotted in the 1960s: "This is the idea that administrators should have nothing to do with instruction."[9]

In sum, what probably occurs too often is what LaRocque and Cole-man (1985) saw in their research and described as a kind of "mutual non-interference pact" between school principals and central office administrators. If this tendency is coupled with the common reluc-tance of principals to supervise and evaluate teachers, the "isolated teacher" syndrome associated with the dearth of supportive *profes-sional* colleagueship in typical schools (Rosenholtz 1985), and the pervasive "treaties" underlying disengagement from teaching and learning (Powell, Farrar, and Cohen 1985; Sedlak et al. 1986), the upshot is "peaceful" but unproductive "co-existence" all around.

In this context, as Murphy and Hallinger (1987: 248) remark, there is increasing recognition that school "administrators are often inept managers of the technical core operations" of their organiza-tions. Clearly, teachers seem to feel that this is often the case (Urban-ski 1986). In fairness to school administrators, though, it should be noted that until recently scholars and preparation programs in edu-cational administration—reflecting the orientation of the field—also have neglected attention to organizational outcomes and student achievement (Erickson 1977, 1979). For example, Bridges (1982: 21–22) found that studies of organizational achievement were much rarer than of organizational maintenance.

Still, to return to an earlier theme, it could be argued that while day-to-day administrative attention to improving instruction and student achievement is infrequent, school managers nevertheless dis-charge their responsibility here through periodic strategic actions, as in budget and allocation decisionmaking. Research on this subject is again thin and again is not encouraging. Part of the problem is that educators have been slow to accept the idea that they have any sub-stantial responsibility for student learning outcomes. Instead, they cling to the view that what schools do is give students an opportu-nity to learn, which they must be able and willing to seize. Even when outcome-oriented approaches such as PPBS (Program Planning and Budgeting Systems) are used, educators may be inclined, as van Geel (1973) found, to persist in taking an access, rather than outcome-oriented stance. Studies of school district budgeting are rare (Hartman 1988a). Those that exist suggest that the process is politicized and that the interests of employees often take precedence over attention to student and instructional needs (Levy, Meltsner, and Wildavsky 1974: 64). Usually, an incremental, bargaining model of budgeting is followed (Guthrie, Garms, and Pierce 1988: 223–35). In this context, discussions of how allocations relate to improved instruction and achievement are few and far between.

Studies of budgeting within school buildings are even rarer. However, we suspect that the findings of a recent comparative case study of budget decisionmaking in four high schools, ranging from working-class to upper-middle-class student bodies, are representative of what usually occurs. In this study, Hartman (1988b) found that

> The possibility of linking distribution of resources to improving student achievement was *never* considered explicitly. No evidence was found that the use of any consistent achievement measures to provide information for decision making had been contemplated. . . . The primary objective of the allocation process in the four high schools examined was equality among teachers in workload and in meeting the teachers' self-declared needs for instructional supplies and equipment. In each school the allocation process worked differently, but functioned to distribute resources in such a way as to minimize conflict among school personnel and to establish a perception of fairness among teachers. Similar to Mann (1981: 4), this analysis found that "The current procedures for resource allocation at the building level have more to do with the equitability of adult working conditions than with the production of responsive learning environments for children."

In concluding this discussion of what school administrators do about productivity, we want to emphasize the strong contrast between descriptions of typical and effective schools. Speaking of elementary school principals, Leithwood and Montgomery (1982: 322) provide a forceful summation:

> Whereas the effective principal acts as an instructional leader, leadership provided by the typical principal is largely administrative. The primary goal of these principals is a smooth-running organization with emphasis on keeping activities in the school manageable in the midst of pressures for change. . . . With respect to teachers, running a smooth ship places the principal's main emphasis on harmonious interpersonal relationships. . . . The typical principal

is quite distant from curriculum or instructional decisions and initiates few changes in the school's program. Emphasis is placed on the existing professional competence of teachers and the value of "leaving teachers alone to teach." . . . [I]n strong contrast to the orientation of the effective principal, there is a lack of achievement orientation.

Similarly, Hord and Hall (1987) describe three types of principal styles: responder, manager, and initiator. They found that effectiveness in facilitating change increases with movement from responder to manager to initiator. Rosenholtz (1985: 369) reports that "principals or their administrative assistants in effective schools are ubiquitous in their efforts to monitor classroom affairs." Some research even suggests they are quite assertive and put pressure on teachers. "One of the principal and clearly controversial findings in this study," says Hubermann (1983: 24), "was that successful implementation often occurred at places where administrators exerted strong and continuous pressure on teachers" (see also Rosenholtz 1985: 361, 363).

On the other hand, Rossmiller's (1987) reading of the research on effective schools emphasizes the role of principals in building consensus and a team approach. He is in agreement with Rosenholtz's (1985) assessment of the literature, which stresses teacher participation in decisionmaking and consensus building regarding shared goals. Moreover, as Deal reminds us, principals cannot focus just on instructional improvement. They cannot risk neglecting any of four major domains to which leaders must attend; they must not only get things done but also meet human needs, manage conflict, and create shared meanings (Deal 1987). Similarly, Cuban (1986) argues that there are three *interrelated* core roles in principaling: instructional, managerial, and political.

It is important to note, however, a strong dissenting view (Rallis and Highsmith 1986)—favorably discussed by Shanker (1988) in a column aimed at the National Association of Elementary School Principals convention—that management and instructional/educational leadership more realistically should be viewed as two *different* jobs that should be divided. This view underlies the increasing tensions between leaders in teachers and principals associations over the respective role each group should play in instructional leadership.[10] Reflecting this problem, Bossert (1988: 346) notes that effective schools not only have strong principals but also teachers with high levels of autonomy, and he asks, "How are strong leadership and autonomy managed simultaneously?" This key question is now a central issue in the evolution of the current school reform movement in the United States.

WHY DON'T SCHOOL ADMINISTRATORS DO MORE TO PROMOTE PRODUCTIVITY?

The discussion so far raises a number of questions about the motivations of school administrators. What are the principal incentives and constraints influencing their behavior? What are their goals and, among these, which are they trying to maximize or optimize? To what extent, and under what circumstances, are they merely trying to "satisfice," both in terms of their own behavior and in terms of organizational outcomes? These generic kinds of questions really apply to managers in general and in all kinds of organizations, public and private. The more germane questions here are, What accounts for the traditional deemphasis of productivity in public schools, and how are school administrators drawn into the ambit of this tradition?

There are a variety of interesting answers to these questions to be found in the literature. Our brief survey of this subject is divided into three categories of explanations: economic-financial, sociological, and political. Our review is suggestive rather than exhaustive, but we believe that each of the explanations we discuss contributes something toward the construction of a comprehensive answer. Thus, we argue in conclusion that just as it would be absurd to disregard well-documented sociological and technological factors inhibiting educational productivity—such as ambiguous goals and a poorly understood technology—it also is no longer possible to disregard the influence of well-documented factors associated with the political economy of public schools, however unpalatable these may be to friends of public education who cling to the idea that the enterprise is essentially an altruistic crusade championed by disinterested public servants.

Economic and Financial Factors

To the extent that our knowledge about the education production function is weak or nonexistent, as some claim, apathy about educational productivity is understandable. As we noted at the outset, economists have directed a great deal of attention to the shortcomings of our knowledge in this arena. But as Brown and Saks (1980) and others have shown, for all their sophistication economists still have been unable to develop models of the production function that are fully appropriate for education. Although the deficiencies of our knowledge in this area represent a major constraint on our ability to operate schools more efficiently, research on systematic instruction, effective schools, use of school time and time on task, and cost effectiveness (Levin 1983) has provided a basis for far more than random or "superstitious" behavior. Consequently, ignorance about the technology of education cannot be used as an excuse for doing nothing to improve the effectiveness of schools and teaching.

Thanks to scholars such as Hanushek, Murnane, Levin, and Brown and Saks, the search goes on among economists for better models of the education production function. For example, in "The Microeconomics of Schooling" Brown and Saks (1981) discuss the complexity of modeling teaching and learning situations. Among other things, they note the problem of assuming optimizing behavior or effort in a classroom or school where the product is not sold at a market price. Here, they direct attention to the value of Leibenstein's (1980) "X-efficiency theory" as a means for dealing more realistically with situations in which optimization is unlikely. "When there is imperfect maximization, Leibenstein posits the existence of 'inert areas,' representing decisions that may not be optimal but from which people may be unwilling to move simply because it is costly to do so" (Brown and Saks 1981: 249). Leibenstein's X-efficiency theory suggests to Brown and Saks (1981: 249–50) that an effective school administrator may provide the motivation for the extra efforts needed to break out of "inert areas" and, more generally, to perform in a less cybernetic and more responsive and efficient manner. In making this point, though, Brown and Saks (1981: 249) touch on a key point influencing administrative behavior, one to which we shall have good reason to return: "Influencing the effort of lower levels requires some effort itself, *a cost that may not be less than the predicted benefits*" (emphasis added).

Spending levels for the financial support for public schools constitute another issue associated with productivity. On one side are those who argue that contemporary "excellence" reforms are being erected on the sands of inadequately funded school systems in some states and locales (Fowler 1988). Overworked teachers in underresourced schools scarcely provide a promising basis for improving the efficiency and effectiveness of public schools. As Kasten (1986: 281) observes, "The prior condition for any effort at redesigning teacher's work is adequate resources in the form of salaries, reasonable class sizes, and supplies and materials. The accountability movement in education has focused on outputs and shown little interest in [such] resources." On the other side are critics, such as Brimelow (1986, 1987), who castigate public educators for a "productivity collapse." They note that spending per K through 12 pupil has nearly quadrupled in the United States since 1945 and output quality seems to have declined. Generally speaking, the critics have been winning the political debate over productivity. Their argument has been bolstered by findings such as those of Walberg and Fowler (1987: 13), who conclude from their statewide analysis in New Jersey that "it appears that it is the educational policies of districts and the instructional practices in classrooms rather than expenditures that consistently determine achievement and efficiency. Thus, changes in educational policies and practices rather than expenditures may offer the best chance of improving efficiency." Similarly, Ginsburg, Noell, and Plisko (1988) observe that the federally sponsored Wall Chart comparisons "reinforced findings that the level of resources in schools—in other words, money spent on education—is not strongly associated with school outcomes. Many high-achieving states had relatively modest expenditures. . . . The news media have publicized these low correlations and questioned whether school systems are using funds to maximum efficiency."

Sociological Factors

Perhaps the most comprehensive sociological explanation for the deemphasis of productivity in schools is found in Meyer and Rowan's (1977, 1978) discussion of schools as "institutionalized organizations." Their starting point is the idea—supported by considerable evidence—that educational institutions tend to be "loosely coupled" organizations (March and Olsen 1976; Weick 1976; Meyer et al. 1978; Hannaway and Sproull 1978-79). As they put it (Meyer and Rowan 1978: 79) this means that "structure is disconnected from technical (work) activity, and activity is disconnected from its effects." This loose coupling is manifested in schools by such characteristics as the strong tendency to "leave instructional activities and outcomes uncontrolled and uninspected." Despite this pattern, Meyer and Rowan argue that schools manage to command legitimacy and support by means of the use of standardized categories of students, teachers and curriculum topics that "give meaning and definition to the internal activities of schools." These "ritual classifications" are "institutionalized in the legal and normative rules of the wider society. Meyer and Rowan (1978: 80) conclude that

> In the American situation, attempts to tightly link the prescriptions of the central theory of education to the activities of instruction would create conflict and inconsistency and discredit and devalue the meaning of ritual classifications in society. Educators (and their social environments) therefore decouple their ritual structure from instructional activities and outcomes and resort to a "logic of confidence": Higher levels of the system organize on the *assumption* that what is going on at lower levels makes sense and conforms to rules, but they avoid inspecting it to discover or assume responsibility for inconsistencies and ineffectiveness. In this fashion, educational organizations work more smoothly than is commonly supposed, obtain high levels of external support from divergent community and state sources, and maximize the meaning and prestige of the ritual categories of people they employ and produce.

To the extent that Meyer and Rowan's analysis is correct, it helps us understand the behavior of school administrators. "Ritual classification" and a "logic of confidence" are useful tools for people operating in loosely coupled organizations characterized by ambiguous goals and unclear technologies. In the absence of a well-understood production function, administrators and society generally may come to rely heavily on "myth and ceremonies" to structure activities in sensitive institutions like schools. Even if there were a better understood technology for effective education, disagreement and shifting priorities about the various goals of public schools can make continuity and effective planning and management quite difficult to achieve (McPherson, Crowson, and Pitner 1986: 80). This is especially a problem within the political structure of decisionmaking for public education, since it lends itself to interest group activity and contestation. Cuban (1975) provides a vivid depiction of what can result in his account of the decisionmaking process in a turbulent period in the Washington, D.C., school district.

This point brings us to the question of what society or its governing segments really expect schools to be accomplishing. On the one hand, U.S. schools are supposed to be promoting social mobility and a democratic, egalitarian society, with a strong emphasis on the civic and collective as well as private benefits of schooling. Yet at the same time, many people, including some educators, continue to believe that students from lower social class backgrounds rarely are capable of much learning or social advancement. Schools and administrators often are caught in the middle of this tension, which manifests itself particularly through patterns of curriculum tracking for students of differing social classes. Many critics of these arrangements agree with Oakes's (1986: 13) assessment: "Even as they voice commitment to equality and excellence, schools organize and deliver curriculum in ways that advance neither."

Murphy and Hallinger's (forthcoming) analysis of "equity as access to learning" underscores the problem. They show that evidence "is growing for the position that pupils in lower ability clusters and tracks not only often fail to receive the putative benefits of grouping, but receive less of many of the important alterable learning resources that promote such important outcomes as achievement and goal aspirations." Murphy and Hallinger conclude that "the lack of rewards gained by teachers working with low groups . . . the perceived need to trade academic expectations for student goodwill [and] a lack of inspection of learning conditions within and among groups and tracks has contributed to the problem, as has a generally reduced sense of accountability for outcomes of non-academic track students." Thus, to the extent that administrators adhere to the old notion of educational opportunity as merely access to schooling (with students shouldering full responsibility for the outcomes) and perceive (rightly or wrongly) that society expects little learning from disadvantaged children, their lack of accountability for results frees them from the burden of worrying about productivity.

This analysis, of course, connects with the Marxist critique of class bias in capitalist schooling systems (Bowles and Gintis 1976). In this interpretation, schools are constrained to be instruments for social control and the reproduction of an unjust structure of social stratification. Schooling maintains inequality by fostering and reinforcing different skills and attitudes that divide people from one another. Because this is done in the name of "meritocratic" competition among students, the process is perceived to be fair, which legitimizes and maintains the system. It follows, in this view, that educational administration becomes far more a "technology of control" than anything to do with genuine education (Bates 1983).

Even if one does not accept this view, one is still left with the disturbing problem of the performance and functions of the tracking system. There is also the troublesome question of whether public schools in the United States really have been expected to provide efficient, high-quality intellectual training. Jill Conway (1987) calls attention to the historic tension between elitism and egalitarianism in U.S. schooling and its resolution toward anti-intellectual egalitarianism. In a provocative interpretation, she argues that this resolution was tacitly abetted by the feminization of teaching and stereotypes about women teachers' limited intellectual capacities and tendencies toward the maternal and emotional rather than the rational and critical mindset necessary for intellectual education. Again, to the extent that society and school administrators have accepted an anti-intellectual form of egalitarianism, this orientation reduces expectations for academic productivity on the part of schools.

If public schools were as loosely coupled and anarchic as some have claimed (Meyer et al. 1978; March and Olsen 1976), school administrators would face nearly insurmountable obstacles in trying to manage them efficiently and productively, even if they were strongly inclined to do so. However, recent research, such as Crowson and Morris's (1985) analysis of administrative control within the Chicago school system, supports Willower's (1979) contention that school systems are neither as loosely coupled nor tightly bureaucratic as some earlier research indicated (Hannaway and Sproull 1978–79; Rogers 1968).

Two sociological theories help to flesh out the arrangements that facilitate the functioning of loosely coupled organizations. "Negotiated order" theory is concerned with how order is established and maintained in organizations through a process of interaction among members who negotiate a variety of rules, agreements, and understandings, most of which are informal and unofficial (Day and Day 1977; Strauss et al. 1963). Much of the informal bargaining that occurs in this interaction and negotiation can be understood in terms of "exchange theory," developed most notably by Homans (1958) and Blau (1964). Based on an economic calculus of benefits, and the need for mutually beneficial accommodations among groups and actors, exchange theory emphasizes the need for reciprocity and *quid pro quo* arrangements in social relationships ("You scratch my back and I'll scratch yours").

Crowson and Morris (1985) found that such negotiations and exchanges were among the key factors promoting coordination and control in the Chicago school system. Moreover, as we have noted earlier, recent scholarship on the problems facing school reformers is replete with evidence of the pervasiveness, throughout the entire hierarchy of school systems, of informal bargaining, "treaties" (Sedlak et al. 1986; Powell, Farrar, and Cohen 1985; Rosenholtz 1985), "mutual non-interference pacts" (LaRocque and Coleman 1985), and the like. Thus, Hubermann (1983: 23) found that "much of the innovation process is taken up with bargaining, both explicit and implicit. One person's 'strategy' for school improvement collides with another person's 'strategy' for avoiding a loss of status or freedom or benefits."

Political Factors

With the salience of bargaining behavior in exchange theory, negotiated order, and "organized anarchy" theory (March and Olsen 1976), we have entered the domain of theories that are political as well as sociological. It is but a short jump directly into the realm of "micropolitics" in organizations, with its focus on the strategic use of influence, manipulation, bargaining, and coalitions (Bacharach and Lawler 1980; Bacharach and Mitchell 1987; Hoyle 1985, 1986; Pfeffer 1978). Even without leaving the bounds of exchange theory we can begin to see why school administrators frequently are reluctant to push for more productive behavior: *The costs of working out such exchanges with subordinates often are perceived to be greater than the benefits received.*

To see why this is the case, one must look at the constraints on the ability of school administrators to direct or motivate teachers. As Hoyle (1986: 135) observes, in his evocative discussion of the micropolitics of schools in the British context,

> The problem for heads [i.e., principals] is that they have a high degree of authority but the legal sanctions which underpin this authority will only be invoked relatively infrequently. Moreover, teachers have a relatively high degree of autonomy supported by professional norms which inhibit the exercise of legally-based authority of the head. Thus the head's administrative

control must depend to a considerable degree on the exercise of latent power and on influence. This would seem to be likely to encourage the head's deployment of micropolitical strategies in the somewhat gaping interstices within the management structure.

In the U.S. context, the power and authority of school principals seems even more limited. Based on interviews with 113 principals in 59 elementary school districts in suburban Chicago, Dan Lortie (*Education News* 1988: 10) concluded that

> The relationships principals find most valuable are not with their superiors [or with parents], but those with teachers. . . . Principals are dependent in many ways for their personal satisfaction and their ability to advance in their careers on their ability to get along well with the teachers in their buildings. . . . This dependency on teachers creates peculiar tensions for principals, largely because of the ambiguous nature of principals' authority. Central offices often possess final authority on many important matters and the principal's autonomy depends on his ability to gain the trust of more highly placed administrators. That relationship is fragile and is often tested. Unhappy teachers can complicate the relationship. As a result, many principals take few risks with new programs and seek to build strong personal relationships with teachers. . . . The strong impression is of persons relying more on their ability to win influence and good relationships than on the assertion of powers being built into the office they hold. It is also consistent with a reality in which formal powers are indeed weak. Principals adapt to those realities in ways that are understandably rooted in interpersonal skills rather than use of powerful rewards and punishments.

Given the conditions in which teachers typically work—as modestly compensated solo practitioners, heavily dependent for occupational survival and personal satisfaction on the cooperative attitudes and academic ability and success of their students (Lortie 1975)—the maintenance of a favorable balance between organizational inducements and their personal contributions is often problematic (Rosenholtz 1985). In particular, the psychic costs teachers face frequently threaten to overwhelm the psychic rewards or "earnings" they receive (Rosenholtz 1985). Thus, it is not surprising that teachers in typical schools are apprehensive about being "supervised" or evaluated and are reluctant to ask for help or advice (Rosenholtz 1985).[11] Consistent with exchange theory, they behave like Blau's (1955) government agents, who were reluctant to ask for help and advice for fear of being thought incompetent or because they did not want to become indebted to those from whom they sought help.

In this context, Hoyle (1986: 125–49) observes that both principals and teachers must be creative in exploiting the limited "goods" they have available for purposes of bargaining and exchange. Thus, a principal may swap lax application of rules and autonomy for a teacher's support and opinion leadership among peers. When the going gets tough, though, a principal may have to resort to bolder micropolitical strategies, such as dividing and ruling, cooptation, displacement, controlling information, and controlling meetings (Hoyle 1986: 140–48). Although concerned about the ethical issues involved, Hoyle notes that administrators sometimes use such tactics as: "rigging" agendas, "losing" recommendations, "interpreting" consensus, and "massaging" the minutes of meetings (1986: 145–46).

Since playing politics or even exerting strong leadership can be risky for school administrators, we need to know more about incentives and disincentives that may foster or discourage more venturesome behavior on their part. Here, theory and research (Barry and Hardin 1982; Niskanen 1971) on rational choice behavior and the political economy of public-sector organizations add considerably to the insights of exchange theory and micropolitics. Interpretations in this body of knowledge range along a continuum that runs from reasonable to strident versions of the same logic. Unfortuantely, the more extreme versions—which unfairly contrast public-sector organizations with idealized versions of efficient, profit-seeking firms—cause many people to dismiss the logic of the whole argument, which is quite consonant with the precepts of exchange theory discussed so far.

Rational choice theory begins with the reasonable assumption that individuals seek to maximize their welfare and, accordingly, make rational choices or decisions toward this end. In assessing the costs and benefits of alternative courses of action, they are sensitive to the incentive or reward structures in which they find themselves. Since public, nonprofit organizations lack a profit motive, this leads to questions about the nature of the incentives that operate in its absence. For instance, given the tenuous nature of principals' authority in public schools and their dependence on the good will of teachers, why should principals risk trying to change and improve things? What are the rewards for doing these kinds of things? As one of our practitioner/graduate students remarked, "How many principals are willing to stir things up and possibly have to move to another job as a result? How often will even risk-takers be willing to do this? And how many times will the superintendent or central office be willing to 'go to the wall' for principals when they stir things up?"

Of course, if there were keen incentives in the school district for improving performance, then one could envision the central office strongly supporting and rewarding principals who "stirred things up" or, better, were able to improve productivity by more harmonious interpersonal and group processes. Note, however, that even the latter approach involves changing things, which can be risky. The question remains, then, about how strong the incentives are likely to be for better productivity. A closer examination of the political economy of public schools provides a disturbing view of this matter.

Analysts using the perspective of market-oriented political economy contend that the nonprofit, government-supported character of public human services organizations tends to create a perverse structure of incentives for employees (Michaelsen 1977, 1981). In the quasi-monopolistic, consumer-insentive setting of such organizations, the reward structure often is not oriented toward performance. "Public choice" theorists emphasize the profound effects of two features of public-sector organizations. First, public managers lack property rights or a profit motive in the successful performance of the organization. Second, the organization receives a tax-supplied budget independent of satisfying individual consumers. From these starting points, much of the behavior of public school personnel that might otherwise appear irrational or "loosely coupled" can be explained. For instance, because there are no profits in public schools to motivate and reward managers (and teachers' salaries are based on seniority rather than performance), educators—as rational, self-interested people seeking to maximize their own welfare—may be inclined to maximize their nonpecuniary benefits. This means that in place of profits (which would depend on satisfied customers) public educators may seek to maximize such things as the size of their budget, the scope of their activities, the ease of their work, and their power and prestige. On the other hand, they will try to minimize their psychic costs by avoiding risks and conflict insofar as possible.

In short, the personal goals of employees in public schools often will take precedence over the official goals of the schools because the costs of inefficient behavior, in terms of the official goals (such as student outcomes or consumer satisfaction), are low. Indeed, in the argot of economists, this state of affairs creates a "demand for inefficiency," since the "law of demand" postulates that demand for various "goods" increases as their cost decreases (Chambers 1975). Thus the discrepancy between personal and official goals that is accentuated by the reward structure in public-sector organizations creates the basis for the distinctive "bureaucratic politics" that characterize such organizations and their relationships with clients and sponsors (Boyd and Crowson 1981; Michaelsen 1977, 1981; Ostrom and Ostrom 1971). From the point of view of productivity, Chubb and Moe's (1988) analysis comparing the attitudes of public and private school teachers and administrators suggests that the political preoccupations set in motion by public education's governance structure have negative consequences for school effectiveness.

Even if one rejects the "public choice" interpretation outlined above, Shapiro and Crowson's (1985) analysis of the supervisory behavior of twenty-four Chicago public school principals shows the value of rational choice theory. This study explored why these principals, on the average, spent only 7 percent of their time in classrooms, even though the observation and improvement of teaching are supposed to be among their most important roles. Although principals themselves were inclined to say that they were "just too busy" to be able to find the time, and that it was neither necessary nor very useful to observe teachers, the ethnographic data in this study suggested a more basic explanation to Shapiro and Crowson: "it is just *not in the best interests* of building principals to engage in classroom observation" (1985: 17, emphasis in original).

In support of this conclusion and consistent with Lortie's observations reported above, they note, first, that "principals intrude infrequently into the classroom teacher's private educational domain because principals need and depend upon the cooperation of teachers, a cooperation endangered by close supervision" (1985: 17). Thus, they found that "teachers may actively sabotage overly close supervision of effort" with such micropolitical tactics as

> forgetting to bring requested materials to conferences, overloading a principal with trivial requests or decisions, constantly arriving late at meetings, neglecting personal duties (e.g., hall monitoring) and exhibiting a general slowdown in report preparation; these are among the subtle cues (plus some not so subtle such as increased numbers of grievances) delivered to principals by teachers to suggest that all is not well in the superior-subordinate relationship.

As a result of these sorts of cues, "principals typically downplay the classroom observation element in the supervisory role in favor of a

tacit understanding that teachers owe them something in return"
(1985: 19).

A second reason that principals did not observe teachers more in
the Chicago school system is that such behavior was not rewarded by
the system. Indeed, Shapiro and Crowson present evidence showing
that sometimes principals were punished rather than rewarded for
rigorous evaluations of teachers or efforts to get rid of true incompetents. Moreover, *the operative values in the system really emphasized
control rather than instruction* as the purpose of classroom observation (1985: 22):

> Although conceivably a mechanism for the improvement of instruction . . .
> the observation of classroom activity serves the principal more as a mecha-
> nism for "keeping the lid on" in the school. Principals are more likely to be
> punished organizationally (e.g., transferred to less desirable schools) for their
> failure to keep their buildings devoid of visible conflict, away from damaging
> publicity and generally free of vocalized parental displeasure than for a failure
> to be instructionally effective.

In sum, school administrators are not irrational. Like most people,
they calculate the benefits and costs of different courses of action in
light of the reward structure that prevails around them. Superintendents and central office administrators, as well as school principals,
are sensitive to the likely consequences of their behavior. They try to
anticipate the reactions and consequences of their acts and seek to
optimize their welfare. Because of the significance of the feelings and
attitudes of teachers, particularly due to the potential power of their
unions, principals and even superintendents may be inclined to be
more solicitous to their concerns than to those of (generally unorga-
nized) parents. Given a reward system for teachers that is insensitive
to performance—and teachers unions' resistance to reforms that
would change this, such as merit pay and career ladders (Malen and
Hart 1987)—those with the most interest in better productivity (parents and citizens) are in a weak position to pursue that interest.

As we noted at the outset of this section, a complete explanation
of the tendency to deemphasize concerns for school productivity
would most likely combine and integrate the various themes we have
covered under several headings. Thus, economic-financial, sociological, and political explanations would be united in a balanced and
theoretically integrated fashion. We presently lack such a framework,
but recent developments in the relatively new field of the economics

of organizations (Barney and Ouchi 1986; Moe 1984; Zald 1987) suggest that we are getting closer to a body of theory capable of handling many of the relevant concerns. Combining a "contractual perspective on organizational relationships, a theoretical focus on hierarchical control, and formal analysis via principal-agent models" (Moe 1984: 739), the new economics of organizations is moving toward a positive theory of hierarchy that illuminates the classical concern for balancing inducements and contributions in organizations (Barnard 1938; Simon 1947). In so doing, it aids the investigation of questions of personal goals, information asymmetry, shirking, monitoring devices, and incentive structures that range up and down a complex, multistage hierarchy of institution and environment (Crowson and Boyd 1987).

POLICY IMPLICATIONS: BREAKING THE PRODUCTIVITY LOGJAM IN EDUCATION

The picture of public education we have sketched out is one in which there is a strong tendency toward "treaties" and "peaceful," but unproductive "co-existence" throughout the hierarchy, from superintendents down to students. Although there are effective schools and pockets of excellence here and there, these seem to be exceptions within the general framework. Insofar as productivity is concerned, school administrators and teachers too often seem to operate as fairly detached actors within loosely coupled systems. With students distancing themselves from schooling, through bargaining and "choosing" what they will learn (McKenzie 1979); teachers generally performing as isolated, solo practitioners; principals walking a delicate line vis-à-vis their ambiguous authority; and superintendents and central office administrators often rather detached about curricular and instructional matters—the actors within the system seem "lonely," not only "at the top" but also the bottom and middle (cf. Jackson 1977).

The contemporary need to diagnose and cure what ails public education has created a virtual growth industry. Depending on one's diagnosis, cures range from "hard" to "soft" prescriptions. If one accepts an unadulterated version of the diagnosis by "public choice" theorists, then the implications argue strongly for healthy doses of market competition—that is, merit pay, voucher plans, and the like.

Although not necessarily connected logically, this approach is super-ficially compatible with hard-nosed recommendations to "get tough," raise standards, root out incompetents, and apply "no-nonsense" business methods. On the other hand, if one is drawn toward more sociological diagnoses, then the prescription is more likely to involve ways to break down the detachment and isolation in school systems, which foster unproductive exchange relationships, and replace them with more collaborative professional arrangements (Rosenholtz 1985). When the problem is seen in this light, competi-tion—which may exacerbate isolated individualism—seems just the opposite of the medicine that is needed (Bacharach, Bauer, and Shedd 1986; Cohen 1983; Johnson 1986; Kasten 1986). Indeed, in some of the most thoughtful analyses of the problem, Murnane (1981, 1985) and Cohen and Murnane (1985) have shown why, in the context of school teaching, merit pay tends not to work as intended.

What both schools of thought agree about, though, is that there is a strong need to "restructure" public schools so that their internal dynamics and incentives are more conducive to productive relation-ships, What is at issue, essentially, is how to achieve a more produc-tive balance of control or integration (via markets or hierarchies or a mix of both) and professional autonomy in school systems (cf. Lortie 1969; Boyd 1988; Elmore 1988; Kasten 1986).[12] The policy recommendations of the so-called first and second wave of the cur-rent reform movement are at odds on this matter. In a nutshell, the first wave reforms emphasized centralized control and standards for schools and teachers, but the second wave has emphasized restructur-ing schools and professionalizing and enhancing teaching as a career, goals that conflict with the first wave's emphasis (Boyd 1987). So far, our states have adopted much more of the first wave's agenda than that of the second wave. Significantly, with the exception of Minnesota and a few other places, proposals to promote competition (such as merit pay and parental choice of schools) have not garnered substantial political support in either wave of the reform effort (Boyd and Kerchner 1988).

Critics of the first wave's tendency to try to "legislate learning" call attention to a vicious circle connecting school governance and school performance (Chubb 1988; McNeil 1986). Schools having problems attract more attention from reformers, who impose addi-tional outside mandates on them, further eroding the organizational autonomy necessary to foster a climate for effective teaching and learning. Thus, Chubb (1988: 47) notes that "schools have not been granted more autonomy; they have had it taken away. . . . Improvement is being pursued teacher by teacher through testing, credentialling, and evaluation, and not through efforts to foster consensus, collegiality, or collective responsibility."

The tension between control and autonomy seen in the first and second waves also lurks in many policy proposals, even those calling for decentralization and restructuring. For example, Cuban (1988: 572) notes that David Kearns (1988), in his "An Education Recovery Plan for America," calls for increased parental choice and teacher autonomy but couples these with a somewhat contradictory set of mandates regarding the length of the school year, required core courses, and the linking of student promotion and teacher pay to student achievement. Rather than being a fault, what this point illustrates is that optimal organizational arrangements may be characterized by what Peters and Waterman (1982) saw in their excellent companies as "simultaneous loose-tight properties." That is, they were "both centralized and decentralized" (1982: 15) and distinguished by "the co-existence of firm central direction and maximum individual autonomy" (1982: 318). The firm central direction sets the key values and parameters that guide activity, but the sphere of activity has an openness that encourages individual initiative and creativity. Analysis of the recent literature on educational policy and management suggests that the optimum approach in school reform also would be characterized by "simultaneous loose-tight properties" (Boyd 1987).

Thus, school site management plans, school improvement efforts, and the restructuring of schools and the teaching profession must inevitably be conducted within the parameters of state and national goals, equity considerations, and legal requirements (Caldwell and Spinks 1988). We may wish to free schools and educators from bureaucratic regulations and release creativity, but, as Albert Shanker's proposal (Olson 1988) to do this illustrates, it is very difficult to escape the need, within the framework of public schools, to attach a number of conditions constraining this very freedom. Although complete freedom is not possible, it is possible to reduce bureaucratic rigidity and provide—at the same time—both more professional autonomy and more emphasis on student learning outcomes. Through judicious combinations of accountability for achievement goals, professionalization, and incentive systems that promote teamwork and reward group efforts, public schools can become more productive. The challenge is to move the politics of educational productivity toward the achievement of such delicate combinations of "loose-tight" properties.

NOTES

1. Baumol (1967) sees more complexity than Brimelow. Noting the difficulties of increasing the efficiency of labor intensive services, such as education, he observes that public sector providers, such as public schools, must compete with the private sector for labor, with the consequence that public-sector labor costs are likely to increase even without gains in economic efficiency.

2. Summarizing his *Forbes* article (Brimelow 1986), Brimelow (1987: 201) says it "argued that the American education industry, like the Soviet agricultural industry, has the systemic flaws of all socialized enterprises operating outside the discipline of market forces. For example: it demands resources to the limit of its political capacity; it allocates them in the interest of its controlling bureaucracies without any particular regard for the result; its productivity is catastrophic; it is continually swept by top-down panaceas (open classrooms, virgin lands, longer school years) peddled to its political masters by assorted hustlers."

3. In his generally supportive response to Kearns (1988), Cuban (1988: 572) notes that increased productivity comes from three sources: labor, management, and technology. "By focusing on labor (and the role of the schools in helping to shape attitudes and skills), you ignore the crucial decision-making role that management plays in deciding whether to develop or apply technologies to production; you also ignore the strategic errors that corporate management has made over the decades. These decisions have had much to do with enhancing or hindering productivity."

4. Address to the National Press Club in Washington, D.C., September 8, 1987.

5. Address to the National Press Club in Washington, D.C., September 8, 1987.

6. Address to the National Press Club in Washington, D.C., September 8, 1987.

7. Indeed, as discussed later, an argument has even been advanced that there may be a legal basis for a case of "educational malpractice" if educators fail to provide documented "effective schools" practices (Ratner, 1985).

8. See the extensive review of research supporting these conclusions in Boyd and Crowson (1981: 336–61).

9. Given the increasing concern for school effectiveness, more recent research might show more attention toward instructional improvement on the part of central office administrators.

10. On the issue of dividing the principal's responsibilities, see Donaldson's (1988) discussion of the principal's moral authority and the need for integrated leadership in the "just school."

11. As Rosenholtz (1985: 378) stresses, "While the product of exchange in isolated settings is often sympathy, the product of exchange in collegial settings is often ideas."

12. Whatever is done, a preliminary step is to expect schools to produce acceptable results with all children, so that they must operate beyond a "logic of confidence" and mere access to schooling.

REFERENCES

Bacharach, Samuel B., Scott C. Bauer, and Joseph B. Shedd. 1986. "The Work Environment and School Reform." *Teachers College Record* 88 (2) (Winter): 241–56.

Bacharach, Samuel B., and E. J. Lawler. 1980. *Power and Politics in Organizations.* San Francisco: Jossey-Bass.

Bacharach, Samuel B., and Stephen M. Mitchell. 1987. "The Generation of Practical Theory: Schools as Political Organizations." In *Handbook of Organizational Behavior*, edited by Jay Lorsch, pp. 405–18. Englewood Cliffs, N.J.: Prentice-Hall.

Barnard, Chester I. 1938. *The Functions of the Executive.* Cambridge, Mass.: Harvard University Press.

Barney, Jay B., and William G. Ouchi, eds. 1986. *Organizational Economics.* San Francisco: Jossey-Bass.

Barry, Brian, and Russell Hardin, eds. 1982. *Rational Man and Irrational Society? An Introduction and Source Book.* Beverly Hills, Calif.: Sage.

Bastian, Ann, N. Fruchter, M. Gittell, C. Greer, and K. Haskins. 1985. *Choosing Equality: The Case for Democratic Schooling.* New York: The New World Foundation.

Bates, Richard. 1983. *Educational Administration and the Management of Knowledge.* Victoria, Australia: Deakin University Press.

Baumol, William. 1967. "Macroeconomics of Unbalanced Growth: The Anatomy of Urban Crisis." *American Economic Review* 57 (June): 415–26.

Bickel, Robert. 1986. "Educational Reform and the Equivalence of Schools." *Issues in Education* 4 (3) (Winter): 179–97.

Blau, Peter M. 1955. *The Dynamics of Bureaucracy.* Chicago: University of Chicago Press.

———. 1964. *Exchange and Power in Social Life.* New York: Wiley.

Bossert, Steven T. 1988. "School Effects." In *Handbook of Research on Educational Administration*, edited by Norman J. Boyan, pp. 341–52. New York: Longman.

Bowles, Samuel, and Herbert Gintis. 1976. *Schooling in Capitalist America: Educational Reform and the Contradictions of Economic Life.* New York: Basic Books.

Boyd, William L. 1987. "Public Education's Last Hurrah? Schizophrenia, Amnesia, and Ignorance in School Politics." *Educational Evaluation and Policy Analysis* 9 (2) (Summer): 85–100.

_____ . 1988. "Balancing Control and Autonomy in School Reform: Competing Trends and Policy Issues." Paper presented at the American Educational Research Association Annual Meeting, New Orleans, April 6.

Boyd, William L., and Robert L. Crowson. 1981. "The Changing Conception and Practice of Public School Administration." In *Review of Research in Education*, vol. 9, edited by David C. Berliner, pp. 311–73. Washington, D.C.: American Educational Research Association.

Boyd, William L., and Charles T. Kerchner, eds. 1988. *The Politics of Excellence and Choice in Education.* New York: Falmer Press.

Bridges, Edwin M. 1982. "Research on the School Administrator: The State of the Art, 1967–1980." *Educational Administration Quarterly* 18 (3) (Summer): 12–33.

_____ . 1986. *The Incompetent Teacher.* New York: Falmer Press.

Brimelow, Peter. 1986. "Are We Spending Too Much on Education?" *Forbes* (December 29): 72–76.

_____ . 1987. "Victorian in Style or Substance? A Comment on Hickrod." *Journal of Educational Finance* 13 (2) (Fall): 198–201.

Brown, Byron W., and Daniel H. Saks. 1980. "Production Technologies and Resource Allocations within Classrooms and Schools: Theory and Measurement." In *The Analysis of Educational Productivity: Vol. 1, Issues in Microanalysis*, edited by Robert Dreeben and J. Alan Thomas, pp. 53–117. Cambridge, Mass.: Ballinger.

_____ . 1981. "The Microeconomics of Schooling." In *Review of Research in Education*, vol. 9, edited by David C. Berliner, pp. 217–54. Washington, D.C.: American Educational Research Association.

Caldwell, Brian J., and J. M. Spinks. 1988. *The Self-Managing School.* New York: Falmer Press.

Chambers, Jay G. 1975. "An Economic Analysis of Decision-Making in Public School Districts." Unpublished paper, Graduate School of Education and Human Development, University of Rochester.

Chubb, John E. 1988. "Why the Current Wave of School Reform Will Fail." *The Public Interest* (Winter): 28–49.

Chubb, John E., and Terry M. Moe. 1988. "No School Is an Island: Politics, Markets, and Education." In *The Politics of Excellence and Choice in Edu-*

cation, edited by William L. Boyd and Charles T. Kerchner, pp. 131–41. New York: Falmer Press.

Clark, David L., L. Lotto, and T. Astuto. 1984. "Effective Schools and School Improvement: A Comparative Analysis of Two Lines of Inquiry." *Educational Administration Quarterly* 20 (3): 41–68.

Cohen, David K., and Richard J. Murnane. 1985. "The Merits of Merit Pay." *The Public Interest* 80: 3–30.

Cohen, Michael. 1983. "Instructional, Management, and Social Conditions in Effective Schools." In *School Finance and School Improvement Linkages for the 1980s*, edited by Allan Odden and L. Dean Webb, pp. 17–50. Cambridge, Mass.: Ballinger.

Coleman, James S., E. Q. Campbell, C. Hobson, J. McPartland, A. Mood, F. Weinfeld, and R. York. 1966. *Equality of Educational Opportunity*. Washington, D.C.: U.S. Government Printing Office.

Coleman, James S., T. Hoffer, and S. Kilgore. 1981. *Public and Private Schools: A Report to the National Center for Education Statistics by the National Opinion Research Center*. Chicago: University of Chicago.

Coleman, Peter. 1986. "School Districts and Student Achievement in British Columbia: A Preliminary Analysis." *Canadian Journal of Education* 11 (4): 509–21.

Conway, Jill K. 1987. "Politics, Pedagogy, and Gender." *Daedalus* 116 (4) (Fall): 137–52.

Crowson, Robert L., and William L. Boyd. 1987. "Rational Choice Theory and the School Administrator." Unpublished paper, University of Illinois at Chicago.

Crowson, Robert L., and Van Cleve Morris. 1985. "Administrative Control in Large-City School Systems: An Investigation in Chicago." *Educational Administration Quarterly* 21 (4) (Fall): 51–70.

Cuban, Larry. 1975. "*Hobson v. Hansen*: A Study in Organizational Response." *Educational Administration Quarterly* 11 (2) (Spring): 15–37.

_____. 1986. "Principaling: Images and Roles." *Peabody Journal of Education* 63: 107–19.

_____. 1988. "You're on the Right Track, David." *Phi Delta Kappan* 69 (8) (April): 571–72.

Day, Robert, and Jo Anne V. Day. 1977. "A Review of the Current State of Negotiated Order Theory: An Appreciation and a Critique." *The Sociological Quarterly* 18 (Winter): 126–42.

Deal, Terrence E. 1987. "Effective School Principals: Counselors, Engineers, Pawnbrokers, Poets . . . or Instructional Leaders?" In *Instructional Leadership: Concepts, Issues, and Controversies*, edited by William Greenfield, pp. 230–45. Boston: Allyn and Bacon.

Donaldson, Gordon A., Jr. 1988. "Management Is Not a Four-letter Word: On the Principal's Moral Authority." *Reflections 1988*, edited by National Network of Principals' Centers, pp. 36–39. Cambridge, Mass.: Harvard Graduate School of Education.

Education News. 1988. "Studying the Work of Principals" Newsletter of the Department of Education, University of Chicago: 10–11.

Elmore, Richard F. 1988. "Choice in Public Education." In *The Politics of Excellence and Choice in Education,* edited by W. L. Boyd and C. T. Kerchner, pp. 79–98. New York: Falmer Press.

Erickson, Donald A., ed. 1977. *Educational Organization and Administration.* Berkeley, Calif.: McCutchan.

_____ . 1979. "Research on Educational Administration: The State-of-the-Art." *Educational Researcher* 8 (3): 9–14.

Fowler, Frances C. 1988. "The Politics of School Reform in Tennessee." In *The Politics of Excellence and Choice in Education,* edited by W. L. Boyd and C. T. Kerchner, pp. 183–97. New York: Falmer Press.

Fullan, Michael. 1982. *The Meaning of Educational Change.* New York: Teachers College Press.

Fuller, Bruce. 1986. "Defining School Quality." In *The Contributions of the Social Sciences to Educational Policy and Practice: 1965–1985,* edited by Jane Hannaway and Marlaine Lockheed, pp. 33–69. Berkeley, Calif.: McCutchan.

Ginsburg, Alan, Jay Noell, and Valena White Plisko. 1988. "Lessons from the Wall Chart." *Educational Evaluation and Policy Analysis* 10 (1) (Spring): 1–12.

Griffiths, Daniel E. 1966. *The School Superintendent.* New York: Center for Applied Research in Education.

Gron, Peter C. 1982. "Neo-Taylorism in Educational Administration?" *Educational Administration Quarterly* 18 (4) (Fall): 17–35.

Guthrie, James W., W. I. Garms, and L. C. Pierce. 1988. *School Finance and Education Policy,* 2nd ed. Englewood Cliffs, N.J.: Prentice-Hall.

Hannaway, Jane, and Lee S. Sproull. 1978–79. "Who's Running the Show? Coordination and Control in Educational Organizations." *Administrator's Notebook* 27 (9): 1–4.

Hanushek, Eric A. 1972. *Education and Race.* Lexington, Mass.: D. C. Heath.

_____ . 1979. "Conceptual and Empirical Issues in the Estimation of Educational Production Functions." *The Journal of Human Resources* 14 (3): 351–88.

_____ . 1981. "Throwing Money at Schools." *Journal of Policy Analysis and Management* 1 (1): 19–42.

_____ . 1986. "The Economics of Schooling: Production and Efficiency in Public Schools." *Journal of Economic Literature* 24 (3) (September): 1141–77.

Hartman, William T. 1988a. *School District Budgeting.* Englewood Cliffs, N.J.: Prentice-Hall.

_____. 1988b. "Understanding Resource Allocation in High Schools." Unpublished paper, Pennsylvania State University (February).

Hodgkinson, Harold L. 1985. *All One System: Demographics of Education—Kindergarten through Graduate School.* Washington, D.C.: Institute of Educational Leadership.

Homans, George C. 1958. "Social Behavior as Exchange." *American Journal of Sociology* 63 (6): 597–606.

Hord, Shirley M., and Gene E. Hall. 1987. "Three Images: What Principals Do in Curriculum Implementation." *Curriculum Inquiry* 17 (1): 55–89.

Hoyle, Eric. 1985. "Educational Organizations: Micropolitics." In *International Encyclopedia of Education*, edited by T. Husen and T. N. Postlethwaite, vol. 3, pp. 1575–82. Oxford: Pergamon Press.

_____. 1986. *The Politics of School Management.* London: Hodder and Stoughton.

Hubermann, A. Michael. 1983. "School Improvement Strategies That Work: Some Scenarios." *Educational Leadership* (November): 23–27.

Jackson, Philip. 1977. "Lonely at the Top: Observations on the Genesis of Administrative Isolation." *School Review* 85 (May): 425–32.

Jencks, Christopher, Marshall Smith, Henry Acland, Mary Jo Bane, David Cohen, Herbert Gintis, Barbara Heyns, and Stephan Michelson. 1972. *Inequality: A Reassessment of the Effect of Family and Schooling in America.* New York: Basic Books.

Jennings, John F. 1987. "The Sputnik of the Eighties." *Phi Delta Kappan* (October): 104–09.

Johnson, Susan Moore. 1986. "Incentives for Teachers: What Motivates, What Matters." *Educational Administration Quarterly* 22 (3): 54–79.

Jones, L. B., and K. A. Leithwood. 1988. "Draining the Swamp: A Case Study of School System Design." Unpublished paper, Ontario Institute for Studies in Education, Toronto, Canada.

Kasten, Katherine. 1986. "Redesigning Teachers' Work." *Issues in Education* 4 (3) (Winter): 272–86.

Katzman, Martin. 1971. *The Political Economy of Urban Schools.* Cambridge, Mass.: Harvard University Press.

Kearns, David T. 1988. "An Education Recovery Plan for America." *Phi Delta Kappan* 69 (8) (April): 565–70.

Kirst, Michael W. 1983. "A New School Finance for a New Era of Fiscal Constraint." In *School in Finance and School Improvement Linkages for the 1980s*, edited by Allan Odden and L. Dean Webb, pp. 1–15. Cambridge, Mass.: Ballinger.

_____. 1984. *Who Controls Our Schools?* New York: Freeman.

LaRocque, Linda, and Peter Coleman. 1985. "The Elusive Link: School-Level Responses to School Board Policies." *Alberta Journal of Educational Research* 31 (2) (June): 149–67.

Leibenstein, Harvey. 1980. *Beyond Economic Man: A New Foundation for Microeconomics.* Cambridge, Mass.: Harvard University Press.

Leithwood, Kenneth A. 1988. "School System Policies for Effective School Administration." Unpublished paper, Ontario Institute for Studies in Education, Toronto, Ontario.

Leithwood, Kenneth A., and D. J. Montgomery. 1982. "The Role of the Elementary School Principal in Program Improvement." *Review of Educational Research* 52 (3): 309–39.

Levin, Henry M. 1974. "Measuring Efficiency in Educational Production." *Public Finance Quarterly* 2 (January): 3–24.

_____. 1983. *Cost-Effectiveness: A Primer.* Beverly Hills, Calif.: Sage.

_____. 1988. "Cost-effectiveness and Educational Policy," *Educational Evaluation and Policy Analysis* 10 (1) (Spring): 51–69.

Levine, Donald M., and Mary Jo Bane, eds. 1975. *The "Inequality" Controversy: Schooling and Distributive Justice.* New York: Basic Books.

Levy, Frank S., A. J. Meltsner, and A. Wildavsky. 1974. *Urban Outcomes: Schools, Streets, and Libraries.* Berkeley, Calif.: University of California Press.

Lortie, Dan C. 1969. "The Balance of Control and Autonomy in Elementary School Teaching." In *The Semi-Professionals and Their Organizations*, edited by A. Etzioni, pp. 1–53. New York: Free Press.

_____. 1975. *Schoolteacher.* Chicago: University of Chicago Press.

Magnet, Myron. 1988. "How to Smarten Up the Schools." *Fortune* (February): 86–94.

Malen, Betty, and Ann W. Hart. 1987. "Career Ladder Reform: A Multi-Level Analysis of Initial Efforts," *Educational Evaluation and Policy Analysis* 9 (1): 9–23.

Mann, Dale. 1981. "Education Policy Analysis and the Rent-a-Troika Business." Paper presented at the American Educational Research Association Annual Meeting, Los Angeles, April.

Mann, Dale, and Deborah Inman. 1984. "Improving Education within Existing Resources: The Instructionally Effective Schools' Approach." *Journal of Education Finance* 10 (Fall): 256–69.

March, James G., and Johan P. Olsen. 1976. *Ambiguity and Choice in Organizations.* Bergen, Norway: Universitetsforlaget.

Martin, William T., and Donald Willower. 1981. "The Managerial Behavior of High School Principals." *Educational Administration Quarterly* 17: 69–90.

McKenzie, Richard B. 1979. *The Political Economy of the Educational Process.* Boston: Martinus Nijhoff Publishing.

McNeil, Linda M. 1986. *Contradictions of Control.* London: Metheun/Routledge & Kegan Paul.

McPherson, R. Bruce, Robert L. Crowson, and Nancy J. Pitner. 1986. *Managing Uncertainty: Administrative Theory and Practice in Education.* Columbus, Ohio: Merrill.

Meyer, John W., and Brian Rowan. 1977. "Institutionalized Organizations: Formal Structure as Myth and Ceremony." *American Journal of Sociology* 83: 340-63.

_____. 1978. "The Structure of Educational Organizations." In *Environments and Organizations*, by Marshall W. Meyer and associates, pp. 78-109. San Francisco: Jossey-Bass.

Meyer, Marshall W., and associates. 1978. *Environments and Organizations.* San Francisco: Jossey-Bass.

Michaelsen, Jacob B. 1977. "Revision, Bureaucracy, and School Reform." *School Review* 85 (February): 229-46.

_____. 1981. "A Theory of Decision Making in the Public Schools: A Public Choice Approach." In *Organizational Behavior in Schools and School Districts*, edited by Samuel B. Bacharach, pp. 208-44. New York: Praeger.

Mintzberg, Henry. 1973. *The Nature of Managerial Work.* New York: Harper & Row.

Moe, Terry M. 1984. "The New Economics of Organization." *American Journal of Political Science* 28 (4) (November): 739-77.

Murnane, Richard J. 1981. "Seniority Rules and Educational Productivity: Understanding the Consequences of a Mandate for Equality." *American Journal of Education* 90 (1) (November): 14-38.

_____. 1985. "The Rhetoric and Reality of Merit Pay: Why Are They Different?" In *Merit, Money and Teachers' Careers*, edited by Henry C. Johnson, Jr., pp. 57-76. Lanham, Md.: University Press of America.

Murphy, Joseph. Forthcoming. "Methodological, Measurement, and Conceptual Problems in the Study of Instructional Leadership." *Educational Evaluation and Policy Analysis.*

Murphy, Joseph, and Philip Hallinger. Forthcoming. "Equity as Access to Learning: Curricular and Instructional Treatment Differentials." *Journal of Curriculum Studies.*

_____. 1987. "New Directions in the Professional Development of School Administrators: A Synthesis and Suggestions for Improvement." In *Approaches to Administrative Training in Education*, edited by J. Murphy and P. Hallinger, pp. 245-81. Albany, N.Y.: State University of New York Press.

Natriello, Gary, and Sanford M. Dornbusch. 1980-81. "Pitfalls in the Evaluation of Teachers by Principals." *Administrator's Notebook* 29 (6): 1-4.

Newsweek. 1981. "Why Public Schools Fail." (April 20): 62-65.

Niskanen, William A. 1971. *Bureaucracy and Representative Government.* Chicago: Aldine.

Oakes, Jeannie. 1986. "Keeping Track, Part 1: The Policy and Practice of Curriculum Inequality." *Phi Delta Kappan* (September): 12-17.

Olson, Lynn. 1987a. "Chiefs Urge that States 'Guarantee' School Quality to Those 'At risk'." *Education Week* 7 (11) (November 18): 1, 17.

_____. 1987b. "Chiefs Unanimously Endorse School 'Guarantees' Policy" *Education Week* 7 (12) (November 25): 1, 16.

_____. 1988. "Saying Reforms Fail Most Pupils, Shanker Argues for a 'New Type' of Teaching Unit." *Education Week* 7 (28) (April 6): 1, 26.

Ostrom, Vincent, and Eleanor Ostrom. 1971. "Public Choice: A Different Approach to Public Administration." *Public Administration Review* 31: 203–16.

Peters, Thomas J., and Robert H. Waterman, Jr. 1982. *In Search of Excellence: Lessons from America's Best-Run Companies.* New York: Harper & Row.

Peterson, Kent. 1978. "The Principal's Tasks." *Administrator's Notebook* 26 (8): 1–4.

Pfeffer, Jeffrey. 1978. "The Micropolitics of Organizations." In *Environments and Organizations,* edited by Marshall W. Meyer and associates, pp. 29–50. San Francisco: Jossey-Bass.

Pitner, Nancy J., and R. T. Ogawa. 1981. "Organizational Leadership: The Case of the Superintendent." *Educational Administration Quarterly* 17 (1): 45–65.

Powell, Arthur G., Eleanor Farrar, and David K. Cohen. 1985. *The Shopping Mall High School: Winners and Losers in the Educational Marketplace.* Boston: Houghton Mifflin.

Purkey, S. C., and M. S. Smith. 1983. "Effective Schools: A Review." *Elementary School Journal* 83 (4): 427–52.

_____. 1985. "School Reform: The District Policy Implications of the Effective Schools Literature." *Elementary School Journal* 85 (3): 353–89.

Rallis, Sharon F., and Martha C. Highsmith. 1986. "The Myth of the 'Great Principal': Questions of School Management and Instructional Leadership." *Phi Delta Kappan* 68 (4) (December): 300–04.

Ratner, Gershon M. 1985. "A New Legal Duty for Urban Public Schools: Effective Education in Basic Skills." *Texas Law Review* 63: 777–864.

Rodman, Blake. 1988. "Administrators Seen to Be Out of Step with General Public." *Education Week* 7 (17) (January 20): 1, 23.

Rogers, David. 1968. *110 Livingston Street.* New York: Vintage.

Rosenholtz, Susan J. 1985. "Effective Schools: Interpreting the Evidence." *American Journal of Education* 93 (3) (May): 352–88.

Rossmiller, Richard A. 1987. "Achieving Equity and Effectiveness in Schooling." *Journal of Education Finance* 12 (Spring): 561–77.

Salley, C. 1979–80. "Superintendents' Job Priorities." *Administrator's Notebook* 28: 1–4.

Sedlak, Michael W., Christopher Wheeler, Diana Pullin, and Philip Cusick. 1986. *Selling Students Short: Classroom Bargains and Academic Reform in the American High School.* New York: Teachers College Press.

Shanker, Albert. 1988. "Teachers Have Leadership Role: Principals' Dual Task Questioned." *Education Week, Conventions in Print* (March 30): 4.

Shapiro, Jonathan Z., and Robert L. Crowson. 1985. "Rational Choice Theory and Administrative Decision Making: Implications for Research in Educational Administration." Paper presented at the American Educational Research Association Annual Meeting, Chicago, April. Forthcoming in *Advances in Research and Theories of School Management*, edited by Samuel Bacharach. Greenwich, Conn.: JAI Press.

Simon, Herbert. 1947. *Administrative Behavior.* New York: Macmillan.

Sirkin, J. R. 1985. "West Virginia: Epic Mandate, Historic Conflict." *Education Week* 4 (39) (June 19): 1, 18–21.

Strauss, Anselm, L. Schatzman, R. Bucher, D. Ehrlich, and M. Sabshin. 1963. "The Hospital and its Negotiated Order." In *The Hospital in Modern Society*, edited by Eliot Freidson, pp. 147–69. New York: Free Press.

U.S. Department of Education. 1987a. *Schools That Work: Educating Disadvantaged Children.* Washington, D.C.: U.S. Government Printing Office.

_____. 1987b. *What Works: Research about Teaching and Learning*, 2nd ed. Washington, D.C.: U.S. Government Printing Office.

Urbanski, Adam. 1986. "Lessons Learned from Evaluating Administrators." *Education Week* 5 (24): (February 26): 24.

van Geel, Tyll. 1973. "PPBES and District Resource Allocation." *Administrator's Notebook* 22 (1): 1–4.

_____. 1987. *The Courts and American Education Law.* Buffalo, N.Y.: Prometheus Books.

Walberg, Herbert J. 1984. "Improving the Productivity of America's Schools." *Educational Leadership* 41 (8) (May): 19–27.

Walberg, Herbert J., and William J. Fowler, Jr. 1987. "Expenditure and Size Efficiencies of Public School Districts." *Educational Researcher* 16 (7) (October): 5–13.

Weick, Karl. 1976. "Educational Organizations as Loosely Coupled Systems." *Administrative Science Quarterly* 21 (March): 1–19.

Willower, Donald J. 1979. "Ideology and Science in Organizational Theory." *Educational Administration Quarterly* 15 (3): 20–42.

Wimpelberg, Robert K. Forthcoming. "Instructional Leadership and Ignorance: Guidelines for the New Studies of District Administrators." *Education and Urban Society* 20 (3).

Zald, Mayer N. 1987. "Review Essay: The New Institutional Economics." *American Journal of Sociology* 93 (3) (November): 701–08.

III RESOURCE ALLOCATION AT MICROLEVELS

11 BUDGETARY THEORY AND REALITY
A Microview

Guilbert C. Hentschke

Budgeting—how individuals in an organization assemble resources to achieve organizational objectives—is considered to be a singularly important educational undertaking in school districts. "The school district budget is central to the successful operation of the educational enterprise. . . . It can provide a systematic means for focusing the efforts of district personnel on district priorities. . . . [It] is an important tool for school administrators to understand and utilize in achieving their basic mission—educating children in the most effective and cost-efficient manner" (Hartman 1988: 1-2).

Unfortunately, actual budgeting practices fall far short of these high aspirations. Budgeting practice in school districts is largely a financial act of balancing revenue and expenditure projections and applying formula allocations to school sites. Study after study portrays school budgeting as a process that escalates and extrapolates the costs of current practices up to a forecasted revenue constraint. Major budget decisions revolve around how wage settlements, changes in tax rates and yields, and changes in staffing levels affect total expenditures. "Decisions" that lead to resource deployment for direct instruction (the heart of the productivity issue) are made by

I wish to acknowledge the helpful comments and suggestions on various drafts of this chapter from Gerald Dreyfuss, James Guthrie, William Hartman, Peter McWalters, David Monk, and John Yagielski.

311

centrally administered allocation formulas with categorical, non-locally funded programs tacked on. In sum, current practice rules out all but the most marginal decisions about improved instructional programming.

This fundamental discrepancy between expectations for budgeting and the reality of budgeting practice led in the 1960s and 1970s to a wave of criticisms of budgeting and proposals for radical changes in budgeting processes with the goal of improving public school productivity. The hope of "budget reforms" during this period—planning, programming, budgeting systems (PPBS), zero base budgeting (ZBB), school site budgeting, and so forth—was to improve decisions about how schooling resources were allocated and hence improve the productivity of schooling. The explicit assumption in these efforts was, "Improve the budgeting process and you improve schooling."

Despite persistent faith in the importance of budgeting practice and the corresponding flurry of redesigns of budgeting processes, today these "reforms" have left virtually no effect on actual budgeting practice. Instead, historical descriptions of budgeting practice are as accurate today as when they were first written. "Better budgeting" in school districts has produced few changes in how resources in school districts are allocated.

Various reasons have been put forth for this, many of which suggest, directly or indirectly, that reforms did not really change the "rules of budgeting"—that is, the rules about who has what kinds of decisionmaking authority over the distribution of which resources. PPBS, ZBB, and school site budgeting approaches modeled how existing spenders should behave in order to achieve scientifically rational, efficient, and effective decisions (Schick 1966). What was not addressed was the corresponding requirement for changes in authority—that is, who can do what to whom with what regarding allocation of resources in schools.

Many districts undertook what they thought to be one or more of these reform efforts, but without any changes in authority relationships. Therefore, under the rubric of reform, the same people (superintendents, central office department heads, principals) made the same decisions, despite the existence of "new and improved" formats or processes. Although these cosmetic changes may have had some utility in the short run (for example, as a "sales document" to pass budgets) (Alioto and Jungherr 1969; Blodgett 1973), they were of no continuing use to educators because the distribution of power had not shifted. One proposition presented in this chapter is that no change in budgeting occurs unless it can be described as an actual change in the formal authority of educators who are involved in budgeting.

This argument requires some elaboration, including examples, because it implies that budgeting is more than a process. Although at one level budgeting can be described as a process that yields an expenditure plan, at a more fundamental level budgeting processes identify two issues of general management: who has the authority to decide what (rules) and what are the likely consequences of these rules (incentives). Budgeting processes are symptoms of rules. Indeed, it is only by changing the formal authority of people to allocate resources (rules) that changes in budgeting practice come about.

Current arguments for and efforts to "fundamentally restructure" schools deal directly with changes in authority relationships among district employees. In particular, they seek to decentralize decision-making authority and place more decisions at the school level.[1] This general concept of school-based management closely follows the rhetoric of an earlier time—"school site budgeting." In both instances, changes in budgeting practice occur as a result of changes in the distribution of authority within the school district and not the other way around. To the extent that this is true, the most useful approach to "improved budgeting practice" is one that improves incentives for more productive behavior by making specific changes in authority relationships.

The first part of this chapter elaborates these arguments. The second part considers five separate examples of changes in authority relationships among three categories of public school educators (building-level educators, central office departments, and district policy officers) and discusses changes in incentives that result from changes in authority. All five suggested changes move in the general direction of increased school site decisionmaking authority. These changes include placing expenditure decision rights closer to the actual teaching process, allowing greater degrees of substitutability among resource inputs, and permitting spend/save authority. The degree to which fundamental and widespread changes in internal authority relationships in public school districts can be implemented is still an open question, although most proposed changes discussed here are drawn from practice in a few districts. These examples argue that it is more useful to seek to improve budgeting practices by securing specific concrete changes in authority relationships that cause educators to invent ways to be more productive than it is to seek ways to make schools more productive by changing budgeting processes.

CHARACTERIZING SCHOOL DISTRICT BUDGETING: ASPIRATIONS VERSUS REALITY

Few activities of management are thought to be more central to organizational success than budgeting. Budgeting is the means whereby the goals and aspirations of the organization are transformed into activities of the organization that will, hopefully, achieve those goals. It seems logical to assume that "better" budgeting processes promise better decisions about how to allocate resources to best achieve organizational goals. Conversely, if current budgeting practice does not convince us that the "best" decisions are likely to result, then those practices should be changed. Given a concern for improving the performance of school districts, a logical first step is to look at the ways school districts budget resources.

Balancing Behavior of School Districts

In general, school districts seek the largest appropriation possible and cut back expenditure plans in order to "balance" them with revenue forecasts. The central features of current school district budgeting practice include estimating revenues from various sources, projecting expenditures based largely on current service levels and estimated prices of future resource inputs, and then "balancing" a few expenditure variables such as staffing ratios and property tax rates on the revenue side. According to Burkhead (1976: 23-24),

> The major steps in school district budgeting represent a series of estimates and revenues and approval of proposed expenditures. In preparing next year's revenue budget, public school district budget makers count the anticipated aid from the federal and state governments, arrange the district's expenditures to give the appearance of fulfilling all matching requirements, and add in miscellaneous revenue. In determining expenditures, they look at the

enrollment projections for the district and personnel salary adjustments that have been mandated or negotiated, make an allowance for the impact of bond amortizations and interests. The typical gap between revenues and expenditures can be closed in one of two ways: class size can be increased, thereby reducing the requirements for instructional staff, or property taxes can be increased.

The major decisions that affect the budget have little to do with "improvement of schooling" as such. Gerwin, for example, in his analysis of budgeting in the Pittsburgh school system, found that the bulk of analysis and decisionmaking clustered around the following six areas: revenue forecasts, number of employees, salary increases, new fringe benefits, expenditure plans for materials, and new debt service (Gerwin 1969: 123–24). Five characteristic types of actors surfaced in his descriptive model of the process: (1) an administrative unit consisting of a single individual who makes allocation decisions; (2) a staff function that prepares revenue forecasts; (3) subunits, not including the two above, and occupational groups that make requests and receive appropriations; (4) a body (for example, a legislature or lay board) that must review the contents of the budget; and (5) the state government, which imposes certain legal restrictions on the organization.

As these actors involve themselves in the budgeting process, the long-run determining importance of revenue on expenditure surfaces. Early in the process initial estimates of future revenues are made, and they are deliberately biased downward to hedge against the uncertain effect of local and state economic conditions on certain tax bases. Subunits and occupational groups request new appropriations at or above the "base," or level of previous agreement, as measured either in terms of number of employees or in dollars for employees. Subunits and occupational groups do not seek less than the previous agreement, and the administrative unit does not allocate more than is requested.

Budget negotiations are highly variable at this point. What follows describes the central tendency but is not all-inclusive. Requests for the base are preliminarily approved, and the focus of discussion shifts to requested increases in the base. New appropriations (above the base) are affected by the interaction of revenue expectations and the ability of the subunit to exert influence. When relatively more revenue appears to be available, subunits and occupational groups are less vigorous in their attempts to seek appropriations, but the effect of their influence is greater. The opposite is true during periods of less revenue (Gerwin 1969: 128).

Salary increases are bargained around percentage changes across job types roughly during the same period of time. The key bargaining unit is usually teachers—that is, the group that can most disrupt schooling. Negotiated salary increases "settle" the preponderance of expenditure planning. New debt service requirements are then evaluated with an eye toward spending as much as possible through the operating budget. New bonds are avoided to the extent possible.

After these major segments of the budget have been assembled in preliminary form, the balance between revenues and expenditures is evaluated. Every attempt is made to avoid having to renegotiate tentative agreements reached between the central administrative unit and subunits. Revenue forecasts are reexamined, moving the numbers from "conservative" to "realistic." If the balancing effects of this are not sufficient, expenditures for capital outlays are reduced as much as possible. If a projected deficit remains, allocations to subunits and programs serving relatively few children are reduced (Gerwin 1969: 127–49).

As mentioned earlier, the above description is one of central tendency only. Variations on this general process of balancing have been described elsewhere and with different emphases. Hentschke and Yagielski (1982), for example, emphasize the balancing of planned revenues and expenditures as a prelude to pursuing a tax rate increase. In that instance, the "base" is constructed around short-run fixed and variable cost elements, such as counseling ratios of 1/350 or elementary class sizes of 1/23. These ratios are then processed through actual student enrollment estimates to determine quantities of resource requirements at current prices. Inflation and contract settlements are then incorporated to get estimates of total future costs implied by extending current instructional practices.

Estimates of all non–property tax revenues are then subtracted from the estimate of total costs in order to determine the amount of revenue required from the local property tax to support existing levels of schooling. At this point district officials evaluate the political feasibility of proposing different levels of changes in the tax rate to support schooling. They go through an iterative process of adjusting short-run fixed and variable cost elements in order to stay within the boundaries of a politically feasibly local property tax rate. "Balancing" in this context is of two types: balancing revenues and expenditures for the upcoming operating year (like Gerwin) and also taking into consideration past and future changes in local tax rates. (The goal in this latter instance is to avoid the need for significant increases in a single period.)

Despite differences among districts in the amount of scientific rationality that is inserted into the budgeting process and in the rhetoric of cost-effectiveness and goal maximization, the basic procedures are the same. These basic "givens" of the way school districts get and spend money greatly influence how money is budgeted, not the other way around.

Budgeting for Instruction in School Buildings

Budgeting processes that allocate resources from central administration to school buildings characteristically assume that there is a single best production process for direct instruction. This one best process is determined centrally and embodied in a set of rules that allocate resources to school buildings based on a variety of algebraic formulas that provide the "resources for instruction" at each of the school sites. Some resources are provided on the following kinds of bases: a certain kind of employee or unit of expenditure per number of children of certain type, and certain amounts of money and number of employees per school site. These allocation formulas greatly simplify the allocation problem faced by central administration. The formulas are also politically useful because they are "objective" and "treat all schools equally." An example of the set of formulas for one school district is provided in Table 11-1.

These formulas are used at two different points in the budgeting process. They are first used to estimate school building resource requirements in the preliminary budget. Some of the most sensitive ratios, such as staff per student, are then adjusted during the balancing phase in order to bring planned expenditures in line with available revenues. The revised formulas then become the basis for allocating resources to schools in the coming year.

Although the quantity (and sometimes the quality) of each of these resources is determined centrally, it is the responsibility of the school site staff to assemble these resources in the most effective

Table 11-1. Line Allocation Formulas for Selected School Accounts.

Account Code	Account Description	Formula
210	Instructional salaries	
211	Principals' salaries	One principal and three vice-principals in each school, except as designated in article VI, section 11-C, page 62, of the Board Policy Manual.
212	Supervisors' salaries	One curriculum assistant for two periods each day in school. District personnel as determined by Board of Trustees.
213	Teachers' salaries	
213.1	Regular certificated staff	A ratio of one certificated staff member for every 22 students except as follows: School A, 21.5; School B, 19.5. The following assignments are exempt from the above ratio and are in addition to basic staff allowance: special education, driver training, curriculum assistant, and teachers given out-of-class assignments by the superintendent of schools. Students enrolled in classes exempt from ratio formula should be deducted from total enrollment figures. Nonteaching activities are deducted from above figure and budgeted under 214.
214	Other certificated salaries of instruction	
214.1	Librarians' salaries	A certificated librarian for each school on basis of actual placement on salary schedule.
214.2	Counselors' salaries	One hour of counseling time for every 75 students. Total counseling salaries are part of basic ratio in 213.1.
220	Classified salaries of instruction	
221	Regular clerical salaries	The following are maximum allowances: Five secretaries and clerks (including mimeo clerk) are allowed as basic staff for each school up to 1,000 enrollment. One of above clerks to be assigned as school treasurer. Add one-fifth time of clerical person for each 100 students in excess of 1,000.

		Library staff is assigned on basis of formula allowing for two classified persons for each school as basic staff and one-fifth time of clerical person for each additional 200 students in excess of 1,000 up to total enrollment of 2,000. Maximum clerical staff for school of 1,000 is 9. Maximum clerical staff for school of 2,000 is 13.
222	Student clerical salaries	Maximum allowance for student clerks for all services should not exceed 80 cents for each student enrolled. Maximum allowance for school of 2,000 enrollment is $1,600.
230	Textbooks	Maximum allowance of $4.00 per student plus $250.00 for book replacement, plus $6.50 per unit of growth over previous year for new schools that have not previously reached capacity. This allowance may be adjusted by borrowing from or adding to the 240 account. The combined total for the two accounts should not exceed the combined allowance for each account.
290	Other expenses of instruction	Total maximum allowance for each school based on the following allowance for each student enrolled: School A, $22.50; School B, $22.50; School C, $22.50; School D, $22.50; School E, $25.50; School F, $28.50; plus additional allowance of $5.00 per unit of growth over previous year in new schools that have not previously reached capacity. Include in the above allowances for attendance office. Additional allowance for conventions as established by administrative policy, article VI, section I-D. Allow $300 additional for EMR classes and allow for blind students on basis of previous experience.
400	Health service	
410	Certificated salaries of health personnel	A full-time nurse in each school.
490	Other expense of health service	Allow 15 cents per unit of enrollment.

(*Table 11–1. continued overleaf*)

Table 11-1. continued

Account Code	Account Description	Formula
600	Operation of school plant	
610–620	Classified salaries of operation Gardening salaries	Two gardeners assigned to each school. District staff to consist of a gardener, foreman, three equipment operators, a gardener leadman, and five gardeners, for a total of ten.
730	Replacement of equipment	Not to exceed five percent of total assessed value of school equipment as reflected on inventory of previous fiscal year. Limitations are placed on school total and not on departmental figures. If total inventory values are not available, limitation of $4.00 per unit of enrollment. Individual items to be listed.
791	Repairs of buildings	Based on survey of needs as shown on work requests but limited to a total cost of $15.00 per unit of enrollment.
793	Repair of equipment	Based on survey of actual need as reflected on work request and experience of previous years but not to exceed a total cost of $3.50 per unit of enrollment.

Source: Hentschke (1975): 314–15.

manner. School site educators do not budget in the classical sense; instead, they are provided with a given mix of inputs. The processes employed by building-level educators to assemble resources within the school building vary greatly. At one extreme the principal makes all major decisions about how staff are to be used, what books are to be purchased, and so forth. At the other extreme teachers are extensively involved with the principal.

Incentives of Public School Officials

The greatest amount of "energy" in school district budgeting goes into decisions that are, at best, only indirectly related to instruction. Proportionately little effort goes into decisions dealing directly with educating children. This is not surprising when we consider the *financial* incentives faced by public school chiefs and how different those incentives are from those faced by private school chiefs (in both non-profit and for-profit schools). This section distinguishes in detail the two sets of incentives because the concluding argument in the chapter deals with ways to change the incentives within the public school district.

The argument presented here in brief is that public school administrators have strong incentives to seek the largest possible budgets for schools each year but have little incentive to use resources efficiently. Private-sector managers, on the other hand, do not face such strong incentives to "maximize budgets."

To paraphrase Niskanen (1973) in his analysis of bureaus, public school districts offer a promised bundle of activities and expected outputs of these activities in exchange for a total budget. (This is in contrast to private-sector managers who sell units of service at a unit price.) Those who provide revenues for the operating budget of the public school district also tend not to be direct users of public schooling, whereas purchasers of private schooling are.

This is not to say that central office administrators are not concerned with parents' perceptions of schooling quality. From a financial perspective, however, having a parent withdraw a child from a public school does not have the same negative consequences that it would in a private school. On the other hand, public school administrators often seek to mobilize parents to lobby for increased public school revenues from city, state, and federal governments.

Providers of revenue to public school districts—that is, various levels of government—are essentially "passive." They know the budget they are prepared to grant for a given quantity of services, but they do not have either the incentive or the opportunity to obtain information on the minimum budget necessary to obtain those services. Consider, for example, state legislators, who provide revenues not only for public schools but also for a wide variety of other public goods and services ranging from highways to welfare, from water projects to jails. They simply cannot become expert enough in schooling to identify the minimum that each district "needs" for its schools. Even if they could, their opinions would carry no more weight than those (higher estimates) from district administrators.

Public school administrators, like the rest of us, seek to maximize personal "utility," but why does this necessarily imply budget maximization in their particular case? Niskanen advances two arguments to support this notion: "rationality" and "survival." Among the several variables that may be among the school administrators' preferences are salary, perquisites of the office, public reputation, power, schooling outcomes, patronage, ease of making changes, and ease of managing the school district or agency. All except the last two are positively associated with the total budget of the school district—that is, the bigger the budget, the bigger the salary, perks, and so forth. (The last two are more associated with *increases* in the budget.) This does not imply that the school administrators' interests are other than "professional." Again to paraphrase Niskanen, most school administrators, by either predisposition or training, undoubtedly try to serve their perception of "the public interest." School administrators, however, are neither omniscient nor sovereign. They cannot acquire all the information on individual preferences and production opportunities that would be necessary to divine "the public interest," and they do have the authority to order an action that is contrary to either the personal interests or the different perceptions of "the public interest" by other bureaucrats or higher-level education officials (Niskanen 1973: 23). Rationally, bureaucrats pursue their preferences via larger and larger budgets.

The survival argument also suggests why chief public school administrators seek to maximize budgets. Two groups of people significantly influence school administrators' tenure in office: the employees of the school district and the "sponsors"—that is, local taxpayers and state and federal education officials and legislatures. To varying degrees, individuals employed by school districts desire budget maximization for reasons similar to those of the chief school administrator, and they also can influence school administrators to seek increased budgets. As Niskanen points out, for all public bureaus, employees "can be co-operative, responsive, and efficient. Or, they can deny information to the [school administrator], undermine his directives, and embarrass him before the [public]. Their behavior depends on their perceived rewards of employment in the [school district]" (Niskanen 1973: 24). The administrator who seeks operating efficiencies without budget increases will have difficulty "buying the cooperation" of employees. From the standpoint of financial incentives, district employees do not gain from being efficient.

Local taxpayers and state and federal education oficials and legislators also have an interest in (public) school district budget maximization, although their reasons are less obvious. Parents' interests in increased spending are a major force for increased budgets, although parents of school-age children constitute a declining proportion of taxpayers in many school districts.[2] Local, state, and federal legislators fully expect local, state, and federal school administrators to aggressively propose additional funding based on increased needs and new activities. State and federal legislatures often lack the time, the information, and the staff necessary to formulate new programs; they depend on local, state, and federal education officials to propose them. "At every state in a multistage review process, the review officers are dependent on the bureaucrat to make a forceful case for his proposed budget, in part to determine whether a previous review had made too large a reduction" (Niskanen 1973: 25).

In contrast to public schools, which derive a larger proportion of their revenues from taxing authorities, profit-seeking and private nonprofit schools derive substantial proportions of their revenue from student fees and gifts. Just like the public school administrator, the private school administrator seeks to maximize personal utility. However, because of the differing financial relationships between school and funding sources in private schools, the focus is not on budget size but on the net present value of future flows of funds. This means that private school administrators make decisions to save (invest) as well as to spend so as to increase net revenues over the long run. The private school administrator's behavior is similarly motivated by rationality and survival criteria, but the incentives are different. Because the sponsors of private schools include fee-paying students as well as donors of money, goods, and services, and not legislatures, they behave differently from their public school counterparts.

Decisions by private school administrators will not necessarily be consistent with budget maximization. "Doing well" in private schools is enhanced by internal operating efficiencies (cost control) for at least three reasons. First, direct savings by effecting internal efficiencies will enhance the value (equity) of the school. Savings can be added to endowment or salaries. Second, private school administrators are motivated to create the impression of fiscal integrity and internal operating efficiency in order to attract donor and client support. Third, they are motivated to minimize unit costs for a given quality level in order to be able to price the educational services of their schools competitively.[3] The incentives of public school officials are different from those in private firms in ways that are not conducive to cost-effective behavior. This observation has not deferred (and indeed has encouraged) many to seek changes in budgeting practices that will yield more productive schooling.

PREVIOUS BUDGET "REFORMS"

We have had a vigorous tradition of attempting to argue for changes in budgeting practices as a means for improving the productivity of educational institutions. Normative or "reform" theories of budgeting arose from a perceived problem with current governance of educational organizations, identified current budgeting and accounting practices that were associated with the problem, and recommended changes in budgeting practices that would solve those problems.[4] The proposition set forth here is that all of those reform efforts failed because they were attempted without changes in the authority relationships within the school district.[5]

More recent normative theories of budgeting have been critical of school productivity in general. They have identified corresponding weaknesses in budgeting practices and have argued for innovations in budgeting practice (Brackett, Chambers, and Parrish 1983). PPBS, ZBB, and school site budgeting are among the most recent of these normative theories.

Program-Oriented Theories of Budgeting. All program-oriented theories of budgeting were constructed on the assumption that current budgeting practices were deficient and that changes in budgeting would improve the operation of schools. Although PPBS, ERMS, and ZBB[6] differ among themselves in many respects, they all are structured around the concept of the program as the nexus of both current problems with schooling operation and their solution.

Even though the disaggregation of budgets into programs was the most visible attribute of these reform theories, the fundamental argument for the theories was the need to link efforts to institutional performance, regardless of the manner in which schooling services were disaggregated. Listen to the words of the early architects of program-oriented budgeting for education. In *Educational Planning-Programming-Budgeting: A Systems Approach*, Hartley (1968: 4) argues that

> [the] underlying premise for this approach is that it represents an improvement over existing educational planning techniques. In very simple terms, *the advantage of the proposed approach over traditional means is that in the new format, emphasis is placed upon the outputs, or programs of the school, rather than on the inputs that are necessary to support these programs* [italics in original].

In this instance "outputs" are programs or services provided, not enhanced student achievement. Nonetheless, the emphasis is on a rational process that attempts to link decisions to desired goals or "outputs." Most of these early blueprints for program budgeting started with a set of scientific principles that described in quite abstract terms how inputs were to be converted most efficiently and effectively into outputs. The following sequence of steps is representative (Foster 1971: 30–31):

1. An assessment of needs.
2. The examination of existing goals.
3. The establishment of a set of priorities.
4. The tentative determination of major progams.
5. The careful analysis of alternatives.
6. The selection of alternatives.
7. The preparation of a program and financial plan.
8. The development of a comprehensive plan for evaluation.

PPBS, ZBB, and other program-oriented budget reforms were designed around the instructional program as the unit of analysis. These systems presumed that more productive schools resulted from more scientific analysis of programs. School site budgeting perceived a different problem—that is, that more discretion should be given to building-level educators to fashion education services.[7]

Although extensively documented and described at their inception, virtually none of these budgeting reform efforts has had a lasting effect on school district budgeting processes. Current descriptions of school district budgeting practices are substantially unchanged from ten- and twenty-year-old descriptions. Why is this? Many explanations have been set forth (Botner 1970; Simmons and Barkdull 1976; Kirst 1975; Hentschke 1978; Wildavsky 1975). The argument set forth here is that, generally speaking, all the reforms were attempted without changes in the authority relationships within the school district. Although spending may have been portrayed in a program-by-program format, no changes were made in authority over spending decisions.[8]

It seems that it is possible to superficially change a district's budgeting process without changing authority over resource allocation. Arguably, it is *not* possible to change fundamental authority relationships in the district without changing budgeting practices. The particular budgeting process employed in a school district is as much a symptom of authority relationships as it is a resource allocation process. To the extent this is so, it may well be more fruitful to seek to improve the productivity of schools through fiscally oriented changes in authority relationships than through budgeting processes per se.

BUDGETING IN RESTRUCTURED SCHOOLS

Concern over school productivity has led to arguments for "fundamentally restructuring" schools (Benveniste 1985; Carnegie Task Force on Teaching as a Profession 1986). Five examples of changes in fiscally oriented school district authority relationships are discussed below. They are described as changes among three categories of employees in school districts: school district policymakers, central office departments, and building-level educators. Each of the five fiscally oriented authority relationships is described in terms of "existing" and "alternative" states, and the implications of the alternative for budgeting are discussed.

Authority over Utilities and Substitute Teachers

Existing Relationship. Central office departments often request resources of district policymakers, and those resources are consumed at the building level as "free goods" provided to school building educators. Two examples of this practice include expenditures for utilities in the school and expenditures for substitute teachers. These resource allocation decisions are set up to "run by themselves" in that they are provided on an "as needed" basis during the school year to resource consumers in the school buildings. The assumption behind this type of mechanism is that because there is little professional discretion associated with the ultimate consumption of these resources, centralized control and distribution of the resource is more efficient.

Under this model utility expenditures are controlled at the building level by policy directives to turn out lights when a classroom is not in use, keep doors closed to prevent heat loss, close down air conditioning systems over the weekend, and so forth. Utility costs will rise and fall as needed, but the decisions about utility usage do not typically enter into the calculus of building-level educators.

Resources required for substitute teachers are often treated similarly. A budget for expenditures for substitute teachers is created and administered centrally, although the resources are expended at the building level. Like the utilities example, expenditures for substitutes under this model are controlled through central directives and union contracts that identify the rules under which teachers may be absent. The actual number of absences that occur in a building, like the amount of utility usage in a building, are "natural" occurrences about which no authority actually makes decisions. Rather, they are phenomena whose financial effects are estimated in a budget, are controlled centrally through policy directives and contracts, and then occur during the year "naturally."

As is typical with this type of practice, when expenditure estimates for the year turn out to be high, remaining resources are used centrally to cover other commitments that have been underestimated. When expenditure estimates for the year turn out to be inadequate, central office departments have to find resources to keep these operations going or issue "emergency" policy directives.

Building-level educators who actually consume these resources under these rules feel little responsibility and have no incentives to conserve resources beyond the boundaries imposed by central office guidelines. They have no incentives to try to conceive and put in place alternative practices that may produce significant savings in the consumption of utilities and substitute teacher resources. To do so would not help them do their job better, but indeed, to devote time to these problems would actually detract from their job. As a consequence, these kinds of resources continue to be managed centrally and consumed locally as if they were "free goods"—that is, in accord with the centralized decision rules established by school district policymakers.

Alternative. An alternative to this distribution of authority is to allocate the dollar value of these resources to the building level and to treat the expenditures for utilities and substitute teachers as if they were decisions to be made at the building level. The full implication of placing those decisions at the building level is that building-level educators can benefit from their conservation efforts—that is, the savings in expenditures for utilities and substitutes can be used to purchase resources that more directly aid in achieving educational goals. On the "flip side," building-level educators would also bear the "risks" associated with unexpected increases in utilities or substitute teacher costs.

With this alternative district policymakers have changed the budget rules that link some central office departments to school building educators. Incentives to conserve expenditures for "necessary" items like utilities and substitute teachers have been increased with the effect of driving more resources to direct instruction at the school site. In order to maintain incentives to conserve, it would be necessary to budget "reasonable" amounts each year and not penalize savings by budgeting less in future periods.

Authority over Staff Development, Curriculum Development, and Other Central Office Support

Existing Relationship. Central office departments request resources of district policymakers in order to "more effectively deliver direct instruction." There are numerous central office departments whose reason for being is, at least in part, to "support" direct instructional activities at the school building level. These departments provide a wide range of services, including staff development services, curriculum development services of various kinds, audiovisual services, liaison services designed to match schools with donated business services and goods, testing and assessment services, supplies and equipment purchasing services, and liaison to parent groups. These services are provided "free" to building-level educators and sometimes even without request from them.

These central office departments behave just like Niskanen's (1973) bureaus, in that they make arguments to district policymakers to expand their budgets. They justify budget expansion by promising to deliver additional services—that is, by "responding to increased needs." Although putatively done to "support" the educational program of the individual school, the form and content and hence overall value of these particular functions are not determined by educators at the school level.

This category of resource has slightly different incentives and effects than those in the first category, although both are provided "free" to the building-level educators. In the first category building-level educators understand the relationship between building-level activity and resources consumption. Colder months require more heat, and absent teachers require substitutes. In the second category, instructional support from the central office is part of the external environment that building-level educators cope with. It constitutes a barrage of other people's "solutions" to the educational deficiencies of the school. Because these "solutions" must be sufficiently generic in order to be minimally relevant for the maximum number of school sites, their effect on a particular school is highly attenuated.

Alternative. The authority redistribution and hence budgeting alternative to this category of resource is to do what many corporations have done—that is, put central office "support functions" in the position of having to sell their services to school building educators. Instead of justifying their services to boards of education in order to get budget appropriations from them, these central office "support" departments would have to sell their services to those to whom they purport to serve—that is, educators at the building level. In a word, these central office "cost centers" would become "revenue centers," vying for the resources that have been allocated to building-level educators.

Building-level educators would then face decisions about how much central office support they wish to purchase. Their decision alternatives include not only how much support to buy to help on staff development versus, say, business partnership linkages, but also whether to buy that support from central office or from other sources such as other districts, other schools, private firms, regional offices of education, and universities.

Much of the talk of accountability has focused on the building level, without much attention to the accountability of central office staff functions. This budgeting alternative would make central office staff functions much more "accountable."

Authority over the Mix of Professionals

Existing Relationship. District policymakers specify a mix of resource inputs at the building level. Building-level educators are themselves the product of a district-level allocation decision. As portrayed in Table 11-1, the quantity and mix of staff and nonlabor resources are usually specified centrally. The number and kind of teachers, classroom aides, vice principals, counselors, and so forth, as well as expenditures for items such as repairs and textbooks, come to the school via formulas.

As an example, the school district formula that allocates one teacher aide for every, say, 100 students in a building has the effect of specifying both the decision rule and the number of teacher aides that will be used in each school during the coming year. This authority relationship differs from the first category, where building-level activity during the school year affected the amount of resources consumed. (In theory, building-level educators could affect the amounts spent on substitute teachers and utilities.) The actual consumption level of *each item* in this category is determined for the year by central office departments. By far the greatest amount of resources employed at the building level are centrally budgeted on a formula basis. In effect the exact resource mix for each school building is specified by a set of algebraic relationships that applies uniformly to all schools in a district. These formula-driven resources are again provided "free" to the building, in that building-level educators did not decide to purchase this particular resource mix.

Alternative. The budgeting alternative to this category is the same as in the first—that is, to provide the dollar equivalent of these formulas to building-level educators and leave the decision as to the mix of resources up to them. The goal of the change in rules would be to permit building-level educators to alter the mix of "free" goods at their building in order to better achieve their objectives. It permits them, for example, to exchange their entitlement for a vice-principal for several teacher aides if they so desire. With this alternative building-level educators would be, in effect, given authority to purchase more of some resources with savings achieved by reducing expenditures for other resources.

For this alternative to have its desired effect it would be necessary to rely on "standard costs" for each position and not the salary figure of a particular individual. All schools deciding to do without a vice principal would then save the same amount of money. Likewise all schools wishing to purchase an additional vice principal would be faced with the same additional expenditures.

One of the side issues that this alternative raises is the employment of part-time versus full-time employees. Many of the retirement and fringe benefit structures in school districts make a full-time employee more expensive than two otherwise identical half-time employees. The overall compensation package associated with half-time employment is disproportionately less. Recent experience in the Dade County schools suggests that when allowing building-level educators discretion in spending for personnel, they will face instances where they will wish to employ the services of part-time employees because by doing so they save and can redeploy some of the associated fringe benefit expenditures.

Authority over the Source of Supply

Existing Relationship. In all three of the above alternatives to existing authority relationships the discussion has been limited to decisions about the mix of centrally provided resources at the building level. In all three cases the alternatives described gave building-level educators more decisions over the ultimate mix of centrally provided resources. The limiting feature in all instances is that the "shopping list" for services is limited to what is provided by the central office. Whether the services are teaching, administering a program, aiding instruction, or providing staff development, the sole source to buy these services comes from an "approved list" from central office. Only professionals hired by the personnel department can be employed in the school. Only furniture and equipment from approved vendors can be acquired. Only textbooks from an approved list can be purchased. The most constraining of these concerns the supply of personnel. The net effect of this "supply constraint" is that building-level educators are locked into the prevailing personnel pool and wage rates of the school district.

Alternative. The budgeting alternative to this is to permit building-level educators to purchase services from individuals who are not necessarily district employees. This is most easily seen as an extension of the second category above (central office support). Building-level educators would be given authority not only over how much to spend on, say, staff development, but also on whether to buy the services from central office departments or from nondistrict suppliers of staff development. The alternative not only could be, but in several school districts already has been, extended into direct instruction (Hentschke 1986: 32). One school in Dade County is employing Berlitz to teach Spanish because building-level educators felt that Berlitz employees would do a more cost-effective job than district employees. In these instances contracts with private firms have been written up wherein those firms provide specialized instruction. In those instances educators decided that the anticipated costs and benefits of contracting outweighed those associated with reassigning school district employees. The concept of building-level authority to contract for direct instruction and instructional support is relatively new, although the general concept is not.

Authority to Carry Over Resources

Existing Relationship. District appropriations and budget policies create incentives for departments to spend all appropriations before fiscal year end. Like Niskanen's bureaus, educators who depend on appropriations seek to avoid a year-end cash surplus because it reduces their ability to argue for larger budgets in the future. Furthermore, these surpluses are often expropriated anyway. (Typical practice near the end of a fiscal year in many, especially large, school districts is for the central office to "vacuum up" unspent funds from the many budgetary accounts in order to pay for unanticipated overspending in other budgetary accounts.)

Alternative. The alternative to this practice is to grant authority to school building educators to carry over unspent appropriations into subsequent budget periods without penalizing units that do this. The incentives to behave then shift from "spending residuals to avoid losing them" to "saving residuals in order to buy high-priority resources in the future."

DISCUSSION

These five changes in authority relationships do not exist in most school districts for several reasons. Although all of these examples give greater decisionmaking authority to public school building-level educators (and also create incentives to have them act fiscally more like private school educators), there is no guarantee that localized discretion leads to more productive schooling. This argument implies, in effect, that district policymakers currently prefer to guarantee a fixed but low level of schooling productivity rather than risk an even lower level of productivity in some schools by delegating more fiscally oriented authority to building-level educators.

For district-level policymakers to delegate such authority to school building educators, they have to be convinced that such an act will increase the productivity of schools. What building-level educators would likely have to promise in exchange for these rights is increased productivity for their building—that is, improvements in student performance beyond what would otherwise be expected.

This "exchange" is, of course, at the heart of current "accountability" discussions—that is, district-level policymakers granting greater authority to building level educators and, in exchange, building-level educators promising more productive educational services for youngsters. This seems to be the direction of experiments in the Rochester, New York and Miami-Dade school districts (Dreyfuss and Whipple 1987). Indeed, the process of implementing these or any other changes in authority relationships would be done through negotiation among interested parties. Changes in authority relationships, if any, would follow from these negotiations. Changes in budgeting practices, if any, would follow from changes in authority relationships.

NOTES

1. See, for example, Carnegie Task Force (1986), for the general argument and Quinones (1986), Syracuse City School District (1987a, 1987b), and New York City Board of Education (1987) for specific examples.
2. Individuals who want to combat budget-maximizing behavior, such as taxpayer groups, are defeating school budgets in increasing numbers. These efforts, however, do not appear to have measurably slowed the rise of public schooling costs or halted the steady decline in student-teaching staffing ratios.
3. The incentives of administrators in profit-seeking and private nonprofit schools is similar. Although the administrators in private nonprofit schools are less able than their for-profit counterparts to appropriate excess revenues that result from efficiency to themselves, their personal utility is directly tied to the net present value of future flows of funds within their term of tenure.
4. Although this chapter focuses on contemporary reforms, this was also the case near the turn of the century with "reforms" that led to public-sector budgeting and control by object of expenditure and later by functional category of expenditure. Abuses of public moneys that had been allocated on a lump-sum basis were reduced somewhat, it was argued, by allocating money for each individual item of expenditure.

    Later in the century, when expenditure controls began to be put in place, the problem shifted to one of efficiency in government. It was not enough to know how much was spent on salaries versus brooms versus books versus heating oil. To run schools efficiently and effectively, it was argued, it was necessary to understand the broad functions to which line item resources were applied—such as instruction, administration, transportation. The "problem" was an inability to easily grasp the relationship between items of expenditure and the functions to which these items were to be applied. As a consequence, expenditures became categorized by "function" as well as by "item." Both reforms remain today in many school district budgets.
5. For an extended elaboration on this argument see Arrow (1971) and Jensen and Meckling (1976).
6. For an extended elaboration on these, see Hentschke (1986: 179-211), Guthrie, Garms, and Pierce (1988: 232-33), and Hartman (1988: 28-30, 39-40).

7. For an extended list of references on school-site budgeting see Guthrie, Garms, and Pierce 1988: 234 n. 13.

8. This generalization has been confirmed in telephone conversations with several school superintendents who had implemented and then discontinued major budget "reforms" in their districts.

REFERENCES

Alioto, R. F., and J. A. Jungherr. 1969. "Using PPBS to Overcome Taxpayers' Resistance." *Phi Delta Kappan* (November): 138–41.

Arrow, Kenneth J., ed. 1971. *Control in Large Organizations: Essays in the Theory of Risk-Bearing.* Chicago: Markham.

Benveniste, Guy. 1985. "The Design of School Accountability Systems." *Educational Evaluation and Policy Analysis* 7 (Fall): 261–79.

Blodgett, Terrell. 1973. "Steps to Success with Zero-Base Budgeting Systems." *Management Controls* 24 (June): 15.

Botner, S. 1970. "Four Years of PPBS: An Appraisal." *Public Administration Review* 30 (July/August): 423–31.

Brackett, John, Jay Chambers, and Thomas Parrish. 1983. "The Legacy of Rational Budgeting Models in Education and a Proposal for the Future." Institute for Research on Educational Finance and Governance, Stanford University, Stanford Calif., August.

Burkhead, Jesse. 1976. "The State of the Economy: Resources and Costs for Educational Services." Paper delivered at the Conference on the Changing Politics of Education: Prospects for the 1970s, University of Virginia, Charlottesville, November 23–24.

Carnegie Task Force on Teaching as a Profession. 1986. *A Nation Prepared: Teachers for the 21st Century.* New York: Carnegie Corporation.

Dreyfuss, Gerald O., and Ida Whipple. 1987. "A Historical Perspective: School-Based Management/Shared Decision-Making Pilot Program." Miami, Fla.: Dade County Public Schools.

Foster, Charles W. 1971. *Educational Resources Management System.* Chicago: Association of School Business Officials.

Gerwin, Donald. 1969. *Budgeting Public Funds: The Decision Process in an Urban School District.* Madison, Wis.: University of Wisconsin Press.

Guthrie, James W., Walter I. Garms, and Lawrence C. Pierce. 1988. *School Finance and Education Policy.* Englewood Cliffs, N.J.: Prentice Hall.

Hartley, Harry. 1968. *Educational Planning-Programming-Budgeting: A Systems Approach.* Englewood Cliffs, N.J.: Prentice Hall.

Hartman, William T. 1988. *School District Budgeting.* Englewood Cliffs, N.J.: Prentice Hall.

Hentschke, Guilbert. 1975. *Management Operations in Education.* Berkeley, Calif.: McCutchan.

_____. 1978. "Evaluating Zero-Base Budgeting in the Light of Earlier Budget Reforms." *Journal of Education Finance* 4 (Fall): 234–47.

_____. 1986. *School Business Administration*. Berkeley, Calif.: McCutchan.

Hentschke, Guilbert, and John Yagielski. 1982. "School District Fiscal Strain: Implications for State and Federal Financial Assistance." *Journal of Education Finance* 8 (Summer): 52–72.

Jensen, Michael C., and William H. Meckling. 1976. "Theory of the Firm: Managerial Behavior, Agency Costs, and Ownership Structure." *Journal of Financial Economics* 3 (October): 305–60.

Kirst, Michael. 1975. "The Rise and Fall of PPBS in California." *Phi Delta Kappan* 56 (April): 535–38.

New York City Board of Education (Office of Comprehensive School Improvement and Planning). 1987. *A Resource Guide for Comprehensive School Improvement and Planning.* New York.

Niskanen, William A. 1973. *Bureaucracy: Servant or Master?* London: Institute of Economic Affairs.

Quinones, Nathan. 1986. "Minimum Performance Standards for the New York City Public Schools: A Blueprint for Excellence through Accountability." New York City Public Schools. Mimeo.

Schick, Allen. 1966. "The Road to PPBS: the Stages of budget Reform." *Public Administration Review* 26: 243–58.

Simmons, William, and Charles Barkdull. 1976. "Why Is Response to PPBS Mostly Bad? An Answer or Two." *School Business Affairs* 42 (November): 280–82.

Syracuse City School District. 1987a. "Performance Standards." Syracuse, N.Y. Mimeo.

_____. 1987b. "School Improvement Plan Packet." Syracuse, N.Y. Mimeo.

Wildavsky, Aaron. 1975. *Budgeting: A Comparative Theory of Budgetary Processes.* Boston: Little, Brown.

12 ARE SCHOOL SUPERINTENDENTS REWARDED FOR "PERFORMANCE"?

Ronald G. Ehrenberg
Richard P. Chaykowski
Randy A. Ehrenberg

The April 1983 report of the National Commission on Excellence in Education, *A Nation at Risk*, focused public attention on the need to reform public education. Among its most hotly debated proposals was one to institute merit pay plans for teachers, despite the fact that historically merit pay plans have not met with much success in public education, at least partially because certain characteristics of public education make their implementation problematic (see, for example, Bacharach, Lipsky, and Shedd 1984 and Murnane and Cohen 1986).

Somewhat surprisingly, less attention has been directed to the role that educational administrators (school principals and superintendents) play in the educational process and their methods of compensation. Given their roles in a variety of areas, including the recruitment and continual motivation of teachers, the design of curriculum, the setting of educational goals, and their management of school district resources, one might expect administrators' actions to be of importance in determining both how much students learn and the

We are grateful to the numerous school superintendents who responded to the survey used in this chapter, to the staff of the Cornell Institute of Social and Economic Research for acquiring a number of the data tapes that we used, to Eileen Driscoll for facilitating our use of these data, and most especially, to Jeffrey Keefe for his assistance coding and analyzing data during the early stages of the project. We are also deeply indebted to numerous colleagues at Cornell, the NBER, and other institutions for their comments on earlier drafts.

cost of public education to taxpayers (see the "effective school" literature, in for example, Bossert, et al. 1982, Kroeze 1982, and Hallinger and Murphy 1982). Yet there has been little public call for formal merit pay plans for school administrators. This is puzzling because studies of individual (as opposed to group) merit or incentive pay plans in the for-profit sector of the economy find that they tend to be concentrated at upper levels of management, where fundamental policy and managerial decisions are made, rather than at levels covering all employees (see Milkovich and Newman 1984).

In fact, although there is a voluminous literature on the determinants of teachers' salaries (see Ehrenberg and Schwarz 1986 and Lipsky 1982), little is known about the forces influencing the compensation of school administrators. In particular, little evidence is available about whether school administrators explicitly or implicitly are rewarded for their school districts' performance by higher compensation and/or greater opportunities for mobility to higher-paying positions.[1] Such evidence is clearly important for policy debate; unless there is evidence that school administrators' compensation is at least implicitly tied to their district's "performance," a case can be made that consideration should be given to building incentives for improving school district performance explicitly into their compensation arrangements.

This chapter presents analyses of the compensation and mobility of school superintendents in New York State during the 1978–79 to 1982–83 period. The focus is on school superintendents because they are the chief operating officers of school districts, their salaries are determined through individual "negotiations" with school boards, and their salary data were made available to us.[2] In contrast, school principals' salary data were not available to us. Especially in large districts, principals tend to be members of a union and their salary increases negotiated collectively, which limits the likelihood of observing individual principals' salaries being related to measures of their school's performance.

The discussion begins in the following section with a description of the characteristics of school superintendents in New York State, including their patterns of mobility and compensation. To provide information on the structure of school superintendents' compensation, multiple regression analysis is used to estimate the extent to which superintendents' salaries are related to characteristics of both their school districts and themselves. Estimates of the extent to which superintendents' probabilities of mobility and salary changes are related to measures of their school districts' "performance" are then discussed. Finally, in the last two sections we discuss whether school superintendents appear to influence these school district "performance" measures and the implications of our findings for public policy.

A crucial element in the study is the definition of *performance.* Because school districts and their school board members are idiosyncratic and evaluate superintendents' performance in a wide variety of ways, our methodology is to focus on a few well-defined outcomes. Specifically, we assume that school districts value high educational performance and low school tax rates, each relative to the comparable outcome in "similar" school districts in the state.[3] The discussion is nontechnical in nature; technical details, including underlying tables of statistical findings, can be found in other work of ours (Ehrenberg, Chaykowski, and Ehrenberg 1986, 1988).

DESCRIPTIVE STATISTICS ON SCHOOL SUPERINTENDENTS IN NEW YORK STATE

To obtain background data on the characteristics of school superintendents in New York State, a survey was mailed to the approximately 700 school districts in the state (excluding New York City) in May 1985, and a follow-up survey sent to nonrespondents in July of that year. We received 496 responses; this represents almost a 70 percent response rate. The sample appears to be representative of superintendents in the state; the response rate did not vary systematically with either school district size or with whether the county in which the district was located was upstate or downstate.

Table 12-1 presents some descriptive statistics for the sample. Respondents averaged nearly forty-nine years of age and first became superintendents at about the age of forty. The typical superintendent had been at his or her job for six years and had close to three years' total tenure in previous superintendents' positions. About 50 percent of the sample had received a certificate of advanced study in school administration, while close to 40 percent had received a doctorate degree.

Table 12-2 tabulates the distribution of respondents by years on their current job. Superintendents in the sample spent between one

Table 12-1. Descriptive Statistics.[a]

Variable	Sample Size	Mean	Standard Deviation	Minimum	Maximum
AGE	466	48.91	7.05	33	69
AGEF	466	40.02	6.56	25	62
TEN	495	6.07	5.04	1	28
NUM	495	0.60	0.98	0	8
EXPS	495	2.76	4.40	0	23
SIZE	192	0.43	0.76	0	2
CDEG	490	0.48	0.50	0	1
DDEG	494	0.38	0.49	0	1

a. Sample sizes are less than the overall sample of 496 due to nonreporting of data.

AGE   = age in years.
AGEF   = age when first became superintendent.
TEN   = number of years at current position.
NUM   = number of previous superintendent positions.
EXPS   = total years tenure at previous positions.
SIZE   = (for individuals who held a previous superintendent position) previous district
         was smaller (0), about the same size (1), or larger (2) than current district.
CDEG   = 1 = has a certificate of advanced study; 0 = no.
DDEG   = 1 = has a doctorate degree; 0 = no.

and twenty-eight years in their current jobs and the longer the job tenure, the smaller the number of superintendents observed. Indeed, a simple semilog function fit the data very well and implies that the number of superintendents with any given level of tenure on the job is roughly 19 percent more than the number with one additional year of tenure.

Finally, Table 12-3 presents data on the total number of superintendent positions held in each respondent's career, by age category of respondent. Although one hears much talk about how mobile superintendents are, the vast majority of superintendents in the sample had held (as of the survey date) less than four positions during their lifetimes (panel A). When they did change positions, they tended to move to larger districts; however, the probability that a job change led them to a smaller district increased as they aged (panel B).

Our analyses of superintendents' compensation use data from the over 700 school districts in New York State during the 1978–79 to 1982–83 period obtained from the New York State Education De-

Table 12-2. Tenure on Current Job.

Years Tenure	Number	Years Tenure	Number
1	81	15	12
2	64	16	8
3	48	17	8
4	54	18	5
5	42	19	5
6	33	20	2
7	24	21	1
8	27	22	1
9	19	23	1
10	15	24	1
11	12	25	1
12	14	26	0
13	10	27	0
14	6	28	1

Note: Fitting a semilog function to the first twenty-five years observations yields

$$\log(\text{number}_i) = 4.688 - .190 \ (\text{years tenure } i) \quad \bar{R}^2 = .946$$
$$\phantom{\log(\text{number}_i) = } (.138) \ (.009)$$

Table 12-3a. Number of Superintendent Positions Held, by Age.[a]

Number of Positions	All	Age Category			
		< 40	40–49	50–59	> 59
1	303	40	117	105	41
2	128	10	51	60	7
3	44	0	10	27	7
4	11	0	3	7	1
5	4	0	0	3	1
6	3	0	0	2	1
7	0	0	0	0	0
8	1	0	0	1	0
9	1	0	0	1	0
Total	495	50	181	206	58

Table 12-3b. Comparison of Size of Current and Last School District for People Who Have Held at Least Two Positions.[a]

Current District Size Is	All	Age Category			
		< 40	40-49	50-59	> 59
Larger	141	10	54	63	9
About the same	19	0	5	13	1
Smaller	32	0	4	21	7
Total	192	10	63	102	17

a. Sum of age categories does not equal entire sample because some superintendents did not report their birth years.

partment's Basic Educational Data System (BEDS) annual school district tapes.[4] Panel A of Table 12-4 reports salary data for the superintendents in the BEDS sample. The mean salary of superintendents in the sample rose from slightly under $35,000 in 1978-79 to over $44,000 in 1982-83. Each year the variation in salaries across districts was large; for example in 1982-83 superintendents in the state earned between $20,000 and $71,000, with the standard deviation in salaries equaling almost $10,000. Much of this variation is clearly due to the wide variation of school district sizes in the sample, however, as we demonstrate below, other factors are also important.

The BEDS data also permit us to track if a superintendent remained in the same school district for two consecutive years, moved from one district to another school district in the state during the period, or moved from one school district in the state to "out of sample" status. In the latter case, the superintendent may have retired or died, may have moved to another superintendency outside of New York State (previous studies suggest the vast majority of school superintendents serve in only one state during their lifetime; see Knezevich 1971), may have moved to a different educational position (nonsuperintendent) in another district in the state, or may have switched to a noneducational position. Alternatively, the school district may simply have failed to report data in the second year.

The data in Panel B of Table 12-4 suggest that the *annual* turnover rates of school superintendents are low, as each year between

Table 12-4a. School Superintendents' Salaries in New York State: 1978-79 to 1982-83.

Year	Number of Districts Reporting	Mean	Standard Deviation	Minimum	Maximum
1978-79	701	34,964	8,325	17,500	58,500
1979-80	700	36,614	8,617	17,500	61,500
1980-81	698	38,936	8,978	18,500	64,500
1981-82	689	41,665	9,479	22,785	71,000
1982-83	675	44,227	9,887	20,000	71,000

Table 12-4b. Mobility of School Superintendents in New York State: 1978-79 to 1982-83.

Years	A	B	C	D
1978-79 to 1979-80	727	610 (84%)	28 (4%)	89 (12%)
1979-80 to 1980-81	719	624 (87)	29 (4)	66 (9)
1980-81 to 1981-82	715	582 (81)	42 (6)	91 (13)
1981-82 to 1982-83	720	634 (88)	28 (4)	58 (8)

Source: Authors' calculations from data on the New York State Education Department's Basic Educational Data System (BEDS) School District Tapes for 1978-79 to 1982-83. Excluded each year are New York City, districts where the position is vacant, and districts that failed to report salary information.
A = number of superintendents in the sample in the first year.
B = number (percentage) of superintendents in the first year who were in the same district in the second year.
C = number (percentage) of superintendents in the first year who moved to another district in the state in the second year.
D = number (percentage) of superintendents in the first year who were not employed in any district in the sample in the second year.

81 and 88 percent of the superintendents continued in their current job.[5] Each year only 4 to 6 percent of the superintendents moved to another district in the state, while 8 to 13 percent of the superintendents dropped out of the sample.

CROSS-SECTIONAL VARIATION IN SUPERINTENDENTS' SALARIES

A superintendent's salary would be expected to be higher in districts that wish to attract and retain outstanding superintendents. These would probably be the larger districts (where more students are affected by the superintendent's action), wealthier districts (where the demand for education is likely to be greater), districts that contain a high proportion of highly educated adults (who are likely to have a strong "taste" for education), and districts whose students have special educational needs (such as those with a large proportion of minority students). On the other hand, characteristics of the superintendent should also matter. More experienced and more highly educated superintendents are likely to be able to command higher salaries.

Table 12–5 reports attempts to see if these forces do matter. Estimates of annual cross-section salary equations of the form

$$\log(W_i) = a_0 + a_1 X_i + a_2 S_i + \epsilon_i \qquad (12.1)$$

where W_i is the annual salary of superintendent i, X_i is a vector of school district characteristics in the employing district, S_i is a vector of characteristics of the superintendent, and ϵ is a random error term, are reported there. As noted in the table, the school district data used in the analyses come from a variety of federal and state sources. The characteristics of the superintendents come from two volumes of *Who's Who in Educational Administration*, the directory of members of the American Association of School Administrators, and the responses to our survey of all school superintendents employed in New York State in 1984–85.[6]

As expected, the characteristics of school districts prove to be important determinants of superintendents' salaries. Other things held constant, in each year larger districts (as measured by the logarithm of total enrollment *LENR*), wealthier districts (as measured by the logarithms of property values per enrolled student *LVAL*), per capita personal income in the county ($LY1$), or census year (1979) median family income in the school district ($LY2$)), and districts that place a high value on education (as measured by the percentage of the district's adult population with greater than a college degree $PHED$) all are associated with higher superintendents' salaries.

In contrast, only two of the superintendents' characteristics, his[7] years of tenure in the current district (TEN) and years since receiving a bachelor's degree ($EXPG$)—the latter a rough proxy for age or total labor market experience—prove to be statistically significant. Moreover, the effects of these variables are very small, with the rate of return per year of tenure being roughly 0.6 percent and that per year since degree being roughly 0.2 percent. Somewhat surprisingly, neither the possession of a doctorate degree ($DDEG$) or a certificate of advanced study in administration ($CDEG$)—the latter an intermediate degree between a master's and a doctorate—nor the total number of years of previous experience as a superintendent in other school districts ($EXPS$) systematically are associated with salary.

Of course, it is well known, and the results of our survey confirm (see Table 12–3), that the typical mobility pattern of a superintendent (at least during the early stages of his career) is from smaller to larger and/or from poorer to wealthier districts. If this is the case, these personal characteristic variables may affect salary indirectly via influencing the characteristics of the school district in which the superintendent is located, rather than directly influencing his salary level, given his district's characteristics.

To test this hypothesis, the logarithm of property value per enrolled student and the logarithm of total enrollment in the superintendent's district were both regressed each year on the personal characteristics of the superintendent (excluding years of tenure in the current district). The results (see Ehrenberg, Chaykowski, and Ehrenberg 1986) suggest that having a doctorate degree, having more prior experience as a superintendent in other districts, and being older were associated with employment in larger school districts, while having a doctorate degree was also associated with being employed in wealthier districts.

These latter findings have important implications for the following analyses of the relationship between superintendents' compensation and school districts' performance. Even if within a given school district one was to find no relationship between a superintendent's compensation and his school district's performance, superintendents

Table 12-5. Determinants of School Superintendents' Salaries in New York State: Annual Cross-Sections (*absolute value of t statistics*).

Explanatory[a] Variable/ Academic Year	Logarithm of Annual Salary (SAL)				
	1978–79	1979–80	1980–81	1981–82	1982–83
LENR	.127 (22.5)*	.113 (20.0)*	.117 (21.2)*	.111 (20.7)*	.110 (20.0)*
LVAL	.045 (5.8)*	.025 (4.1)*	.028 (4.8)*	.019 (3.9)*	.011 (2.3)*
LY1	.191 (5.2)*	.228 (6.5)*	.228 (6.3)*	.273 (8.4)*	.294 (9.3)*
LY2	.151 (3.6)*	.146 (3.4)*	.189 (4.3)*	.152 (3.6)*	.120 (2.9)*
PNW	.178 (2.6)*	.072 (1.2)	.032 (0.4)	-.071 (1.0)	-.111 (1.7)
PHED	.357 (2.5)*	.449 (3.0)*	.367 (2.5)*	.445 (3.1)*	.494 (3.4)*
PCHL	.200 (2.0)*	.009 (0.0)	.027 (0.3)	-.001 (0.0)	.074 (0.8)
POOC	-.073 (1.0)	.022 (0.3)	-.049 (0.7)	-.036 (0.5)	-.080 (1.0)
PCOL	.185 (1.8)	-.147 (1.3)	.105 (1.1)	.224 (2.2)*	.218 (2.1)*
PURB	.014 (1.0)	.025 (1.6)	.000 (0.0)	-.019 (1.2)	-.012 (0.9)
DDEG	-.008 (0.7)	.006 (0.6)	.010 (1.0)	.013 (1.4)	.023 (2.3)*
CDEG	.000 (0.0)	-.016 (1.4)	-.014 (1.3)	-.032 (3.1)*	-.016 (1.7)
EXPS	.002 (1.1)	-.000 (0.3)	.001 (0.6)	-.000 (0.1)	-.000 (0.2)
TEN	.006 (5.3)*	.006 (5.0)*	.006 (5.5)*	.004 (3.6)*	.007 (5.7)*
EXPG	.002 (2.1)*	.003 (3.3)*	.002 (2.1)*	.002 (2.2)*	.001 (0.8)
$\bar{R}^2$	.842	.845	.840	.836	.828
n	590	557	558	570	574

Sources: Authors' computations from:

1. Salaries, LENR, LVAL—New York State Education Department, Basic Educational Data System (BEDS) School District Tapes for 1978–79 to 1982–83, and New York State Education Department, Financial Data System (ST3) School District Tapes for 1978–79 to 1982–83.

2. LY1—U.S. Department of Commerce, Bureau of Economic Analysis, unpublished tabulations for 1978 to 1982.

3. LY2 to PURB—U.S. Bureau of the Census, 1980 Census of Population, School District Data File for New York State.

4. DDEG to EXPG—American Association of School Administrators, Who's Who in Educational Administration, 1976–77, 1980–81 editions, and the survey of school superintendents in New York State conducted by the authors in the summer of 1985.

a. Also included were an intercept term and dummy variables for nonreporting of the superintendents' previous experience, current job tenure, and year of bachelor's degree. Experience and job tenure were available for 35 to 65 percent of the sample each year, while year since degree was typically available for 70 to 80 percent of the sample.

*Coefficient statistically significantly different from zero at the .05 level; two-tail test.

LENR = logarithm of total enrollment in the district in the year.
LVAL = logarithm of the full value of property in the district per enrolled student in the year.
LY1   = logarithm of per capita personal income in the country in the year.
LY2   = logarithm of median family income in the district in 1979.
PNW   = 1979 percentage of the district's population that was nonwhite.
PHED = 1979 percentage of the district's adult population with greater than a college education.
PCHL = 1979 percentage of the district's households with children at home.
POOC = 1979 percentage owner-occupied housing in the district.
PCOL = 1979 percentage of the district's adult population with some college or a college degree.
PURB = 1979 percentage of the district's population residing in urban areas.
DDEG = 1 = superintendent had a doctoral degree in the year; 0 = no such degree in year.
CDEG = 1 = superintendent had a certificate of advanced study in the year; 0 = no such degree.
EXPS = superintendent's total number of years experience in other school districts as a superintendent.
TEN   = superintendent's years of tenure in the current district.
EXPG = superintendent's years since receiving a bachelor's degree.

might still be rewarded for district performance by increased opportunities for mobility to better paying positions.

EVALUATING THE "PERFORMANCE" OF SCHOOL DISTRICTS

We assume that school boards value high academic test scores (high educational output) and low school tax rates (more money available for other public and private uses), each relative to the comparable outcome in "similar" school districts in the state and that they evaluate a superintendent (at least implicitly) by his district's performance on these criteria. It is natural to ask how these measures correspond to criteria superintendents believe school boards actually use in their evaluation. In a survey of school superintendents we asked respondents to list criteria they believed their school boards used in their evaluation. Although we gave keeping test scores high and tax rates low as two examples of criteria that might be used, the question asked was open ended and superintendents were free to respond however they wished. In cases where a formal evaluation instrument existed, the superintendent was asked to attach it to his response. Approximately 80 percent of the respondents (397 of 496) included a list of criteria in their responses and about 25 percent of these (86) attached formal evaluation instruments.

A preliminary scanning of the responses suggested that the criteria mentioned could be classified into twelve broad categories, and a count was made of the number of times each category was mentioned. These responses are tabulated in Table 12-6; because most superintendents mentioned more than one category, the total count across categories far exceeds the number of respondents.

Most striking (because we gave keeping test scores high and tax rates low as examples on the questionnaire of criteria that might be used), the most commonly mentioned criteria was community/public relations and school board relations. Fiscal management (the category that would include—but which is not limited to—keeping tax rates low) came in fourth on the list and was mentioned by about two-thirds of the respondents. Academic performance and achievement (the category in which keeping test scores high would fall) was eighth on the list and was mentioned by less than one-third of the respondents.

Table 12-6. New York State Public School Superintendents' Perceptions of the Criteria School Boards Use in Evaluating Their Performance.[a]

Responses	Number
Overall response to the survey	496
Response to questions on criteria used in evaluation	397
Mentioned that criteria included:	
Community/public relations	318
School board relations	294
Staff and Personnel management	287
Fiscal management	267
Curriculum development, educational planning and leadership	202
Professional and personal development	132
General management and administration	129
Academic performance and achievement	125
Facilities management	50
Student services and relations	49
Student discipline	26
Parent relations	25
Included a formal evaluation instrument	86

a. Responses from the approximately 700 school superintendents in New York State (excluding New York City) to a survey conducted by the authors in May to July of 1985.

What are the implications of these findings for the use of the objective performance measures that we propose? On the one hand, it is hard to envision objective measures that are readily available for the other ten criteria; measures of fiscal management and academic performance and achievement may be the best one can do. On the other hand, it is clear that the specific measures we use are measured with considerable error; if these errors are random, the coefficients of our performance variables will be biased toward zero in our analyses of mobility and compensation change. Furthermore, given that more than twice as many respondents mentioned fiscal management as did academic performance, one might expect that, on average, the former will prove to be more important than the latter in explaining compensation and mobility.

To give the reader a feel for how the performance measures were actually constructed, Table 12-7 presents estimates of tax rate and educational outcome equations for 1979-80 (separate equations

Table 12-7. 1979–80 Tax Rate and Educational Outcome Equations (*absolute value of t statistics*).

Explanatory Variables/Outcome	log (T)	log (GM)	log (AS)
LVAL	-.100 (7.0)*	-.036 (1.2)	-.033 (1.6)
LY1	-.001 (0.0)	-.243 (1.3)	-.029 (0.2)
LY2	.180 (1.8)**	-.253 (1.2)	-.397 (2.8)*
PNW	.691 (4.6)*	1.351 (4.2)*	1.111 (5.2)*
PHED	1.009 (2.8)*	-1.331 (1.8)**	-1.801 (3.5)*
PCHL	.979 (3.7)*	.670 (1.2)	.374 (1.0)
POOC	-.417 (2.1)*	-.689 (1.7)**	-.653 (2.3)*
PCOL	.388 (1.4)	-.685 (1.2)	-.634 (1.7)**
PURB	.271 (7.6)*	-.042 (0.6)	-.009 (0.2)
D	.006 (0.1)	.278 (2.9)*	.205 (3.1)*
$\overline{R}^2$	.457	.184	.349
n	573	565	568

Sources: Authors' calculations are from:

1. *LVAL* to *PURB*—defined as before, see Table 12-5.

2. *T, D*—New York State Education Department, Financial Data System (ST3) School District Tape for 1979–80.

3. *GM, AS*—New York State Education Department, Pupil Evaluation Program (PEP) Test Scores.

*(**) = coefficient statistically significant from zero at .05 (.10) level of significance; two-tail set.

T = full value property tax rate in the school district in 1979–80.

GM = percentage of the district's students who scored below the state reference point on standardized 6th grade mathematics exam in 1979–80.

AS = average of the percentages of the district's students who fell below the state reference point on standardized third- and sixth-grade reading and mathematics exams in 1979–80.

D = 1 = city school district (school board sets tax rate); 0 = other school district (voters approve school budget in annual referendum).

were estimated for each year and the results are very similar across years). The tax rate variable is the logarithm of the *full-value* property tax rate in the school district (total school district property tax revenue/total value of taxable property in the school district). The educational outcome variables are the logarithms of the percentage of the district's students who fall below the state reference point on a standardized sixth-grade mathematics examination and the average (which we computed) of the percentages who fell below the state reference point on standardized third- and sixth-grade reading and mathematics examinations.[8] Students who fall below the state reference point are deemed to require remedial services, and state aid is increased to help fund these services. Because these outcome scores measure the proportion who "fail" these tests, we are focusing on the bottom tail of the academic achievement distribution.[9]

For each of these three outcomes (O), equations were estimated of the form

$$\log O_{ji} = b_{0j} + b_{1j}Z_i + u_{ji} \qquad j = 1, 2, 3 \qquad (12.2)$$

where O_{ji} is outcome j in school district i, Z_i is a vector of school district characteristics in district i expected to influence these outcomes, and u_{ji} is a random error term. In fact, the variables in (12.2) are assumed to be identical to those school district variables that enter the superintendent salary equation, except that a (1, 0) "city school district" dummy variable replaces the continuous size of district variable. The latter is included here because in the large city school districts during this period the property tax rate was set by an elected school board (subject to constitutional limitations), while in the smaller school districts the tax rate was set each year by a voter referendum. One might conjecture, ceteris paribus, that in the latter situation direct voter control will lead to lower tax rates.

In the main, the estimates in Table 12-7 conform to one's prior expectations and provide reasonable explanations of the tax rates and test scores. For example, with respect to tax rates, although wealthier ($LVAL$) districts have lower tax rates, they also raise more revenue to finance education because of their higher wealth. Similarly, richer in terms of current income ($LY2$) districts have higher tax rates; districts with higher proportions of nonwhites (PNW), and thus special needs, have higher tax rates; districts with higher proportions of adults with more than a college education ($PHED$), and presumably greater taste for education, have higher tax rates; and districts in which a greater percentage of the households have children at home ($PCHL$), and thus greater interest in spending on education relative to keeping taxes down, have higher tax rates.[10]

Similarly, with respect to test scores, wealthier districts, districts with higher current income and districts with highly educated adults, ceteris paribus, all have lower failure rates on the tests, while districts with a higher proportion of nonwhites have higher failure rates. Failure rates, but not tax rates, also appear to be higher in the "city" school districts. It is worth noting that the equation used to predict the average test failure rate "fits" much better than the equation used to predict the sixth-grade math test failure rate. Although it would be preferable to use the former in our analysis, as noted above (note 8) only the latter can be used in analyses that exploit the longitudinal nature of the data.

Given these estimated coefficients, corresponding to $\hat{b}_{0j}$ and $\hat{b}_{1j}$ in (12.2), one can obtain *predicted* values of the logarithm of each outcome for each school district i from

$$\hat{\log} O_{ji} = \hat{b}_{0j} + \hat{b}_{1j} Z_i \qquad j = 1, 2, 3 \qquad (12.3)$$

The school district's performance is then defined as the difference between the predicted and actual values of the log of each outcome.[11]

$$P_{ji} = \hat{\log} O_{ji} - \log O_{ji} \qquad j = 1, 2, 3 \qquad (12.4)$$

Positive values of P_{ji} indicate positive performance for the district, as positive values would occur only when predicted tax rates (or failure rates on tests) would exceed actual tax rates (or failure rates on tests) in the school district.

It is worth reemphasizing that (12.2), (12.3), and (12.4) are estimated separately each year. Thus, the equations that generate the performance measures are allowed to vary across years, as are the estimates of tax and test score performance in the district.

SCHOOL DISTRICT PERFORMANCE AND SUPERINTENDENT MOBILITY

As noted above, each year roughly 5 percent of the superintendents in the sample moved to another school district in New York State, while roughly 10 percent dropped out. Among the former group, approximately 80 percent received salary increases, while 20 percent received the same salary after moving or suffered a salary cut. Finally, approximately 85 percent of the sample continued in their same positions. What determines whether each superintendent moves to another district with a higher salary, moves to another district with the same or lower salary, leaves the sample, or stays in the same school district each year?

To econometrically model this joint process of wage change, job change, and leave the sample would be extraordinarily complex because both school boards and superintendents are involved in this decision process. What one would ideally like to do is estimate a complete structural "matching model" that contains both employer (school board) and employee (school superintendent) decision rules. Given our limited data, we instead estimated simpler reduced form models of the form

$$\log\left(\frac{P(\text{state}=k)}{P(\text{state}=4)}\right) = d_{0k} + d_{1k}Y + d_{2k}S +$$

$$d_{3k}T + d_{4k}E + \epsilon_k$$

$$k = 1, 2, 3 \tag{12.5}$$

where Y is a vector of characteristics of the school district (a subset of the X in (12.1), S is the vector of superintendent characteristics, and T and E are the relevant tax rate and educational test score performance measures. The notation $P(\text{state}=k)$ denotes the probability that an individual is in state k, with the four states being change districts with a salary increase, change districts with the same or a lower salary, leave the sample, and continue on in the same district, respectively. Under suitable assumptions about the distribution of the error terms (logistic), the system in (12.5) represents a multinomial logit model and can be estimated by standard maximum likelihood methods. Each estimated coefficient in equation k ($k = 1, 2, 3$) tells us how the explanatory variable associated with it affects the logarithm of the ratio of the probability of the superintendent's being in state k relative to the probability of his continuing in the same district.

What relevant tax rate and educational test score performance measures should be used in this analysis? On the one hand, one might argue that relevant measures would involve *changes* in performance over time. That is, a superintendent's mobility probabilities might be influenced by whether his school district's tax rate and test score performance measures had improved or worsened over time. On the other hand, one might argue that keeping test score and tax rate performance at a constant but high (low) level might lead to higher probabilities of moving to a higher- (lower-) paying job. Ultimately, whether a *change* in performance measure or a *level* of performance measure is correct is an empirical question; we discuss results of experimenting with various specifications below.

Suppose, however, that the focus is on the level of performance measures; the dating of the performance measures to use must still be decided. To clarify this issue, suppose we are looking at potential mobility between 1979–80 (the *base* year) and 1980–81 (the *new* year). The base-year math test (for 1979–80) was given in the spring of 1980, and a district may have received its own test results back shortly thereafter. However, there is very little chance that it would have received data on the test scores in other districts in the state prior to the next academic year (the fall of 1980). Such information would thus come too late to be used to estimate test score performance indexes that could then be used in decisions to retain the superintendent for 1980–81 and/or to try to attract a superintendent from another district whose district had high test score performance. In fact, the latest (in a temporal sense) test score performance measure that could be used in potential mobility studies between 1979–80 and 1980–81 is the index for 1978–79; we refer to this as the *lagged* year district test performance level index below.

Using a similar line of reasoning, one can show that potentially the *base* year tax level performance measure *is* available to be used in mobility decisions from the base to the new year. However, if information on school district performance is processed by school districts only with a lag, the *lagged* year tax rate performance index may again be the relevant one to use.

When equation (12.5) was estimated using the lagged year performance level measures, the lagged tax level performance measure was positively associated with the odds of moving to a higher-paying job (relative to staying) and negatively associated with the odds of moving to a lower-paying job (relative to staying).[12] Put another way, among movers the better lagged tax level performance is, the more likely the individual will move to a better job. A school district's financial performance *does* affect its school superintendent's future. The math performance variable, however, was always insignificant, perhaps because of the reasons discussed in the previous section.

As suggested from the cross-section results discussed above, having a doctorate degree was shown to increase a superintendent's chances to move to a better-paying job relative to his chances to not move. Older superintendents, as measured by years since receiving a bachelor's degree, were less likely to move to another job and more likely to leave the sample, both relative to staying in the same district. The former clearly reflects voluntary mobility declining with age, and the latter reflects retirement rates increasing with age. Superintendents with more previous experience as a superintendent in other districts were more likely to move to both higher- *or* lower-paying jobs relative to staying in the same district; this may well reflect heterogeneity of turnover probabilities. Finally, being employed in a school district with high median family income reduced the probability of moving to a higher-paying job relative to the probability of staying. As indicated in Table 12–5, higher-income school districts pay more, thereby reducing the likely gain to mobility.

In fact, this latter result suggests that some measure of the superintendent's potential gain from mobility should be directly included in these equations. We experimented with four such measures: the logarithm of base year salary, residual from a base year log salary equation that included only superintendents' characteristics, residual from a base year log salary equation that included both superintendents' and school district characteristics, and residual from a comprehensive base year log salary equation that also included performance measures. None of these measures proved to be statistically significant (when they were included one at a time), nor did their inclusion affect the pattern of signs and significance of the other coefficients.

We also tested for the sensitivity of our mobility results to the specification of the performance variables. Four specifications were tested: base year level, lagged year level, both base and lagged year levels, and change between the base and new year. Results (see Ehrenberg, Chaykowski, and Ehrenberg 1986) indicate quite clearly that only the lagged level of tax performance matters, with better performance leading to an increased (decreased) probability of mobility to a better-paying (not better-paying) position relative to the probability of remaining on the same job.

SCHOOL DISTRICT PERFORMANCE AND SUPERINTENDENT SALARY CHANGES

The previous section focused on the determinants of school superintendents' mobility. According to the results discussed, the higher a school district's estimated tax rate performance in the lagged year, the greater the probability that the district's superintendent would move to a better-paying job and the lower the probability that he would move to an equal or lower-paying job, both relative to the probability of remaining in the district in the next year. Thus, superintendents in school districts with high (low) values of the tax performance measure appear to be rewarded (punished) for their district's performance. No such relationship was found, however, between a district's lagged math test performance measure and its superintendent's mobility prospects.

This section treats the mobility status of superintendents as given and examines how salary increases for both superintendents who remain in the same district for two consecutive years, and those who move to another district in New York State, were related to the lagged year tax rate and test score performance measures in the base year school district.

We estimated two salary change equations for superintendents who remained in the sample over two consecutive years. In the simplest model, salary change was postulated to be a function only of the year we were looking at (because average salary increases varied across years) and a variable that indicated whether the superintendent changed jobs during the year. The results suggested that mobility mattered; on average superintendents who changed jobs received salary increases that were 6 percent higher than those who remained in the same position. To say that on average "movers" gain is not to say, however, that mobility always pays. In fact, as noted above, approximately one-fifth of the movers each year failed to increase their salaries; some of these suffered salary losses as large as 30 percent.

We next estimated a model in which a superintendent's salary change was also postulated to be a function of the lagged tax rate and math test score school district performance measures in the superintendent's base year school district, as well as the changes in the logarithms of county income, school district enrollment, and school district full value of property per student, from the base year to the new year school district. (For stayers, the latter three variables are simply the within district changes in the variables between the base and new years.) The coefficients of each of these change variables and the performance measures were allowed to differ between movers and stayers in this model.

The results of this analysis suggested that, other things held constant, movers suffered salary *losses* in the range of 5 to 6 percent relative to superintendents who did not change jobs. This occurred because among the other things held constant were school district income, enrollment, and wealth per student. In fact, the changes in each of these variables was positively associated with salary changes for movers (but *not* for stayers). Hence, in order for superintendents to have gained from mobility, they must have moved to either higher-income, larger, or wealthier school districts; this result is fully consistent with the cross-section salary equations presented in Table 12–5.

Focusing on the performance variables, the lagged math test performance variable coefficient suggested that superintendents who were "stayers" in school districts with above-average math test performance received larger salary increases than other superintendents who did not change jobs. In contrast, being employed in a district with above-average tax rate performance was positive but insignificantly associated with the salary increases of stayers.

What about the effects of performance on the salary changes of superintendents who changed jobs? Here the evidence was more mixed. Lagged tax performance in the superintendent's base year school district was positively associated with earnings gains for superintendents who change jobs, but lagged math test performance was negatively associated. We have no explanation for this latter finding, which is not consistent with the other results reported here and in the previous section.[13]

HAVE SCHOOL SUPERINTENDENTS'
ACTIONS INFLUENCED SCHOOL
DISTRICT PERFORMANCE?

Our presumption is that school superintendents can affect our measures of school district performance and that the provision of appropriate financial incentives will encourage them to do so. One may wonder, however, whether superintendents' actions per se have had *any* influence on these school district performance measures in the past. A simple way to address this issue is to assume that a school district's estimated performance in a year depends only on the district *and* the particular superintendent employed in the district in the previous year.[14]

Operationally, this is equivalent to specifying a regression model in which the dependent variable is an estimated performance measure for a school district in year t and the explanatory variables are a set of dichotomous variables (one for each of the approximately 1,000 superintendents in the sample), each of which takes on the value 1 if the superintendent that it denotes worked in that school district in year $t - 1$ and 0 otherwise, as well as a set of school district dichotomous variables (one for each of the approximately 700 school districts), each which takes on the value 1 if the school district it represents is that school district and 0 otherwise. If superintendents per se matter, at least some of the coefficients of the "superintendent variables" should prove to be nonzero.

To estimate such a model requires one to estimate an equation with approximately 1,700 coefficients, no simple computational task. However, if one takes the first difference and thereby obtains an equation for the change in performance in a school district between year t and year $t - 1$, all the school district variables and those superintendent variables that represent superintendents who never changed jobs during the period drop out of this model. This simplifies the estimation considerably, and when we estimated this latter model we found *no* evidence that knowledge of who the school superintendent was in a district in the previous year helped to predict the school district's tax rate or math test score performance measure in a given year (see Ehrenberg, Chaykowski, and Ehrenberg 1988 for details). Put another way, superintendents per se did not appear to influence our measures of school district performance.

A more complete analysis would experiment with a variety of different lags and use larger sample sizes (more years' data).[15] In addition, the weakness of our educational performance measures should be reemphasized. Data limitations restricted us both here and in the previous sections to focusing on the lower tail of the achievement distribution in mathematics for one elementary grade level. More complete measures would focus attention on the upper tail, on other subjects, on achievement measures for older students (test scores, drop-out rates, high school graduation rates, and college attendance rates) and on variables that are less easily measured (teaching students to think critically or instilling them with a sense of social responsibility). It is clear that our educational performance measures are measured with considerable error; this may well cause us to understate both superintendents' effects on them and their effects on superintendents' salary changes and mobility.

CONCLUDING REMARKS

Are school superintendents in New York State rewarded for their school districts' "good performance" by larger salary increases and/or greater opportunities for mobility to higher-paying positions? Although the evidence presented here is somewhat ambiguous, our tentative answer is yes. Higher scores on the tax rate performance index in the prior (lagged) year were associated with greater (smaller) probabilities that a superintendent will move to a better- (poorer-) paying job relative to the probability of staying in the same district and, for "movers," larger salary increases. Higher scores on the third-grade mathematics test index in the prior year were associated with larger salary increases for stayers. However, contrary to our expectations, this index was also negatively associated with salary increases for movers. It is this latter finding that gives us some pause as we draw conclusions.

Moreover, to say that the market for school superintendents is at least implicitly rewarding superintendents for their district's "good performance" is *not* to say that the implicit incentives to perform that superintendents face is sufficiently strong. Given the responses to our survey's question on the criteria that school boards use in their evaluation of superintendents (Table 12–6), our estimates suggest that these incentives are quite modest.

For example, our estimates suggest that a superintendent who remained in the same district while his district's math test performance index remained one standard deviation above the mean performance index (which is zero), would receive an annual salary increase that was only 0.3 percentage points higher, other things equal, than a "mean performer." If the district maintained this level of performance over a ten-year period, the superintendent's salary level at the end of the period would be only slightly more than three percentage points higher than that of the mean performer. Similarly, our results suggest that, among superintendents who moved to another position, those whose district's tax rate performance index was one standard deviation above the mean tax rate performance (which again is zero), would receive a salary increase on moving that was only 1.7 percentage points higher, ceteris paribus, than the salary increase that a "mean performing mover" would receive. Neither of these magnitudes provides a strong incentive for superintendents to perform well.

On the other hand, our estimates suggest that a district's tax rate performance substantially influences its superintendent's prospects for mobility. Other things equal, a superintendent whose district's tax rate performance was one standard deviation above the mean would increase the ratio of his probability of moving to a better-paying job relative to the probability of staying in the same district by 40 percent and decrease the ratio of the probability of moving to a poorer-paying job relative to the probability of staying by 37 percent. These ratios, however, on average are very small (.038 and .016, respectively), so one may question whether even these mobility effects are of sufficient magnitude to provide the appropriate incentives for performance.

Indeed, taken at face value, the results discussed in the previous section suggest that superintendents per se do not appear to influence our measures of school district performance. One may interpret this finding in a number of ways. First, it is possible that the incentive effects estimated here are not sufficiently strong to provide adequate incentives for superintendents to try to influence these performance measures. Second, it is possible that school superintendents actually have little control over these measures (given the effective schools literature referred to in the introduction that stresses the important roles school administrators play, we doubt that this interpretation is correct). Third, as noted in the previous section, the limited number of years' data we had available and errors in the measurement of our educational performance measures may have caused us to understate both superintendents' effects on school district performance and the latter's effect on superintendents' salary changes and mobility. Resolution of which interpretation is correct will require additional research that is beyond the scope of our data set, although we have discussed throughout the chapter the form that some of these analyses might take.

Assuming that one agrees with the normative propositions that school districts should value high educational performance and effective fiscal management, the appropriate policy recommendations that follow will depend on which interpretation proves correct. Our own inclination is to take the results of both our econometric research and our survey findings at face value (the first interpretation) and to suggest that local school boards build more incentives into school superintendents' compensation arrangements to encourage superintendents to improve educational and financial measures of school district performance.

NOTES

1. Some case studies and statistical analyses of superintendents' turnover and mobility have been conducted; see Berger (1983), Knezevich (1971), and March and March (1977, 1978). Some comparative data on superintendents' salaries has also been published; see American Association of School Administrators (1979) and Knezevich. None of these, however, attempted to measure "performance" and to see if it matters; indeed, March and March (1977) argued that the mobility of superintendents is almost a random process. Their approach, however, was criticized by Schmittlein and Morrison (1981).

2. We must caution, however, that the "effective schools" literature has tended to focus on the role of building administrators (principals) and not on the role of school superintendents.

3. A district can simultaneously have high test scores and low tax rates, relative to "comparable" districts in the state, if the district's administrators efficiently manage both financial and educational (that is, staff) resources and effectively motivate school district personnel.

4. Unfortunately, no data on nonsalary compensation items are available on the BEDS tapes; we were limited to analyzing salaries rather than total compensation. Excluded from the sample each year were New York City (because the size of its school system and its large number of local district school boards make it noncomparable to any other district in the state), districts in which the superintendent's position was vacant, and districts that failed to report salary information.

5. These turnover data are consistent with what the superintendents themselves reported in Table 12-2.

6. Because less than half of the superintendents in the sample belonged to the professional association and the response rate of incumbents to the survey was about 70 percent, there was a substantial number of observations with missing data on some, or all, of the superintendents' characteristics. We also could not obtain school district characteristics data for some of the districts. As a result, we excluded observations from the sample if either

the school district's characteristics or the superintendent's degree information was missing. As Table 12–5 indicates, this reduces our sample sizes to between 550 and 600 observations each year.

7. We use *his* hereafter because over 97 percent of the approximately 1,010 superintendents who appear in our sample during the 1978–79 to 1982–83 period were males.

8. We isolate the sixth-grade mathematics test because it was the only one of the four tests that did *not* undergo revision during the period and that was given in all five years. As a result, while the entire battery of tests can be used to construct a performance measure when analyzing a single year's cross-section, subsequent sections' longitudinal analyses, which pool data across years, are restricted to using the single sixth-grade mathematics test.

9. These, unfortunately, were the only test score data that the New York State Education Department could provide us as they are the only tests that *all* students in the state are required to take. It obviously would have been preferable to have test scores for older students and also to focus some attention on the upper tail of the achievement distribution. For example, data on high school graduation rates or on the fraction of seniors going on to higher education would have been desirable. Our focus on the lower tail of the elementary school student test distribution imparts additional error to our educational performance measures, as does our ignoring other aspects of educational performance that are not easily measured (such as teaching students to write or instilling a sense of social responsibility in them).

10. A number of people have pointed out that in many communities businesses pay a substantial share of property taxes. Because only residents vote on school taxes, it would be desirable to include the share of property owned by residents in the total tax base as an additional explanatory variable in the tax rate equation. Discussions with officials in the New York State Education Department and Division of Equalization and Assessment indicated that (a) residential property data are *not* readily available at the school district level in New York State and (b) such data would not capture what we are after because some business property may be owned by residents and some residential (rental) property may be owned by non-residents.

11. A similar "residual approach" to estimating performance was used in Goldstein and Ehrenberg (1976) in a different context.

12. See Ehrenberg, Chaykowski, and Ehrenberg (1986, 1988) for tables of statistical results that support the statements made in this and the next two sections.

13. As in the previous section, inclusion of the superintendent's salary in the base year as an additional explanatory variable did not alter any of the other coefficients. For the subset of school districts for which we had

teacher salary data, we also attempted to test if school superintendents' salary changes were related to the salary changes of teachers in their school districts. This variable, however, never proved statistically significant.

14. The one-year lag is assumed in the case of the tax rate measure because the tax rate in year t is determined by the school board and superintendent in year $t - 1$. Although test scores in year t conceivably could depend on the superintendents' actions in year t, a year lag here also seems reasonable. Longer panels of data than we have would permit experimentation with a variety of lag lengths.

15. For example, we found similar results (school superintendents per se do not appear to influence school district performance) when we assumed that performance in period t was a function of the superintendent in period $t - 2$.

REFERENCES

American Association of School Administrators. 1979. *Compensating the Superintendent.* Arlington, Va.: AASA.

_____. 1979–80. *Who's Who in Educational Administration.* Arlington, Va.: AASA.

Bacharach, Samuel, David Lipsky, and Joseph Shedd. 1984. *Paying for Better Teaching: Merit Pay and Its Alternatives.* Ithaca, N.Y.: Organizational Analysis and Practice.

Berger, Michael. 1983. "Predicting Succession under Conditions of Enrollment Decline." Paper presented at the Annual Meeting of the American Educational Research Association, Montreal, Canada.

Bossert, S., D. Dwyer, B. Rowan, and G. Lee. 1982. "The Instructional Management Role of the Principal." *Educational Administration Quarterly* 18: 34–64.

Ehrenberg, Ronald G., Richard P. Chaykowski, and Randy A. Ehrenberg. 1986. "Merit Pay for School Superintendents?" Cambridge, Mass.: National Bureau of Economic Research Working Paper No. 1954.

_____. 1988. "Determinants of the Compensation and Mobility of School Superintendents." *Industrial and Labor Relations Review* 41 (April): 386–402.

Ehrenberg, Ronald G., and Joshua L. Schwarz. 1986. "Public Sector Labor Markets." In *Handbook of Labor Economics,* vol. 2, edited by Orley Ashenfelter and Richard Layard, pp. 129–68. Amsterdam: North Holland.

Goldstein, Gerald, and Ronald Ehrenberg. 1976. "Executive Compensation in Municipalities." *Southern Economic Journal* 43 (3): 937–47.

Hallinger, Phillip, and Joseph Murphy. 1982. "The Superintendents Role in Promoting Educational Leadership." *Administrator's Notebook* 30 (6).

Knezevich, Steven. 1971. *The American School Superintendent.* Washington, D.C.: American Association of School Superintendents.

Kroeze, David J. 1982. "Effective Principals as Instructional Leaders: New Directions for Research." *Administrator's Notebook* 30 (9): 1–4.

Lipsky, David. 1982. "The Effect of Collective Bargaining on Teacher Pay: A Review of the Evidence." *Education Administration Quarterly* 18 (1): 14–42.

March, James C., and James G. March. 1977. "Almost Random Careers: The Wisconsin School Superintendency: 1940–72." *Administrative Science Quarterly* 22 (3): 377–409.

_____. 1978. "Performance Sampling in Social Matches." *Administrative Science Quarterly* 23 (4): 434–53.

Milkovich, George, and Jerry Newman. 1984. *Compensation.* Plano, Tex.: Business Publications.

Murnane, Richard J., and David Cohen. 1986. "Merit Pay and the Evaluation Problem: Why Most Merit Pay Plans Fail and a Few Survive." *Harvard Education Review* 56 (1): 1–17.

National Commission on Excellence in Education. 1983. *A Nation at Risk: The Imperative for Educational Reform.* Washington, D.C.: U.S. Department of Education.

Schmittlein, David, and Donald Morrison. 1981. "On Individual Level Inference in Job Duration Research: A Reexamination of the Wisconsin School Superintendents Study." *Administrative Science Quarterly* 26 (1): 84–89.

13 THE INTERNAL ALLOCATION OF RESOURCES WITHIN U.S. SCHOOL DISTRICTS
Implications for Policymakers and Practitioners

Michael W. Kirst

THE POLICY CONTEXT

Internal allocation of school resources emerged in 1987 as a major national issue. *U.S. News and World Report* was typical of the media coverage with its headline story, "Beating Back the Education 'Blob'" (Solorzano 1987), and Secretary of Education William Bennett called the growing education bureaucracy a "blob that continues to grow no matter what." A key allegation was that the portion of school spending devoted to teachers' salaries dropped from 50 percent to 41 percent between 1970 and 1987. In an enterprise like public elementary and secondary education, which spends about $200 billion a year, this is a very sizeable reallocation. Bennett's uncontrollable blob of bureaucrats oversaw instructional costs that increased by 67.7 percent between 1960 and 1980 and administrative costs that more than doubled (Montague 1987). According to the Education Department, between 1960 and 1984 the number of teachers grew by 51 percent, principals and supervisors grew by 79 percent, but other staff such as curriculum supervisors and guidance counselors skyrocketed by 500 percent.

School administrators and board spokespersons shot back with equally florid rhetoric. Thomas Shannon, executive director of the National School Boards Association, claimed that without administrators to check up on teachers our schools would become "an educational Beirut, a form of neoanarchy" (Solorzano 1987). Administrators produced their own studies that contended the administrative blob was "an illusion." The highest rates of spending they claim is in areas such as retirement plans and fringe benefits. Such "fixed charges" rose from 7.4 percent in 1960 of the total spending to 13.6 percent in 1980 (Montague 1987). The Secretary of Education's press secretary retorted that the education bureaucracy is trying to "count itself out of existence by defining many administrative employees, such as curriculum planners, as instructional staff" (Montague 1987). The same issues erupted at the state level when California Governor George Deukmejian debated with State Superintendent of Instruction Bill Honig. Deukmejian succeeded in rebating $1 billion of state taxes in 1988, claiming the schools had enough money if they would more efficiently allocate and spend the dollars in the classroom rather than on overhead like administration.

After reviewing some broader policy issues raised by this debate about the allocation of resources, this analysis will return to the specific issue of alleged administrative inefficiencies. Subsequent sections will demonstrate how difficult it is to define and measure such terms as the budget for teachers, instruction, and administration as well as the most efficient allocations among such categories. Despite the political rhetoric, internal allocation of resources within school districts attracts surprisingly little scholarly attention, as the citations of the authors in this chapter demonstrate (Thomas 1971; Gerwin 1974). In 1988–89 school districts will spend about $200 billion or 5 percent of the GNP on K through 12 education. In the past the lack of policy implications from research on education production functions has tended to discourage micro economic education policy research. The bulk of the research continues to focus on equity and adequacy of distribution among school districts or on such emotional issues as vouchers. There was a brief upsurge of research interest in internal issues in the early 1980s as total resources for schools were restricted by property tax revolts and the economic recession (Kirst 1982, 1983: 1). But the education reforms from 1983–88 spurred by concerns about international economic competition helped to produce school spending increases of 21 percent after inflation for the nation as a whole (Odden and Marsh 1987). Finance research was directed to paying for "reform" and financing new concepts like career ladders for teachers. The robust U.S. economic growth probably accounted for more of this astounding total

Figure 13-1. The Rewards of Teaching: Average Annual Earnings of Teachers and All U.S. Workers in Constant 1987 Dollars (*in thousands of dollars*).

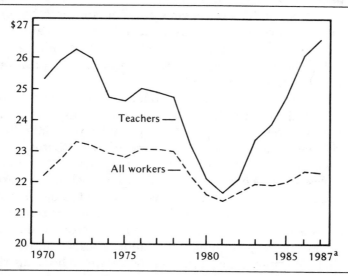

Source: American Federation of Teachers.
a. The 1987 figure for all workers is estimated.

education expenditure growth than the academic reform movement, but this has not been carefully explored either.

It is unlikely that school expenditures can continue to increase as rapidly as they have since 1983. For example, as Figure 13-1 demonstrates, teacher pay has increased much faster than the average annual earnings of all workers ever since 1982. Adjusted for inflation, teacher pay is up only 2 percent from its previous peak in 1972, but the average U.S. worker has not recovered all of the real wages lost in the inflationary 1970s. This growth is bound to slow down, and perhaps the next decade will stimulate more scholarly attention to internal spending decisions.

SCHOOL DISTRICT BUDGETING

A review of the budget processes used in school districts reveals some common techniques that transcend district variations (Brackett 1983). The budget process is generally a centralized process and incremental. Initial responsibility for the budget usually lies with the business manager, who is paid much less than his counterparts in industry for similar size total budgets.

Internal school budgeting depends primarily on three components: (1) formulatic ratios, (2) centrally controlled budget categories, and (3) pay scales (Guthrie 1988). Enrollment projections are crucial because they determine the number of professional positions allocated to functions at each school.

Most districts use two formula concepts: (1) a staffing formula and (2) a funding formula for supplies, materials, and textbooks. Most administrators reported that the formulas were inherited from their predecessors and there was little relationship between the formula level and quality measures or costs (Brackett 1983). In general, the formulas are based on a per student basis, although custodians may be based on the number of rooms or square footage in the buildings. There are no standard formulas for allocation of central district office administrators. Staffing ratios and class size are different because the hiring ratio is simply the student/teacher ratio within a school that determines the hiring needs of the school district. Because teachers often teach five classes and students take six in secondary schools, the class size and hiring ratios differ. Most districts use a formula with more teachers for secondary school classes than elementary. There is no clear research base for this decision because elementary students might benefit more from smaller classes than secondary school pupils. Other personnel are based on increments of students—that is, one counselor for each 500 students.

The funding ratios for supplies and materials are based on ADA per school and the amount increases by grade level. But these formulas are not based on actual costs. In fact, when budget reductions are necessary, the ratio is ignored and a flat-rate concept is used (Brackett 1983).

Another key concept in school district budgeting is the use of centralized allocations whereby a part of the budget is held centrally for use of districtwide administration and functions that serve two or more schools such as legal or transport services. This is the allocation that has engendered so much recent media concern, but again we find that past experience is frequently given as the justification for any particular amount. For instance, the past five-year average for maintenance is adjusted by a cost-of-living adjustment to determine the current budget (Guthrie 1988).

Pay scales are the third pillar of school district budgets. Pay is almost always based on the number of years employed and educational credit beyond the bachelor's degree. Education salaries are rarely based on any direct relationship to the teacher's ability or performance evaluations (Guthrie 1988). If senior teachers prefer particular schools, this will create a very high cost per pupil compared to the average school. Senior teachers can often choose where they want to teach under the collective bargaining contract.

School decisionmakers talk in terms of expenditures, not configurations of resources that reflect actual costs, program needs, or performance outcomes. Consequently, school budgets do not reflect a school's program or delivery system. Few administrators outside the cabinet are aware of district revenue projections, so the school site requests exceed the available funds by quite a bit. The superintendent's cabinet then engages in decremental cuts to reach a balanced budget. The list of reductions is presented to the board who takes responsibility for assigning priorities. As Brackett (1983: 17) observes:

> Faced with unclear goals and technology, board members and administrators use only the most subjective measures of effectiveness when deciding which reductions to make. No cost-effectiveness studies are made, since true costs are seldom known.

School boards are confronted with value-laden decisions about whether instructional materials or school social workers are most important with little data to help them. For instance, California schools cut back after Proposition 13 with the general guideline of "cut as far from the classroom as possible." This caused a lot of cutting in equipment, maintenance, and facilities that over the long term has proven to be a false economy. Guthrie (1988: 23) summarized the decisionmaking in this way:

> These decisions are seldom scientifically determined. Class size controversies have been alluded to above. However, there is, if anything, even less credible research evidence in other personnel areas, such as conventionally assumed counselor-pupil ratios or the number of students that can aptly be served by a librarian.
>
> Allocation ratios generally owe their origins variously to unexamined past practice, comparisons with similarly unscrutinized practices of surrounding school districts, collectively bargained agreements with employee unions, the pronouncements of self-serving professional associations, and the dicta of

administrators. In effect, allocation ratios are a crucial coin in the political exchange process which determines school resources. Citizens, thus, must speak at school board meetings, and with their elective representatives to ensure that the implied assumptions behind allocation ratios are made public and publicly examined. Otherwise, important decisions can be made about the resources that will flow to individual schools and a false appearance will be given that the procedure is politically fair and simply mechanical in nature. Unless such procedures are fairly questioned, inequity can thus travel under the guise of science.

Almost all attempts to implement PPBS, MBO, and ZBB have failed. School districts rarely state objectives explicitly or then allocate funds specifically to achieve the objectives. There may be objectives for educational purposes (such as improved reading scores), but there is little linkage to the budget. Negotiated personnel agreements and mandated fixed costs consume 85 percent of the total school budgets in the typical California district. Such contracts along with employee tenure and school building commitments make it unlikely that school districts could implement zero-based budgeting in its theoretical form. Budget categories are large conglomerations of programs like administration, instruction, and fixed charges.

Brackett, Chambers, and Parrish (1983) developed a local cost model for school budgets that specified educational programs in terms of their resource requirements and directly linked programs and budgets. But local administrators have not evidenced much interest in such information or the complex process of creating such a budget (called the resource cost model) from the bottom up. Consequently, it is very difficult to align budgetary decisions to curriculum policy decisions. Moreover, there is no budget format that links the amount of administrative services needed to implement particular programs or collections of services, so there is no clear way to assess charges of an excessive administrative blob. School boards and the public are unable to easily analyze cost and service tradeoffs.

These shortcomings, however, are very difficult to overcome. PPBS started in a large federal agency and ZBB in private industry. Neither model could be easily adapted to fit the school context. As Brackett, Chambers, and Parrish (1983: 37) concluded,

> the complexity of the procedures, the esoteric nature of the terminology, the potential for overwhelming paperwork, and the inapplicable nature of several key concepts oppose acceptability.

Incremental budgeting has enormous support from political and organizational routines that have helped to preserve the existing system for many decades. Perhaps more devolution of budget authority to the school site could shake up some of the current incrementalism.

WHERE DOES THE MONEY GO:
A CALIFORNIA CASE

In order to rebut charges in the press about internal inefficiency and criticism by various politicians, the California State Department of Education prepared the cost of an average California school 1985–86 (see Table 13–1). The completion of such an analysis was a major undertaking that had never been done before. In the past, policymakers had not been provided with standard expenditure categories for this type of analysis. Some of the allocations among categories raise interesting policy issues. Is 5 percent of the money for operations and maintenance, or 7 for instructional aides, an optimal amount for these services in a total school budget? Given the large class sizes in California (a student/teacher ratio of about 30 to 1), perhaps more teachers would be more cost effective than aides. Several of the categorical restrictions that encourage the original employment have been eliminated recently, but California schools have made few changes in their personnel mix. Some teacher aides have developed strong political ties to local political groups around specific school sites.

Note the very small allocation for equipment that might substitute capital for teachers—such as computers ($51,000 for equipment out of a total of $2 million overall). The operations and maintenance budget consumes 12 percent of the total, but some school superintendents claim they could save substantially by contracting out many of these services to private vendors. Collective bargaining agreements with custodians, however, typically prohibit outside contracting. California statistics do not support Secretary Bennett's view that there is a gigantic administrative blob. Administrators beyond the school site consume 6 percent of the budget, and there were fewer than two administrators per site. California's expenditures per pupil, however, are slightly below the national average and are not representative of the high-spending states where the "blob" may exist.

Table 13-1. Cost of an Average California School, 1985-86.

The average school in California had 578 students in 22 classrooms—21 regular classrooms with 568 students and one special education day class with 10 students. The total operating budget was $2 million, of which 63 percent was spent on direct classroom expenditures, 31 percent was spent at the school site, and 6 percent was spent for district, county, and state administration. The following table explains these costs in more detail:

Cost Category	Dollars (in thousands)	Percentage of Total	Description
Classroom Costs	$1,286	63%	33.5 people—24.5 teachers, 7 instructional aides, and 2 pupil support professionals
22 classroom teachers 21 regular teachers 1 special education teacher	906	44	On a statewide basis, *classroom teachers* taught in 162,900 classrooms. Of these, 151,700 were regular classes, 9,600 were special education full-day classes for the severely handicapped, and the full-time equivalent of 1,600 were for summer school instruction. The average teacher salary in 1985–86 was $30,000, and related health and retirement benefits amounted to $7,600. In addition, payments were made for teaching responsibilities that extended beyond the regular school day such as coaching sports activities and supervising student clubs, and hiring substitutes when teachers were ill.
2.5 specialized teachers 1.5 special education 1 resource specialist, curriculum teachers, music and art teachers	101	5	Special Education and Compensatory Education are supplemental services provided by *specialized teachers* in various fields and made up the bulk of the cost in this category. The 2.5 people in this average school represent 9,000 special education resource teachers and speech therapists, 3,400 compensatory education teachers and reading specialists, and 4,600 specialist teachers in other areas such as art and music.

2 pupil support personnel 1 counselor 1 psychologist, nurse, or librarian	85	4	*Pupil support* personnel help to assure that students receive the maximum benefit from a program of instruction suited to their individual needs. Pupil support staff included 5,000 school guidance counselors, 1,250 psychologists, 1,300 librarians, and 3,000 teachers with extra instructional duties such as homerooms and study halls.
7 instructional aides 3 special education 2 compensatory education 2 regular aides	94	5	Over 50,000 *instructional aides* provided supplementary assistance to at-risk children; 23,000 aides helped special education students; 13,000 aides worked in compensatory education programs; and 13,500 assisted reading specialists and regular classroom teachers in meeting the needs of individual students. In our hypothetical school, there are 7 instructional aides. However, this will not hold true for high schools, and will be more reflective of elementary schools because the majority of compensatory education funding is for elementary grades.
Books, supplies, and equipment $2,400 per classroom, or $86 per pupil for textbooks, workbooks, supplies; $2,300 per classroom for projectors, laboratory equipment, computers	100	5	Of the $100,000 spent by the average school on *books, supplies, and equipment,* about $49,000 was spent on books, paper, pencils, and other instructional materials. In 1985–86, California schools spent $28 per pupil for textbooks. In addition, it cost each school about $51,000 annually to buy or lease instructional equipment such as projectors, computers, and laboratory supplies.

Note: The information in this table is based on 1985–86 CBEDS counts and 1985–86 financial reports, as submitted by school districts and county offices of education.

Table 13-1. continued

Cost Category	Dollars (in thousands)	Percentage of Total	Description
School Site Costs	$630	31%	15.5 people—1.5 administrators, 1 teacher, 13 support personnel
Operations and maintenance			
Buildings	395	19	Nearly $400 million was spent statewide for gas, electricity, and water for our schools, or about $200 per month per class; insurance costs accounted for $98 million. Nearly 42,500 people worked on school _buildings_, at a cost of $1.3 billion for salaries, benefits, equipment, and materials. They repaired and maintained school buildings and property valued at approximately $60 billion.
6 carpenters, painters, gardeners Utilities; insurance; maintenance and supplies	241	12	
Food	85	4	_Food services_ in schools provided 2.5 million meals a day at an average cost of $1.54 per meal. About $43,000 was spent by each school on salaries for cooks and cafeteria workers, and another $42,000 was spent for food and cafeteria supplies.
2 cafeteria workers Food and supplies			
Transportation	69	3	_Transportation programs_ operated by school districts and county offices of education transported 910,000 students to and from school in 15,000 buses, traveling 215 million miles. This program cost approximately 6 cents per mile per student (20 cents for special education students and 4 cents for regular students).
1.5 bus drivers Buses, fuel and supplies			
Instructional support	95	5	_Instructional support_ activities involved 7,000 science, math, history, and other teachers working to improve curriculum and instruction; 2,500 curriculum leaders and 5,600 secretaries assisted teachers.
.4 curriculum leaders 1 teacher; 1 secretary			
School site leadership	139	7	_School site leadership_ was provided by 8,500 principals and vice-principals, who were responsible for the instructional leadership and management of the schools. Over 18,000 secretaries and clerks assisted by keeping attendance, typing, and performing other office duties.
1 principal 0.2 vice-principal, other supervisors 2.5 secretaries and clerical staff			

	%	$	People / Description
District/County Costs	5.5%	$119	3 people—1 administrator, 2 secretaries

District/county administration
0.9 district administrators, including superintendents;
2 secretaries and clerical staff
Equipment and office supplies

Each *district* serves on the average, 7 schools consisting of slightly over 4,000 students. There were 1,600 superintendents and assistant superintendents almost 1,700 classified administrators, and 14,500 secretaries who worked in school districts and county offices of education. These people were responsible for providing leadership and policy direction, and legal, personnel, and financial services to their schools. Equipment and office supplies, personal service contracts, travel and other office expenses were included here.

	%	$	People / Description
State Department of Education Costs	0.5%	$ 11	.16 people—.09 instructional support and .07 administrators

.016 state level administrators and instructional support staff

1,200 people worked for the *Department of Education*, 400 of whom were professional educators. They provided services in such areas as curriculum and test development, and the allocation of state and federal funds at a cost of $80 million.

	%	$	People / Description
Total costs	100%	$2,046	52 people—27.5 teachers, 22 classified employees, 2.5 administrators
School facilities		$133	

Expenditures for the modernization and reconstruction of our oldest facilities (1/3 of our schools are over 30 years old) accounted for nearly $1 billion in 1985–86. Total expenditures for facilities construction operation and maintenance equalled $2.3 billion for the 425 million square feet of school facilities; this is 4 percent of the total value, or about 50 cents per square foot per month, compared with about 10 percent of total value, or $1.00–$1.25 per square foot per month to lease comparable space.

But these states have much lower student/teacher ratios that probably account for the difference in expenditures for the highest-spending states.

COMPARING THE INCOMPARABLE

Comparable definitions are crucial for valid comparisons of financial data reported by different states, localities, or other education agencies. However, many governmental agencies use different definitions that only partly overlap, and states cannot even agree on what the term average daily membership means (Education Research Service 1987: 34–35). The function of "instruction" is particularly surrounded by different definitions and perspectives. Administrators are sometimes included as part of instruction if they perform mostly curricular duties or are department chairs. Other states allocate part of department chair time to instruction and part to administration. The lack of program budgets in education results in an inability to consider priorities among such areas as reading, history, or driver training on a cost basis. Attempts to implement PPBS in U.S. schools have never been successful, and all similar reforms including management by objectives (MBO) have met the same fate. The California study cited above allocated percentages of time to "instruction" on a judgmental basis but still ends up as a function or object analysis devoid of programmatic conclusions.

These definitional issues can lead to misleading or debatable conclusions. For example, the Education Research Service (1987: 39–41) disputes the conclusion that budget emphasis on instruction is declining. These charges rest on what it considers a misuse of the concepts concerning the total budget for classroom salaries that is declining but ignores other instructional objects.

> The use of teacher salary data in this way ignores increases in the portion of budgets assigned to *auxiliary instructional services* such as guidance, testing, and school libraries. These are certainly important instructional services. However, the associated costs are not included when *classroom teacher salary* data are used in isolation.
>
> Compounding this problem of the use of expenditures for teachers' salaries as a proxy for trends in percent of budget allocated to instruction is the *method* used to compute the teachers' salary portion. Sherman, in his study of resource allocation patterns in the public schools, used figures for average

teacher salary, number of classroom teachers, and total operating expenditures to arrive at the percent of budget figures. However, this method, in addition to excluding the cost of employer retirement contributions and fringe benefits for teachers, also failed to account for costs associated with part-time teachers or substitute teachers.

According to the Educational Research Service (ERS) the average percentage allocated to "teachers" is 51.7 percent and to "administrators" only 4.9 percent, but then one must go along with their inclusion of fringe benefits in the teachers' portion and other allocations of fixed charges. The ERS average allocation of 1986–87 school district operating budgets appears in Figure 13-2. ERS uses its own sample of 1,000 local education agencies and its own definitions to compute these figures. The point is that it is difficult to discuss the proper allocation within schools and districts if the debate bogs down initially over definitions of terms. Secretary Bennett's administrative blob, however, is probably not as big a fiscal concern as he suggests. ERS (1987: 44) concluded that

> In 1986–87, if the typical school district had taken *all* of the money it budgeted to pay *salaries* for central office administrators (which was 2.2 percent of the total budget) and applied it to teacher salaries, it would have increased

Figure 13-2. Average Allocation of 1986–87 School District Operating Budgets.

Other Current Expenditures 3.0%

Heating, Cooling, Utilities

Maintenance and Operation

Central Administration/ School Board Services 4.8

Student Services 7.

School Site Leade

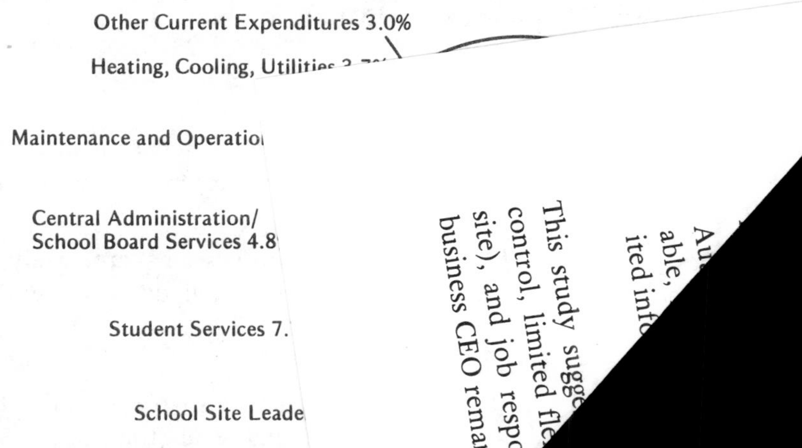

Source: Local School District Budget
unpublished data.

teacher salaries on average of only 5.0 percent. Likewise, if the typical school district took *all* of the money it budgeted to pay *salaries* for central office administrators and used it to hire more teachers to reduce class size, it would result in a reduction of only one pupil per class, from an average of 24 pupils per class to 23 pupils.

A group of North Carolina business leaders analyzed internal operations of schools from a different perspective. They hired a management consulting firm to conduct structured interviews and time analysis studies through time use records of 349 teachers, 27 principals, 21 assistant principals, and 32 school secretaries for four weeks (Public School Forum 1987). Obviously, this limited sample in one state is not generalizable, but their findings are provocative as presented by three different content areas.

1. *Time analysis study*

    Major job functions are reduced to a limited proportion of the week (for example, teachers spend 48.2 percent on direct instruction; principals spend 10.4 percent managing instruction; office personnel spend 32.2 percent on direct clerical responsibilities).

2. *Working conditions survey*

    Noninstructional monitoring and excess of paperwork dominates teachers' concerns.

    An insufficient number of personnel are at the school site to accomplish the supportive evaluation, training, and administrative overload.

3. *Applications transfer study*

    Work overload is caused in part by the absence of information management systems that address fundamental school and administrative needs.

    ...tomated instructional management systems are rarely avail... leaving teachers to make instructional decisions with lim... ...rmation.

    ...sts that such basic issues as span of administrative ...xibility at the operating level (that is, the school ...ibilities deserve serious consideration. As one ...(Public School Forum 1987: 1),

I found it ironic that the school secretary is the school's chief financial officer—compiling reports, completing the school's accounting work, and generally running the financial operation of the school—while teachers are typing tests.

MAJOR TRADEOFFS AMONG INTERNAL ALLOCATIONS WITHIN SCHOOL DISTRICTS

Economists for many years have lamented the inability of education to save money by substituting capital for expensive labor. Charles Benson wrote in 1975:

> Education has long been regarded as particularly vulnerable to inflationary pressures, the reason being that schools are "labor-intensive." That is, most of education is provided by teachers and not by machines. In industries where physical capital is very important, improvements in technology can offset the effects of paying higher salaries to workers. . . . In education, there have been no great advances in process that economize on teacher time while holding quality constant. . . . The result is that education (along with other state and local services, which are also, generally speaking, labor intensive) becomes ever more costly as compared with the general run of goods and services.

Kent Halstead (1983) developed the School Price Index (SPI) in 1977 to reflect a "market basket" of goods and services used in public elementary and secondary education. This SPI went up faster than the Consumer Price Index (CPI) between 1975 and 1986. Any price index suffers from the nearly irresolvable problem of eliminating the effects on prices of quality changes in the commodities purchased. His analysis demonstrates which types of school inputs are increasing the fastest from 1975 to 1982.

> As shown, six of the nine SPI components sustained *less* inflation than the overall SPI rate—professional salaries, nonprofessional salaries, services, supplies and materials, equipment replacement, and library materials and textbooks. However, the three other SPI components—fringe benefits, utilities, and fixed costs—had exceptionally high inflation rates. Thus, although these three components account for only 14.23 percent of expenditures, their inflation rates were sufficiently high to raise the overall SPI above all the other components.

The rapid rise in fringe benefits suggests that there might be economies of scale in group purchasing by small school districts. California has formed such cooperatives with significant savings.

Another problem with a cost index is that declines in enrollment result in per pupil expenditures *increasing* at a faster rate than the total dollars of current expenditures. Schools have not been able to cut staff and "lumpy" expenditure categories on a commensurate basis with school enrollment decreases. This is a crucial problem for educators to explain when one considers that declines in student/teacher ratios (from 29 to 1 in 1959 to 17 to 1 in 1988) have not resulted in increases in pupil achievement. Again, these fiscal issues are attracting popular attention. For example, a *Forbes* magazine article (Brimelow 1986) castigated the schools this way:

> The educational establishment's sanctimoniousness might be excusable if educators could point to results from increased spending. But the statistics all show a catastrophic and continuing productivity decline. . . .
>
> U.S. education is in essence a socialized business, the American equivalent of the Soviet Union's collective farms. In such a setup the power of the educational lobby and the sympathy that the media extends to educators become the decisive factor rather than the results. . . .
>
> Are there $600 toilet seats in American education? Well, the New York City Board of Education, heavily influenced through the mid-1970s by the local Democratic machine, has $62,000 a year custodians—and teachers in ghetto schools who have to scrounge textbooks from friends.

Although these comments are obviously journalistic, they do reflect the conservative view of internal allocation issues. Education researchers can retort that the achievement scores are not precise indicators of output and that special education programs that are very costly account for some of the decline in the student/teacher ratio. But without more comprehensive research on cost-effectiveness, these statements sometimes appear self-serving.

Guthrie (1988) advocates questioning some other typical local budget assumptions in order to provide more efficiency. He suggests decentralizing the lump sum budget for teacher substitutes, thereby creating a school site incentive to hold down these costs. Unspent site funds could be used for other school site purposes. At present, districts allocate an amount for substitutes at the central office level, and teachers call in to the central office for a replacement. There is not a school-based disincentive not to use this central pool of resources. This is only one example of how decentralized decisionmaking can contribute to efficiency. See Hentschke's chapter in this volume for further elaboration on this as well as other possibilities.

Table 13-2. Number and Ratio of Central Office Administrators and Other Professionals, Selected California School Districts.

District	Enrollment	Central Office Professionals	Ratio of Students to Professionals
Oakland (1)	50,300	177	284:1
San Jose (3)	30,700	84	365:1
Mount Diablo	30,679	64	479:1
Fresno	54,305	109	498:1
Sacramento	41,151	78	527:1
Long Beach	61,919	80	733:1
San Diego	100,353	124	809:1

Source: Oakland Unified School District Strategic Planning Project, August 1984– March 1986, James W. Guthrie, Director.

If we return to our original issue of the "administrative blob," there are some comparisons that will be useful despite the complexity of school budget categories. In addition to comparisons of administrative costs over time, comparisons should be made with similar expenditure categories in other districts and other kinds of organizations (Guthrie 1988). For instance, large city districts or small suburban ones in the same region can be compared over time for their percentage of administrative expenditures. Comparisons with private schools and noneducation agencies may be useful. For the latter category, food service costs may differ among schools and hospitals, and fringe benefits are much lower in city government. Table 13-2 displays such a comparative analysis for administrators.

PAYING FOR EDUCATIONAL REFORM

Despite these conceptual and definitional issues there are some estimates of costs that could enhance the thinking of policymakers about improving schools. Odden (1984: 312) compiled a list of "low-cost" versus "high-cost" reform strategies. Low-cost strategies include

1. Technical assistance programs to improve the effectiveness of teachers and administrators;

2. Incentive programs including grants for innovative programs or bonus programs for gains in productivity at the school level;
3. The application of money toward research to improve school effectiveness.

High-cost strategies, many of which have been both recommended by education commissions and funded by state legislatures, include

1. A variety of teacher compensation packages;
2. Increase in the school day or year;
3. The addition of new programs such as mandatory kindergartens.

After estimating that an extension of the school day from 6.5 to 8 hours would cost U.S. taxpayers more than $20 billion, with a cost of an additional $20 billion to increase the school year from 180 to 220 days, Odden recommended that attention be focused instead on using the time available more effectively. One possibility of using time more effectively—in line with a suggested low-cost strategy—would be "altering the way teachers use time through inservice training that focuses on effective teaching strategies and good classroom management." Another would be to use the attributes of effective school leadership that can be distilled from research syntheses (Lane and Walberg 1987).

Business leaders were particularly active in the Carnegie Forum on Education and the Economy that recommended a drastic "restructuring" of the internal operations of schools (Task Force on Teaching 1986). This group proposed "lead teachers," school site devolution, peer review of teachers by other teachers, and new forms of collective bargaining such as policy trust agreements. What do these kinds of innovations cost, and could savings from centralized operations be used to finance some of this school site decentralization? So far the discussion about restructuring has focused on teacher behavior and experimentation with scant attention to finance concerns.[1] Under the Carnegie Forum plan, experienced lead teachers would make $56,000, and advanced certificate holders would make $35,000 after certification by a proposed National Teacher Standards Board. The Task Force implies that money could be reallocated from current noninstructional uses to help pay for these higher salaries, but as the preceding analysis suggests, this will be difficult.

The school restructuring agenda contains other potential cost implications. For example, concerning space and support staff, the Carnegie Task Force recommends:

1. *The use of space.* The traditional character of the teacher's classroom is so ingrained, the physical organization of schools so well established, that it is hard to grasp how school space might be differently used. Yet the collegial approach to school organization is unlikely to work, and additional staff are unlikely to contribute, unless some classes can be small and others large. Usage of space must be flexible so some students can work alone and others in small groups or with teachers or a tutor.

2. *Staffing ratios.* The Task Force emphasizes that support staff should be added to existing teacher staffing levels, not substituted for teachers. The ratio of students to professional teachers must remain stable.

   It would be far more efficient to establish most school district instructional and other services as "cost centers" that have to sell their services to the schools in order to survive. Put another way, most of the budget for school district instructional services should be allocated to the school level, and the principal and teachers should together decide what services to buy and where.

Presumably there would be incremental costs for the more flexible space arrangements and the added support staff. The school site purchase of central district instructional support services, however, might save some money. Overall, we have no idea what the net cost would be from this group of recommendations.

IMPROVING TEACHING THROUGH
FINANCING STAFF DEVELOPMENT

A major focus of the 1983–87 reforms was on raising academic standards. In my 1983 article, I stressed the need to build a closer merger between local academic policies and school finance. For example, students tend to learn what they spend time studying in school (that is, students who take French know more French than those who take Spanish). Changing the content pupils study can be an important policy change with more direct achievement impacts than many mar-

ginal increases in state aid to lower class size. Curricular alignment of
district tests, texts, and curricular guides costs money in terms of the
production of new or revised content, and the retraining of teachers
to teach such areas as problemsolving in math (Kirst 1983). The first
stage of academic reform, however, has been to change the path of
students through the curriculum so that they take more traditional
academic courses. We are not sure what the incremental costs are
from such reallocations that include more science and foreign language classes and fewer vocational education and music classes. The
next stage probably still will be one of intensifying the existing
model of schooling but also will entail upgrading the academic curriculum to include critical thinking, problemsolving, inferential statistics, and more active learning (Odden and Marsh 1987).

This upgraded curriculum will require extensive and intensive staff
development (ten to twenty days a year) that has rarely been studied
for its financial implications. For example, many teachers want to
teach mathematical problemsolving, but are unable to do so. In
1987 Policy Analysis for California Education (PACE) completed an
overall study of California staff development (state and local) and
reached eight major conclusions (Little et al. 1987).

1. Categorical staff development programs for California's teachers and administrators consume approximately 2 percent of total
education funding, a total of $357 million during a one-year period.

- The taxpayers' direct contribution to staff development programs
  is made up of four parts: (1) approximately $87 million in funds
  targeted specially for staff development; (b) an estimated $35
  million for staff development linked to other categorical aid programs; (c) an estimated $35 million for staff development associ-
  ated with federal categorical aid programs administered by the
  state; and (d) nearly $200 million in local allocations primarily
  from district general fund budgets.

- The average annual local district expenditure for staff development activities was slightly over $1,300 per participant, or about
  $16.51 per participant hour of staff development. Public dollars
  spent directly on staff development acitvities go first to support
  the salaries of district specialists who plan and lead staff development services, and second to pay for substitute teachers who take
  responsibility for classrooms when regular classroom teachers are
  away.

2. The salary advances that teachers accrue as a result of advanced university coursework or salary credits awarded by the district are the taxpayers' largest investment in staff development.

Categorical program support constitutes only one portion of total taxpayer investment in staff development. The direct state appropriation for formal staff development programs, together with the share of state and federal categorical programs devoted to staff development, approximates $200 million, or less than one-fifth of the total staff development-related resources.

- The bulk of taxpayer investment in teachers' professional development—nearly $600 million during a one-year period—is in the form of future salary obligations made to teachers who accrue credits by enrolling in university coursework or by attending district-sponsored activities outside the salaried work day. When future salary increments are taken into account, the total taxpayer investment exceeds 4 percent of total education funding and approaches $1 billion per year.

- Linking continuing education to salary advances by the use of uniform salary schedules is a widespread feature of school governance. In California, the average salary value of a semester unit is $1,400. Local and state policymakers exert control over this expenditure insofar as they establish criteria and procedures to regulate the award of credits that teachers apply toward salary increases. This is a major area where funds might be redirected for greater efficiency to other staff development approaches than salary schedule increments.

3. California teachers and administrators demonstrate a firm commitment to improving their own knowledge and practice.

4. Local school district capacity to organize and deliver staff development has grown steadily.

5. Selected staff development activities have sound prospects for favorably influencing classroom performance and the overall quality of school programs. On the whole, however, the current array of staff development activities and incentives is unlikely to yield substantial change in the thinking or performance of California's classroom teachers.

6. California's staff development resources are spent in ways that mainly reinforce existing patterns of teaching, conventional struc-

tures of schools, and long-standing traditions of the teaching occupation.

7. California's staff development activities go largely unevaluated, in comparison with other educational initiatives.

8. The state appropriates staff development funds for teachers, schools, districts, counties, and universities but reveals no comprehensive or consistent policy orientation toward staff development or toward the institutions that provide it.

Some obvious policy issues are raised. Why spend so much on teacher salary increments for completion of university courses that districts have minimal influence over? Should central district offices play a more specific role in designing and operating staff development at the central district level? In this way, the districts would make more precise cost estimates and exercise more oversight over cost effectiveness. Teachers can submit courses from local universities that may be unrelated to current district priorities.

Can staff development be moved to the summer when teachers can do it full time for an extended period? What are the costs of this arrangement given that substitute teachers would not have to be paid for during the school year? Staff development programs that are held for one or two days during the school year are not very effective, according to the PACE study.

Another major fiscal policy issue in the 1983–87 reform era concerned time in terms of increasing the school day or year. The *A Nation at Risk* report recommended a much longer school year and pointed out that the Japanese attend school for at least sixty days more than the average U.S. student. Obviously, the cost implications of this are sizeable, once again raising the cost effectiveness issue. On the one hand, summer sessions can help prevent summer learning loss, but on the other, there is the fiscal concern about air conditioning facilities for summer climates. As for a longer school day, a Stanford study of (1) lowering class size, (2) tutoring (peer and adult), (3) computer-assisted instruction, and (4) increased instruction time found that increasing instructional time by one-half hour a day has the smallest effect per unit of cost (Levin, Glass, and Meister 1984).

This type of cost-effectiveness research requires combinations of scholars, including economists, educational psychologists, and subject matter curricular experts. Such scholarly aggregations are still rare in most school finance research and would provide an additional perspective to the psychological and statistical "effects" studies of various interventions on student achievement. Walberg (1984: 19) and others have recommended such educational emphases as more graded homework and cooperative learning but provide no data on costs. Walberg (1982) synthesized research on the impact of time allocations and ability grouping on student learning and found several positive effects, but the effects vary for different types of students. Again, the issues of costs are left unanalyzed, so it is hard to pick the best instructional alternatives based on a combination of academic *and* fiscal criteria. Walberg stresses that engaged learning time and teacher-directed study may be taken to such an extreme that student tasks become boring and tedious. "Effective teaching is like music in that the combination, sequence, and pacing of the elements is as important as the quality and quantity of the elements" (Walberg 1982).

CONCLUDING THOUGHTS

The internal allocation of school resources and expenditures is a cyclical issue that tends to increase in intensity with eras of fiscal restraint. The 1983–87 education reform era and recent economic growth in the U.S. stimulated concern about increasing resources for schools rather than efficiency issues. The nation's economic growth permitted more money for schools to be linked with political demands for higher academic standards and school improvement. Often omnibus reform bills were loosely coupled packages of ideas that were not costed out individually but rather allocated through general state education aid formulas. It was unclear how much added requirements of science and math would cost or how raising standards for teacher candidates would impact university costs. Expenditures rose 21 percent after inflation in three years, and the problem in 1988 became one of sifting and sorting among the numerous new initiatives to weed out the least desirable. Teacher salaries shot up dramatically, and there was less concern about substituting technology or machines for expensive labor.

By the close of the first wave of reform, more questions were being raised about the most appropriate mix of internal expenditures. But this debate remains hampered by lack of agreement on expenditure definitions, accurate program costs, and input/output relationships. It is unlikely that professional educators will lead the search for new knowledge. They are comfortable with the existing fiscal information system and have not been enthusiastic about such new systems as PPBS or MBO. The pressure for change will have to come from elected officials, the media, and such groups as the business community. This pressure is more likely to build if school spending remains level or is constrained by slow economic growth. The search for more efficiency through better internal allocation of funds is not as intense when there is a surplus in the overall state budgets, which occurred in 1983–86.

NOTES

1. A good start on some of these issues is in Alexander and Monk (1987). An earlier treatment of finance issues concerning teacher compensation is in Gerwin (1974).

REFERENCES

Alexander, K., and D. H. Monk. 1987. *Attracting and Compensating America's Teachers.* Cambridge, Mass.: Ballinger.

Benson, C. 1975. *Education Finance in the Coming Decade.* Bloomington, Ind.: Delta Kappan Foundation.

Brackett, J. 1983. "Budgeting: A Synopsis of Current Priorities." Stanford, Calif.: Institute for Education Finance and Governance.

Brackett, J., J. Chambers, and T. Parrish. 1983. "The Legacy of Rational Budgeting Models in Education." Project Report 83–A21. Stanford, Calif.: Institute for Education Finance and Governance.

Brimelow, P. 1986. "Are We Spending Too Much on Education?" *Forbes* (December 29): 56.

Educational Research Service. 1987. *Cost of Education.* Arlington, Va.: ERS.

Gerwin, D., ed. 1974. *The Employment of Teachers.* Berkeley: McCutchan.

Guthrie, J. 1988. "Understanding School Budgets." Washington, D.C.: U.S. Department of Education.

Halstead, K. 1983. *Inflation Measures for Schools and Colleges.* Washington, D.C.: U.S. Department of Education.

Kirst, M. W. 1982. "How to Improve Schools without Spending More Money." *Phi Delta Kappan* (September): 6–8.

_____ . 1983. "A New School Finance for a New Era of Fiscal Constraint." In *School Finance and School Improvement*, edited by A. Odden and L. D. Webb, pp. 1–16. Cambridge, Mass.: Ballinger.

Lane, J., and H. Walberg, eds. 1987. *Effective School Leadership*. Berkeley: McCutchan.

Levin, H., G. U. Glass, and G. R. Meister. 1984. "Cost Effectiveness of Four Educational Interventions." Stanford, Calif.: Institute for Educational Finance and Governance.

Little, J. W., et al. 1987. *Staff Development in California*. Berkeley, Calif.: Policy Analysis for California Education.

Montague, W. 1987. "Administrators Rebut Bennett's Critique of Burgeoning Bureaucratic Blob'." *Education Week* 7 (September 9): 7.

Odden, A. 1984. "Financing Educational Excellence." *Phi Delta Kappan* January 65 (5): 311–318.

Odden, A., and D. Marsh. 1987. "How State Education Reform Can Improve Comprehensive Secondary Schools." Berkeley, Calif.: Policy Analysis for California Education.

Public School Forum of North Carolina. 1987. *The Condition of Being an Educator*. Raleigh: Public School Forum of North Carolina.

Solorzano, L. 1987. "Beating Back the Education 'Blob'." *U.S. News and World Report* (April 27): 39.

Task Force on Teaching as a Profession. 1986. *A Nation Prepared: Teachers for the 21st Century*. New York: Carnegie Corporation.

Thomas, A. 1971. *The Productive School*. New York: Wiley.

Walberg, H., ed. 1982. *Improving Educational Standards and Productivity*. Berkeley: McCutchan.

Walberg, H. 1984. "Improving the Productivity of American Schools." *Educational Leadership* 41 (May): 19–27.

NAME INDEX

SUBJECT INDEX

Ability groups
  class size and learning and, 192–195
  inequality in achievement and, 195
  learning models and, 187–188
  opportunities for learning and, 194
  resource allocation and, 235–236, 240
  slower learning students and incentive systems and, 132
  sociological research on, 207–208
Absenteeism of teachers, and motivation, 246–247, 248
Accountability, and productivity, 272–273
Achievement
  ability groupings and, 195
  class size and, 192–193
  family and, 207
  need for, 243
  resource allocation examples of, 216–225
  schooling inputs and, 186–187, 190–191
  student motivation and, 247–248
  student/teacher ratios and, 380
Achievement tests
  learning curve studies and, 185
  merit pay proposals and, 121

Administrators, *see* Principals; School administrators; Superintendents
Admission policies
  resource allocation decisions and, 92–94
  unit expenditures and, 93
Adopt-a-school program, 66–67, 71
Africa
  financing mechanisms in, 87
  teacher utilization in, 108
  see also specific countries
Aid to education, *see* State aid to education
Algeria, 99, 107
  boarding expenditures analysis in, 100, 102, 103, 108, 109
  financing mechanisms in, 87
  size of institution and total expenditures in, 96, 98
  size of institution and unit expenditures in, 105, 106
Allocation of resources, *see* Resource allocation
American Association of School Administrators, 347, 361 n. 1
Aptitude, and resource allocation, 239, 240
ARCO, 66

ABOUT THE EDITORS

David H. Monk is associate professor of educational administration at Cornell University. He joined the Cornell faculty in 1979 after earning his Ph.D. at the University of Chicago. He has taught at the University of Rochester, the International Institute for Educational Planning in Paris, and l'Institut de Recherche sur l'Economie de l'Education at the University of Burgundy in Dijon, France. His interests in the economics and financing of education are reflected in numerous research articles that have appeared in professional journals. His book *Educational Finance: An Economic Approach* will be published in 1989.

Julie Underwood is an assistant professor of educational administration at the University of Wisconsin-Madison. Previously she taught at the University of North Dakota, Center for Teaching and Learning, and the University of Florida, College of Law. She received her J.D from Indiana University and her Ph.D. from the University of Florida. She has served on the national membership committee of the National Organization of Legal Problems of Education and on the board of directors for the American Education Finance Association. In addition, she has written a number of monographs, chapters in books, and articles. She currently serves as finance coeditor for the *Journal of Education Finance* and is on the author's committee for the *Education Law Reporter.*

ABOUT THE CONTRIBUTORS

William Lowe Boyd is professor of education at the Pennsylvania State University, University Park, Pennsylvania. He specializes in educational administration and educational policy and politics. He is president of the Politics of Education Association and coeditor of the first yearbook of the association, *The Politics of Excellence and Choice in Education* (1988). He also coedited the recent volume entitled *Educational Policy in Australia and America: Comparative Perspectives* (1987).

Byron W. Brown is professor of economics at Michigan State University. His research interests are the microeconomics of schools, especially the study of the allocation of time among students in classrooms, and the public choice aspects of educational spending by school districts.

Richard P. Chaykowski is assistant professor and Queen's National Scholar at the School of Industrial Relations, Queen's University, Kingston, Ontario. He received his B.A. and M.A. degrees in economics from Queen's University, and his Ph.D. from Cornell University in industrial and labor relations. His published research has dealt with industrial relations and educational issues and has appeared in the *Industrial and Labor Relations Review, Relations Industrielles*, the

419

Journal of Labor Research, and a National Bureau of Economic Research conference volume.

William H. Clune is a professor of law at the University of Wisconsin Law School. Professor Clune is a recognized expert on education law with a strong background in sociology. He had directed most of his research toward the effects of implementation and regulation on educational organizations and applies that background to his research on student standards and school site autonomy for the Center for Policy Research in Education. He has also worked with the National Institute of Education group on educational policy and organization and with two educational policy organizations: The Wisconsin Center for Education Research and the Institute for Finance and Governance at Stanford. He has published implementation case studies in such diverse areas as school finance, special education, school disciplines, and public employee interest arbitrations and is an editor of the *Interdisciplinary Journal* (law and policy). His experience as a policy analyst includes consultant activity with the Illinois Bureau of the Budget, the New York State Commission on Elementary and Secondary Education, and the Wisconsin Task Force on School Finance.

Randy Ann Ehrenberg is the vice-principal at DeWitt Middle School (Ithaca, New York) and chairperson of the Ithaca City School District Language Arts Curriculum Committee. She received a B.A. from Harpur College (State University of New York at Binghamton), an M.A.T. in English education from Northwestern University, and a C.A.S. in school administration from the State University of New York at Cortland. She has presented numerous papers at professional association meetings. Her previous publications on topics relating to teaching English and school administration have appeared in the *English Journal, The Idea Factory*, and the *Industrial and Labor Relations Review*.

Ronald G. Ehrenberg is the Irving M. Ives Professor of Industrial and Labor Relations and Economics at Cornell University, director of research at Cornell's School of Industrial and Labor Relations, and a research associate at the National Bureau of Economic Research. He is an internationally recognized scholar and has authored or co-authored over fifty-five articles and eight books. His research interests include the study of public sector labor markets, wage determination in regulated industries, the evaluation of labor market programs and legislation, analyses of compensation policies, and resource allocation issues in education.

Richard Elmore is a professor of education and political science at Michigan State University and senior research fellow with the Center for Policy Research in Education. He received his bachelor's degree in political science from Whitman College in Walla Walla, Washington; his master's degree in government from Claremont Graduate School in Claremont, California; and his doctorate in policy from the Graduate School of Education, Harvard University. Prior to assuming his position at Michigan State University, Professor Elmore was associate dean and associate professor in the Graduate School of Public Affairs, University of Washington, Seattle, where he was on the faculty for eleven years. He received the University of Washington's Distinguished Teaching Award in June 1985. His current research is focused on the effects of state and local policies on the structure and content of public schooling and on policies directed at the labor market and educational problems of disadvantaged youth. He also maintains a professional involvement in education programs for public sector executives.

Susan Fuhrman is a research professor at the Eagleton Institute of Politics, Rutgers University and director of the Center for Policy Research in Education (CPRE), a consortium of Rutgers, The State University of New Jersey, Michigan State University, Stanford University, and the University of Wisconsin-Madison. CPRE is sponsored by the United States Department of Education to conduct research on state and local policy to improve schooling.

Dr. Fuhrman is the author of numerous articles, research reports, and monographs on education policy and finance. She coauthored two monographs on legislative education leadership in the states. She was a consultant to the Ford Foundation's program on educational management and finance for ten years. She currently serves as a school board member in Westfield, New Jersey.

Adam Gamoran is assistant professor of sociology at the University of Wisconsin, Madison. He received his Ph.D. in the sociology of education at the University of Chicago in 1984. His areas of interest include stratification in school systems, resource allocation in school systems, and institutional effects of education. Currently, he is involved in a two-year study of instruction and ability grouping in eighth and ninth grade English and social studies.

William Hartman is an associate professor at The Pennsylvania State University, where he teaches educational finance, school business administration, economics of education, and microcomputer applications in educational administration. He has an M.B.A. from Harvard University and a Ph.D. in administration and policy analysis from Stanford University. He is the author of *School District Budgeting* and numerous articles in the *Journal of Education Finance* and other journals. His current research interests include special education finance, financial modeling, resource allocation in education, and educational finance policy analysis. He is also a member of the board of directors of the American Education Finance Association.

Guilbert Hentschke is dean and professor at the University of Southern California School of Education. He has held academic and administrative positions at the University of Rochester, Teachers College, Columbia University, and The Chicago Public Schools and was a high school teacher in The East Side Union High School District, San Jose, California. His previous publications include *School Business Administration: A Comparative Perspective* and *Management Operations in Education.*

Stephen A. Hoenack is presently working at the World Bank, on leave from the University of Minnesota, where he is a professor in the Humphrey Institute of Public Affairs and serves as director of the Management Information Division. His research interests include education, organizations, and economic development. He has published extensively on the economics of higher education and is the author of *Economic Behavior Within Organizations.* He received his Ph.D. in economics from the University of California at Berkeley.

Michael W. Kirst is the chair of administration and policy analysis, School of Education, at Stanford University. He has had an extensive career in government, including positions as president of the California State Board of Education, staff director of the U.S. Senate Subcommittee on Manpower and Poverty, and associate director of the

White House Fellows. His recent books include *Who Controls Our Schools* and *Schools in Conflict.* Professor Kirst is codirector of Policy Analysis for California Education.

Bettye MacPhail-Wilcox is associate professor and coordinator of elementary and secondary school administration at North Carolina State University. She currently serves as president-elect of the American Education Finance Association and associate editor of the *Journal of Education Finance.* Prior to her current academic position, she was an industrial manager for Texas Instruments, a secondary school administrator, and a science teacher. Her research interests in school finance, organizational theory, and administrative practice are broad, including equity, resource allocation, motivation, decisionmaking, and change processes in public education.

Milbrey W. McLaughlin received her Ed.D. in education and social policy from Harvard University in 1973. From 1973–83, she was senior social scientist at the Rand Corporation. In 1983, Dr. McLaughlin joined the faculty at Stanford University as associate professor in the School of Education. Currently, she is also the director of the Center for the Study of Teachers and Teaching in the Secondary School Context. She is the author of numerous books, monographs, and articles in the areas of policy implementation and planned change, politics of education, organizational behavior, and intergovernmental relations in education. Her most recent books include *Steady Work: Policy Practice and the Reform of American Education* (1987) and *Teacher Evaluation: Improvement, Accountability and Effective Learning* (1988).

Susan J. Rosenholtz, associate professor of education at the University of Illinois, Champaign-Urbana, received her Ph.D. from Stanford University. Her recently completed study, *Teachers' Workplace: The Social Organization of Schools*, will be published in January 1989. Her main fields of interest are the sociology of teaching and teacher policy. She is presently engaged in a national study of teachers' workplace conditions and the effects of education reform for the National Education Association.

Kenneth A. Strike is professor of philosophy of education at Cornell University. He is coauthor, with Emil Haller, of *An Introduc-*

tion to Educational Administration: Social, Legal and Ethical Perspectives; with Jonas Soltis, of *The Ethics of Teaching*; and, with E. Haller and J. Soltis, of *The Ethics of School Administration*. He has also written numerous articles linking conceptions of distributive justice with questions of educational policy.

Claude Tibi, after having worked in the field of short-term economic forecasting at the National Institute of Statistics and Economic Studies in France and having contributed to the establishment of the National Institute of Statistics and Applied Economics in Morocco, joined the International Institute for Educational Planning in Paris in 1969. There he was responsible for studies, carried out in North Africa and Latin America, on the financing of educational systems, and later he conducted research on training needs and strategies for educational planning and cost analysis within educational institutions.

AMERICAN EDUCATION FINANCE ASSOCIATION OFFICERS 1988-89

Officers

President	Kern Alexander
President-Elect	Bettye MacPhail-Wilcox
Secretary-Treasurer and Executive Director	George R. Babigian
Immediate Past President	William E. Sparkman

Directors

Michael Addonizio	Deborah Inman
Wilfred Brown	K. Forbis Jordan
William E. Camp	Betty Malen
Koy M. Floyd	David H. Monk
James Fox	Robert Pearlman
Deborah Gallay	Deborah A. Verstegen
Steven Gold	Bill Walker
William T. Hartman	

Editor, Journal of Education Finance

Kern Alexander

Sustaining Members

American Association of School Administrators
American Federation of Teachers
National Education Association
National School Boards Association